CITIZEN EMPLOYERS

CITIZEN EMPLOYERS

Business Communities and Labor
in Cincinnati and San Francisco,
1870–1916

Jeffrey Haydu

ILR Press

an imprint of

CORNELL UNIVERSITY PRESS **ITHACA AND LONDON**

Cornell University Press gratefully acknowledges a grant from the University of California, San Diego, which has aided in the publication of this book.

Copyright © 2008 by Cornell University

First published 2008 by Cornell University Press
Printed in the United States of America

Library of Congress Cataloging-in-Publication Data

Haydu, Jeffrey.
  Citizen employers : business communities and labor in Cincinnati and
San Francisco, 1870–1916 / Jeffrey Haydu.
    p. cm.
  Includes bibliographical references and index.
  ISBN 978–0–8014–4641–2 (cloth : alk. paper)
  1. Industrial relations—Ohio—Cincinnati—History.   2. Industrial relations—California—San Francisco—History.   3. Middle Class—Ohio—Cincinnati—History.   4. Middle class—California—San Francisco—History.   5. Small business—Ohio—Cincinnati—History.   6. Small business—California—San Francisco—History.   7. Labor unions—Ohio—Cincinnati—History.   8. Labor unions—California—San Francisco—History.   9. San Francisco (Calif.)—Social conditions.   10. Cincinnati (Ohio)—Social conditions.   11. United States—Social conditions—1865–1918.   I. Title.
  HD8085.C563H39 2008
  331.09771'7809034—dc22   2007036945

Cornell University Press strives to use environmentally responsible suppliers and materials to the fullest extent possible in the publishing of its books. Such materials include vegetable-based, low-VOC inks and acid-free papers that are recycled, totally chlorine-free, or partly composed of nonwood fibers. For further information, visit our website at www.cornellpress.cornell.edu.

Cloth printing   10 9 8 7 6 5 4 3 2 1

To Kath, finally

Contents

Preface

At first I had planned to write a book about employer conceptions of workplace justice. What did American employers believe they owed their employees? What worker rights did they feel obliged to respect? Pitching this idea to friends and colleagues elicited a common response: "That will be an awfully short book." Although my topic has evolved over time, I continue my effort to take employers' professed principles seriously. This is not easy. Particularly in recent years, corporate leaders (and their political allies) seem to have become especially shameless in self-righteously portraying as a public service their pursuit of sordid self-interest. And closer to my own subject matter, contemporary American employers' claims about union rights and wrongs are easily dismissed as so much window dressing for their real interests. Yet such pronouncements often seem to be sincerely made. More important, they are widely accepted. Egregious polluters, after all, are not the only ones who believe that environmental regulation threatens the nation's liberties, and employers fighting organizing drives are not alone in finding unions un-American. It is worth asking what cultural resources and social conditions make such rhetoric plausible to speakers and their chosen audiences. And while base self-interest may always be with us, the dazzling variety of public veneers poses a sociological puzzle. Why, given the extensive rhetorical tool kit at their disposal, did employers in specific times and places adopt such different tools for denigrating—or, much more rarely, legitimizing—unions?

For the employers I studied, the answers had more to do with business communities than with personal circumstances. Their thinking about labor at work, moreover, proved to be closely linked with their recipes for good government in politics. My title thus echoes David Montgomery's *Citizen Worker* in highlighting the influence of civic ideals on workplace ideology, while shifting the focus from labor to capital. And by adding the plural—Citizen Employer*s*—I mean to emphasize the importance of employers' collective organization and identities in shaping their approach to unions and employees within their individual firms.

As I developed my ideas and tried out my arguments for this project, many colleagues tried to set me straight. Some—including Jim Atleson, Bruce Carruthers, Jeff Goodwin, Rebecca Emigh, Phil Scranton, and Theda Skocpol—did so at talks and conference presentations. Others took time to comment on drafts, answer e-mail queries, or listen to musings, notably Rick Baldoz, Emily Beaulieu, Charlene Bredder, Lis Clemens, Steve Cornell, Ellen Dannin, Paul Frymer, Jack Goldstone, Larry Isaac, Howard Kimeldorf, Tom Klug, Caroline Lee, William Roy, Kathy Thelen, Rhys Williams, and Mayer Zald. And department colleagues Amy Binder, Mary Blair-Loy, Isaac Martin, Akos Rona-Tas, Gershon Shafir, and John Skrentny have been especially generous with comments and encouragement. Special thanks, finally, to Howard Kimeldorf and Howell Harris for their detailed and constructive reviews of the penultimate manuscript.

I also thank staff members at the Cincinnati Historical Society; the Cincinnati Public Library; the University of Cincinnati; the California Historical Society; the San Francisco Public Library; the Bancroft Library, University of California–Berkeley; and the Geisel Library, University of California–San Diego, particularly the long-suffering workers in its Interlibrary Loan and Periodicals departments. Financial support came from the National Humanities Foundation; the University of California's Institute for Labor and Employment; and the University of California–San Diego Academic Senate. Others provided support in kind, including Ben and Kay Schneider (materials relating to Uncle Herman Schneider), Robert Manley (minute books kept by grandfather John Manley, secretary of Cincinnati's Metal Trades Association), and especially John and Peggy Mooney (ready hospitality during my research visits to San Francisco). And I appreciate the good judgment and the heroic stints of microfilm reading contributed by research assistants Caroline Lee, Larissa Leroux, Dorothy Pizzaro, Rebecca Sager, and Eric Van Rite. At Cornell University Press, Fran Benson gave my work an enthusiastic welcome and steady support, Cameron Cooper and Teresa Jesionowski guided it toward publication, and David Schur gave it some final spit and polish.

I have learned more from Colin Haydu than he thinks, although it is impossible to pinpoint where in this book that influence shows. The influence of Kathy Mooney, by contrast, is easy for me to see but impossible to acknowledge in full. She started asking me "what about employers" a long time ago, and has helped me refine my answers—and my prose—ever since. The book is dedicated to her.

JEFFREY HAYDU

San Diego, California

CITIZEN EMPLOYERS

BUSINESS IDEOLOGY AND CLASS FORMATION

Businesspeople are no more fond of taxes than the rest of us. Their objections, however, are anything but personal. "It's dumb to tax investment capital," one Connecticut manufacturer recently complained when the legislature opened the door to property taxes on machinery. The state is "discouraging us from hiring new people," another employer argued, and "preventing us from being more profitable." "We prefer they tax the egg and not the goose." Public officials often agree. Pennsylvania governor Edward Rendell boasted in 2006 that reducing business taxes benefited the state as a whole. "For nearly four years now, we've led the way in creating a more attractive business environment—one where our companies can grow and compete in global markets," the governor told the Schuylkill Alliance Chamber of Commerce. "After cutting business taxes by $1.1 billion, launching one of the nation's most aggressive stimulus packages, and directing new resources to workforce development, more and more businesses are now choosing to set up shop and expand in Pennsylvania." Turning back challenges to such use of taxpayer money in North Carolina, that state's supreme court ruled that the expenditures, "while providing incidental private benefit, serve a primary public good."[1]

Employers tend to see no such public benefits in the activities of unions. During an organizing drive at Amazon.com in 2000, managers advised employees ("associates") that it was the union, not the company, that was "a greedy, for-profit business." Amazon's internal website reminded workers that unions are interested more in the dues than in the welfare of their members and would only make matters worse by working to "actively foster distrust towards supervisors" and "limit associate incentives. Merit increases are contrary to union philosophy." Reflecting on efforts to organize Houston janitors in 2005, one employer representative emphasized that the higher wages a union might win are, like taxes, as much a public as a private burden. "I don't see how [unionization] is going to help Houston. It has the potential of raising the cost of doing business." Ads run by the anti-union organization Union Facts made the point more bluntly. "The New Union Label," reads the headline over a padlocked factory gate: "Closed."[2]

These public-spirited business sentiments are common fare. Fifty years after Charles Wilson's claim that what is good for General Motors is good for the country, GM no longer seems the best example. But business leaders still agree that fostering private enterprise serves the public interest. By contrast, unions are portrayed as "special interests," grabbing power and dues at the expense of the common good. And just as unions poison relations between employees and supervisors at work, so in the larger body politic: business leaders would surely back Republican charges that rival politicians are inciting "class warfare" when they present the interests of working families and the rich as at odds.

Few social scientists take such claims seriously. The identity of business and public interests, the self-serving nature of thuggish unions, the unpatriotic character of class conflict, all are easily written off as rationalizations deployed to curry public favor and discredit opponents. This book agrees that these articles of business faith are indeed self-serving, but it still takes them seriously as powerful social forces. The business of America is business, and the ideologies through which merchants, manufacturers, and managers publicly justify their positions have exerted tremendous influence on our culture and institutions.

That influence is clearest in the ways we think about and regulate class relations in the United States, or fail to do so. It is no surprise, for example, that the wealthy would attribute their success to their own individual merits—their hard work, their consummate skill, their religious faith—rather than to their class advantages. But as many scholars have shown, that interpretation of success and failure is widely shared where one might least expect it, among those with few resources and dim prospects.[3] Nor is it surprising that businesspeople should prefer to keep class off the political agenda, particularly if that agenda includes higher taxes on the rich or closer regulation of business behavior. But this taboo is not broken much more often by the self-proclaimed representatives of "working families" than it is by those flush with corporate political action committee (PAC) contributions. "Class," comparativists suggest, is simply alien to our national language;[4] it is a topic raised more by disaffected sociologists and muckraking journalists than by real Americans. Similarly, the congenial view that business and public interests are identical enjoys wide political support. It justifies the use of public resources—tax dollars, land—to subsidize private investment as state and local governments compete to attract business. In my own state, it supports a double standard in university budget-making: a modestly funded University of California institute for labor research drew attacks for being partisan and pro-union; the much larger budget for business schools to train future managers is an unquestioned public service.

America's labor history reminds us that class cannot always be kept invisible. Here too, however, business ideology matters. In recurrent battles over labor rights, employers have demonized unions on many grounds. At different times, they have charged that unions constitute threats to "law and order," to free enterprise, to individual employees' "right to work," to cordial relations between management and workers, and to flexibility and competitiveness. These dire views of unions have helped employers prevail in two ways. At least since the 1890s, businesses have usually been able to win over a broad middle class to their criticisms of unions. That political alliance, in turn, has often put local police, the judiciary, and the media at their disposal during strikes.[5] The construction of dire union threats has also provided businessmen of varied backgrounds and interests with a common rallying cry. This ideological common ground was especially important before World War I. In our own time, Wal-Mart or Amazon.com may be able to fend off unions single-handedly, but when most firms had fewer resources, effectively fighting labor required a collective crusade. These ideological weapons matter, finally, for the peculiar shape of U.S. industrial relations. Part of the puzzle of American "exceptionalism" has been the relative weakness of the country's labor unions. After keeping pace with comparable economies through the nineteenth century, union growth stalled in the early 1900s, reached a peak well below European counterparts in the 1950s, and has since dropped off by more than half. Scholars have offered many reasons for the exceptional weakness of unions in the United States.[6] But many agree that American employers have been unusually resistant to, and successful in rolling back, unionization and collective bargaining. Their practical ability to win may have little to do with ideology, but their principled determination reflects particular ideological constructions of the union menace.

This book examines an important early chapter in this larger story of business ideology and labor. The focus is on the period between the Civil War and World War I and on capitalist enterprises of small size and proprietary character.[7] During this period, I argue, three developments in business ideology and class relations came together. First, the generic claim that business serves the general good took a particular form. A variety of merchants, manufacturers, and independent professionals, adapting older standards of republican citizenship, identified their interests with those of the municipal community, and they did so in a highly personal way. It was not merely by successfully building up their enterprises, and not yet by exercising *corporate* responsibility, that they contributed to the community; by virtue of their economic position, they also claimed a responsibility to take the lead in public affairs. Second, they applied this standard of selfless public service—what I will call business citizenship—to unions. Much of the rhetoric of anti-unionism in this period, depicting unions as enemies of law and order and as purveyors of class discord, reflected businessmen's broader criteria for good citizenship. Third, they practiced what they preached. By the early twentieth century, these competitive proprietors were acting together, in local business communities, to rid their trades of union "dictation." And it is this early-twentieth-century open shop movement that marks the beginning of America's "exceptional" industrial relations.

Against this backdrop, consider Cincinnati and San Francisco, my two case studies. The cities resembled one another in many significant ways. Small-scale, proprietary capital dominated both local economies. The same leading industries (such as clothing, brewing, and machinery) could be found in the cities' manufacturing sectors. And although San Francisco was justly known as a commercial city, its manufacturing employment in 1880 ranked ninth in the nation, only two places behind Cincinnati.[8] Yet despite such similarities, the two cities differed dramatically in businessmen's class alignments, approach to unions, and civic ideology.

In all three respects, Cincinnati stands as the more typical American case. Its diverse manufacturing and commercial capital increasingly organized together under the banner of business citizenship and in opposition to organized labor. San Francisco offers a striking contrast, more in line with employers in western Europe. Its businessmen remained divided through most of the pre–World War I years. More puzzling, at the same time that Cincinnati was moving in the direction of the open shop, most San Francisco manufacturers were moving in a more "European" direction: recognizing unions, accepting collective bargaining, and relying on industry-wide agreements to regulate labor relations. Corresponding to these strategic choices, moreover, was a thoroughly un-American business ideology, which I summarize as practical corporatism and discuss in part 2. Practical corporatism acknowledged class divisions as inescapable facts of life, both at work and in city politics. The public interest was best served, in this view, if both sides were tightly organized, with responsible leaders willing to make deals and to enforce them on their constituents. Where Cincinnati's business citizenship kept class out of politics and industry, San Francisco's practical corporatism treated unions and business organizations as essential units of economic and municipal governance.

The book thus confronts a historical and sociological puzzle. Why did two bourgeoisies, located in comparable cities in the same country at the same time, differ so dramatically in their displays of unity, in their civic ideologies, and in their reigning views of labor unions? The answers hang together as contrasting stories of class formation. Both the question and the answers indicate that, while I take business ideology seriously, I do not consider it an expression of essential and enduring American values—a view exemplified in the work of Seymour Martin Lipset, among others. Instead, I tie these interpretations of good citizenship and bad unions to particular groups, times, and places. Cincinnati's business citizenship was the ideological work of a specific social stratum rather than an expression of some classless national character. And while elements of that civic ideology have proved enduring, others were specific to the period, as elites selectively adapted republican traditions to meet the challenges of their times. The San Francisco contrast confirms that business discourse could also vary dramatically *within* the United States, depending on local conditions of class formation.

To simplify the presentation of these contrasting patterns of class formation and to highlight causal mechanisms that may be found in other cases, I divide these stories according to three analytical themes. Part 1 focuses on the problem of collective action among capitalists, using social movement theory to explain bourgeois solidarity and division. Part 2 zeroes in on business ideology, highlighting the path-dependent ways in which capitalists constructed particular civic identities and social boundaries from among wider repertoires. Part 3 treats employer views of unions as one example of how social actors transpose cultural scripts across institutional borders. Each of those parts is introduced by an overview of the larger historical debates to which the case studies contribute. The rest of this chapter develops the sociological tools used to explain differences between Cincinnati's and San Francisco's business communities.

CLASS FORMATION AND SOCIAL MOVEMENTS

Over twenty years ago, Michael Burawoy opened his *Politics of Production* by acknowledging that the working class was "unfashionable," and he recommended "bringing workers back in" to sociology.[9] That defensive tone still runs through studies of class, despite persistent findings that class shapes social networks, lifestyles, government policies, cultural orientations, and more.[10] But if the working class has gone out of scholarly fashion, over the years it has still garnered more attention than has the bourgeoisie. This may reflect a populist preference for the underdog. Studying labor offers the satisfaction of restoring the historical agency and alternative voices of neglected workers. Businessmen, by contrast, are usually history's winners, and often quite voluble in victory. Yet winners deserve attention too, especially when their triumphs have such lasting consequences for the ways that citizens think about the relationship between business and the public interest and for the chronic weakness of the American labor movement. And understanding both the bourgeoisie's victories and the ideological baggage that comes with them requires a closer look at bourgeois class formation.

As a first approximation, by *class formation* I mean an increasing alignment between economic hierarchies,[11] on one side, and cultural practices or collective action on the other.[12] I say cultural practices *or* collective action, because these need not go together. Research on the contemporary U.S. working class much more often finds shared cultural traits than common action or even a sense of solidarity. At the same time, individual workers who join a union or engage in strikes may do so out of quite varied motives, with no unifying ideology or shared identity. The same holds true for members of employers' associations, and this is one additional justification for analytically separating the treatment of business action and organization (part 1) from business discourse (part 2). Even by this minimalist standard of class formation, there might be two good reasons why the literature on bourgeois class formation in the United States is so sparse. One is that business class formation never happened, and the second is that it did not even need to happen. The first claim comes from comparative perspectives on U.S. capitalists. These suggest that employers resemble American workers in their "exceptional" lack of solidarity and class consciousness.[13] The second claim originates with Claus Offe and Helmut Wiesenthal's venerable contrast between the strategic positions of capitalists and workers.[14] The latter, Offe and Wiesenthal argue, can reach common understandings of their interests only through collective dialogue. Employers have the advantage that each one's interests are made visible and unambiguous by their calculations of profit and loss. And because capital itself comes together in production, its owners need not do so in order to pursue those interests.

This claim may seem plausible when the main economic actors are large corporations. It makes little sense at a time when proprietary capital still dominated industrial communities. Entrepreneurs of the late nineteenth century certainly faced common problems, including union challenges, "ruinous competition," and urban disorder. But they lacked the resources to solve those problems single-handedly. Nor did the bottom line unambiguously address such questions as whether it was better to cooperate with or to fight against unions. Each alternative had its advantages and costs, some of them contingent on what *other* employers did (would competitors stand by you in a strike, or poach your customers?) and some impossible to quantify (were union workers better trained? less easily disciplined?). And as with workers, *collective* responses to challenges—agreement on what was to be done and a willingness to act together—were not assured by the mere fact that entrepreneurs occupied the "same" position in economic relations of production. All sorts of conflicts made joint organization and action difficult, including those between direct competitors, among businessmen in rival trades, and between old money and new. The pooling of capital in the labor process hardly did away with such frictions.

Perhaps, then, comparativists are right, and bourgeois class formation in the United States never happened? In fact, proprietary capitalists often *did* cooperate in fighting unions and regulating prices, despite divergent interests and the temptation to free ride. To take an especially important example, the open shop movement of the early twentieth century was largely the work of middling firms banded together in trade-based groups (like the National Metal Trades Association) and citywide organizations of employers.[15] Bourgeois solidarity also extended well beyond the labor market. Case studies often tell the story of an emerging upper class, relatively cohesive and exclusive in their residence, refinement, and politics.[16] But we know much less about how proprietors came to organize and act together than we do about solidarity among corporate capitalists or more rarefied elites,[17] and far less still than we know about working-class formation.

To learn more, Cincinnati and San Francisco are good places to look. Proprietary firms of modest scale dominated both local economies. Particularly in confronting labor, these firms faced the classic dilemmas of collective action: singly, they could rarely win, but differences in market position and short-term interests made it difficult to stick together. The cases are also useful because they diverge so dramatically. In Cincinnati, a wide range of businessmen came to organize and act in tandem, including in opposition to labor. Their San Francisco counterparts remained sharply divided, manufacturers from merchants, smaller firms from a handful of large corporations. And, most acrimoniously, they squared off as either allies or enemies of organized labor. Differences in businessmen's unity and in their ties to other groups can also be found beyond industrial relations, in the cities' politics and high culture. Moreover, these contrasts, coming as they do from two communities *within* the United States, offer analytical leverage missing from comparisons between other countries and the United States as a whole.

As is appropriate for cases that highlight proprietary capital, my account of class formation pays primary attention to those who in the early twentieth century would have been described as members of "the business community." This category was narrower than "the middle class" but broader than the economic "elite." Its members included self-employed professionals and high-level managers, but most important and numerous were owners (including partners) of manufacturing companies, commercial enterprises, retail establishments, and transportation firms. They varied in the scale of their operations and the extent of their power over local economic life. By the early twentieth century, however, contemporaries viewed them as reasonably distinct from the teeming ranks of wage earners in factories and offices.[18] The distinctiveness of this grouping was itself an outcome of class formation, a process of realignment in which business-men's relations with one another and with other groups shifted.

In explaining differences in bourgeois class formation between Cincinnati and San Francisco, I will draw on two lamentably distinct literatures, one on working-class formation and the other on social movements. The first provides my criteria for bourgeois class formation and an appreciation for how group formation can occur in different sites as well as along different lines. The second helps explain how those multiple possibilities get sorted out.

Studies of working-class formation have become far more flexible over the last few decades, moving away from a narrow focus on white male industrial workers and a reliance on orthodox assumptions inherited from Marxism.[19] Three cau-tions offered by revisionist treatments of working-class formation are applicable as well to the bourgeoisie. We are advised, first, to abandon fixed expectations of what a "formed" class will look like. To the extent that some common discourse *does* develop among individuals in similar economic positions, there should be no prior assumptions about the content of that discourse. "Class conscious-ness" may take many forms, including, in Cincinnati, a strong ideological claim to being "above class." Whatever the content of the class discourses, however, revisionist studies depict working-class formation as involving the extension of social ties, common experiences, and shared cultural orientations among wage earners, and their differentiation from the ties, experiences, and orientations of men and women in upper classes. Turned around, the same applies to the bour-geoisie. Treatments of working-class formation also encourage us to ask the fol-lowing questions: How pervasive is this process? Are members of different classes differentiated in the same way in politics, at work, at school, and so forth? For example, as Ira Katznelson has shown for nineteenth-century American workers, class lines may be clearly drawn on the job but less salient than ethnic differences in electoral politics.[20]

There is a second bit of conventional wisdom in recent approaches to working-class formation: do not assume that the economy is where class "happens." Orthodox Marxist accounts had highlighted the effects of economic transforma-tions—changing standards of living, de-skilling at work, the concentration of capital—on the experiences of workers and their relations with employers. With the cultural turn in academe, scholars more often focus on class differences as constructed through politics, leisure, or language.[21] For example, artisans might develop shared sensibilities or engage in collective action on the basis of their work-related experiences and networks. But they may do so, instead, through political dialogue, family structures, or cultural institutions—arenas in which experiences and interests may be less divisive than they are in economic relations. In adapting this literature to my purposes, I add two points. The first is definitional. Solidarity might be constructed in any number of social settings and take widely varying discursive forms. Unless the individuals involved share a common economic position, however, there is no point in labeling it "class formation." Whether economic position actually *shapes* class formation is a separate and contested issue. The disagreements may be exaggerated by the conventions of academic debate, however. Even those who would thoroughly deconstruct class let economic constraints sneak in the back door—allowing, for example, that narratives of class are limited by the distribution of power or must be plausible in light of workers' experiences.[22] My second point involves a difference in approach. Some scholars make the valuable observation that, regardless of the social setting in which class differences are constructed, working-class formation is "relational."[23] The insight applies as well to the bourgeoisie. Merchant, manufacturer, banker, and professional came together, if at all, in response to challenges to business as usual. Some of these challenges came from below, in the form of urban riots, union pressure, or political insurgences. Others had little to do with class, such as competition with other cities for regional supremacy. Capitalist class formation was relational, too, in that it involved boundary work between businessmen and other groups, although neither the identities businessmen embraced nor the groups they looked down on were necessarily defined in terms of class. My relational account differs from that of Margaret Somers or Marc Steinberg in one other respect. For those authors, workers develop some class consciousness as they interact with their adversaries. In Cincinnati, the ideological content of class formation developed less through relations with workers than through relations *among* employers, as they constructed shared meanings of "the labor problem" or the nature of good and bad citizenship.

A third piece of advice from students of working-class formation is perhaps the most basic: do not assume that it will happen at all. The possibilities for group alignments are multiple, and the outcomes contingent and transient. Individuals may act jointly or develop cultural affinities with others in similar economic positions. But they may as readily do so with others of similar church membership, ethnic background, or sexual orientation. The salience of one or another locus for group formation defies theoretical generalization—a hard pill for most sociologists to swallow. The best we can do is reconstruct the mix of generic causal mechanisms and historical serendipity that comes together to steer group formation in one direction or another. This advice, too, applies to capitalists no less than to workers. There is one possible difference in outcomes, however. For workers, status distinctions such as those based on ethnicity, skill, or religion are typically obstacles to class solidarity. Cincinnati's proprietors, like those in many U.S. industrial cities of the time, were more homogeneous in ethnic background and religious affiliation. For them, class formation and status closure could (and did) go hand in hand.

It is particularly in sorting out why collective action and organization develop along class lines, rather than on the basis of any number of other social attributes, that I will draw on a second scholarly resource: social movement theory. One thing that makes the study of social movements a distinct subfield is its focus on "contentious" action and challenges to authority, and for that reason we should not say that late-nineteenth-century businessmen engaged in a "social movement." But class formation is in many ways *like* a social movement. Both involve groups coalescing in response to "grievances," although in bourgeois class formation these consist of threats from below rather than injustices from on high. For social movements, as in class formation, there are also any number of lines along which group solidarities may develop, so that even among similarly aggrieved individuals, collective organization and action is more the exception than the rule. Accordingly, analysts may begin with the character of grievances but move quickly on to how the structure of opportunities fosters or discourages mobilization; how changing social ties bring individuals into a movement or shunt them aside; and how casual contacts and half-hearted engagements can lead to stronger bonds and deeper involvement with the cause.[24] In my interpretation of business class-formation, I also emphasize more strongly than most social movement theorists the organizational settings within which individuals respond to challenges, expand their networks, and cultivate new identities.

Class alignments in Cincinnati and San Francisco moved in opposite directions. My account of Cincinnati begins with the character of challenges facing businessmen, among which political corruption and relative economic decline were usually more troublesome than unions. Mobilization took place around issues of municipal improvement and through broadly based civic associations. Those agenda and organizational vehicles, in turn, proved particularly favorable to business unity. Most associations of merchants or manufacturers before the 1880s had been limited in their membership to specific industries (liquor dealers, iron manufacturers) and specialized in their focus on regulating the trade or fighting strikes. The Commercial Club (founded in 1880) and the Businessmen's Club (1892) had a different character. They enrolled businessmen from diverse economic sectors, and the issues they dealt with further aided in bridging divisions among them. Clean streets and clean government did not pit competitors against one another, as price regulation could; these organizations brought businessmen into regular contact, as episodic strikes did not; and these clubs had considerable appeal across industries. Organizational settings, then, are a key part of the story of bourgeois class formation in Cincinnati, and as in revisionist labor studies, the organizations that matter most were not economic ones.

Class relations took a very different turn in San Francisco. To begin with, race divided not just workers—a familiar story—but also businessmen. Because of the ways in which Chinese workers and proprietors entered into local industry in the 1860s and 1870s, the conflicts engendered by changes in the scale and methods of production ended up pitting small manufacturers and white craft labor against both large firms and "coolie" labor. Other challenges facing local businessmen, above all strong unions and domineering monopolies, reinforced an alliance of a "great middle" against the Chinese below and big capital above. Less broadly representative civic associations, finally, did little to offset conflicts among factions of capital. Instead, manufacturers organized first and foremost to deal with unions, and *these* organizations both segregated them by trade and foregrounded issues that divided them according to their short-term interests in the labor market.

One further comparison, not between Cincinnati and San Francisco, but between San Francisco before and after 1911, reminds us to take seriously the contingency of class formation. My analysis highlights several kinds of contingencies. The institutional setting within which businessmen forge some degree of unity may vary from one case to another. So too may the ideological grounds on which they make distinctions between themselves and other social groups. And there is no reason to assume any trend toward an alignment between economic position and collective action or organization. For these reasons, it also makes little sense to think of class formation as something that happens once, much less once and for all. What we will see, instead, is a re-formation of class, as new challenges and changing institutional settings disrupt old alignments, favor different ways of drawing social boundaries, and create new bases for group solidarity. In the last years before World War I, class boundaries and alignments shift again in San Francisco, this time in the direction of greater business unity and a turn against organized labor. This shift, too, reflects changes in challenges faced and in the organizations through which businessmen mobilized in response.

CLASS DISCOURSE AND PATH DEPENDENCY

Part 1 of this book highlights one side of class formation, the degree of solidarity in organization and action displayed by the two cities' bourgeoisies. Part 2 shifts the focus from broad social alignments to the specific ideological content of class formation. On what basis did proprietors distinguish themselves from some groups and ally themselves with others? What public identities did they construct for themselves? Part 1 also sets a flexible standard for class formation: Do collective actions (such as organizational affiliations) or cultural practices (such as methods of child rearing) align with economic position? Part 2 sets a similarly low threshold for "class consciousness." Individuals *may* be aware of differences in collective action or cultural practices and use those differences to distinguish between how "we" behave or what "we" believe and how "they" behave and think. To the extent that this boundary work coincides with economic divisions, we can dub it "class consciousness," even if there is no explicit reference to class or to the economic positions of us and them. For example, contemporary Americans often mark class distinctions but do so using languages of gender or race.[25] Much of part 2 describes the ways in which languages of citizenship did (in Cincinnati) or did not (in San Francisco) line up with class differences. A broader theoretical puzzle raised by this boundary work is recognized—but not solved—by treatments of collective identity and framing in the social movements literature. Why, out of the many identities and frames that actors might put to use, do particular ones become more prominent? To properly answer that question, social movement scholars can usefully borrow the model of path dependency in historical explanation, profiting especially from its attention to mechanisms which "lock in" particular trajectories. This explanatory task is the other main focus of part 2.

"Collective identity" and "framing" carry a heavy analytical burden in the social movements literature. The first plays pivotal roles in social movement mobilization, leading individuals to redefine personal troubles as collective injustices, plugging them into activist networks, and giving them an emotional investment in their causes.[26] The concept of framing, in turn, has focused scholarly attention on how movement organizers and participants interpret grievances and opportunities, dramatize messages through their tactics, and justify goals.[27] These issues are as important for elites as they are for protesters. When their authority or interests are challenged, elites may, like protesters, more clearly define what unites them and sets them apart from others. They may also draw these lines as part of the more routine business of constructing social hierarchies and pursuing status closure.[28] And whether in responding to insurgences or in erecting status boundaries, identity work and framing operate together. On one side, drawing boundaries involves the construction of similarities (I am like them . . .) and differences (. . . and unlike them), these being the most basic features of collective identities. On the other, those similarities and differences do more than designate who is on which side of the boundary. They also pick out and highlight—frame—the characteristics, motives, and worth of us and them.[29] If I were to identify as a Hungarian American, for example, I would not merely be distinguishing myself from others on the basis of national origin but would also be imputing to Hungarians some virtues and not others (their cuisine or music, for example, but not their military prowess).

That selectivity reminds us that at any given time there will be a large tool kit available for constructing identities and interpretive frames, enabling individuals to draw boundaries along many different lines. A number of sources keep the tool kit well stocked. One source is our multiple social relationships. Identities are constructed through our relations with others, and those ties are many and mutable.[30] Another source is our participation in a variety of social institutions, each with its own cultural logic for allocating honor and stigma.[31] But the fact that we have multiple identities—as parents, spouses, religious believers, citizens—is only half the story. Not only are our potential identities varied; so are the meanings of any one of them. There are a wide array of models for the role of "father," for how being a father sets an individual apart from mothers and childless men, and for what kinds of relationship between fathers and their children are appropriate. The cultural scripts characteristic of different social institutions, similarly, can be read in different ways. As is painfully clear from contemporary U.S. politics, there is little consensus on appropriate relationships and rules of the game within "the family," or even what kinds of relationships qualify as families. Similarly, we might say, with Roger Friedland and Robert Alford,[32] that the defining logic of the economy is one of commodification and accumulation. But this hardly dictates the specific characteristics of "capitalists" which individual businessmen might invoke to identify themselves and to draw contrasts with noncapitalists. The repertoire, to be sure, is not inexhaustible. At any historical moment, some ways of classifying enemies and characterizing "people like us" are readily available. Others may have dropped from the menu, their labels for stigma and honor no longer familiar. Employers in the early twentieth century had many choices for drawing the line between virtuous businessmen and reprehensible unions. But other choices, common enough in other eras, would have seemed fusty or meaningless (and thus useless for scoring points). In contrast to the early nineteenth century, for example, identifying unions as secret societies that threatened the republic was no longer a viable (or even well-known) rhetorical option. Still, the repertoire is extensive and forces the questions of why actors adopt the particular identities and frames that they do, or why they choose some lines along which to draw social boundaries, and not others.

It is in answering those questions that social movement theory needs some help. If analytical tools from this literature are useful to the study of class formation, as I argue in part 1, then the literature on class formation can return the favor by imparting a more historical sensibility to the understanding of identities and frames. Historians who examine class are likely to think in terms of cumulative causation over time. Classes do not necessarily (or even usually) "happen"; there are other social attributes that may be more salient grounds for organizing identities and relations with others. Historical explanations for how class does emerge as a prominent basis for social experience and social relations tend to involve complex conjunctures of long-standing traditions, immediate contexts, contingent events, and human agency. The usual way of summarizing this style of explanation is through the metaphor of path dependency, in which multiple possibilities are winnowed down and one of those possibilities gets locked in over time.[33] Social movement theorists would do well to think in similarly path-dependent terms, focusing on mechanisms which select and reinforce particular identities and frames from among wider discursive menus. These mechanisms will vary from case to case. But they will likely include some mix of challenges to which particular frames are adapted, events which keynote specific identities, and collective organizations in which selected identities and frames are embedded.

Some examples of these lock-in mechanisms may be useful. A path-dependent account of frame selection might begin by asking which inherited cultural tools from the past are effective in coping with current problems. Individuals, after all, do not so much *have* identities and frames as *use* them to situate themselves in their social worlds and to make sense of those worlds. Depending on historical settings, some may be more effective than others in this work of diagnosing experiences and mapping social relations. For example, stereotypes of African Americans as lazy and irresponsible as compared to whites are a persistent part of the American cultural repertoire. That way of drawing boundaries and framing differences, perhaps with some encouragement from political entrepreneurs, may be particularly favored among working-class whites when their local schools and neighborhoods are deteriorating. It provides an explanation (and a scapegoat) for troubles, and it justifies exclusionary practices. Under these conditions, from among the larger menu of identities and frames, racial boundaries and stereotypes "work." In social movements, workable frames would also be stabilized by consistency in their *opponents'* framing—as in the steady back and forth between pro-choice and pro-life abortion frames—because that consistency both reinforces boundaries and makes strategic shifts in framing unnecessary.

A second type of lock-in mechanism consists of those serendipitous events that defy conventional causal explanation. Social movement scholars have long allowed for "precipitating events" that give a movement a final push when other, more fundamental conditions are ripe. But events may do more than nudge a group the last inch over the threshold to protest. They may also crystallize the boundaries that define a group to begin with. In Traugott's account of the 1848 June Days in Paris, an accidental discharge of a rifle leads nervous soldiers to fire on the crowd, "suddenly transform[ing] reformist protest into hardened resistance."[34] It did so, in part, by sharply defining the boundaries—in this case, the literal battle lines—between "the people" and the monarchy, and by reinforcing a particular interpretation of the regime's character. Here too, there is ample room for activists to put their own interpretive spins on events and to widely publicize their interpretations.[35]

The organizations to which individuals belong further narrow and lock in choices from available repertoires of identities and frames. For one thing, they bring people together in particular groupings. The less obvious point here is that individuals may come to participate in voluntary associations (parent-teacher associations, unions, clubs, neighborhood groups) for all sorts of reasons, such as a desire to accompany friends, gain material advantages, assert social status, or comply with occupational pressures. Involvement in these organizations, however, builds new social ties and new ways of identifying insiders and outsiders. This insight is familiar from institutionalist analysis: institutions constitute interests and identities as much as they reflect them.[36] Studies of interlocking directorates, for example, argue that participation in multiple corporate boards and peak associations transforms businessmen's identities. By virtue of their contact with a wider range of executives and owners, individuals come to perceive class interests that transcend their own parochial concerns.[37] Organizations also have their own standards of merit or rules of evaluation—wealth, in some circles, but professionalism or cultural literacy or physical prowess in others. These rules divide people into categories of more or less worthy, privileging particular boundaries (from among many possibilities) between us and them.[38] The manifest purposes and activities of specific organizations, finally, may serve as a model for participants' choices of identities. Unions, for example, organize employees to deal, in more or less adversarial ways, with employers. Homeowners' associations highlight property values and "law and order," interests ostensibly shared by neighborhood residents. Those organizational settings favor different ways of dividing up the social world and different selections from among potential identities, including, as David Halle shows, boundary work that foregrounds class in the workplace and race at home.[39] Finally, different organizations survive or disappear for reasons that have little to do with the views of their members—another reason why such organizations must be considered independent influences when we try to determine why certain identities become entrenched over time.

These selective mechanisms operate in conjunction and in cumulative fashion to steer boundary work into particular paths and keep it there. An analytical narrative of each road taken, accordingly, will combine long trajectories (such as inherited cultural repertoires), more immediate influences (a changing distribution of resources among different social actors, for example, or reliance on specific forms of collective organization), and serendipitous events. The upshot will be that particu-lar identities and frames become more salient and enduring than others.[40] Given this complex mix of constraints and contingency in the way that actors' boundary work adapts the past to deal with the present, it is also particularly important to follow Robert Benford's advice and study framing comparatively.[41]

It may seem that I have gone to great trouble lining up my tools when there is little use for them. Surely business identities and ideological frames in the Gilded Age hold no surprises. Cross-national comparisons suggested to observ-ers like Louis Hartz and Seymour Martin Lipset that America's middle class was unusually attached to property rights, hostile to government authority, and blind to class. And if liberalism holds sway in U.S. society, its most enthusiastic sup-porters would have been the Gilded Age bourgeoisie, whose laissez-faire ideol-ogy is contrasted both to earlier republicanism and later corporate liberalism and Progressive reform.[42] But we will see that a modified republicanism lived on in businessmen's social maps of vice and virtue. And much as workers and employers could interpret republicanism in quite different ways, so Cincinnati and San Francisco businessmen could put republican traditions to different uses. In Cincinnati, as in many other industrial cities,[43] they continued to preach the duty of civic participation, the need to elevate public over private interest, and the importance of good government for a healthy community. They put these standards of good citizenship to work as they stigmatized corrupt office holders, political demagogues, and the rabble that backed them both. And they claimed for themselves the corresponding virtues, assuming responsibility for promot-ing good government and the public interest against corruption and class partisanship—with the public's and business community's interests being iden-tical, and class partisanship being the mischief of labor. San Francisco's business community had no such consensus. But a substantial faction, at times domi-nant politically, took republicanism in a different direction. No less concerned with good citizenship, this faction instead stigmatized the Chinese as servile and degraded labor, unworthy as either producers or voters. Political virtue lay with a great middle class of white craftsmen and proprietors. And unlike their Cin-cinnati counterparts, they viewed both monopolies and unfit citizens as loom-ing threats to republican virtue. San Francisco and Cincinnati businessmen also departed from Gilded Age stereotypes in placing the public good above selfish interests. They defined the public good in different ways, however. In Cincinnati, it proved identical with the needs of the business community and incompatible with any voicing of class interests. In San Francisco, a majority of proprietors before 1911 distinguished the public good from the interests of *either* labor or capital. More, they saw it as best served when *both* classes were well organized and regularly involved in governing industrial and political affairs.

Businessmen of similar types, drawing on similar ideological repertoires at roughly the same time, thus ended up drawing boundaries along different lines and embracing rival civic identities. In explaining this divergence, I will be emphasizing the path-dependent character of identity selection. Contrasting uses of republicanism were guided, in part, by challenges facing businessmen. Rival definitions of the primary threats to political virtue, for example, had some real grounding in businessmen's experiences with local machine politics or Southern Pacific Railroad power. Investing organizational energy in civic improvement or collective bargaining, similarly, reflected realities of economic decline or union power that could not be wished away. Those organizational investments, in turn, helped consolidate particular ways of framing public interests and constructing civic identities. They did so in part by their express purposes—cleaning up government or coping with unions—but also by embedding those identities in rules and routines, such as specialized committees for dealing with city problems or for monitoring compliance with trade agreements. And serendipitous events could underscore particular definitions of civic problems and public heroes. Cincinnati's 1884 Court House riot, we will see, provided a focal point for businessmen's horror of mobs and contempt for political demagogues. The failed 1901 lockout of unions in San Francisco reinforced the view that acting "responsibly" meant consulting with unions, not driving them from the workplace. The cumulative effect of these challenges, institutional settings, and keynoting events was to move business identities from similar starting points along different paths.

INSTITUTIONS, IDENTITIES, AND TRANSPOSITION BETWEEN POLITICS AND WORK

Part 1 assesses differences in bourgeois unity, and part 2, differences in boundary work and civic ideology. Part 3 explores the movement of collective identities and interpretive frames across the border between politics and work. That border crossing is of interest in part for understanding managerial ideology in the United States, and particularly how employers have justified their exceptional hostility to unions. It also sheds light on the problem of "cultural transposition"—the application of a common cultural script across social settings. Cultural transposition does important theoretical work for sociologists. Sewell's "transposable schemas" are the cultural models that, paired with material resources, make up what we call social structures. Applied in new ways, they are also the keys to social transformation.[44] Institutionalists, who cut their teeth accounting for persistence when change (adaptation to markets or improvement for greater efficiency, for example) might have been expected, rely on cultural transposition to bring change back into the theory.[45] The cultural scripts of interest in my study of bourgeois class formation are frameworks for defining identities and assessing worth in particular institutions and organizations.[46]

Cincinnati most clearly illustrates what cultural transposition looks like in practice. The city's businessmen (much like wage earners in some revisionist accounts of working-class formation) forged broader ties among themselves *outside* the market- or workplace. It was especially through civic associations that they cultivated closer relations and shared ideas. Those shared ideas, moreover, did not privilege the roles of employers but of leading citizens, standing above the fray of class interests. I will argue, however, that this pristine civic discourse carried over into the realm of work. It appeared in businessmen's thinking about the character of good workers, the proper approach to vocational education, and the obligations they had to their employees. Most important, it also gave ideological shape to a virulent anti-unionism.

Such border crossing took a different direction in San Francisco. Social alignments there—the persistent coalition of proprietors and craft labor—were driven in large part by relations at work, whether these involved conflicts between whites and the Chinese or between proprietors and increasingly powerful trade unions. And work relations, not civic uplift, were the main focus of collective organization by the city's manufacturers. But these experiences and organizational efforts at work are echoed in San Francisco businessmen's civic ideology. In city politics as in labor relations, business leaders came to accept the legitimacy of class and the virtues of resolving differences through orderly negotiation between leaders from both sides. In effect, they applied the same script of class representation to both collective bargaining and municipal governance.

At first glance, this seems as it should be. We might reasonably assume that employers' thinking about their workplace obligations or civic duties would reflect some more general cultural orientations. Anthony Wallace's study of Rockdale,[47] for example, found that employers' approach to workplace discipline was strongly colored by a pervasive evangelicalism. Late-nineteenth-century German industrial management, similarly, has been interpreted as one among many manifestations of upper-class patriarchal authoritarianism.[48] But there are some good reasons to expect businessmen's thinking about work relations to be thoroughly insulated from their roles as citizens. One large-scale historical trend in nineteenth-century Western societies, after all, was to separate work from the household, and markets from political or religious regulation, each sphere having its own distinct norms and standards of legitimacy.

There are still more general reasons to expect cultural transposition to be more the exception than the rule. The separation of norms and standards is sustained both by the cultural practices of social actors and the character of social institutions. Social actors learn early on to switch hats as they move from one setting to another.[49] Those that have not learned this lesson—most often, but alas not only, children—may be said to be "acting inappropriately." The settings that cue us to appropriate behavior may be our different roles as parent, employer, voter, choir member, sports fan, and so on. And as much as we might like to assume, with Robert Putnam, that choir members make better citizens and more cooperative businessmen, social actors may practice civility and teamwork in singing together and then skewer their political opponents and economic competitors.[50] We also routinely switch hats as the character of our social relationships change. As students of "bounded solidarity" have reaffirmed, norms applicable to the in-group may not be applied to others. Ethnic or club ties among businessmen, for example, may support levels of trust and sharing of confidential information that would be deemed highly imprudent vis-à-vis businessmen outside these circles.[51] Role definitions and social boundaries change. As they do, so do the occasions for hat-switching. Workplace roles may come to accommodate some parental responsibilities, with employers offering "family friendly" leave policies or daycare programs. Redrawn social boundaries may also alter notions of who does and does not merit our trust or deserve our respect. At certain times, San Francisco and Cincinnati employers lumped themselves with some of their employees as whites (as opposed to the Chinese) or as mechanics (as opposed to unskilled labor and the idle rich). Changes in production practices and managerial hierarchies favored a redrawing of boundaries to more clearly divide workers from wage earners, making it less obligatory to extend to workers the same consideration owed to fellow businessmen. The important point here is that social actors often do not apply scripts across roles or group boundaries, and so cultural transposition cannot be assumed. Institutionalists make a similar point from the top down. Institutions are characterized by distinct cultural logics which are, normally, *non*transposable. In liberal democracies, norms of obedience and discipline suitable for military life are not considered appropriate for politics. A disposition to truck, barter, and exchange may properly guide our behavior in the market, but not our relations with family members.[52]

Yet as chapters 5 and 6 illustrate, cultural transposition does sometimes happen. Cincinnati employers, for example, applied the same basic cultural frames in the arena of work that they deployed in their civic lives. Or, in Michèle Lamont and Laurent Thévenot's terms,[53] the standards for evaluating worth, which normally vary from one kind of relationship to another, in this case lined up. Are there any theoretical tools available for explaining *how* such transposition happens? Yes—but there is more to the question. Institutionalists emphasize that societies have multiple cultural codes because there are multiple institutions, each with its own characteristic script.[54] But single institutions themselves have multiple scripts or cultural repertoires. For example, in the United States, competing norms, including familial paternalism, Christian tutelage, and cash nexus, were available to govern early-nineteenth-century employment relations. So we must ask not only how scripts transpose but how specific scripts are selected for transposition, or why individuals keep wearing *particular* hats from their collections.

Institutionalists offer one answer. There are "logics of appropriateness" that restrict the application of cultural scripts from one institution to another, but these logics are neither immutable nor impermeable. What were once well-insulated scripts may converge. Arlie Hochschild's study *The Time Bind* provides one illustration: some aspects of domestic life, including child care and food preparation, are increasingly commodified and rationalized as job demands intensify, blurring the boundaries between family and work.[55] And institutional scripts may be sufficiently similar that actors can stretch one in order to advance their interests in another setting. In Elisabeth Clemens's account of the early-twentieth-century suffrage movement, women invoked maternalist ideologies, rooted in the family, to legitimize their right to vote. Whether in Hochschild's case or Clemens's, institutional logics are close enough to allow social actors to carry the same scripts back and forth. Something like this can be seen in San Francisco. Owing to the clout of organized labor, industrial relations and municipal politics featured very similar configurations of class forces. Businessmen experienced much the same sets of allies and adversaries in each sphere. They also learned a consistent lesson, whether they were trying to cut wages or change the city charter: unions could be neither ignored nor defeated. An alternative script better served their interests in both settings. Negotiation minimized disruptive conflicts, and having an agreement with labor leaders usually delivered the rank and file as well. Theodore Koditschek's study of Bradford, England,[56] offers another example of organizational forms and social cleavages lining up across institutions and fostering a transposable script. Bradford's industrialists waged parallel struggles against the religious establishment *and* political oligarchy *and* economic monopoly. In each field, they found themselves in a dissenting position and faced with the same Anglican, Tory elite. This institutional alignment led them to generalize particular grievances—particular both in the sense of institution-specific and in having been selected from a broader menu—into a transposable ideology of "liberty."

We can add to institutionalist accounts of transposition by generalizing not from San Francisco but from Cincinnati. Here the key was not any symmetry between institutions or any convergence in logics of appropriateness, but instead the character of collective identities. Cincinnati businessmen came together through civic organizations that involved them in a wide range of activities—building art museums and extending sewer lines, soliciting new investment and rooting out political corruption. These diverse roles, moreover, were not only housed in single organizations; they were also subsumed within a generalized identity as leading citizens, responsible for boosting the economy, reforming city government, and fostering high culture. With such an all-purpose identity, hat-switching is unnecessary: Cincinnati employers could proudly wear the same "good citizen" hat from social club to board of education to political reform meeting and on into their own "private" business domain. Depending on how such organizations are constructed, moreover, including their membership criteria and their manifest purposes, they are likely to privilege particular identities and scripts. That selective highlighting helps explain why some items from the cultural menu, and not others, transpose across institutional boundaries.

In some cases, these two sources of transposition—parallel institutions and generalized identities—go together. Consider one generalized identity familiar to sociologists, namely, class consciousness. A major source of class consciousness, at least among subordinate groups, is the experience of multiple, symmetrical disadvantages—denial of trade union rights at work, voting rights in politics, and dignity in the status order. Those overlapping experiences, in turn, *may* give rise to a master frame in which social life in still other institutional sectors (schools, churches, sports) is interpreted according to a common narrative of class inequality and oppression. The development of such master frames underpins major accounts of the origins of working-class radicalism.[57] The contrast between Cincinnati and San Francisco bourgeoisies makes it possible to clearly distinguish these sources of transposition.

Tracking the movement of cultural scripts between politics and work also sheds new light on old debates about U.S. managerial ideology. Comparative studies suggest that American employers have been unusually hostile to unions and exceptionally strident in their assertion of an unfettered "right to manage."[58] A forceful case in point is the open shop drive between 1902 and World War I, which stymied labor organizing and marked the beginning of a clear divergence in industrial relations between the United States and leading European economies. The main question in scholarly debates has been why American employers have so vehemently opposed unions; a separate question worth asking is why they justified their opposition in the particular ways that they did.

Explanations for the cross-national differences in managerial strategies fall into three main camps. One emphasizes characteristics of U.S. economic development, which gave employers either extra incentives or enhanced capacity to dispense with unions.[59] A second stresses a national culture which sanctifies unencumbered property rights and undermines any sense of noblesse oblige toward employees.[60] And a third highlights the political advantages enjoyed by U.S. employers. On one side, the absence of a political challenge from labor freed capital from the need to compromise with moderate unions; on the other side, a sympathetic political regime gave employers support in fighting labor organization.[61] The latter explanation fits my two case studies reasonably well. Labor's political clout in San Francisco, and the corresponding reluctance of municipal politicians to use government power on capital's behalf, encouraged the city's employers to concede union rights. Most of their Cincinnati counterparts, facing no such political constraints, imposed the open shop.

The rationale for insisting on open shops is another matter. Over a long and colorful history of fighting labor organization, U.S. employers have advanced any number of reasons why unions cannot be tolerated: they preach atheism, mount secret conspiracies, foment violence, threaten private property, impede efficiency, disrupt personal ties between owners and employees, serve only the selfish interests of union leaders, violate the natural laws of the market, infringe on exclusive management rights, undermine discipline, deprive individuals of the right to work, and more. From this extensive rhetorical arsenal, why do employers choose some weapons and leave the rest in storage? I argue, first, that we have been looking in the wrong place for an answer to such questions about management rhetoric. The strategic circumstances of individual employers only go so far in explaining how they frame unions or justify their unfettered control of the workplace. It is also necessary to examine the collective identities employers cultivate as part of larger business communities. My second argument concerns how such collective identities favor particular anti-union frames over others, and here I return to cultural transposition. Cincinnati businessmen's civic identities embodied certain standards of good government and criteria for distinguishing worthy from unworthy citizens. Those same metrics guided their choice of frames for demonizing unions, condemning them above all for partisan agitation, workplace tyranny, and mob violence. Other elements of employer ideology—the characteristics of the good worker, the proper approach to employee training, and the best ways to represent Cincinnati's manufactures at industrial expositions—similarly mirrored civic identities and their changes over time.

In San Francisco, business views of labor differed dramatically. Particularly between the late 1890s and the early 1910s—a period when the nationwide open shop movement was gathering steam—most local businessmen reached a pragmatic accommodation with labor power at work and in politics. In both spheres they, like their Cincinnati counterparts, applied a common standard of governance. But that model treated classes as legitimate actors, called for balanced organization by labor and capital, and insisted that their unavoidable conflicts be settled by bargaining rather than irresponsible action on either side. They applied this model of practical corporatism not just in labor relations but in such areas as charter reform and the promotion of "home industry." The lion and the lamb did not lie down together. But this approach did remove from the agenda of industrial relations some of the most contentious issues of the time, above all labor's right to union representation and collective bargaining. Indeed, by explicitly organizing representation around class, practical corporatism on the national level might have made worker rights more secure than they later proved to be under the New Deal system. But San Francisco's alternative would be a road not taken. Even during the 1900s, with labor's power at its peak and businessmen at their most conciliatory, there was no consensus behind practical corporatism. A consensus did develop after 1911, but one of a very different kind, and some familiar causal culprits were at work. The 1906 earthquake and a slippage in the city's economic position relative to West Coast rivals posed new challenges; the 1911 consolidation of business associations into the civic-minded Chamber of Commerce created a new organizational framework for addressing those challenges; and critical events in 1916 (the "irresponsible" waterfront strike and the Preparedness Day bombing) gave anti-union business leaders the opportunity to "reframe" organized labor. It is at this point that San Francisco's "exceptionalism" ends, as employers declare for the open shop, and do so on much the same ideological grounds as did their counterparts in Cincinnati.

San Francisco's reversal might tempt readers to think that there is really no puzzle here: the city differed from Cincinnati only by lagging behind along the same trajectory. But this conclusion would be a mistake. Neither the principles of practical corporatism nor the practice of trade agreements were characteristic of Cincinnati at some earlier point in time, to be discarded later on. And from the 1890s, the comparative pattern is one not of leads and lags but of *increasing* divergence, as Cincinnati moved toward the open shop and San Francisco consolidated union recognition, industry-wide bargaining, and class-based political representation. This stark contrast in local businessmen's civic ideologies and views of labor thus warrants a closer look.

COMPARISONS, LOCAL AND TEMPORAL

Why local case studies, as against a broader national survey? The reasons are historical, practical, and methodological. Historically, in this period the local community remained the primary stage for class formation among proprietary capitalists. Even if they bought and sold in national markets, they generally thought of themselves as part of a local economy, what Chamber of Commerce speakers and publications would refer to as "the home market," with its own imports and exports. And even if they thought first of the fortunes of their own enterprises, businessmen saw those fortunes as linked to the progress of home industry. They were also more likely to belong to regional than national trade groups and employers' associations. A similar local orientation prevailed in civic life, with prominent businessmen in Cincinnati and San Francisco involved mainly in citywide reform organizations, cultural institutions, and social clubs.[62] Were bourgeois class formation to happen in the same way in each city—which it clearly did not—there would still be a practical reason to zero in on local cases. Reconstructing businessmen's organizational lives and cultural practices takes time: the sources are scattered and often recalcitrant, and there are not enough case studies by historians to permit freeloading by "big picture" sociologists. On some important issues, finally, there are methodological advantages in local studies. Many of the claims about U.S. employer characteristics—their fragmentation, their hostility to unions, their ideological (if not practical) aversion to government regulation—are based on cross-national comparisons. We can gain some additional explanatory leverage by focusing on variations in class formation or business ideology *within* the United States. For example, comparing Cincinnati and San Francisco makes it possible to "hold constant" some potential influences, such as the legal framework and electoral system, and concentrate on others, such as the character and strength of labor organization.

In making use of these cases for explanatory purposes, my starting point will be John Stuart Mill's hoary method of difference, in which potential causes of contrasting outcomes are highlighted or ruled out on the basis of similarities and differences between the cases. Mill, however, cannot stand alone. As his critics have pointed out, it is possible to infer causes from Millian comparisons only by making dubious assumptions about the equivalence and independence of cases and about causal uniformity across cases and time periods.[63] In search of firmer ground, I will complement Mill in three ways. One is to look more closely at historical sequences within each case. Rather than treating "racial conflict" as a variable that was present in San Francisco's industrial structure but not in Cincinnati's, and thus a causal factor in class alignments, I will show how the intensification of anti-Chinese agitation in the 1870s was followed by collaboration between small proprietors and craft unions. Race mattered, then, not merely as a causal variable in comparing the cases, but as part of a causal narrative in one case.[64] The second way of complementing Mill is to attend as far as possible to the workings of causality through historical actors. A Millian comparison can correlate active participation of Cincinnati businessmen in civic associations with class solidarity against unions, as against the absence of both in San Francisco. We gain confidence that this is a causal connection to the extent that Cincinnati businessmen themselves express the view that civic associations helped bring them together and to the extent that we find members of these associations *also* cooperating with one another in fighting unions. A third supplement to Mill is to identify and make use of variations over time *within* individual cases—adding cross-period to cross-city comparisons. The key temporal cases are San Francisco before and after about 1911, and the final section of chapter 6 reinforces the general causal claims by contrasting developments in these two periods.

Available sources do not make it easy to develop these arguments. Employers generously recorded their views of commodity prices, product specifications, tariffs, and the like; they much more often kept their views of work and labor to themselves. What evidence does exist may also be unrepresentative, the product of unusual businessmen (who paid uncommon attention to labor matters) or exceptional circumstances (such as strikes, when labor managed to catch employers' attention). To get around this problem, my basic strategy is to look for recurrent patterns of expression. If, for example, there are signs of a shift in employer identities from "mechanic" to "businessman" in multiple settings—civic clubs, business-sponsored vocational programs, industrial expositions—then we can be more confident about the trend even though direct evidence is fragmentary. There is virtue in this necessity. By following the traces of business thinking into club dining rooms, apprenticeship classes, and exposition planning committees, we can get a fuller sense of their class culture. A good place to start is with Cincinnati and San Francisco businessmen's ability to overcome their own internal divisions, the topic of part 1.

Part I

SOLIDARITIES

The introduction set a low threshold for "class formation": an alignment between collective action or cultural practices, on one side, and economic hierarchies on the other. Sociologists and historians routinely make some broad distinctions between more and less privileged groups in a given era's economic structure—recognizing that the analytically useful dividing lines will vary from one time and place to another. In late-nineteenth-century American cities, a key distinction is between those who worked for wages, mostly in manual employment, and those who earned a living through self-employment or the control of property. These broad categories encompass a wide array of occupations, whose occupants might disagree on all sorts of issues. And the distinction between these categories might turn out to be largely irrelevant to social life. But it is also possible that individuals on one side of this economic divide came to differ from those on the other side, and to be more closely tied to one another, in their collective action or cultural preferences. That dual movement of increasing separation between economically defined groups and extended ties within them are what I mean by class formation. The questions posed regarding the late-nineteenth-century American bourgeoisie concern whether class formation in this sense "happened": If so, how? And in what ways did this process resemble or differ from working-class formation? The chapters of part 1 focus on one aspect of this story: how collective action and organization aligned with class divisions. Part 2 takes up the cultural thread in the story of bourgeois class formation.

Even the low threshold that the introduction set for class formation is a tall order. Solidarity among capitalists was no more securely anchored in their economic positions than it was among wage earners. All sorts of conflicting interests undercut joint organization and action among businessmen. Some pitted one city's business against another's, including competition for regional supremacy. Others divided firms in the same industry. Efforts to curb price competition, for example, regularly fell victim to free riders.[1] And while capitalists are sometimes thought to unify more readily against the common enemy of unions than against the threat of competition, a common complaint before World War I was that "some employers have reaped considerable profit by yielding to the demands of labor during a strike in which their competitors, by refusing to surrender, were unable to transact any business."[2] These are all examples of tensions between shared long-term interests and individual short-term advantage. In other areas, however, businessmen simply lacked common rallying points. The tariff concerns of many manufacturers, for example, left railroad men indifferent; transportation costs were not of equal concern to manufacturers producing for local as against national markets. The labor process could also fragment employers to an even greater degree than it did workers. Uneven development within an industry or disparate workforce requirements created very different challenges and opportunities for manufacturers, as both Cincinnati and San Francisco show. And in contrast to its effects on workers, the labor process neither brought businessmen together in one place nor, in the event of conflict, did it pit them *as a group* against employees.

These obstacles to common organization and action mainly involved economic relationships. Businessmen, like workers, also had other social bases for affiliation that ran counter to class unity.[3] Old money often had disdain for new, Republicans for the occasional Democrat, Protestants for Jews, whites for racial minorities. Even if businessmen shared important economic interests, there is no reason to assume that these would trump the identities that divided them. In San Francisco, as we will see, "whiteness" often outweighed class, aligning small proprietors and skilled labor against the Chinese and their employers. In general, however, compared to workers, business owners were more homogeneous in ethnicity and religion (being predominantly white Anglo-Saxon Protestants).[4] In late-nineteenth-century industrial communities, accordingly, status closure and business unity could coincide: when Cincinnati businessmen drew boundaries on the basis of taste or good citizenship, they reinforced rather than cut across class solidarity. Still, bourgeois unity faced formidable obstacles.

How can we tell when these hurdles have been overcome? The key for capital, as for labor, is a realignment of solidarities, in which vertical ties between classes weaken and horizontal ties within classes broaden. This dual movement may be visible in organization, in action, and in ideology, and shifts in these areas may reinforce one another. Are businessmen forming or participating in more exclusive organizations—social or business clubs with restricted memberships, for example? Are they moving beyond sectional organizations, along the lines of trade-based economic bodies, to more encompassing ones, such as citywide employers' associations? Do they stick together in practice, notably by providing mutual support in combating labor? Such shifting alignments in organization and action are the main focus of chapters 1 and 2. A third key measure of class formation is harder to pin down, but no less important: the growing salience of common identities and ways of framing the social world, identities and frames that were different from and perhaps at odds with those of other groups. These might include a shared conventional wisdom about the causes of urban disorder or a growing taste for high culture, with these understandings both providing common ground among diverse businessmen and distancing them from the rabble. These overlapping cultural boundaries are explored in part 2.

By these standards, a common comparative judgment is that bourgeois class formation in the United States never happened. Explicitly comparative treatments of American businessmen as a class are far fewer and less systematic than studies of working-class "exceptionalism." The conclusions, however, are roughly the same. U.S. capitalists, comparative observers suggest, have generally displayed less solidarity in organization and action than their European counterparts. As usual, Tocqueville made the point early on. "Although there are rich men, a class of rich men does not exist at all," because these rich men "have neither corporate spirits nor objects in common."[5] James Livingston summarizes (without endorsing) the more recent views of business and New Left historians alike, that "businessmen are simply too worried about their short-term profits and sectoral interests to think or act, rationally and systematically, as a class."[6] Martin Sklar highlights other American circumstances which inhibited collective action among businessmen, especially on a national scale. Most important were "the expanse of the nation and the market . . . the diversity of the capitalist class . . . and the multiplicity of legal jurisdictions."[7] As for a separation *between* classes in collective action or culture, comparative analysis of associational life and race relations also implies limited bourgeois class formation. From Tocqueville through to Robert Putnam and Theda Skocpol, it has been argued that American society is particularly rich in voluntary associations, and membership in many of those organizations crosses class lines.[8] In addition, the commonplace generalization about U.S. workers—that race usually has trumped class and aligned white wage earners with more privileged whites—can be turned on its head. Across a wide range of social organizations and networks, U.S. property owners have been tied to lower-class whites through shared antipathy to minorities.[9]

When historians zero in on specific communities, however, a different picture emerges.[10] These case studies often characterize the Gilded Age as a time of growing social distance between industrial workers and a broadly defined "class" of proprietors, managers, professionals, and white-collar workers. Within this class—the boundaries of which vary from one study to another—historians also see evidence of the "corporate spirits [and] objects in common" that Tocqueville found missing among the early-nineteenth-century rich. There is no *necessary* contradiction between these case studies and cross-country comparisons, because the latter privilege national over local class relations and formal organization over informal networks. Still, the difference in emphasis between case studies and comparative generalizations makes it particularly useful to examine contrasts in bourgeois class formation *within* the United States. Doing so checks the tendency of cross-national analysis to oversimplify "the" U.S. pattern, while providing leverage to sort out causes of variation. Chapter 1 shows that outcomes in Cincinnati resemble those described in some of the other community studies, while the unusual case of San Francisco (chapter 2) better fits cross-national generalizations about the weakness of American bourgeois class formation. Comparing the two calls special attention to the role of civic associations and racial dynamics in businessmen's solidarity with one another and in their separation from the lower classes.

Consider first the late-nineteenth-century decline in cross-class ties found in other case studies. Patterns of collective action and organization in Cincinnati appear consistent with this trend. Important cross-class ties after the Civil War had included common trade identities in small manufacturing establishments and the free labor republicanism that brought together wage earners and at least the petite bourgeoisie.[11] And as in Herbert Gutman's narrative of industrialization, these ties diminish over time. The culprits are familiar. They include changes in the workplace division of labor and the scale of production that Steven Ross emphasizes in his account of Cincinnati working-class formation. These shifts more sharply demarcated the skills, prospects for advancement, and economic fortunes of ordinary workers from those of their employers. Although the timing of these developments varied from one industry to another, by the late nineteenth century, few local industries bore much resemblance to the artisan ideal of a few tradesmen applying their varied skills in the company of the "practical mechanic" who employed them. Cincinnati also illustrates how intensified social unrest in the 1870s and 1880s undercut the republican alliance of wage earners and petite bourgeoisie, favoring a realignment of middle and upper classes under the banner of "law and order."[12] And Cincinnati certainly resembled other cities in its separation of the "respectable classes" from workers in residence and in cultural preferences (as chapter 3 shows).

What the Cincinnati case also highlights, however, are associational responses by local businessmen to threats *other* than labor, including urban misgovernment and economic competition from rival cities. Although these organizations—above all, Cincinnati's Commercial Club and Business Men's Club—did not develop in opposition to challenges from below, they included few members outside the ranks of property owners and self-employed professionals. It might be argued that the appearance of such class-exclusive business clubs in the 1880s and 1890s was part of a wider flourishing of associational life, one which *also* included cross-class groups such as fraternal orders.[13] But in Cincinnati, at least, the popularity of such cross-class groups could hardly have offset the impact of businessmen's civic organizations. For one thing, case studies of fraternal lodges in the period suggest that the order most favored by leading Cincinnati businessmen—the Masons— had a more elite membership than did others.[14] More important, civic clubs simply mattered more than fraternal orders for Cincinnati's bourgeoisie. They were featured more often in obituaries and other biographical sketches as badges of an individual businessman's status,[15] and they were the main vehicles for businessmen's involvement in local politics, economic boosterism, and cultural philanthropy.

Collective organization and action among San Francisco businessmen displayed more durable cross-class ties. Those ties did not originate in the "bridging social capital" of uplifting voluntary associations, however. We will see that the city's businessmen, and manufacturers in particular, were significantly less engaged in such associations than their Cincinnati counterparts. Nor did San Francisco resemble Burlington, the Iowa railroad town in Shelton Stromquist's comparative study where businessmen's long-standing local roots supported cross-class alliances against "outside" unionists.[16] Instead, San Francisco's leading merchants and manufacturers were upstarts compared to Cincinnati's. And it was surely not harmonious labor relations which preserved ties across class lines, because, of the two cities, San Francisco saw more intense industrial conflict.

The comparison supports two alternative explanations. First, the combination of small-scale proprietary capital and a handful of overbearing corporations kept alive a shared opposition to "monopoly" in San Francisco politics. That republican coalition of small business and skilled labor in a "great middle" matches Gutman's narrative—but it lasted longer than in most industrial cities. Second, shared hostility to the Chinese reinforced this alliance. Chapter 2 traces that hostility to a peculiar conjunction of demographic and industrial change. The short story is this. In Cincinnati, blacks were largely excluded from unionized trades, and employers relied on women for de-skilled jobs.[17] Here, new methods of production put capital and union labor at loggerheads. In major San Francisco trades, by contrast, large employers hired cheap Chinese labor, and low entry costs opened the door to Chinese-owned sweatshops. This configuration made the Chinese a common enemy for white craftsmen and proprietors. Cross-class opposition to the Chinese spread well beyond the manufacture of clothes, cigars, and shoes, however. And here civic association of a different kind proved relevant after all. The "social capital" bridging class divisions flourished not in high-minded improvement clubs but in white label leagues and anti-coolie associations.

As Cincinnati businessmen distanced themselves from wage earners, they also organized and acted together on a more inclusive basis. Such expanded horizontal ties (or their absence) are commonly discussed in studies of labor, where overcoming divisions of skill, race, gender, or trade are rightly seen as essential parts of working-class formation. Sometimes in self-conscious imitation of this literature, students of more privileged classes have taken the same tack. Stuart Blumin, for example, describes the making of a distinct middle class in mid-nineteenth-century U.S. cities, tied together by common consumption practices, voluntary associations, and identities as mental rather than manual workers.[18] Closer to home are a handful of studies of the re-formation of urban upper classes in the late nineteenth century. The common narrative in these studies is the emergence of a more coherent business class, fusing older merchant capital and respected professionals with newer manufacturers and a still newer stratum of corporate managers. The best example is *Monied Metropolis,* in which Sven Beckert shows how developments in politics, elite culture, and labor unrest helped overcome prior divisions among New York City's bourgeoisie.[19]

Beckert draws the line between the bourgeoisie and a relatively modest middle class whose members did more work with their hands, experienced more economic instability, and had the means for only the budget version of gentility. In cities like Cincinnati and San Francisco, where small-scale capital prevailed, the dividing line between bourgeoisie and middle class was even less clear. Members of Cincinnati's Commercial Club resemble Beckert's main characters, but the city's Business Men's Club brought smaller property owners and young professionals into the local "business" class. Although the scale and boundaries of Cincinnati's bourgeoisie differed from New York City's, in both cases many of the same developments that divided businessmen from workers also built bridges *among* diverse businessmen. Social clubs like the Queen City Club fostered networks and standards of propriety across iron manufacturers, merchants, and railroad managers, while excluding the rabble. Art museums and music societies not only divided more from less prosperous Cincinnatians in leisure activities; they also cultivated among the former shared canons of good taste and common philanthropic obligations. In these developments Cincinnati's story echoes those of Chicago, Pittsburgh, and Boston, as well as of New York City.[20] It also contrasts with San Francisco, where institutions of high culture developed later and involved relatively few of the city's manufacturers.

My comparison of horizontal ties among the two bourgeoisies, like my account of cross-class alliances, diverges from others' accounts in its emphasis on race and businessmen's civic associations. We are often reminded that racial cleavages tended to undermine class solidarity among American workers; the same was true for San Francisco's capitalists. Merchants and manufacturers in late-nineteenth-century U.S. cities, of course, had little of the labor force's racial diversity. Race divided San Francisco businessmen in a more circuitous fashion, as commonplace tensions between importing merchants and local manufacturers or between owners of large factories and small shops overlapped with frictions between the beneficiaries and perceived victims of Chinese immigration. As for business associations, other case studies note how involvement in civic reform and other types of public service have helped forge networks and build solidarity among economic elites.[21] I emphasize, in addition, how the specific organizational vehicles for civic reform made them particularly well suited to bridging divisions among businessmen. These associations at once excluded lower classes and brought together businessmen from different sectors, manufacturers from different trades, owners and managers, proprietors and professionals. They directed attention away from sectional interests to some putative general goods, such as the relative economic standing of the city. They brought businessmen together on a regular basis for informal socializing. And as I argue in chapter 3, they placed members in a series of alternative roles—acting on behalf of clean government and vocational education and cultural improvement—and thereby fostered a common identity as leading citizens rather than as individual dry goods merchants or carriage makers. In all these areas, San Francisco lagged behind. Its main business reform organization was not broadly representative, did not have as wide-ranging an agenda, and did not provide members with the same club-like center for leisure and camaraderie as its Cincinnati counterpart. Only after 1911, as chapter 6 shows, did San Francisco see business associations combining similarly broad membership and civic scope.

This argument for the role played by civic clubs suggests that for businessmen, as for workers, economic relations do not provide a favorable terrain for class formation. It is not just that, as Michael Mann points out,[22] market ties are diffuse and weak. More important, the economic associations commonly formed in this period to regulate prices or fight unions tended to reinforce rather than surmount sectional differences. They organized employers on the basis of trade interests and identities, and they often focused on issues that, at best, held little interest for businessmen outside the trade and, at worst, actively divided them.[23] Another kind of economic relation also failed to unify businessmen: militant labor movements could as easily split employers as provide a common enemy to rally against. It was San Francisco's businessmen, not Cincinnati's, who confronted the more powerful challenge from unions, and they consistently squabbled about whether to accommodate or fight back. At the very least, the impact of labor militancy on business unity will depend on the character of the challenge and the alternatives open to different groups of businessmen in meeting it. In San Francisco, unions were strong but, in *some* trades, "responsible";

protected markets gave employers in *some* industries extra leeway for concessions; and labor's political leverage raised the costs of confrontation beyond what smaller capital could bear. In all these ways, economic relations did little to build bourgeois solidarity.[24] It was instead in the civic arena of political reform, city boosterism, and cultural philanthropy that businessmen organized more broadly and, through those organizations, focused collective attention on a more consensual agenda.

This comparison focuses, of course, on the local level, where class formation among proprietary capitalists "happened," if at all. It can say nothing of bourgeois class formation on a regional or national scale. Chapters 1 and 2 also concentrate on class alignments as evidenced by collective organization and action. They leave for part 2 the ideological content of bourgeois class formation—the cultural boundaries and identities through which businessmen distinguished themselves from lower classes and allied themselves with one another.

1

BUSINESS UNITY IN CINCINNATI

The dilemmas of capitalist class formation are well displayed in post–Civil War Cincinnati. Individual firms, generally of modest size, could hardly discipline markets, train future workers, or fend off unions single-handedly. Cooperation did not come easily, however. Efforts to join forces were regularly undermined by competitive rivalries, status conflicts, and mutual indifference. At the same time, in smaller firms, personal ties to employees, together with a persistent producer ideology, helped sustain cross-class solidarities. This chapter examines these dilemmas and then traces the social realignments in late-nineteenth-century Cincinnati that broadened horizontal solidarities among businessmen and frayed vertical ones with workers. Much of the story is a familiar one for Gilded Age America, in which businessmen organized collectively in response to social upheavals. Particularly in Cincinnati, labor was only one such threat, and often not the most pressing. Similarly, the most important forms of collective organization were neither trade-based nor concerned with fighting unions. They were instead civic groups with broad memberships and wide agendas. Ultimately, however, these high-toned associations helped satisfy strategic industrial relations needs. By the early twentieth century, most local employers were well organized on a citywide basis to deal with unions. And as chapter 5 will show, they also shared a common understanding of what was wrong with unions and what were preferable ways to manage workers.

THE QUEEN CITY OF THE WEST

Nineteenth-century Cincinnati elites took justifiable pride in their city's rise to national prominence as a center of trade and industry. First settled in 1788, Cincinnati's early growth built on its location as a gateway to the west, and its easy access to the Ohio and Miami rivers. By the 1830s, Cincinnati had become a major center for processing and shipping agricultural products—its leading role in meat packing earned it the nickname Porkopolis alongside the more dignified Queen City—and for the distribution of manufactured goods. The next three decades saw a boom in the city's own industries. Manufacturing employment climbed from 9,010 in 1840 to 28,527 in 1850 and to 59,827 in 1870.[1] With a diverse industrial base that included boot and shoe manufacturing, printing and publishing, furniture making, metalworking, and clothing production, the city ranked as the nation's third largest manufacturing center in 1860. Expansion continued after the Civil War, but at a slower pace and amidst an increasing sense of relative economic decline. As railroads replaced river transport, growth lagged behind that of both earlier years and current rivals, including Pittsburgh, Chicago, and St. Louis. By the turn of the century, local success stories (notably in soap and machine tools) were matched by equally impressive failures, such as the continued loss of pork packing to Chicago, beer making to Milwaukee, and carriage manufacturing to the Detroit auto industry.

Several features of Cincinnati's history recommend it as a case study in class formation. Most important, proprietary capital still dominated the local economy in the late nineteenth century. This characterization is based in part on the size of local enterprise. The average manufacturing firm had 14 employees in 1880, and 15 a decade later; among all establishments, Cincinnati averaged 12.3 employees in 1900 as compared to Cleveland's 20.1 and Pittsburgh's 36.1.[2] Industries varied substantially in this respect. Breweries and foundries, for example, had far more employees than did publishing houses or clothing manufacturers. The trend in Cincinnati, as elsewhere, was toward a greater concentration of capital. In labor relations, however, the key actors in most industries were numerous firms of modest size rather than a handful of large corporations. Cincinnati capital had a proprietary character in a second sense: the principal owners still played leading roles in management. Here too, the trend was toward a separation of ownership and control. However, given the typical firm's size, extended administrative hierarchies and professional management were neither feasible nor useful. As of 1880, moreover, nearly half of the *largest* 10 percent of local enterprises remained in the hands of individuals or at most three partners.[3] And even some of the local giants remained under the close personal control of a single family—the Procters at Procter and Gamble, the Geiers at Cincinnati Milling, the Wulsins at Baldwin Piano. The *local* source of this control further reinforced Cincinnati capital's proprietary character. Cincinnati residents rather than representatives of a national economic elite owned and controlled most of the city's firms. Community roots went beyond residence. Businessmen like Fred Geier and Lucien Wulsin played prominent roles in the city's cultural and political life.[4] These proprietary characteristics of local industry made a difference for class formation. The size of firms put a premium on collective action, and employers' local roots supported a tight ideological link between business and community interests.

Two other idiosyncrasies of Cincinnati history are relevant to class formation there. First, the timing of its development made for an unusual ethnic makeup in the late nineteenth century. During its years of rapid expansion, the city absorbed large numbers of German and Irish immigrants. By the 1890s, both groups had become fairly well integrated, with substantial representation through most levels of the class structure.[5] The waves of more stigmatized immigrants from eastern and southern Europe, by contrast, arrived after Cincinnati's boom years. These men and women were drawn instead to such fast-growing cities as Pittsburgh, Cleveland, and Detroit. Cincinnati did have a black minority, one both stigmatized and marginalized. But it was also largely excluded from local industry. Of the 5,405 "Negro" adult males recorded in the 1900 Census, only 743 worked in manufacturing.[6] As a result, class distinctions in general, and relations between manufacturing workers and employers in particular, were not *also* divisions between ethnic or racial groups.

Second, in an era of unsavory municipal politics, Cincinnati's government distinguished itself for the power of its political machine, earning a prominent place in Lincoln Steffens's exposé of "bossism." By the standards of the day, the reign of George ("Boss") Cox was relatively efficient and even helped adapt city management to the challenges of urban growth.[7] Still, issues of political corruption and municipal governance regularly demanded the attention of Cincinnati's business leaders. That agenda, particularly in combination with Cincinnati's relative economic decline, shaped class formation. In the absence of serious working-class political challenges or sustained, citywide union threats, employers mobilized broadly around issues of civic order, not industrial conflict. This pattern of broad organization to deal with municipal governance rather than with labor differed from the situation in San Francisco. There, employers' priorities were nearly the reverse. As chapter 3 will show, the agenda in Cincinnati also steered the ideological content of class formation in the direction of "business citizenship."

HANGING SEPARATELY: OBSTACLES TO BUSINESS CLASS FORMATION

Since E. P. Thompson's reorientation of labor history, the standard narrative of class formation notes inequalities in economic assets—property, skills, earnings—but does not assume that these make a difference for alliances and identities. Even when there is a wide gap in economic position, classes may not be "made" because cross-cutting solidarities and divisions are more salient. This agnostic approach to class formation is equally appropriate for employers. In the years immediately after the Civil War, a variety of divisions among Cincinnati capitalists, and links between them and workers, made capitalist class formation an unlikely prospect.

Persisting Vertical Ties

Cincinnati's proprietors and their employees were drawn together in part by a strong producer ethic, rooted in both republican traditions and the character of local manufacturing.[8] In its early years, the city's mechanics' institute actively promoted this ethic. Founded in 1828, the Ohio Mechanics' Institute sought "to facilitate the diffusion of useful knowledge," benefiting in equal measure "the mechanic, artisan, and manufacturer."[9] This republican vision blurred the distinction between wage-earning craftsmen and propertied employers. Both enjoyed respect as productive workers and solid citizens, socially distinct from either dependent common labor and slaves on one side, and the idle rich on the other. For some years after the Civil War, public rhetoric and rituals continued to reinforce this common ground between craftsmen and manufacturers. Those attending an 1870 meeting of "manufacturers, mechanics, and inventors" declared themselves all "practical working men," superior to mere "talkers."[10] Published profiles of leading entrepreneurs, similarly, extolled them as men with craft experience who were thus both competent and trustworthy. "It is a noticeable feature of Cincinnati," the secretary of the Chamber of Commerce boasted in 1878, "that they who are managing our industrial establishments are generally men who are thoroughly acquainted with the practical features of their business. They are mechanics themselves."[11] This lumping together of entrepreneurs, skilled workers, and inventors also appears in the city's industrial expositions during the early 1870s. The call for contributions to the 1872 Expo, for example, solicited "works of art, new inventions, the products of the soil and mine, and of skilled labor in every branch of industry."[12] And even the growing numbers of manufacturers who lacked practical training themselves often paid lip service to the ideal by having their sons do a tour of duty in the industrial trenches. From small shops to Procter and Gamble, having the heir "learn the business" from the ground up before taking control was a recognized and valued career path.[13] In this ideal of the mechanic, then, owners and employees shared a common status as producers and practical men.

Elsewhere, a shared producer ethic, associated as it was with free labor ideology, began to fade after the Civil War.[14] Yet in Cincinnati it was sustained for a time by the character of local industry. It remained common in the 1870s for local manufacturers to have craft roots. Steven Ross calculates that 35.8 percent of business leaders in 1880 had worked their way up through the ranks—down from 70 percent in 1850, but still a substantial fraction of proprietors in manufacturing.[15] Laudatory references to owners who worked "side by side with their men" are also sufficiently numerous to suggest that this was a lingering practice rather than a vanished ideal. And to the extent that production continued to involve craft skills and small-batch output, as in the machine tool industry, this occupational trajectory and common craft identity persisted. Such ties were also sustained in a local economy dominated by small enterprise. Several major Cincinnati industries featured large firms where personal contact between owners and manual workers was unlikely. But these same industries were apt to have a wide range of firms, from bespoke shops to large plants. Among respondents to Ohio's Bureau of Labor Statistics 1877 survey, the number of employees in local carriage firms ranged from 4 to 117, and in furniture from 8 to 315.[16] In this setting, no single line divided workers and employers into separate, homogeneous masses.

Other ties linked employers and wage earners outside of work. Some key Cincinnati industries, including furniture, brewing, and machine tools, were heavily German, giving capital and labor a shared "minority" status.[17] And in Cincinnati as elsewhere, the two decades after 1870 saw rapid growth in the membership of fraternal orders—led in Cincinnati by the Masons and the Odd Fellows. The Masons were the most elite fraternal order, yet case studies still find lodges to have had cross-class memberships. Scattered rosters show that businessmen dominated the ranks of officers in Cincinnati's Masonic lodges. But the order strongly emphasized the equality of all members, and unless Cincinnati departed from Masonic norms, local lodges' public entertainments and private rituals would have included significant numbers of skilled men. Biographical profiles and memorials for Cincinnati businessmen indicate that they also belonged to more plebeian fraternal orders.[18] The fact that they were mostly local residents, not absentee owners, further helped preserve some shared ties to Cincinnati and its home industry.

Divisions among Businessmen

Cincinnati businessmen, tied in these ways to wage earners, were also divided among themselves: merchants from manufacturers, members of one trade from another, one firm against its competitors. As was the case for their ties to workers, particular divisions among businessmen varied in salience over time, by economic sector, according to the controversy at hand, and even from one businessman to another. Theoretical generalizations about their relative importance, or about their social weight as compared to common class position, are thus unwarranted. The goal here is more modest: to identify some competing interests and identities within "the bourgeoisie" in Cincinnati, and thus some reasons why social alignments did not necessarily run along the lines of class.

As in other cities, Cincinnati's early fortunes came from trade and real estate. Merchants were also quick to organize for self-regulation, establishing the Chamber of Commerce in 1839 and dominating its administration and membership. Those who grew rich from manufacturing, by contrast, generally did so later and represented "new money"—men like David Sinton, who prospered during the Civil War by hoarding the output of his modest iron works until the price shot up.[19] Some of the same things that brought manufacturers closer to artisans in Cincinnati also set them apart from merchants, including their self-image as "practical men" and the fact that many operated on a very small scale. It was not uncommon for observers in the 1860s to distinguish among Cincinnati's "manufacturers, merchants and citizens" or to claim that "What the Chamber of Commerce is to the merchants ... the Ohio Mechanics' Institute is to our mechanics and manufacturers."[20] And there are occasional signs of friction between the two groups over matters of organization and public policy. One impulse behind the formation of Cincinnati's Board of Trade in 1869 was a sense that the interests of manufacturers were not adequately represented by the Chamber of Commerce. In contrast to commerce, the board's major promoter argued, manufacturing represented "stationary capital" and was, accordingly, more closely identified with the interests of the city.[21] Tensions between elite and mechanics' cultures also show up in debates over pedagogy. Manufacturers argued that schools should provide training in drawing, applied math, and shop skills. The existing curriculum, by contrast, "wast[ed] years of labor upon Greek tragedies and Latin odes"; these were fine for leisured gentlemen, but not for practical men who had to earn a living.[22] High culture and practical men squared off again in 1884 over the use of a proposed new music hall by Cincinnati's Industrial Exposition. The arrangement seemed to elevate musical festivals above the annual business of promoting local manufactures, and critics griped that "we are a mechanical people, not a race of fiddlers."[23]

Those mechanical people, of course, were divided among themselves, both by industry and by competitive rivalries. What may have been a burning issue for manufacturers in one industry (temperance for local distillers, for example) might leave others utterly indifferent. One trade's profit could be another's loss, as when the city's tanners organized against butchers in 1873 in hopes of reducing the price of hides and getting them "minus the horns [and] sinews."[24] The uneven development of local industry also meant that manufacturers had different needs and faced different pressures—or similar ones but at different times. Some firms competed in national markets and ran factory operations with an extensive division of labor and, increasingly, semiautomatic machinery; others produced smaller batches for local markets using craft production methods.[25]

Competitors in the same industry, finally, were plagued with all the usual free-rider problems that afflicted capitalists who hoped to curb "ruinous competition." Efforts by brewers to set the price of beer sold to local saloons repeatedly broke down, sometimes amid charges that price controls benefited well-known brands at the expense of smaller firms.[26] Even the sharing of information could fall victim to competitive rivalries. Owing to "the selfishness of many, and the jealousy of a much greater number," the Chamber of Commerce found it difficult to compile its annual survey of local manufacturing.[27] Faced with the common enemy of organized labor, businessmen might be expected to rally together. Yet here too, differences in manufacturing practices, firm size, and general disposition toward unions could prevent cooperation. In 1882, manufacturers and unions associated with the Knights of Labor agreed to settle future disputes in the boot and shoe industry through a joint arbitration committee. The pact fell victim to disagreements among employers two years later. One line of conflict pitted established members of the trade against newcomers to the business, unsympathetically described by an old-timer as "a new class of men engaging in the business who entered for the purpose of making money and had no previous training. . . . They were forever and eternally complaining that we were paying too much for labor. . . . They at last predominated [on the board] and succeeded in carrying their cranky notions so far as to break up nearly all good feeling between the employes [sic] and the manufacturers."[28] In addition, proprietors operating on a modest scale resented the big firms, arguing that they had used arbitration "to crush out the smaller manufacturers."[29]

HANGING TOGETHER: THE DEVELOPMENT OF A BUSINESS COMMUNITY

The story of class realignment among Cincinnati employers roughly parallels narratives of working-class formation. It is a story of challenges to employers' political and economic positions, and their mobilization to meet those challenges.

I tell this story in two chapters: the present one focuses on collective organization and action, the next (chapter 3) on collective identities and framing. The first part of the story highlights the development of civic associations which were broadly representative of Cincinnati capital and involved businessmen in common activities on a wide range of local issues. These developments set Cincinnati apart from San Francisco, where capital remained more divided both in organization and in action. They also set the stage for the second part of the story, in which I trace the elaboration of a class discourse of business citizenship. Collective organization and discourse together undercut ties between businessmen and lower classes, whether "lower" referred to their income, their taste, or their citizenship. The character of organization and discourse also helped bridge many of the divisions among capitalists described above. This simultaneous cutting of vertical ties and generalizing of horizontal ones warrants the summary term "class formation."

Challenges

Between 1870 and 1900, Cincinnati's manufacturers suffered economic setbacks, popular insurgences, political troubles both acute and chronic, and a range of new problems and opportunities within the workplace. These differed only in degree, not in kind, from challenges facing capital elsewhere. In Cincinnati, economic and political difficulties were probably more severe, and labor rebellion less so, than in most other industrial cities. Together, however, they pushed businessmen to organize in self-defense.

On the economic front, the depressions which began in 1873 and 1893 highlighted the usual dilemmas of capitalist markets: how to expand them (by improving trade policies and transportation facilities, for example) and how to curb the "ruinous competition" they imposed (by regulating prices and output, for instance). More important, and more distinctive to Cincinnati, was the city's *relative* economic decline. Compared to the glory years before 1870, the pace of growth slowed in the last three decades of the nineteenth century.[30] Worse still, the city lost its edge over rival cities. Prior to the Civil War, Cincinnati had been the region's leading transportation hub and manufacturing center. That position gradually eroded. With railroads replacing river transport, Chicago displaced Cincinnati as trade and transportation center of the Midwest. And in key industries that had helped fuel Cincinnati's growth, other cities took the lead—Chicago in meat packing, Pittsburgh in steel, Milwaukee in beer. Overall, too, industrial output and population in centers like Chicago, Pittsburgh, and Cleveland caught up with Cincinnati or even surpassed it.[31] These were not obscure statistical matters reconstructed by economic historians. Instead, they were closely monitored and well publicized by local businessmen. They were also the subject of endless hand-wringing. A typical dinner speech at the Carriage Makers' Club in 1890 indicted Cincinnati for its "old fogyism" and held up as an instructive contrast the energy and civic spirit of Chicago. Most businessmen would have heard similar speeches on many other occasions.[32]

Much like the cycle of economic boom and bust, the arc of labor militancy in Cincinnati differed only in degree from that in other cities. A major wave of unionization and strikes hit Cincinnati between 1864 and the 1873 panic; and a more powerful one still came in the late 1870s and 1880s, peaking in 1877 and 1886. Ross estimates that Cincinnati workers formed one hundred new unions between 1878 and 1884, with membership shooting up from one thousand to twelve thousand. And as compared to between two and five strikes annually in 1873–76, Cincinnati averaged fourteen per year between the 1877 railroad uprising and the 1894 Pullman strike. Labor action then dropped off between the 1893 depression and the turn of the century. Many of the same trades that dominated union activity elsewhere did so in Cincinnati as well. Building tradesmen, metal workers, and shoe makers led the way in repeated battles over wage rates, hours of labor, and union recognition. Other hotspots, flaring up less frequently, included cigar making, brewing, and carriage building.[33] Cincinnati commentators often remarked that the city's workers were less prone than others to strikes and, if striking, to violence. During the 1877 railroad strikes, the *Cincinnati Enquirer* joined the general hysteria over anarchy and mob violence, but it also boasted that "Cincinnati may well be proud of her citizens. Not another city in America has less of that sort of population called the dangerous class."[34] Still, union demands and strikes became common enough in major local industries that employers had to reckon with "the labor problem," whether through temporary expedients like the funding of special police by the Chamber of Commerce in 1886,[35] or through more enduring counterorganization. And the conclusion they likely drew from sensational newspaper accounts of labor violence elsewhere was probably not that things were better in Cincinnati, but that things could get worse.

The worst did not come in 1877, 1886, or 1894, however; and it did not come from organized labor. The reference point for elite fears of social upheaval was instead the 1884 Court House riot. Although sparked by a lenient sentence meted out for a murder, the riot had deeper roots in the 1880s. Like residents of other large cities, Cincinnatians felt besieged by urban social ills, from intemperance and prostitution to violent crime. And they criticized city officials for being too corrupt or incompetent to maintain order. At the dedication of the new Chamber of Commerce building in 1889, the Reverend Chidlaw voiced many citizens' prayers. "We beseech Thee, O God, to . . . grant unto us just and good men as magistrates and judges, righteous officers of courage and judgment to execute our good and wholesome laws, that immorality, vice, and crime may be suppressed, society protected, and violence cease in the land."[36] Not waiting for divine intervention, school officials developed a new curriculum to better socialize the city's youth. Rote memorization of uplifting literary passages, the school superintendent hoped, would improve their morals, and physical education would improve their discipline. For those who remained unimproved, the obvious solution was more efficient social control. A Police Court judge drew up plans in 1876 to better screen, train, and supervise patrolmen, and to more closely monitor the city's "transients."[37]

The Court House riot occurred in the context of these more general fears of immorality and misgovernment. In March 1884, a jury convicted William Berner of manslaughter. Neither the offense nor the verdict was extraordinary. Berner and an accomplice had murdered their employer, and they were among twenty-three individuals facing murder charges that month. The lenient verdict was also typical: local newspapers regularly denounced crooked lawyers, corrupt judges, and craven juries for finding murderers guilty only of lesser charges, or not at all.[38] In response to what the presiding judge himself condemned as a "damned outrage," leading citizens called a public meeting for March 28 to denounce the verdict and demand reform. Those who signed the call were prominent businessmen and professionals. But after a packed meeting in the city's Music Hall, a lynch mob went to get Berner from the jail. Thwarted, the crowd then set fire to the Court House. Two days of confrontation with police and national guardsmen left fifty-four dead, hundreds injured, and the Court House in ashes.

Most rioters were manual workers, but Cincinnati newspapers and businessmen did not depict the riot as pitting labor against the forces of order. Instead, both Democratic and Republican newspapers portrayed the mob as made up of decent men who had lost their heads in reaction to a genuine moral outrage, combined with a smaller contingent of criminals, opportunists, and drunkards. "The men active and earnest in the movement were not, as a rule, of the vicious classes. They were largely workingmen—a good example of the plain people."[39] To be sure, they went too far, but they went in the right direction. "Although the law of the land, the best interests of society and good morals are not in sympathy with mob violence . . . the people of this community have every reason to doubt the ability of existing methods for punishing crime to cope with the army of evil doers which seems to have taken possession of our city."[40] And once passions cooled, the *Gazette* predicted, rioters and leading citizens might be able to work together. "The good and true men on both sides of the barricades can reach a basis of agreement. The demand for justice is just. The wrath against the doers of iniquity was righteous, but the methods were fatal to social order, to public prosperity, to private rights. What we want is that good citizens shall all march one way."[41] The Court House riot, then, dramatized problems of moral order and civil unrest in Cincinnati. And the prominent men who took the lead in protesting Berner's sentence probably regarded rioters as pursuing the right goals by the wrong means. But the riot sharpened the ideological distinction between respectable citizens and those prey to demagogues and irrational action. It also encouraged business leaders to take countermeasures to restore order.

If the Court House riot raised doubts about the plain people, less ambiguous threats came from above, in the form of alarming political developments in Cincinnati and Ohio. One common complaint was that taxes were excessive and targeted manufacturing goods unfairly. Some local industries, such as tobacco and beer, faced special levies that certainly did not unite them in misery with other businesses. But the general importance of tax and trade policy for Cincinnati industries reminded businessmen of the need to bring their "practical experience and matured judgment" to bear on state and national legislators.[42] State laws in 1866 and again in 1886, defining a day's work as eight hours long, also caused general concern. The laws inconvenienced employers regardless of industry, less by compelling them to cut hours (the statutes were not enforced) than by inciting workers to demand compliance. In both taxation and the eight-hour laws, at least some businessmen saw the heavy hand of an oppressive state. An 1893 tax amendment worked one member of the city's Manufacturers' Association into a fine republican lather: "the position of a legislator under this law would be more tyrannical and smell stronger of anarchy than any of the laws of England." At the very least, such bills showed employers that on important matters of public policy, their "matured judgment" might not prevail.[43]

Cincinnati in the mid-1880s conformed to national trends in experiencing formidable labor mobilization on the electoral as well as the economic front. Barely two years after the Court House riot, and building from the 1886 May Day strikes, leaders of the Knights of Labor and Central Labor Union in Cincinnati joined middle-class reformers to launch a local branch of the United Labor Party. The party championed Henry George's single tax, government control of "natural" monopolies, and enforcement of Ohio's eight-hour law. The campaign also exposed and attacked the unequal benefits of economic growth in Cincinnati. All this was anathema to business leaders, who then had the additional shock of seeing the United Labor Party nearly win the April 1887 city election, despite the Democrats throwing their support to the Republican mayoral candidate.[44]

The United Labor Party quickly lost support—plummeting from 36.7 percent of the vote in April 1887, to 1.2 percent in November 1888.[45] And despite the scare in 1886–87, Cincinnati businessmen could take some comfort in the relative moderation of local workers. But business faced a more enduring political problem in Cincinnati's machine-ridden municipal government. As one early local historian of Cincinnati's elite recalled, city elections in the 1870s and 1880s could "flush an honest voter's cheek with shame," with multiple voting, selective distribution and counting of ballots, and outright bribery of election judges.[46] In 1886, the state's Republican governor gained control of Cincinnati's key Board of Public Affairs, and he put George Cox in charge. Cox, a saloon keeper and party hack, proved a skillful boss. With judicious use of kickbacks, patronage, and careful coalition building, Cox built a political machine which would dominate city government until 1911.[47]

Cox brought a kind of order to Cincinnati government. He systematized corruption and rationalized control of local politics by the Republican Party. These achievements made him a useful ally for key figures like Andrew Hickenlooper, president of the local gas company. For some other businessmen, the predictability of municipal government under Cox overcame their scruples over his methods. As one of his enemies put it, Cox at least "demands reasonably good service" from his patronage appointments, and cooperation between Cox and business organizations proved possible on certain administrative reforms.[48] And if nothing else, Cox guaranteed continued Republican rule. But particularly against the backdrop of union mobilization and civic disturbances, many leading citizens—including reform-minded Republicans—found the disadvantages of Cox's regime outweighed its benefits. For one, Cox's power rested in some small part on Cincinnati's construction trades unions, which gave labor a political voice that businessmen preferred to silence.[49] And while municipal government under Cox may have been more orderly than under his predecessors, the machine's reliance on patronage and political appointments seemed to be a recipe for high taxes and poor performance—a source of particular concern to affluent residents settling into new suburbs and demanding prompt attention to city services, from sewers to schools. At the very least, reformers argued, Cincinnati deserved "a dollar's worth of government for every dollar's worth of taxes." Lastly, the Cox machine was an embarrassment. It was hard enough that Cincinnati lagged behind its rivals in economic growth. For the Queen City to also have a national reputation for misgovernment was an added insult, and one that might compound the city's difficulties by scaring off potential investors.[50]

Relative economic decline, political threats from above and below, and even much of Cincinnati's labor mobilization besieged employers from "outside" the workplace. A last set of dilemmas confronted them from within their own businesses and represented opportunities as well as challenges. Economic organization in Cincinnati moved in familiar directions, albeit at a slower pace. As Ross has documented, manufacturing in Cincinnati increasingly took place in factories employing large numbers of hands and taking the form of corporations rather than partnerships.[51] Production techniques also changed. A more extensive division of labor narrowed the range of skills exercised by employees, and some of those skills began to be built into machinery. New styles of supervision also appeared, with foremen replacing both the increasingly distant owners and the autonomous job control of craftsmen. The contributions of these changes to worker unrest are well known. But they could also reshape capitalist alliances and identities, both by cutting vertical ties across class lines and by forcing employers to confront new problems of labor management—and, perhaps, to develop new collective solutions for those problems.

Consider de-skilling. "Foolproof" machinery, subdivided labor, and routinized tasks helped employers in several key industries substitute semiskilled workers or children on work customarily done by craftsmen. Thanks in part to machine stitching, for example, local shoe manufacturers in the late 1870s were able to greatly expand output while assigning to specialized jobs "a bevy of happy girls, who sing merrily above the rattle of their sewing machines."[52] A large manufacturer of barrels in 1886, similarly, could produce in high volume because of "labor saving devices, the use of machinery, and the system of interchangeability, so that every thing when assembled together, fits."[53] These changes had obvious costs for craftsmen, including pay cuts, job insecurity, and injured pride. The gains accrued to employers in the form of lower labor costs and greater leverage in dealing with trade unions. A carriage firm answered state Bureau of Labor Statistics inquiries about prospective strikes with the assurance that neither wage hikes nor strikes were likely because machinery had blurred the line between skilled and unskilled workers. "Most skilled men can be replaced by unskilled labor on short notice."[54]

It might be expected that, as the composition of the workforce changed, ties between employer and craftsman, based on a shared identity as "mechanics," would atrophy. But de-skilling also created new problems for employers. Skilled men may have been expensive and ornery, but they knew their work and could undertake "management" tasks—planning out the work, maintaining tools, co-ordinating jobs with other craftsmen. Less-skilled specialists could not. These responsibilities, accordingly, fell to management. Another new problem involved training. Factories still required *some* skilled men. As de-skilling advanced, however, individual employers no longer had much incentive to maintain traditional apprenticeship programs. Instead, they took on "apprentices" as learners at low wages, quickly got them up to speed on narrow tasks, and taught them no more. For those jobs that continued to call for versatility and experience, the supply of labor became a real concern.[55]

Two other major trends in late-nineteenth-century manufacturing—toward large-scale production and corporate organization—also appear in Cincinnati, if to a lesser degree than in comparable industrial cities. The main indicators are an increasing number of employees in the average enterprise and a relative decline in the number of proprietary firms. Ross has compiled figures for both. The proportion of Cincinnati's labor force in firms employing more than one hundred workers, for example, grew from one-third to almost one-half between 1870 and 1880; and where two-thirds of the top manufacturing firms in 1850 were owned by individual families or two to three partners, this proportion was down to less than half by 1880.[56] The obvious implication for class formation is that proprietors found it more difficult to maintain direct ties with employees as their sheer numbers increased and as owners became more distant from the shop floor. But much as with de-skilling, changes in industrial organization raised the problem of what would take the place of customary controls. Whether or not proprietors had ever worked side by side with their men, they were likely to have been closely involved with the details of both production and personnel. Increasingly, they had to find substitutes for "the personal touch"—ways to handle hiring, firing, and grievances in the absence of face-to-face contact with, or personal knowledge of, workers.[57] Post–Civil War Cincinnati employers' positions and experiences became less and less consistent with either a self-image or a public role as "mechanics." The labor process, however, did not dictate what took its place, particularly because the transition to mass production proceeded at very different paces in Cincinnati industries. Craft skills and small-batch production remained the norm in construction, the machine tool industry, and lithography well into the twentieth century. At the other extreme, pork packing was undertaken on a (dis)assembly-line basis before the Civil War, and the shift to large-scale, mechanized production was mostly complete in furniture manufacture by the late 1870s and in brewing in the 1890s. Other industries, notably those making shoes and carriages, were divided between a dominant mass production sector and bespoke shops.[58]

The varied challenges facing Cincinnati employers following the Civil War—economic slowdown, labor unrest, civil disorder, political mismanagement, workplace growing pains—did not simply "lead to" new employer solidarities and ideologies. They did strain the vertical ties of interest and identity that existed between proprietors and wage earners. And some of the peculiarities of Cincinnati, such as the relative moderation of its organized labor and the comparative venality of its government, may have encouraged employers to define their enemies and allies more in terms of civic and political roles than in terms of class. But the links between challenges and class realignment are much more complicated than this. A given employer, after all, could define and respond to the "same" threats in different ways. And, as noted in my earlier discussion of public policy and workplace change, some problems facing employers could as easily divide as unite them. Finally, the relative salience of different challenges could change from one historical moment to the next.

Employer Organization

The causal path from challenge to response runs through organization. Employers met new problems by organizing. They often did so in an ad hoc way, and they had varying motives for joining. Institutions, however, develop a dynamic of their own. It was ultimately the character of business organization that consolidated new alliances. The history of employer organization after the Civil War follows Bertolt Brecht's dictum: grub first, then morals. Most of the organizational growth in the first ten to fifteen years centered on immediate economic interests. Associations aiming to regulate trade affairs or fight labor continued to occupy manufacturers for the rest of the century. Spurred by economic decline and political challenges, however, much new organizational activity in the 1880s and 1890s centered instead on civic improvement. Both the membership and the purposes of these associations brought together a wider range of businessmen than had organizations focused on trade matters. If what we mean by *class solidarity* is that diverse individuals who happen to occupy similar economic positions organize and act in concert, then capitalist class solidarity in Cincinnati developed through civic engagement, not through the pursuit of pressing economic interests.

TRADE ASSOCIATIONS

The main preoccupations of manufacturers' associations after 1865 were with "ruinous competition" and unruly workers. Managing relations among competitors had long been the main concern of the city's Chamber of Commerce. Pork packers, grain traders, distillers, and other merchants relied on the Chamber of Commerce to provide central exchange facilities, to codify standards for grading and measuring commodities, and to discipline those guilty of "unmercantile conduct." The Chamber of Commerce played little role in manufacturing, however, and it was in this sector that collective organization flourished after the Civil War.

Prompted in part by economic slowdown after 1867 and by growing conflict with unions over wage reductions, Cincinnati manufacturers formed trade associations at a rapid pace over the next decade. Iron producers came first, in 1867, followed by manufacturers of tobacco (1868), cigars (1869), horseshoes (1872), leather (1873), boots and shoes (1873), beer (1874), and furniture (1877). The construction trades joined their ranks in 1878. Like the unions they often fought, these were unstable organizations. Some disappeared as labor unrest died down or economic pressures eased, reappearing when conditions warranted. Others persisted in form but changed in purpose. Cincinnati iron manufacturers first formed a local association in 1867, posting notices that they would cut molders' wages and ignore their work rules. Less than a year later, the same body turned its attention to the "ruinously low" price of iron. Cincinnati brewers reversed the sequence. They organized in 1874 and again in 1877 to fix the price of beer, trying to maintain a united front against the tavern owners. The Brewers' Protective Association then coordinated responses to union wage demands in 1879.[59]

Other associations focused specifically on labor relations, but during the 1870s and 1880s they were no more consistent in their policies. Depending on union strength and market conditions, the same group of employers might move back and forth between belligerent anti-unionism and more or less grudging acceptance of collective bargaining. Organized cigar makers came to terms with unionists in 1870, launched an unsuccessful lockout to break the union in 1880, and won the open shop in 1884.[60] Boot and shoe manufacturers covered a still wider range. In May, 1882, they established a Board of Arbitration, with representatives from the association and the local Knights of Labor, to settle disputes. The board successfully resolved several grievances and wage claims over the next two years. Owing in part to divisions among employers, the board ceased operations in 1884, but organized manufacturers continued to bargain in good faith with the Knights. Only in 1889 did employers repudiate the union.[61]

Whether they treated unions as enemies or allies in their efforts to regulate trade, employers' associations sought to solve basic problems of collective action. Manufacturers in each industry had a common interest in regulating prices and preventing unions from getting the upper hand. They also had common enemies—particularly unions, but sometimes also organized buyers or suppliers, such as the tavern owners for brewers, or butchers for tanners. Brewers and tanners were also competitors, however, who stood to gain in the short term from underselling rivals or cutting a separate deal with the union.[62] The trade associations formed after the Civil War, accordingly, were liable to breakdown, and they self-consciously adopted measures to maintain unity. Some followed the custom of requiring members to post a bond, to be forfeited if they broke ranks. They also catered to members' social as well as business needs. Several labeled themselves "clubs" in their early years, and most organized picnics and visits to other cities to build camaraderie. Even formal meetings allowed time for good meals and relaxed fellowship—accompanied, in the case of the Metal Trades Association, by performances of the Machine Tool Quintet.[63] Economists would recognize these activities as selective incentives to curb defections. Participants at the time were less cynical, viewing their dinners and recreations as ways to build solidarity in place of competitive rivalry. At bimonthly dinners of the Carriage Makers' Club, members left behind "the troubles and cares of business" and "forgot competition," focusing instead on the "enjoyment of the occasion" and "what would benefit the trade."[64] Later associations, notably in the metal trades, would widen the circle of fellowship to include engineers and professional managers as well as proprietors. But driven by immediate economic interests and constructed on the basis of industry affiliation, these institutions rarely brought employers together across trade lines. Particularly in the area of industrial relations, it would not be until the founding of the Employers' Association in 1904 that a wider coalition of businessmen organized, *as employers*, under one roof.

Employers built trade-based associations such as these to deal with pressing market or labor crises. Those motives account for the timing of organizational foundings. Most can be traced to economic downturns beginning in 1867 and 1873, with revivals during labor's insurgency between 1877 and 1886. The roots of trade organization in market and labor upheavals also meant that these associations waxed and waned as going concerns. Their fundamental purposes, finally, narrowed their constituencies to members of specific industries. More inclusive organization came later, addressed different problems, and in important instances proved more enduring. Two arenas for more encompassing employer group formation were particularly important: cultural enrichment and civic improvement. Neither was wholly distinct from prosaic economic concerns. Enhancing Cincinnati's reputation as a cultural mecca, for example, promised to attract new investment. And civic improvements included railroad facilities and lower taxes as well as civil service rules and charter reform. The economic benefits of symphonies and railroad lines were not restricted to particular trades, however. Instead, they helped rally a wider constituency and fostered a broader view of business interests.

CULTURAL INSTITUTIONS

Art museums and music festivals obviously were not direct responses to strikes on the part of businessmen, acting in their capacity as employers. But these institutions, too, addressed concerns over Cincinnati's economic standing and civic decay. And they were both products of business leadership and vehicles for enlarging businessmen's networks and civic roles. In both the visual arts and music, the 1870s saw a crusade to build new cultural institutions. Planning for an art museum got underway in 1873. The initial push came from the wives of prominent businessmen; their husbands took on the manly tasks of organizing and fund-raising. Following a donation of $150,000 from a retired merchant and generous subscriptions from other local magnates, the museum opened its doors in 1882. An art academy complemented the museum's exhibitions with educational programs to train local artists and encourage art appreciation. Cincinnati's claim to be the cultural center of the West rested especially on its musical offerings. Local notables inaugurated a Musical Festival Association in 1873, building in part on the city's German choral societies. The festival featured an annual series of concerts directed by acclaimed conductor Theodore Thomas, with world-renowned soloists joining Thomas's New York–based orchestra and a local chorus. The Music Hall Association followed in 1875. Organized to raise funds for a permanent center for performing arts, it completed its work in 1878. The College of Music began accepting students that same year.[65]

These institutions fit a familiar pattern in Gilded Age urban centers: the elaboration of cultural hierarchy.[66] The hierarchy distinguished refined from popular culture (Shakespeare versus vaudeville, for example, or classical music versus "pops"), and it prescribed rules of decorum for the consumption of high culture (such as reserved contemplation as opposed to effusive participation). These changes were part of a larger process of status closure. An emerging upper-middle class (the exact boundaries of which vary from one historical study to another) set themselves apart from the urban rabble in residence, manners, and education, as well as taste.

Two other motives for cultural institution-building have more to do with post–Civil War challenges to urban upper classes. One concerned moral order. Studies of late-nineteenth-century refinement often note that it involved a disciplinary response to an increasingly foreign and unruly urban population. The same standards that erected distinctions between social groups served the purposes of education, uplift, and discipline. The United States of America, after all, was a democracy. Even the humble clerk could learn to practice good manners and appreciate Beethoven. With the aging of new money, moreover, came a sense of obligation to perform good works. Cincinnati was no exception. Alongside its institutions for presenting works of art were those designed for broader cultural uplift. For example, the College of Music would not only train performers, but inculcate a broader "taste for music" through instruction and public performances.[67]

Art and music were seen as antidotes to economic as well as moral decay. At a time when leading citizens lamented Cincinnati's fading fortunes relative to industrial rivals, building the city's reputation for cultural excellence had great appeal. It provided one area in which Cincinnati could still claim superiority over upstarts like Chicago or Cleveland. A College of Music publication took considerable pride in quoting charges by Chicago critics that festival conductor

Thomas "plays 'over the heads of people.' They can find nothing that would appeal to the popular taste in the programs of his 'Popular Concerts.'" Cincinnatians knew better. Thomas deserved praise for instilling an "appreciation of the highest forms of instrumental music."[68] Here, cultural hierarchy served to distinguish the relative refinement of cities rather than classes. There was a more practical benefit to high culture, however. It might attract new capital. As the business-oriented *Daily Gazette* editorialized shortly after the organization of the Musical Festival, "intelligent lovers of music and all who are interested in the encouragement of musical taste and advancement will be glad of the opportunity to place the Cincinnati orchestra on a permanent basis. The advantages to the city and its citizens, flowing from such an act, are easily perceived."[69] Planning for the city's music hall underscored the link between cultural and industrial betterment. As the directors of the Ohio Mechanics' Institute emphasized, the plan was for "the erection of a Grand Central Building, to be known as a Music Hall, but to be . . . expressly adapted for Expositions of Industry."[70]

Both the organization and the purposes of Cincinnati's cultural institutions separated businessmen from the lower classes and drew them closer to one another. The membership rosters of organizing committees and governing boards contain no surprises. There sit a very narrow range of Cincinnati society, with many of the same worthy citizens—department store owner John Shillito, wool merchant A. D. Bullock, the manufacturer W. H. Davis, brewer Herman Goepper, Merchants' Exchange member A. T. Goshorn—appearing in one cultural enterprise after another. Predictable, too, is the fact that the biggest donors were successful merchants and manufacturers. But on a more modest scale, other businessmen were the key "stockholders" of these institutions. Under Ohio law, the museum and music hall were nonprofit corporations which raised funds by issuing stock. Shares bore no interest and could not be transferred, but they entitled owners to elect trustees and review yearly reports. Lists of shareholders, not surprisingly, read "like a 'Who's Who' of Cincinnati's business, social, and industrial leaders."[71]

While segregating businessmen from those with fewer resources and different tastes, cultural philanthropy also brought together proprietors and managers who would never have crossed paths in trade associations. Of 124 shareholders in the Cincinnati Museum Association in 1882, for example, 80 percent were in the city's Blue Book for 1879 or 1886. No rubbing shoulders with the common man here. Yet the occupants of this exalted circle came from a wide range of businesses. Trustees included a railroad executive, a jeweler, an insurance executive, a machine firm owner, a gas utility president, a banker, a retailer, a physician, and a brewery proprietor, among others. Social pressures certainly encouraged businessmen of varied backgrounds to participate in cultural improvement.

Memorials written by members of the city's leading business associations, for example, consistently praise former colleagues for their liberal support of the arts. And philanthropic impulses aside, appearing on the lists of donors served as a badge of social status, recognizable and honored regardless of trade. The etiquette of cultural patronage also helped neutralize any conflicts of economic interest. The fact that stock ownership in the art museum and music hall neither earned interest nor permitted sale signaled that in this sphere, at least, narrow self-interest should not apply.[72]

Among Cincinnati capitalists, then, status closure—which among workers often contributes to craft monopolies or racial divisions—fostered a broader class formation. Belonging to cultural organizations and idealizing art helped bridge economic divisions among businessmen. They also eroded vertical ties. Cultural philanthropy excludes those without suitable wealth, networks, or taste. Business associations devoted to civic improvement had similar effects, but they involved an even broader class base than did patronage of the arts.

CIVIC IMPROVEMENT ASSOCIATIONS

Trade associations in Cincinnati were organized by members of an industry to meet particular economic needs. Art museums and symphonies had wider constituencies but fairly narrow purposes. Civic improvement associations were especially important responses to challenges facing Cincinnati businessmen because they both enlisted a cross-section of the city's proprietors and pursued a broad agenda. Of the three types of organizations, they were also the last on the scene, with foundings clustering in the 1880s and early 1890s.

Among the city's important civic associations, the Commercial Club came first in time and rank. Founded in 1880, the Commercial Club originally focused on trade with the South and, specifically, freight rates out of the city. But it soon diversified to address questions of economic infrastructure, civic amenities, and municipal governance. It also combined the functions of a social club and a political lobby. Like a social club, it was exclusive. The roster was limited to fifty, and admission required nomination by a current member, screening by a special committee, and a nearly unanimous vote of approval. Two other unwritten prerequisites seem to have been that the candidate be a gentile and a current member of Cincinnati's preeminent Queen City Club. *Within* the city's economic elite, however, the Commercial Club strove to be broadly representative: no more than two members could come from any one company. Like a social club, finally, the Commercial Club provided a center for fellowship and gentlemanly indulgence. At monthly dinner meetings, members and their guests gathered (often at the Queen City Club) for gourmet meals, wine and cigars, and casual conversation. Once or twice a year, the club also made excursions to resorts or to sister institutions in other cities, explicitly mixing business and pleasure.[73]

The Commercial Club was also a political organization, however. In the time between lavish dinners, much of the Club's activity devolved on specialized committees. A sampling of committee names indicates the organization's main concerns: Municipal Legislation, Water Supply, Taxation, City Park, Street Improvements, Terminal Facilities, Technical School, Smoke Prevention, and Sanitation. These working committees (organized and disbanded as topics of the day changed) made recommendations to the membership, sometimes hired lawyers to draft legislation, lobbied on behalf of the club, and reported on progress at the monthly dinners. The dinners also featured talks by members or invited specialists (the police chief, a hydraulic engineer, prominent politicians) on pressing public issues. By combining features of an exclusive social club with those of a political lobby, the Commercial Club gave its members a civic education and a potent voice in local government. Among its many achievements, the club helped draft and win passage of a new city charter in 1891. The charter created a new, bipartisan administrative board, intended to end patronage appointments in favor of civil service rules. This change, Club participants argued, would reduce corruption and improve municipal efficiency.[74]

Compared to the Commercial Club, Cincinnati's Committee of One Hundred was an ad hoc and short-lived body. But in its heyday from 1885 to the early 1890s, it played an important role in rallying businessmen for political reform and in popularizing the gospel of nonpartisanship. The committee seems to have coalesced from an informal network of "concerned citizens" protesting the Berner murder verdict in 1884 and egregious violations of electoral laws in 1885.[75] Much of the committee's work in the first few years continued this preoccupation with "law and order." With funds contributed by its wealthy members, the committee hired detectives to gather evidence of electoral fraud and lawyers to prosecute the offenders. In part because the committee found the city's police singularly unhelpful in these investigations, police reform came next. The committee successfully lobbied to limit political control of the force and to substitute merit for patronage in department hiring and promotions. And in several public meetings during 1886, committee members sought to persuade a larger public of the evils of partisanship and the need for civil service reform.[76]

The Committee of One Hundred included lawyers and a sprinkling of other professionals, but the core membership consisted largely of local merchants and manufacturers. The range was broad, from manufacturers of cigars, hardware, beer, and wigs to real estate moguls, utility company executives, and clothing dealers.[77] Despite its name, the committee's executive also tried to broaden its constituency well beyond one hundred. Chairman I. J. Miller claimed "several hundred" members in 1886, although the $5 initiation and $5 annual dues probably limited enrollments from outside business and professional circles.[78] But it had neither the formal organization nor the extensive social functions of the Commercial Club. By the mid-1890s, businessmen devoted to civic improvement had alternatives, less makeshift than the Committee of One Hundred and less exclusive than the Commercial Club. The Young Men's Business Club stood first among them.

Like the Commercial Club, the Young Men's Business Club combined fellowship with good works. The club debuted in 1892, with sixty "prominent young businessmen" agreeing (over a "sumptuous repast") to regular monthly dinners "for the purpose of becoming better acquainted by frequent association."[79] Along with good meals and camaraderie at the club went membership education and public service. Dinners often featured speakers on local and national issues; club excursions were pitched to members as good opportunities, not just to make deals, but to learn of business and government practices in other cities. The main task, however, was to apply these lessons to Cincinnati. As in the Commercial Club, specialized committees involved members in the work of developing proposals for municipal improvements and lobbying on their behalf. The Young Men's Business Club became a leading champion of a wide range of civic projects, from a fall festival showcasing the city's manufactures to improved public education and a new union depot.[80]

The Business Men's Club (as it became known in 1899) also devoted itself to improving the efficiency of city government. For this purpose the club (in partnership with the Chamber of Commerce and the Commercial Club) organized and financed a Bureau of Municipal Research. Staffed by experts in accounting and public policy, the bureau acted both as a watchdog to uncover government waste and corruption and as a think tank for developing efficient alternatives.[81] The Business Men's Club coupled advocacy of municipal reform with even sharper criticism of the Cox regime than that voiced by the Commercial Club. The Business Men's Club also differed from the Commercial Club in its social base. Members of the Business Men's Club were generally younger and less prominent than those in the Commercial Club. They were also far more numerous. The roster grew from 100 in 1892 (already double that of the Commercial Club) to 1,000 by 1904, and to 1,600 in 1912, making it by far the most popular of Cincinnati's business organizations.[82] With its less elite membership, its reformist spirit, and its greater willingness to cooperate on civic projects with nonbusiness groups, the Business Men's Club exemplified early-twentieth-century business progressivism.[83]

The Commercial Club, Committee of One Hundred, and Business Men's Club were the most important late-nineteenth-century associations in which Cincinnati businessmen worked together on civic issues, but there were many others. Some focused their energies more narrowly, such as the Civil Service Reform Association (1881), the Taxpayers' Association (1886), and the Good Government League (1899). Some confined themselves to neighborhood affairs, including the improvement associations which appeared in affluent residential districts like Avondale and Walnut Hills in the 1880s. Only the Chamber of Commerce rivaled the Commercial Club and the Business Men's Club as an agency for civic improvement, and it was a late convert. For its first sixty years, the Chamber of Commerce devoted itself to trade and finance, getting involved in issues of public policy mostly on an ad hoc basis or where public services—such as shipping facilities or street railways—had direct economic consequences for business. In the late 1890s, however, the Chamber of Commerce expanded the scope of its civic activities and began to work more closely with other business associations on behalf of civic reform and municipal efficiency.[84] Cooperative relations among businessmen in these and other civic improvement associations took formal shape in 1905, when the Cincinnati Associated Organizations brought together delegates from most major civic bodies and trade groups to discuss measures for advancing "the general improvement and welfare of the city."[85]

Cincinnati's leading civic clubs were well suited to forging a broader class solidarity. They were *business* clubs, composed exclusively of proprietors, professionals, and managers, but among men in these positions, the clubs drew from a wide range of economic sectors. They did so in large part because of their multipurpose quality, which gave businessmen any number of reasons for joining. Among the many issues addressed by the Commercial Club or Business Men's Club were some narrowly utilitarian ones, such as improving water supplies to newly developed suburbs, lowering tariffs on manufactured goods, or extending street railways to hilltop residential areas. Self-serving interest in issues like these may have spurred some businessmen to enroll. Others were probably driven by status considerations. The Commercial Club was widely recognized as *the* elite business organization, and the Business Men's Club, while less exclusive, had all the amenities of a downtown social club. Some businessmen, finally, may have signed on out of political interests, given the reputation of these associations for championing municipal reform. Even among this group, motives might have been mugwumpish (replacing corrupt bosses with "the best men") or partisan (purging Cox in order to get the Democrats back into office). Whatever their initial attraction, involvement in civic associations familiarized businessmen with a wide range of public issues, as observers and often as participants. They engaged those issues, moreover, in a setting which brought them together with their counterparts in other industries, in commerce as well as manufacturing, and among managers as well as other owners. Among the 137 gentlemen who belonged to the Commercial Club between 1880 and 1907, 68 had interests in manufacturing, 33 in mercantile pursuits, 28 in finance, 24 in railroads and transportation, and 20 in the professions. The Business Men's Club was similarly representative of society's second tier. The 120 officers and executive committee members serving between 1892 and 1910 included 50 associated with manufacturing, 16 with financial services, 16 with mercantile activities, 14 with the professions, and 8 with railroads and transportation.[86]

These civic bodies cannot be interpreted as developing in response to labor insurgency. Such an argument might apply to employer associations actually involved with labor relations.[87] Organizations like the Business Men's Club, however, while they were arguably *more* important for employer class formation, were not part of a countermobilization against working-class protest in the workplace or in politics. Strikes and unionization were not only less prominent in Cincinnati. They were also effectively repelled by other means (particularly the courts) and other kinds of organization. Nor is there any evidence that civic associations paid much attention to labor matters in their early years. Much higher up on their agenda were Cincinnati's economic woes, its misgovernment, and, to a lesser degree, civil disturbances which were not defined in class terms. Yet for just these reasons, civic associations were especially important for reshaping class alignments, fostering a collective identity as business citizens (see chapter 3), and structuring proprietors' understanding of "the labor problem" (see chapter 5).

THE EMPLOYERS' ASSOCIATION

To the trade associations, cultural philanthropy, and civic clubs in their tool kit, Cincinnati businessmen added an organization of a different type. Late in the year 1903, they founded the Employers' Association, dedicated to resisting "unjust demands on the part of labor unions" throughout the city.[88] The association had counterparts in other cities. All were part of a nationwide open shop movement, sparked by the American Federation of Labor's own surge in membership and strike activity after 1898.[89] But the debut of the Employers' Association also can be seen as a point in a local trajectory of class formation.

Even allowing for exaggeration on the part of its enthusiastic backers, the claim of 2,750 members in 1904 indicates that Cincinnati's Employers' Association dwarfed San Francisco's Employers' Association, which in its short life enrolled only a small minority of that city's firms. The constituents of

Cincinnati's Employers' Association also represented a cross-section of local industry, a sharp departure from all prior union-fighting bodies in Cincinnati. No membership list has survived, but there are indications that the association brought together businessmen from most of the major local industries. Newspaper accounts of a 1904 luncheon given by the association to honor visiting open shop spokesmen David Parry and John Kirby include a partial list of the hosts. They were leading owners or executives of companies making machine tools, pianos, furniture, clothing, tobacco, food, and soap as well the heads of a print shop, a railroad line, and the streetcar company. The association also counted among its members the Business Men's Club.[90]

The Employers' Association had more than an inclusive roster. It also had a great deal of clout, proving itself a formidable enemy of unions in a variety of local industries. In battles for the open shop waged by employers in specific trades, the association regularly played supporting roles. It provided financial and tactical assistance in offensives against unionized butchers, iron molders, carriage makers, and cab drivers. It helped organize boycotts of union printing shops and of firms using union teamsters. It supplied "police protection" to local firms fighting union recognition, including Western Union, and may have lent a hand in maintaining blacklists against unionists. In most of these disputes, moreover—and in sharp contrast to outcomes in San Francisco—the association's anti-union policy prevailed.[91]

The trajectory in businessmen's institutional responses to post–Civil War challenges is noteworthy. Trade associations in the years immediately after the war addressed issues and enrolled businessmen on an industry-specific basis. To the extent that they focused on problems *other* than labor unions, they might also preserve a trade community and a "mechanics'" identity that encompassed skilled workers as well as proprietors. As union mobilization in the late 1870s and 1880s changed the agenda to "the labor problem," that inclusive trade community became more obviously mythical in most industries. By the 1890s, associations more broadly representative of owners and managers—and few others—assumed greater importance. Cultural philanthropy and civic boosterism built ties among businessmen with quite varied economic interests, in part by shifting the objects of collective action away from those economic interests. Only with the Employers' Association in 1903 did businessmen come together in an organization that combined stricter exclusion of lower classes, broader inclusion of one another, and a steady focus on a pressing industrial issue: defeating unions.

That issue, however, did not dominate employers' public personae. Nor did later forms of organization supersede earlier ones. Businessmen continued to belong to trade associations, and they continued to make use of them for fighting unions. The important trend in class formation was that over time many *also* became involved in more inclusive and civic-minded bodies. As they did, they articulated a more general identity as members of Cincinnati's "business community," one which carried over to their thinking about the workplace and *why* unions had no legitimate place there. But before taking up these themes in chapters 3 and 5, we will consider San Francisco, where employer organization and collective action took a different path.

2

RACE AND CLASS ALIGNMENTS IN SAN FRANCISCO

San Francisco in the summer of 1907 was worlds away from Cincinnati. Employers in most sectors recognized and bargained with unions. That summer, even the metal trades—one of the most resolutely open shop industries in Cincinnati—fell into line. There were holdouts, notably Patrick Calhoun's United Railway Co., which waged a violent battle with streetcar operators from May through July. Despite the efforts of San Francisco's Citizens' Alliance to rally local capital behind Calhoun's open shop stance, leading business associations refused to go along; the Civic League instead joined with the Labor Council to try to mediate. The political scene that summer also differed dramatically from Cincinnati's. The Union Labor Party ran city government, as it had for the previous six years. Mayor Schmitz would soon be leaving office amid a corruption scandal. That scandal might appear to have been a golden opportunity to purge the party, but as in labor relations, San Francisco businessmen were divided. Some championed clean government. Others opposed the prosecution of Schmitz and his co-conspirators, in good part because those co-conspirators included such prominent businessmen as Patrick Calhoun.

These contrasts appear between two cities that had much in common economically around the turn of the century. Their manufacturing sectors were of similar size; they were composed of many of the same industries; and they featured proprietary firms of small to middling size (the statistical details are offered later in this chapter). Despite these similarities, class alignments developed in nearly opposite directions. San Francisco businessmen in the summer of 1907, as in prior decades, neither belonged to common organizations nor subscribed to common principles in their dealings with labor. Using Cincinnati as the yard-stick, class formation in San Francisco did not happen until after 1910. *Working*-class formation, by contrast, most certainly did. Thanks in part to divisions among capitalists, San Francisco labor achieved remarkable degrees of unity and power at work and in politics.

This chapter explores the distinctive path of class alignments in San Francisco. Many of the obstacles to class formation differed little from those found in Cincinnati. Here too, manufacturers stood apart from merchants, industries followed competing interests, and small businessmen resented large corporations. San Francisco businessmen, however, utterly failed to overcome these obstacles. Significant groups of local capitalists aligned themselves, not with other capitalists, but with organized labor. That alignment, in turn, can be traced back to San Francisco's race relations, to the relative timing of manufacturing development and union growth, and to the weakness of solidary civic institutions. Operating in a cumulative historical sequence, these factors divided capital and allied many entrepreneurs with skilled white unionists. As chapter 4 will argue, they also led San Francisco businessmen to construct social identities and boundaries and to embrace a civic ideology quite different from that of their Cincinnati counterparts.

SAN FRANCISCO EXCEPTIONALISM

The gold rush made San Francisco an "instant city,"[1] driving both the hectic pace and peculiar character of its early growth. A settlement of 1,000 in 1848, the city's population reached 36,151 by 1852. Initially, the city acted as the miners' main base for services—small businesses loaned them money, sold them equipment and provisions, and for the lucky few, exchanged gold for cash. These early activities gave San Francisco a head start as the West's financial center and as the gateway for Pacific trade. The city's growth continued unabated, expanding from 56,802 residents in 1860, to 149,473 ten years later, to nearly 300,000 by 1890.[2]

San Francisco's gold rush roots and pell-mell growth shaped the city's social character. Whether captivated by its democratic charms or appalled by its crudity, observers then and scholars now see San Francisco's early social structure as departing from East Coast norms. The 49ers were a mixed lot. Few unskilled workers could afford to travel to California and equip themselves as independent miners. Among those who could, however, clerks and professionals mingled with mere mechanics. Moreover, for these transplants, standards of refinement that maintained status boundaries back home (including the genteel stigma against getting your hands dirty) temporarily fell away in the scramble for gold. In some ways, this more fluid social structure survived the gold rush. Rapid economic expansion and exaggerated swings of boom and bust as new mines opened and old ones gave out supported unusually high levels of social mobility in San Francisco. Over a third of the city's merchants in 1852 began their careers as clerical or blue-collar workers; as late as 1880, over half of manufacturers had similar roots in clerical or manual labor.[3] This relative openness extended from class to ethnicity. As a powerful magnet for fortune seekers throughout the country and around the globe, San Francisco's population had unusually high proportions of the foreign born and, even by American standards, high levels of ethnic diversity. Among the largest ethnic groups, both the Italians and the Irish moved quickly into small business, and the Irish could be found widely distributed through San Francisco's occupational strata, residential areas, and city government.[4] Their good fortune rested in large part on the great exception to San Francisco egalitarianism, the Chinese, who accounted for 8 percent of the city's population in 1870.[5] This group, too, was drawn by gold, and later by jobs building the transcontinental railroad. Once those opportunities disappeared, most returned to San Francisco. One important theme in the city's history, discussed later in this chapter, is the way hostility against this group crowded out ethnic, religious, and even class differences among whites.

The gold rush also left its mark on the character and timing of San Francisco's commercial development. Since the city was a conduit for men and materials, trade and finance dominated its early economy, and San Francisco remained the West Coast's mercantile hub for the rest of the century. That commercial role also dominated residents' self-image. In the 1860s, however, San Francisco began three decades of rapid development in manufacturing, starting with industries which catered to mining and miners (who needed pumps, tools, and clothing). Compared to Cincinnati, this was a late start, but San Francisco quickly narrowed the gap. In 1860, the city had but 1,564 manufacturing employees, compared to 30,268 in Cincinnati. Ten years later, local industry employed 12,377; in 1880, 28,442; and in 1890, 48,446, roughly half of Cincinnati's total manufacturing employment. That same year, measured by the value of its products, San Francisco ranked as the nation's ninth-largest manufacturing city—two places behind Cincinnati. San Francisco's distinctive balance between manufacturing and other sectors persisted, but the differences from Cincinnati are not dramatic. In 1870, 32 percent of San Francisco workers were employed in manufacturing, 41 percent in services, and 26 percent in trade and transportation. The corresponding percentages for Cincinnati are 44, 33, and 22.[6]

If manufacturing did not play the leading role in San Francisco's economy that it did in Cincinnati's, it still took similar forms in the two cities. The typical

San Francisco firm, like its Cincinnati counterpart, had proprietary ownership and relatively few employees (11.94 in 1890, compared with Cincinnati's
12.35). In San Francisco's case, "typical" hides substantial variation: alongside
the usual small to middling firms stood such large ones as the California and
Hawaiian Sugar Refining Co. and the Union Iron Works. As individuals, however, most San Francisco and Cincinnati employers operated on a comparable
scale and dealt with similar numbers of employees. They also operated in many
of the same trades. Among the leaders in both cities were clothing, slaughtering
and meatpacking, cigars, brewing, boots and shoes, and metalworking. These
leading industries gave the cities a similar mix of production methods. Foundry
work and machine-making, along with the building trades, continued to rely on
craft skills past the turn of the century. Footwear manufacturing and cigar making, by contrast, typified trades moving rapidly toward mechanized production.[7]
The key difference, and the subject of the next section of this chapter, is that
these contrasting labor processes overlapped with racial cleavages. San Francisco
industries marked by the greatest de-skilling in the 1870s and 1880s were also
heavily Chinese.

On balance, the same obstacles to business class formation that were seen
in Cincinnati appeared in San Francisco, but they assumed different forms or
carried different weights. Consider, first, the usual impediments to broadened
solidarities among capitalists. One of these, the friction between old money
and new, appears to have been less pronounced in San Francisco. The city never
lacked a social elite, from residents of Rincon Hill in the 1850s to Nob Hill in the
1870s and Marin and Oakland in the 1880s. And as in Cincinnati, they formed
exclusive enclaves like the Pacific Club (1852) and policed the higher circles with
a social registry (1879). However, consistent with the greater social mobility
found in San Francisco, capitalists there relied more on market opportunities
than on social closure to secure privilege. Rincon Hill itself was leveled, with
little protest from residents, to improve shipping facilities and foster industrial
development. Day-to-day markers of status also appear to have been less keenly
observed. Robert Issel and William Cherny note the lack of clear distinctions
between "places of entertainment [and] places for the appreciation of arts,"
and one local newspaper, *The Argonaut,* complained in 1884 of businessmen's
excessive informality in dress and etiquette.[8] Whether this was, as the *Argonaut*
thought, a throwback to the mining camps, other observers agreed: "nowhere else
will such bad manners be found in families possessing so much wealth."[9] This
sounds like the standard complaint against the nouveau riche, men like Charles
Crocker and Leland Stanford, using their indecent fortunes to build showy man-
sions atop Nob Hill. The difference from Cincinnati was simply that there were
so few of the old-moneyed to be appalled.[10]

In other respects, however, horizontal solidarity among San Francisco capitalists faced greater obstacles than in Cincinnati. In both cities, merchants and
manufacturers had distinct economic interests. In San Francisco, however, the
close public identification of the city with commerce irritated many manufacturers, particularly as industry boomed but remained, in their view, unappreci-
ated. "One manufactory," grumbled the *Mechanics' Fair Daily Press* in 1864, "does
more towards enriching and building up a State, than a thousand mere traders."[11]
Twenty years later, members of the Manufacturers' Association still complained
of the "want of that fellowship and unity of interest which should properly
prevail between manufacturer and merchant."[12] The lack of full integration into
the national economy divided San Francisco businessmen along other lines. Most
manufacturers were oriented toward local markets and sheltered from national
competition. Others, fewer in number, sold their wares in wider markets and
faced corresponding competitive pressures. The Union Iron Works, for example,
bid for government contracts against East Coast firms, while the Tubbs Cordage Company peddled its ropes around the country.[13] In some cases, this split
between local and national orientations reinforced strains between merchants
and manufacturers—a sore point for cablemaker Andrew Hallidie, who regularly
groused that the importing merchant, "in his desire to increase his volume of
imported goods [is] willing to sacrifice home industries."[14] More importantly,
firms competing in national markets or affiliated with large corporations back
east clashed with local businessmen over how to deal with labor unions, a clash
explored more fully below. This source of conflict among businessmen overlapped with yet another one, between firms of modest size and the few giants.
Hallidie sounded the alarm in 1875 over "great corporations" overwhelming
proprietors and "discouraging the efforts of more humble persons."[15] But the
chief villains, for many local businessmen, were "monopolies" like the Spring
Valley Water Company and, worst of all, the Southern Pacific Railroad. For most
of the period, these companies exercised a monopoly hold in industries essential
to the city's growth, water and rail shipping. Merchants and manufacturers alike
complained that as a result, "San Francisco was having the life squeezed out of
it by excessive rates."[16] These companies also had the resources, the connections,
and the ruthlessness necessary to ensure that city and state government usually
satisfied their interests, and those interests appeared to be at odds with good
government. Summarizing the view of many reform-minded businessmen, the
prominent banker James Phelan pronounced the railroad "the source of most, if
not all, of our industrial and political ills."[17] The reprehensible activities of such
firms did not, however, unify local capitalists in shared moral outrage. Some
joined the Southern Pacific at the political trough; others, more dependent on the
railroad for importing goods or shipping out manufactured products, regularly

charged the firm with using its monopoly to levy excessive freight rates and sub-
orn government officials. When "several hundred young merchants" gathered
in 1892 to promote a competing rail line, one speaker cast the conflict in much
broader terms. "It is universally acknowledged," W. H. Metson thundered, "that
in the last quarter of a century, no . . . section of the country has been so tyran-
nically overridden and publicly robbed and defrauded by the rapacious band
of conscienceless monopolies and the debauchery of public officers . . . as our
own California. . . . The interests and resources of our great and noble State are
everywhere crushed and stunted in the interests of corrupt and unscrupulous
monopoly."[18]

Merchant and manufacturer, local and national capital, small firm and large
corporation, all were potential obstacles to business solidarity. Class formation also involves breaking vertical ties between capital and labor. These ties,
too, had a different character in San Francisco than in Cincinnati. By the late
nineteenth century, manufacturing in the latter city had a long history. In many
cases, "practical men" still ran the firm and cultivated a sense of trade community
with their employees. San Francisco proprietors and workers were less likely to
share venerable craft traditions. The city's later and more compressed industrial
development provided less support for trade communities, and San Francisco
manufacturing drew to a larger degree on capital from outside the trade, particularly profits in mining and real estate.[19] As a result, one powerful stimulus to
class formation elsewhere—the disruption of craft traditions by changes in the
technology and scale of production—was weaker in San Francisco. Even in local
industries that moved most fully from hand labor to mechanized production,
such as boot and shoe manufacturing, craft practices were a far less important
focus of contention than were demands for shorter hours and the closed shop.
But if craft ties bound manufacturers and skilled men less tightly in San Francisco, "race loyalty" could bring them closer together. Conflicts between whites
and Chinese in San Francisco were far more frequent, more pervasive, and more
institutionalized than white-black hostilities in Gilded Age Cincinnati. These
conflicts *could* be the basis for persisting ties across class lines.

Could deserves special emphasis. We should no more assume that race will
trump class than that property ownership will be decisive, in the last instance,
for group formation. The construction of a cohesive business community in San
Francisco may have faced greater obstacles than in Cincinnati, but in both cases
divisions could be muted by a common enemy, bridged by new forms of organization, or skirted by new agendas. Ties between employer and employee based
on race, similarly, might be broken by technical changes, by economic crises, or
by demographic shifts. The challenge is to trace historically why some divisions
and ties rather than others became the bases for collective organization and action

in San Francisco and Cincinnati. The most important parts of San Francisco's
story involve racial dynamics, labor conflicts, and civic engagements.

RACE AND CLASS AMONG THE BOURGEOISIE

Race is often held to have divided American workers, especially in circumstances
where racial cleavages coincided with economic rivalries, such as competition for
scarce jobs, divisions based on skill, or unequal access to union representation.[20]
In San Francisco, race had similarly divisive effects on capitalists. Mere bigotry
is not the issue: Cincinnati's blacks were as stigmatized as California's Chinese.
Instead, prejudices—fanned by opportunistic politicians, businessmen, and union
leaders—interacted in particular ways with industrial change to align small businessmen with, rather than against, skilled workers.

Cincinnati offers an instructive contrast. We saw that key industries there
moved from artisanal to factory production between the Civil War and the 1890s.
Employers introduced new machinery, subdivided labor, standardized commodities, and increased the scale of production. Skilled workers responded by
defending customary privileges as best they could. They tried to limit the ratio
of apprentices to journeymen, in order to prevent employers from overstocking
the labor market. They demanded that jobs be staffed by qualified craftsmen,
in hopes of preventing displacement by cheaper hands. The stage was thus set
for repeated battles over work rules, with employers identifying unions as the
chief threat to economical production and managerial rights. In this, Cincinnati
resembled many other late-nineteenth-century industrial cities. Partly for want
of the political means to protect their interests, skilled workers sought control
over local labor markets and workshop practice. That attempt only strengthened
employer opposition to trade unionism.[21]

In San Francisco, contrasting labor processes, between and within industries,
overlapped with racial cleavages. The Chinese accounted for 16.3 percent of
California's manufacturing labor force in 1870, a time when most of the state's
manufacturing took place in San Francisco. But they were concentrated in those
industries that were marked by the greatest de-skilling. In 1870, they accounted
for 2.9 percent of carpenters and .3 percent of iron and steel workers. By contrast,
they made up 91.5 percent of tobacco workers, 64 percent of woolen mill workers,
and 19 percent of boot and shoe workers,[22] all industries with rapidly expanding
factory sectors. Racial divisions also appeared *within* mechanizing industries.
The clothing, boot and shoe, and cigar industries all included a craft sector,
small shops specializing in bespoke tailoring, custom footwear, and hand-rolled

cigars. In these sectors, skilled white labor and white owners predominated. But these trades also included sweatshops relying on low wages to compete in the mass market, and here Chinese labor prevailed. Boot and shoe firms with a Chinese workforce paid annual wages of $311 in 1870, compared to $715 for small shops with white labor. The latter, however, turned out products valued at $2,463 per worker, as against $1,506 for companies with Chinese labor. Because small firms using unskilled labor had small startup costs, Chinese ownership also became common. By the late 1860s, half of the city's cigar-making firms had Chinese owners, and among their five hundred employees were only fifty whites. Large factories complete the picture. These were generally white-owned, with an average of five times as many hands as Chinese-owned firms. The white-owned factories also made greater use of machinery, a more advanced division of labor, and less-skilled workers to turn out standardized shirts, shoes, and cigars. Chinese labor came cheaper than white, so they were often the preferred factory hands. At Golden Gate Woolen Mills in 1880, white men earned $1.75–2.50 a day; "Chinamen" earned $1. The mill manager noted another bonus: Chinese employees did not continually make "unreasonable demands."[23]

The interweaving of industrial change and racial cleavage gave class alignments a peculiar shape in San Francisco, fostering cross-class alliances in opposition to the Chinese and dividing capitalists among themselves. For white owners of smaller firms and for skilled white labor, the Chinese appeared to be a common enemy. White workers saw them as competitors for scarce jobs, and beginning in the 1860s, they mobilized to defend their occupational turf. The Workingmen's Protective Organization tried to blacklist employers of Chinese labor, and shoemakers organized in the Knights of Crispin held mass meetings to oppose "the Asiatic locusts."[24] Proprietors, for their part, resented both Chinese-owned sweatshops and the larger firms that combined new technology and cheap Chinese labor to produce low-price shoes or cigars. Shoe manufacturer Abram Altemeyer, at a state Senate hearing in 1878, acknowledged the attractions of cheap Chinese labor, but warned employers that hiring the Chinese only "put a nail in [their] own coffin," because these workers would learn the trade and go into business for themselves.[25] Organized labor and employers, accordingly, joined forces. The Cigar Makers' Association combined proprietors and journeymen in boycotting Chinese-made goods; more broadly, white labor and marginal manufacturers formed the Pacific Coast Anti-Coolie Association in 1867, a federation of trade- and neighborhood-based clubs pledging not to patronize employers of Chinese labor. Although the 1870s were the most active years for agitation by working-class men and small proprietors, the alliance continued through the 1880s and 1890s. It took many ingenious forms. The Associated Boot and Shoe Manufacturers lent financial support to the Boot and Shoemakers

White Labor League and encouraged them to police competitors to make sure none employed Chinese labor. Butcher-shop owners and workmen organized a boycott of Chinese pork to drive Chinese butchers out of town. Laundrymen and their union employees struck a deal: employers would raise wages, and the union would put Japanese and Chinese laundries out of business. The most sustained and varied cooperative efforts were in cigar making. Beginning in 1878, organized employers and the union used a "white label" (certifying the product as free of Asian labor) to enforce a boycott of cigars made with Chinese labor. In 1884, some of the unrepentant manufacturers finally fell in line when their Chinese employees went on strike. One response was to organize programs to train white boys and girls, among them Mrs. Murray's Cigar School for Young Ladies. The next year, manufacturer and union representatives formed a delegation to go east to recruit white cigar makers. They welcomed the first crop in January 1886, with a procession from the wharf through the city and a handsome banquet, put on by the cigar makers' and seamen's unions and presided over by one of the leading owners.[26]

These cross-class ties, then, were not rooted in a common trade community. Instead, familiar conflicts over industrial change were reconstituted as conflicts between races. The same forces aligning small proprietors with union labor, moreover, divided capitalists. Frictions between larger, more mechanized firms and their small-fry competitors were not unusual during the late nineteenth century. However, in San Francisco they were reinforced by the tendency for larger manufacturing firms to flout "community sentiment" and hire cheaper Chinese labor. Smaller firms, by contrast, more often demonstrated "fidelity to their own race,"[27] whether out of conviction or, given their greater vulnerability to boycotts and union pressure, pragmatism. The presence of San Francisco Chinese deepened another familiar cleavage among capitalists, that between merchants and manufacturers. From surviving records, we know that businessmen endorsed laudable principles of equal opportunity, economic expansion, and the public good. How those principles led them to take one side or the other in debates over Chinese labor turned on less lofty interests. The secretary of the Merchants' Exchange, testifying at an 1877 U.S. Senate hearing, spoke eloquently of the importance of judging the Chinese on their individual merit and of giving them the same immigration rights enjoyed by Englishmen.[28] That position happened to accord with the desire of importing merchants not to antagonize an important trading partner. Manufacturers like Andrew Hallidie and fellow members of the San Francisco Mechanics' Institute, by contrast, defended "American" standards and the progress of local industry against the Chinese and their grasping white allies—whose low-wage products undercut their own. In this view, merchants' shortsighted pursuit of free trade with China led them "to sacrifice home industries [and] the employment of the home mechanic and workman."[29] White retail merchants, for their part, championed the right of American workmen to well-paying jobs. Those workmen, more than lower-wage Chinese laborers, patronized white retail shops, and so these merchants often joined white label campaigns against offending manufacturers. And whatever their reasons for opposing the Chinese, a wide array of small businessmen found an easy target in the Southern Pacific Railroad, both for its employment of "mongol" labor and for the political clout with which it opposed restrictions on Chinese immigration.[30]

In Cincinnati, neither the social location of blacks nor the timing of racial conflict worked to unite small capital and skilled white labor. Blacks were a smaller proportion of Cincinnati's population than were the Chinese in San Francisco (2.7 versus 8.0 percent in 1870). As we saw in chapter 1, they were also largely excluded from local industry. Thus at the time when Cincinnati trades began moving to factory production, there were few black firms or black manufacturing workers to give small proprietors and white craftsmen a common scapegoat for their economic insecurities.

Demography and market advantages go only so far in explaining the alignment of race and class in San Francisco, however. To be sure, it was small employers and white labor in cigars, boots and shoes, and clothing who had the most direct interest in opposing the Chinese, and these were the centers of cross-class cooperation against Chinese workers and proprietors. Yet whiteness trumped class on a broader basis. Unions not directly affected by Chinese competition joined white label campaigns; proprietors from other industries participated in neighborhood-based anti-coolie clubs in the mid-1870s and the Workingmen's Party in the late 1870s; and anti-Chinese mobilization went well beyond industrial relations, targeting (for example) the rights of Chinese children to attend public schools. Ultimately it was this broader coalition of unionists, proprietors, and politicians that successfully pushed for tighter restrictions on immigration, culminating in the Chinese Exclusion Act of 1882.[31]

This generalization of racial boundaries and conflict reflects, in part, the happenstance of timing. Battles in the most contested industries coincided with periods of sharp increase in unemployment and in the local Chinese population. Conflicts in clothing and cigar making over white labor in the 1860s, for example, came at a time when Chinese workers left the mines in large numbers. As East Coast competition put the squeeze on cigar makers in the 1870s, San Francisco experienced a new wave of immigration from China and a period of high unemployment following the 1873 panic.[32] These coincidences broadened the potential audience for scapegoating of the Chinese. In contrast to Cincinnati, there was another kind of political opportunity for anti-Chinese mobilization in San Francisco. Prejudice against the Chinese was probably no more vicious than that against African Americans, and it recycled some of the same stereotypes.[33] But it could also be focused, as racism against blacks could not, on the political cause of exclusion. And here another factor helped steer class alignments: there was no shortage of self-serving actors eager to exploit these opportunities. As Alexander Saxton shows, California's Democratic Party sought to restore its electoral fortunes by playing the Chinese race card at a time when the black one offered little political leverage. Union leaders, too, put the Chinese enemy to good use. Protesting the Chinese threat to well-paying American jobs and wholesome American families (and denouncing the rapacious plutocrats who insisted on open immigration) brought white workers into unions. The same rhetoric helped ambitious labor politicians like Denis Kearney build a coalition far broader than the craft aristocracy.[34] Political strategy thus complemented economic interests to align small proprietors with white labor and pit them both against larger firms oriented to national and international markets. These racial dynamics also contributed to San Francisco labor's formidable industrial and political clout—a second key influence on class alignments in the city.

CAPITALISTS' COMMON ENEMY: THE SAN FRANCISCO LABOR MOVEMENT

Looking back from 1918, San Francisco's Chamber of Commerce president, Frederick Koster, ruefully noted the city's "reputation of being dominated by the labor unions."[35] He had a point. A fortuitous mix of geography, industrial structure, and race-based solidarity allowed San Francisco's white workers to wield formidable power in the city, both through their unions and through electoral politics. That power also shaped business class formation. Far from unifying in the face of a common class enemy, San Francisco capital was divided between grudging allies and frustrated enemies of organized labor.

Labor's power in San Francisco owed much to geography. The city's distance from East Coast industrial centers, even after the completion of transcontinental railroad links, made for acute labor shortages during boom years. That geographic isolation also made it more difficult for employers to break strikes by importing scabs. There were compensations for many employers. The same long distance and high costs that protected unionists from cheap East Coast labor also protected manufacturers from cheap East Coast products. Manufacturers were thus in a position to concede to union demands for high wages, shorter hours, or fewer apprentices without fear of pricing themselves out of the market. San Francisco's geographic cocoon benefited labor in another way. By keeping national competition out, and by the same token limiting most San Francisco manufacturers to local markets, the city's relative isolation preserved an economy of small firms and craft production. This combination of scarce labor, employers with the leeway to cut deals, and production methods that put a premium on skill provided an ideal setting for American trade unionism.[36]

In a perverse way, labor's solidarity and clout also benefited from the city's racial and ethnic relations. Among white workers, demographic patterns minimized ethnic cleavages. With newcomers from wide-ranging backgrounds settling the city over a short period of time between the gold rush and the 1880s, no one ethnic group had either the tenure or the numbers to monopolize a privileged position in the labor market. Even the Irish found that access to skilled jobs and upward mobility came relatively early. By the time of the next wave of immigrants, from southern and eastern Europe, San Francisco was expanding much more slowly, so it was spared the tensions between old and new immigrants found in most East Coast cities.[37] The great exception was the Chinese, next to whom ethnic differences paled. By allowing white workers to concentrate in more skilled occupations and by providing a common enemy against whom to close ranks, the Chinese strengthened craft unionism in San Francisco. Indeed, during the 1870s and 1880s, several major unions were organized as much to fight the Chinese as to battle employers. The coincidence of labor and racial solidarity is indicated by the very names of labor organizations during this period, including the Boot and Shoemakers' White Labor League, the White Cigarmakers' Association, and the White Cooks and Waiters.

On these foundations, San Francisco workers built the most powerful labor movement in the country. Labor's strength in San Francisco, as compared to Cincinnati (and almost all other U.S. cities) was well established by the mid-1880s. Consider one standard measure, union density. Statistics for the proportion of workers organized in specific trades are not very reliable for this period, colored as they are by the wishful thinking of union officials. There is no reason to think that San Francisco unionists told taller tales than their counterparts in Cincinnati, however, and the differences in membership are impressive. In their 1887 reports to the state Bureau of Labor Statistics, locals claimed to enroll 90 percent or more of eligible members in such major industries as baking, brewing, bricklaying, marine engineering, and iron molding. Boot and shoe workers, stevedores, sailors, and printers, all large groups in the city, were at least 50 percent organized.[38] By 1910, San Francisco unionists totaled 70,000 in a city of just over 400,000; Cincinnati, with a similar population that year and with its larger manufacturing sector, had fewer than half as many union members.[39] The contrast is more striking still in such key sectors as the metal trades. This industry, solidly organized in San Francisco, was 95 percent open shop in Cincinnati on the eve of World War I.[40]

More impressive than quantitative indicators are San Francisco workers' substantive achievements. Among craftsmen in particular, solidarity seems to have been a matter of both organization and habit. In key industries, federations of local unions developed early and effectively coordinated action among constituents. Chief among them was the Building Trades Council (BTC, 1890), with nearly dictatorial power to set conditions and discipline unions in construction. The metal trades had its Iron Trades Council (ITC, 1885), and unions active around the docks (Longshoremen, Teamsters) formed the City Front Federation in 1891 (successor to the Wharf and Waves Federation of the 1880s). And although the powerful BTC stood apart, most other unions belonged to and were guided by the San Francisco Labor Council (established in 1892). These were much more than token councils to which union officials reported news of their trades at poorly attended monthly meetings. They had real authority to approve strikes, levy assessments and orchestrate boycotts to support them, and intervene to settle them. An 1886 dispute illustrates a common dynamic. Boilermakers at the Union Iron Works went on strike that summer over the firm's use of non-union labor. The year-old Iron Trades Council, after issuing an obligatory reprimand to the workers for going on strike without prior ITC approval, came to their aid and pulled other crafts from the firm. Owners of the Union Iron Works responded in kind, helping form an Engineers' and Iron Founders' Association to meet the ITC on equal ground. The San Francisco Labor Council elevated this approach beyond single industries in 1904, requiring constituent unions to submit all demands for Council review before levying them on employers. Compliance entitled member unions to support in the event of strikes, while renegades risked expulsion.[41] Here too, San Francisco's geographic position played a part. With the headquarters of individual unions distant and (some local officials felt) indifferent, the city's labor leaders relied more on one another, sometimes following local councils and federations in defiance of their own national executives.[42]

San Francisco craftsmen not only surpassed most other city labor movements in the extent of their cooperation with one another. The local labor movement also was precocious in its unionization of less-skilled workers. As early as 1861, unionization among waiters prompted the formation of the city's first employers' association. Each of the major trade councils included less-skilled constituents alongside craft unions. Thus the BTC had its building laborers, the ITC its foundry and later shipyard helpers, and the City Front Federation its dock laborers. Organization among these workers was certainly more fragile, and collective bargaining successes more limited, than among traditional American Federation of Labor unions. But by the turn-of-the-century boom in unionization, significant numbers of less-skilled workers had become regular members of local unions, giving the San Francisco labor movement an organizational range and depth unequaled in the United States.[43]

To their formidable industrial power San Francisco labor added political clout. Alexander Saxton provides one measure of working-class political influence: between 1892 and 1910, of 120 city assemblymen, 49 were laborers, semiskilled, or skilled workers, as compared to 23 lawyers and 31 businessmen or professionals.[44] Between the Civil War and 1901, workers' political power turned in large part on a highly competitive electoral system, in which both parties had to appeal to working-class constituents in hopes of gaining office. In two eras, however, independent labor-based parties gained offices and promoted certain labor interests. The Workingmen's Party grew out of anti-Chinese agitation and the 1877 railroad strike, and it rested heavily on working-class voters. In addition to promoting the 1882 Chinese Exclusion Act, the party sponsored candidates and constitutional reforms to curb corporate influence in state government.[45] Between 1901 and 1911, the Union Labor Party dominated city government. The name exaggerated the party's roots in local unions, but workers provided the bulk of its electoral support and the party was a fairly reliable defender of union interests—backing the eight-hour day, for example, and discouraging strong-arm tactics by employers during strikes.[46] As these examples suggest, San Francisco's labor politics hardly counts as "radical." Union Labor Party politicians eschewed municipal socialism in favor of supporting union standards (and feathering their own nests). The city's Labor Council took a similar political line, attacking syndicalists and socialists (such as Socialist Party leader Max Hayes, "the noisy little microbe from Cleveland") as unrealistic utopians, at best, or as demagogues who disrupted the legitimate work of the labor movement.[47] Conservatism, however, did not mean renouncing independent labor politics. Elsewhere, labor or socialist parties tended to prosper when rooted in "inclusive" unions.[48] In San Francisco, craft unions, particularly the powerful building trades, led the labor movement. The fact that they nonetheless supported independent electoral politics can be traced partly to the long fight against Chinese immigration—another way in which racial cleavages and class power formed a cumulative historical sequence.

This mixture of geography, industrial structure, and race relations produced a powerful labor movement, and a formidable threat to employers. The interaction over time of capital and this unusual labor movement, in turn, shaped employer class formation. We have seen that San Francisco businessmen divided along several lines, including those between merchants and manufacturers, between small firms and large corporations, and between manufacturers oriented to the local economy and those competing in national markets. A robust labor movement, presenting businessmen with a common class enemy, might be expected to have rallied them together. Instead, it aggravated existing divisions.

Retail merchants, for example, selling shoes, cigars, or beer, were particularly vulnerable to Labor Council boycotts of non-union or non-"white" products. Small firms found it difficult to hold out during strikes and often defected from employers' associations. Local manufacturers had the luxury of granting union demands because they could pass costs along in protected markets. For firms in this position, unions could even be useful. They could standardize wages across competitors, and they could help limit unrest. The employers' Metal Trades Association also got assistance from the Iron Trades Council in promoting home industry and in lobbying for military contracts.[49] By contrast, larger firms, competing in national markets, had more reason to oppose unions, in part because they could not raise prices to cover higher labor costs. Thanks to the city's strong unions and, until the late nineteenth century, its geographic isolation from most national markets, these capitalists were in the minority.

Occasional campaigns against San Francisco trade unions tended to fracture along these lines. In the three main cases before World War I, some business leaders, representing larger firms and national capital, mobilized on behalf of the open shop. In varying degrees, they failed to rally their colleagues; in all cases, they failed to deal unions more than temporary setbacks. The first major effort came in 1891. Outraged by numerous boycotts and by an iron molders' strike, employers from several industries formed the Board of Manufacturers and Employers of California. The association declared that "the time has come when a universal and systematic effort should be made to put an end to boycotts and the pernicious interference of . . . unions with the internal affairs of trade."[50] Whether or not the effort was "systematic," it did yield victories against the iron molders, brewers, and boot and shoe workers. The effort was hardly "universal," however; it was "the largest employers in the city" whom the Board's secretary claimed to have enrolled.[51] And the more effective, if temporary, cure for labor militancy was the 1893 depression. When strikes and boycotts revived later in the decade, the Board no longer existed. San Francisco affiliates of the nationwide Citizens' Industrial Alliance mounted a similar offensive in 1907, promising an end to strikes, boycotts, and union dictation.[52] Against these grand plans, however, the Alliance's achievements were meager. It played a modest role in helping employers' associations impose open shops on weak unions, as in local stables and restaurants. It claimed some credit, as well, for union defeats at the hands of the American Can Company and the Kutz shoe factory. Its more ambitious efforts were in the building trades and in printing, and both were utter failures. And as with its predecessor, the victories won in 1904 were mostly reversed within a year.[53]

The most important case, the Employers' Association of 1901, deserves a closer look.[54] This was the most potent offensive of the three; the timing of its failure was particularly important, coming when employers elsewhere in the United States were beginning successful counterattacks against recent union gains; and it helped bring about a decade of Union Labor Party dominance in city politics. The case also neatly illustrates many of the fault lines running through San Francisco's business community and the ways that unions widened those faults.

The Employers' Association was organized in April, during strikes by cooks and waiters, carriage makers, and bakers. Little is known of the association, and this itself is symptomatic. Fear of exposing members to union boycotts led the association to keep its membership secret and to communicate only through an attorney. Investigative reporting by the *San Francisco Examiner* did turn up some information, however. The core membership came primarily from among wholesale merchants and large manufacturers, particularly those producing for national markets.[55] This split between anti-union firms with national ties and more conciliatory locals is consistent with the more general pattern in the city. The Employers' Association was able to enlist some of the latter in its campaign only through a combination of bribes and blackmail. The bribes consisted of material and strategic support to employer associations willing to take a hard line against unions. The blackmail consisted of cutting off supplies to noncooperating firms—oysters to restaurateurs, meat to butchers, iron to carriage makers.[56] Even so, some employers refused to comply.

In the Employers' Association's public statement, it claimed not to oppose unions per se, but only to defend employers' right to hire whomever they pleased, union or non-union. This position clearly appealed to many employers, particularly in industries like restaurants and drayage, where less-skilled workers were newly organizing and pressing new demands for the closed shop. The Chamber of Commerce and the Merchants' Association (an organization of prominent businessmen devoted to municipal improvement) also signaled their support for the Employers' Association's principles. For a time, capital seemed to be closing ranks. By late July, however, support for the Employers' Association waned as the scope and impact of industrial conflict widened and as the Employers' Association abandoned all pretense of compromise.

In May, the battle over union conditions involved baking, restaurants, and the metal trades. In June, butchers joined the ranks of strikers, and sailors threatened to do so. July brought the most serious escalation of the strike; first teamsters and then stevedores and sailors walked out. With the waterfront tie-up, in particular, threatening to paralyze the local economy, calls grew for a more conciliatory approach. In early July, the presidents of local improvement clubs (whose members were mainly small-scale businessmen) formed the Municipal League and offered to mediate. At the end of the month, Mayor James Phelan summoned employers and union leaders to his office in an effort to end the stalemate. Even as political leaders and small proprietors made these conciliatory gestures, however, the Employers' Association was digging in its heels. Its stated position of accepting unions but not the closed shop came to mean, in practice, that it refused to allow members even to meet with unions to discuss the issue. It also rejected offers of arbitration on the grounds that, where employer rights to hire and fire were concerned, there was nothing to arbitrate.[57] And it won mayoral support for deputizing hundreds of additional police to protect strikebreakers and, labor leaders charged, intimidate strikers.

With the stakes so high and the Employers' Association so inflexible, opposition from within the business community grew. The Retail Grocers Association publicly criticized wholesale merchants for their supporting role in continuing the strike. Members of the Merchants' Association urged the Employers' Association not to interfere if the Draymen wanted to cut a deal with the Teamsters. Drayage proprietors, for their part, made overtures to the Teamsters despite the Employers' Association's claim that there was nothing to discuss. Ultimately, intervention by California Governor Henry Gage sidelined the Employers' Association altogether. Gage called together Draymen and Teamsters—pointedly excluding the Employers' Association—and brokered a settlement which more or less affirmed the status quo.[58] The Draymen's Association and the Teamsters accepted the compromise and resumed work without bothering to get the Employers' Association's approval. Within a year, even some of the Association's inner circle had given up. Shirt and overall manufacturer Neustadter Bros., for example, had a representative on the Association's Executive Committee. But early in 1902, it forfeited its Employers' Association deposits, signed up with the United Garment Workers, advised employees to join the union, and even offered to pay their initiation fees. Others, like Levi Strauss, followed suit. After all, taunted the *San Francisco Examiner,* "no Sansome-street merchant can bear to see his rival get away with business, whether it be under a union label or without it."[59]

The terms of settlement in the teamstering dispute indicate the successes and limits of the Employers' Association's campaign. On one hand, had the Association not directed and supported the Draymen, Teamsters would have won better terms, probably including the closed shop. On the other hand, the inflexible opposition to unions shown by the Employers' Association ultimately cost it the support of other business groups, including such one-time allies as the Merchants' Association and the Draymen's Association itself. Most of the labor gains blocked in 1900, moreover, came anyway within another year or two, as union power at work and in politics waxed and the Employers' Association waned. And here the 1901 episode illustrates a final point, namely that the political as well as the industrial arm of San Francisco's labor movement made it difficult for the city's business community to rally around the open shop. Owing to labor's electoral presence and, during the Union Labor Party's reign, its direct voice in municipal government, employers usually could not count on the typical tools of the trade, such as police protection for strike breakers and injunctions against unions. Indeed, labor's political power raised the costs of anti-unionism, because open shop battles sparked political reprisals. The Employers' Association's offensive in 1901 contributed to the Union Labor Party's mayoral victory at the next election; four years later, the party used resentment against the local Citizens' Alliance to expand its majority on the city council.[60]

DISENGAGEMENT AND DISUNITY

Tensions between old money and new, between merchants and manufacturers, and between larger and smaller firms were common in Cincinnati as well as in San Francisco, even if they were not aggravated by racial divisions or strong unions. In Cincinnati, however, cultural and political dynamics fostered class formation, further eroding vertical ties and building bridges among businessmen. One way this happened was through the elaboration of distinctions between high and popular culture, which closely paralleled class divisions. San Francisco does not seem to have developed such clearly defined boundaries; light entertainment and serious art mixed carelessly in the same facilities. And in contrast to Cincinnati's highbrow musical festivals, the major public concerts in San Francisco took place during the annual mechanics' fairs and betrayed what Theodore Thomas would have considered an appallingly popular character. As for the visual arts, as late as 1904, the Bay Area had "no art gallery or museum worthy of its name."[61]

Civic institutions also fostered class formation in Cincinnati, bringing businessmen from different sectors together and focusing their attention on more consensual issues. The character of civic issues and institutions had, if anything, the opposite effect in San Francisco. Consider some of the leading issues on the agenda. In Cincinnati, general alarm over the city's relative economic slippage was a powerful stimulus to civic boosterism among local businessmen. Relatively weak unions and the trauma of the 1884 Court House riot also favored a definition of the challenges they faced in terms of civic unrest and political corruption rather than labor struggle. This ideology of standing above class partisanship smoothed the way for business solidarity. The construction of San Francisco's problems played out quite differently. Trade unions commanded the attention of the city's businessmen, and anti-unionism provided no grounds for consensus; businessmen instead split, sometimes bitterly, over how best to deal with the labor problem.

San Francisco's leading citizens did have their worries over the city's economic standing relative to West Coast competitors. These worries came later than in Cincinnati, however, and they had different implications for business unity. Who was to blame for San Francisco's failure to maintain its economic preeminence? Not, at least at first, labor unions. The preferred culprits from as early as the 1870s until the early 1910s were, instead, rapacious corporations, above all the Southern Pacific—described with such hyperbolic labels as "the most avaricious monopoly the world ever saw."[62] Transportation costs were one major concern, but they also were one point of friction among businessmen. For importers and manufacturers who sought to reach national markets, shipping costs could be a matter of financial life or death; for many small manufacturers, the SP's stranglehold on rail traffic protected local markets from low-cost competition. There were other stakes, including "monopoly" control over the city's economic destiny. In Cincinnati, reversing economic decline required improvements in rail links and wharves, with businessmen even joining forces to organize a municipal line, the Cincinnati Southern Railway.[63] There was plenty of bickering over the funding and governance of the Southern Railway, but in general it was both testimony to businessmen's capacity for collective action and a source of civic pride. The Southern Pacific was neither. In San Francisco, securing control over the city's economy meant fighting the railroad and its allies. And that struggle could both pit reform-minded businessmen against the beneficiaries of municipal corruption and ally them with workers in populist outrage against Southern Pacific tyranny.[64]

The civic associations that helped Cincinnati businessmen develop closer ties and a common culture also played a lesser role in San Francisco. In part, this was a matter of different organizational trajectories. San Francisco merchants had organized "vigilance committees" in the 1850s to protect the city's business (and credit rating) from political corruption and urban disorder,[65] and their rhetoric resembles that of Cincinnati's Committee of 100 or Commercial Club. By the time manufacturing developed in the 1860s and 1870s, however, the most pressing problem confronting employers was a powerful and well-coordinated labor movement. Among these employers, early efforts to mobilize on a citywide basis tended to focus on industrial relations. And organizing to deal with unions did little to enhance business solidarity in San Francisco. As the fate of the Employers' Association and Citizens' Alliance showed, organization devoted to the open shop divided the business community according to their market positions and national affiliations. And neither these nor more conciliatory employer bodies directed attention to classless civic virtues around which businessmen might rally.

Still, by the late nineteenth century, San Francisco was host to the full range of reform groups and improvement clubs, devoted to civil service rules, lower taxes, cleaner streets, charter amendments, and much more. It appears that they neither mobilized nor united San Francisco businessmen as they did in Cincinnati, however. In part, this was a matter of representation. Manufacturers were much less likely to belong to the leading civic improvement organization, the Merchants' Association. Out of a cumulative list of 137 members of Cincinnati's Commercial Club, 1880–1907, 75 can be identified as manufacturers. The 332 members of the Merchants' Association in 1896, by contrast, included only 45 manufacturers.[66] And among those who *did* belong to the association, the level of engagement appears anemic in comparison to that found in Cincinnati. The body's elected officers regularly lament members' lack of involvement in the organization's affairs and their failure to attend quarterly business meetings. A more quantitative, if indirect, measure of involvement is the extent to which association membership overlapped with other forms of civic engagement. Commercial Club members have far fuller associational lives than their Merchants' Association counterparts. Seventy percent of the club's members *also* belonged to the Chamber of Commerce, 29 percent served in some cultural organization (museum trustee, Literary Club member), 36 percent held political office or belonged to another political club, and 72 percent had memberships in the city's leading social club, the Queen City Club. Among a sample of 142 Merchants' Association members, the corresponding figures are 2 percent, 8 percent, 13 percent, and 8 percent.[67] The Merchants' Association, then, failed to provide what businessmen found in Cincinnati's Commercial Club—an institutionalized network of ties within their class, crisscrossing the domains of civic uplift, cultural improvement, and political reform.

This evidence of civic disengagement, particularly on the part of San Francisco manufacturers, confirms the judgment of contemporaries and historians. The city's businessmen looked chiefly after their own private affairs. Leather manufacturer J. C. Johnson seems typical: "the principle of his life on which he prides himself, is that of minding his own business."[68] It may be that the city's gold rush roots and pell-mell development produced a local culture oriented toward the fast buck rather than public service.[69] With a history at once short and characterized by extreme booms and busts, moreover, late-nineteenth-century San Francisco lacked a key ingredient of Cincinnati's business citizenship: the city had no stable social elite with a self-defined duty to assume civic leadership.[70] But institutions also matter, and the chief institution for civic action was not designed, like its Cincinnati counterpart, to foster civic involvement. To begin with, the norms for participation were quite different. The Commercial Club held monthly dinners, from which three unexcused absences merited expulsion from the club. The Merchants' Association held its first banquet dinner in 1898, five years after its founding.[71] San Francisco businessmen also had few incentives to come. The Merchants' Association lacked the basic functions of a social club; it had neither facilities for leisure nor an appropriate air of exclusiveness. These were an important part of the draw of the Commercial and the Business Men's clubs, where membership required nomination by existing members and conferred such benefits as the use of dining rooms and inclusion in recreational excursions. Nor was the Merchants' Association involved in such cultural uplift as sponsoring a local symphony or art museum.[72] In Cincinnati, by contrast, cultural philanthropy was an important part of business club life. Patronage of the arts conferred social status, but it also transcended members' narrow economic interests and bolstered their identities as public-spirited citizens of the community.

Racial dynamics, class power, and civic practices came together to divide San Francisco businessmen and sustain cross-class alliances with craft workers. Prejudice against the Chinese did not make the difference. What was crucial in San Francisco was the way that racial cleavages coincided with typical divisions among businessmen, between larger and smaller companies, between more and less technically advanced manufacturers, and between merchants and industrialists. Employers also confronted a powerful adversary in local unions. They could not rely on the city government as an ally. And they faced political reprisals for anti-union offensives. These circumstances encouraged many to reach an accommodation with trade unions and to rely on collective bargaining to stabilize their industries. Strong unions and labor parties in San Francisco, rather than helping capitalists set aside their differences, divided them into supporters and opponents of class accord. San Francisco manufacturers, finally, were less involved in class-wide civic organizations than their Cincinnati counterparts. Their collective agenda focused less on relatively consensual issues, such as cultural betterment or reversing economic decline, and more on divisive issues such as coping with unions or battling "monopolies." These factors did their causal work through historical sequences rather than as independent variables. Early mobilization against the Chinese not only aligned employers and craft workers in particular ways; it also strengthened trade unionism by crowding out divisions of ethnicity and skill among white workers. A powerful labor movement, in turn, deepened divisions among local employers—but also prompted businessmen to organize with a focus on industrial relations rather than on civic issues more favorable to capitalist solidarity. As we will see in part 2, these contrasting social alignments were associated with very different ways of defining collective identities and civic worth.

Part II
IDENTITIES

There is a familiar image of the Gilded Age capitalist. His stomach is round, his watch chain is gold, and his God is Mammon. In defense of his stature and wealth, he invokes the basic tenets of laissez-faire liberalism. That ideology erects a thick wall between economy and state. The government has minimal responsibilities, the most important of which are preserving order and protecting property. Within the economy, there should be maximum freedom for the pursuit of individual self-interest, disciplined only by the laws of supply and demand. Under this beneficent regime, ample stomach and gold watch chain are just rewards for masterful competition. In Eric Arnesen's summary, "the dominant business creed of the Gilded Age . . . staunchly upheld laissez-faire economics . . . condemned any interference in the 'natural' workings of the economy as unwise, dangerous, and immoral . . . and celebrated the unbridled acquisition of material wealth."[1]

This stereotype of Gilded Age ideology appears to be sustained by two comparative perspectives. The first contrasts U.S. businessmen with their counterparts abroad, and the second distinguishes Gilded Age entrepreneurs from earlier proprietors and later corporate leaders. Cross-national generalizations deem American businessmen especially hostile to political meddling in their affairs, disdainful of politicians, and insistent on market solutions for public problems.[2] Temporal comparisons add some nuance but do not change the basic picture. One such comparison emphasizes the fate of earlier republican traditions which had provided common ground for small employers and skilled employees. On one side, labor radicals reworked these traditions as weapons of class struggle. On the other, and partly for that reason, the bourgeoisie turned to a more congenial liberalism. For Gilded Age business spokesmen, the much-prized independence of the republican mechanic, merging economic sufficiency and political self-direction, was redefined as freedom of individual contract, unconstrained by governments or unions. And as against the subversive uses of republicanism by labor politicians, business leaders offered little praise for political participation, social equality, or the prerogatives of the community over selfish individuals.[3] A comparative look forward to Progressivism reaches a similar conclusion. Where Progressive businessmen found a role for state-mandated reform and preached social responsibility, Gilded Age entrepreneurs sided with free markets against government regulation and glorified self-interest, sometimes tarted up as social Darwinism. In one pointed formulation, "the new Gilded Age elite was both ignorant and contemptuous of the public realm."[4] These differences in businessmen's civic ideology, scholars often claim, parallel the transition from entrepreneurial to corporate capitalism.[5]

Perhaps because they focus on municipal politics, historical studies of Gilded Age businessmen and urban reform paint a different picture. In local battles for civil service reform, more efficient delivery of city services, or an end to machine politics, business leaders are commonly found in the vanguard. Their professed commitment to public service, moreover, hardly fits the image of privatized individualism. And these men were at most selective proponents of laissez-faire. Even if lured by the prospect of higher property values, they actively supported local government initiatives to clean streets, extend sewer systems, and build parks. Nor, finally, have urban historians confirmed early judgments, notably Richard Hofstadter's, that business reformers were curmudgeons rooted in the old order, driven by status decline, and superseded by a new cadre of Progressives. Gilded Age urban reformers differed from their successors less in demographic base or commitment to political reform than in their relative indifference to issues of social justice.[6]

Cincinnati is a better fit with studies of urban reform than with broad comparative generalizations about the civic ideology of Gilded Age businessmen. Far from embracing a market liberalism distinct from their republican forebears and corporate descendants, Cincinnati proprietors blended republican and liberal themes in their efforts to make sense of new challenges. In their eyes, the most important of these was not labor militancy but rather economic competition, urban disorder, and political mismanagement. And the ideological solutions—which I summarize as *business citizenship*—involved definitions of social boundaries and public identities which complemented the organizational trends described in chapter 1. Although for analytical purposes I tease the two apart and discuss them in separate chapters, organizational changes and cultural boundary work were two aspects of a single process of class formation.

In their boundary work, Cincinnati businessmen selected certain items from the republican tool kit and neglected others. Some tools sharpened distinctions between classes and smoothed out divisions among businessmen. These figured prominently in business citizenship. Others, highlighting producer virtues or egalitarian principles which crossed class lines, saw less service. One theme in Cincinnati's business citizenship was a strong claim to standing above class, and a corresponding condemnation of class interests as grounds for collective action or public policy. This theme was, paradoxically, at the heart of bourgeois class consciousness. It was one important way in which businessmen distinguished themselves from lesser social groups and, in the comfort of their exclusive civic clubs, affirmed the virtues that they had in common.[7] In one respect, business citizenship thus confirms a familiar contrast between Gilded Age and Progressive thought: the pluralist recognition of group interests and representative rights gaining ground among corporate liberals and corporate lawyers made little headway in Cincinnati business circles.[8] But the claim that class interests and class action subvert good government draws more on republican traditions than on classical liberalism.

A second theme of business citizenship celebrates *individual* rights and duties, and this individualism can be seen as a liberal alternative to working-class republicanism. Here too, however, Cincinnati businessmen adapted more than abandoned republicanism. The "independence" that they praised in good citizens no longer included economic self-sufficiency, but neither had it been reduced to freedom of individual contract. Independence involved as well a "manly" character, enabling the individual to stand firm against partisan pressures. And while civic participation was to be individual rather than corporate, it remained obligatory. The individual citizen, like the republican mechanic, had a duty to put personal interests aside and work on behalf of the commonweal. This praise of individual citizenship also had its uses for class formation. On one side, it involved boundary work against those deemed selfish or lacking in "character." On the other, the stigma on self-serving behavior provided a sturdier foundation for class solidarity than did the privatized individualism of market liberalism.

Another insistent theme in Cincinnati's bourgeois ideology made the interests of the business community and of the city as a whole identical. Business spokesmen make this link in all periods, of course, but they do so in different ways. Classical liberalism invoked the invisible hand, transforming private vice into public virtue. In popularized versions of social Darwinism, rapacious competitive struggle is held to winnow out the less efficient companies and less capable entrepreneurs. And Progressive corporate liberals pointed to the ethic of social responsibility which animated professional managers of large corporations. Cincinnati businessmen identified their interests with the general good in a different way. They linked their investments—in energy and intelligence as well as money—in the "home economy" to a more general local patriotism. They also identified personal with community interest through their dual roles as leading businessmen and leading citizens. And here they departed from classical liberalism in another way. Far from erecting a barrier between civic and economic spheres, business citizenship blurred the boundaries between them. One's status as a prominent business figure warranted a privileged role in community life. It did so, in part, because the same qualities that defined the successful businessman—his manly command of economic affairs, his businesslike efficiency, his steady judgment—also defined the virtuous political leader. Cincinnati businessmen certainly were no champions of government economic regulation. But as described in chapter 5, for both government and economy they used the same standards for assessing worth and legitimating authority.

The need to rise above class; the individual's civic obligations; the identity of business and community interest—none of these was a new theme in business discourse. Together, however, they offered ideological common ground for diverse businessmen confronting new challenges. Their republican roots also deserve emphasis. The continuing adaptation of republicanism for collective struggle is a familiar topic in labor studies. It has received much less attention in business history. The uses of republicanism by Cincinnati's bourgeoisie also depart from a familiar story of class realignment in this period. Scholars have seen republicanism as uniting workers and the middle class in many communities against the depredations of industrial capitalism. The shift toward an alliance of middle class and capital against labor militancy, in turn, is said to have been paralleled by a shift from republican to liberal political discourse.[9] Cincinnati class formation does not fit this narrative. Rather than contrasting middle- and upper-class liberalism to artisan republicanism, it is more appropriate to compare workers' and employers' different adaptations of republicanism. And it was the reworked republicanism that I call business citizenship, and not liberalism, which helped bring together a broad bourgeois coalition.

Cincinnati's employers made less use of other themes in the republican repertoire. The ideal of the mechanic as the productive and respected citizen of the republic was one to which craftsmen and "practical" manufacturers could still subscribe after the Civil War. Cincinnati factory owners gradually relinquished that identity. By the 1890s, they appear as businessmen, whose social status and civic responsibilities align them not with craftsmen but with other manufacturers, merchants, and even such unproductive men as bankers and lawyers. The mechanic also had been closely linked to republicanism's egalitarian principles. By virtue of their independence and their productive contributions, mechanics and yeomen merited the political voice and social status previously monopolized by elites. That egalitarian ideal appeared but faintly in late-nineteenth-century business discourse. The businessmen who redesigned Cincinnati's system for industrial education believed that talented and hard-working individuals should be able to better themselves. But they also assumed that these individuals would be the exceptions. And their criteria for measuring social worth in cultural life and civic affairs did not entitle productive labor to equal authority in politics or industry.

These selective adaptations from the republican repertoire, chapter 3 will argue, were locked in over time by local challenges, events, and organizational contexts. The city's slipping economic standing and notoriously corrupt government alarmed businessmen in the 1880s and 1890s more than did labor, with the 1884 Court House riot a focal point for elite anxieties. These perceived challenges, in turn, channeled businessmen's collective energies into organizations devoted to economic boosterism and civic betterment. Through these clubs, manufacturers and merchants practiced particular kinds of boundary work. They assumed for themselves the roles of leading citizens standing above class and working for the good of the community; they saw arraigned against them men whose venality, partisanship, and susceptibility to demagogues threatened Cincinnati's "miniature republic."[10]

If artisans and their employers can take republicanism in different directions, so can different bourgeoisies. An alternative trajectory of challenges, critical events, and collective organization led to very different uses of republicanism in San Francisco. In contrast to Cincinnati, middling businessmen coexisted with a handful of hulking corporations. Those corporations used their formidable power to set rates (for shipping into and out of the city, for example) and policies (to allow continued Chinese immigration) which antagonized a broad range of city business and labor groups. The demographics of the local economy also differed from Cincinnati's. The particular position of the Chinese in key trades, both as small owners and as unskilled employees, aligned white proprietors and craftsmen against them—and against the large firms that employed them. That alliance, in turn, took root in neighborhood associations and party politics, giving the "anti-coolie" coalition a durable institutional base well beyond the industries that employed the Chinese. Under these conditions, San Francisco businessmen made different selections from the republican tool kit, and they used them to construct social boundaries along different lines.[11] At a time when the "mechanic" was splitting into skilled labor and manufacturers in Cincinnati, San Francisco businessmen continued to celebrate the virtuous middle. That great middle of small proprietors and craftsmen represented both economic and political virtue, with invidious comparisons on either side. Above loomed parasitical corporations, corrupting state and local politics. Below swarmed the Chinese, unworthy as producers and unfit for citizenship. Within the great middle, however, proprietors and skilled labor were highly ecumenical, cooperating across class lines and, among white workers, developing a powerful labor movement without regard for merely ethnic differences.

In another respect, San Francisco's proprietors had more in common with the lawyers and enlightened managers of corporate liberalism than with good republican citizens.[12] Facing a powerful labor movement, San Francisco manufacturers organized in self-defense. Chapter 2 showed how that organization tended to divide them by trade and market position. But it also involved them in regular dealings with trade unions and taught them the advantages of collective bargaining over uncompromising industrial warfare—a lesson sharply reinforced by the failure of the city's big firms to win the open shop in the 1901 lockout. By the early 1900s, most businessmen seem to have conceded that industrial relations and politics would be the work of groups, not individuals, and above all the organized representatives of labor and capital. They certainly deemed class actors "partisan" in the sense that these actors pursued sectional rather than general interests. But this was true of organized employers no less than organized labor; business claims to represent the community good, in contrast to class-mongering unions, gained little traction in San Francisco before the 1910s. Among local manufacturers and merchants, the assumption instead was that the public interest stood apart from class actors. It was best served when both sides were organized, had levelheaded leaders, and worked out their differences through peaceful negotiation.

I refer to this model of labor relations as *practical corporatism*. It was a corporatism that in some ways resembled the more familiar corporate liberalism of the early-twentieth-century National Civic Federation (NCF).[13] Led by top executives from some of the nation's largest firms, the NCF took what was, for the time, an enlightened view of unions. They recognized that unions as well as corporations were part of a general trend toward organization in modern economies, and they invited national union leaders to join them in high-level diplomatic relations. But the differences are more striking. As the name *corporate liberalism* suggests, it was an ideology associated with corporations, not proprietors. The professionals who ran these corporations were in a better position than most proprietors to view unions with statesmanlike detachment, and they felt some need to improve the public image of their "trusts." Because of the market power of their firms, corporate managers also had less to fear from competitors if they made agreements with unions. San Francisco employers did not enjoy the same luxury: collective organization on *both* sides was necessary to ensure that trade agreements did not fall victim to free riders. Lastly, and most important, corporate liberals rarely practiced what they preached. The National Civic Federation's well-publicized conferences with responsible labor leaders, declaring in general terms that labor and capital each had rights and deserved respect, were one thing. Collective bargaining involving their own employees was an entirely different matter. Most members of the NCF ran open shops.

San Francisco employers had much less to say in public about union rights and industrial peace than did NCF leaders like George Perkins and August Belmont, but behavior matched rhetoric more closely in San Francisco. The "practical" corporatism of local employers was "practical" because they were not articulating a formal doctrine so much as adopting practices more or less consistent with corporatist ideology.[14] Their corporatism was also practical in the sense of pragmatic. To take the most important example, those employers who accepted union representation at work in most cases did so not on principle but in deference to a fact of life: unions appeared to be an unavoidable part of doing business. Practical corporatism generalizes this fact of life into a set of assumptions about who the legitimate actors are in the public sphere and how those actors should behave.

There was, then, little high-minded idealism in this civic ideology. Practical corporatism was a self-interested response to the realities of labor power at the ballot box and the workplace. And by highlighting businessmen's strategic interests rather than urging them to put these aside and cooperate for the public good, practical corporatism did little to bridge divisions among them. Instead, it fostered and ratified the cross-class alliances described in chapter 2. Self-interested pragmatism had its virtues, however. San Francisco employers' civic ideology may not have done much for their republican souls, but it legitimated accommodation with unions and justified good faith efforts to settle differences through collective bargaining. Cincinnati businessmen were, in comparison, men of lofty ideals and civic virtue. Applying those standards of worth to industrial relations, however, provided ideological cover for denying workers any union rights.

3

BUSINESS CITIZENSHIP IN CINCINNATI

At Cincinnati's 1882 Industrial Exposition, ward residents constructed parade floats to celebrate "the Queen of the West." The Twenty-first Ward's contribution captured several key features of the city's history and self-image. Labeled "Paris of America," the float arranged beer kegs and packing crates in the form of a music stand; from atop the kegs and crates, a giant pig wielded his conducting baton.[1] Today, this might seem an odd juxtaposition. For late-nineteenth-century Cincinnati businessmen, though, packing pork and performing music were parts of a single script. The discourse of business citizenship celebrated their contributions to economic growth, artistic excellence, and good government. Those contributions were not at odds. Instead, they were nurtured by a common identity as good citizens and tied more tightly together by the presence of the same businessmen atop the three hierarchies of economic position, cultural refinement, and civic worth.

Chapter 1 described Cincinnati businessmen's organizational responses to a variety of challenges, from economic decline to labor unrest to municipal misgovernment. Those responses included, in rough historical sequence, trade associations, cultural institutions, and civic organizations. To an increasing extent, each successive type extended ties among businessmen and separated them from wage earners. And these organizational developments reinforced familiar social changes favoring class realignment in the late nineteenth century. The growing scale of factories separated the workaday lives of proprietors and employees; changes in urban geography set them apart in residence and leisure; private schools and eastern colleges in the East afforded the wealthy different training and credentials. None of these changes, however, tells us in what specific ways businessmen defined their shared identities and their differences from other groups.

This chapter looks more closely at Cincinnati businessmen's boundary work, the collective identities they cultivated and the corresponding distinctions they drew between themselves and lower classes. These boundaries were by no means settled after the Civil War. The struggle for "free labor" had invoked a common bond between northern workers and proprietors. Even as industrial establishments got bigger and their owners richer, manufacturers were not necessarily grouped—by themselves or by others—with other owners of property. On one side, manufacturers represented new money, and money earned in ways that seemed less than genteel to older elites. On the other side, they retained ties to artisanal workers through both social origins and republican ideology. Many began their careers "in the trade," and for some time after the war, manufacturers and their skilled employees were still assigned to the single category of mechanics, the productive labor that supported a healthy republic.[2]

In Cincinnati, the category of "mechanic" gradually disappeared, replaced on one side by "artisan" or "skilled hand" and on the other by "manufacturer." By the 1890s, manufacturers were more likely to label themselves "businessmen," a label closely tied to the status of "leading citizen" of the community. Both the generic term *businessman* and the emphasis on their roles as leading citizens highlighted what manufacturers had in common with merchants or self-employed professionals rather than what they shared with fellow members

FIGURE 1. Exposition Float, Cincinnati, 1882. Courtesy, Cincinnati Museum Center.

of their trade. The shift can be seen in their boundary work. As they elaborated hierarchies of cultural refinement and civic worth, businessmen increasingly distanced themselves from the less worthy—those with poor taste, bad character, and limited capacity to act responsibly. Their own virtues as leading citizens followed accordingly: they appreciated the arts, displayed manly character, and behaved reasonably. Like the organizational changes described in chapter 1, this construction of boundaries and identities redrew class alignments: distinctions and identities based on cultural refinement and civic worth *also* divided wage earners from business owners and brought the latter closer together. This reworking of boundaries powerfully contributed to class formation because it merged the criteria—and personnel—of economic, cultural, and civic leadership in Cincinnati. It did so even while "class" itself remained taboo as a category for mapping social differences and similarities.

After describing the categories businessmen used to stigmatize "them" and celebrate "us," this chapter explores the ways in which criteria of cultural, civic, and economic worth cohered. It concludes in a more explanatory vein, emphasizing the path-dependent process by which particular business frames and identities came to be selected from a larger menu. Distinctions and boundaries do not construct social inequalities out of whole cloth. Social realities do limit the menu, and choices from the menu are constrained. Which differences are made the basis for social alignments and invested with meaning depends in part on institutional settings, inherited as well as created. Both by virtue of their manifest purposes and their social composition, institutions favor some ways of drawing boundaries over others. The cultural institutions formed in the 1870s and the civic associations launched in the 1880s and early 1890s drew lines between more and less worthy Cincinnatians. These institutions and associations did not define worth in the same way, but the two sets of boundaries ran close together.

FRAMING LOWER CLASSES
Cultural Hierarchy

Consider, first, cultural hierarchy. In building specialized cultural institutions during the 1870s, Cincinnati's elite was also elaborating social distinctions based on taste.[3] Contrasts between refined and popular sensibilities are clearest in Cincinnati's music scene. The choice of Theodore Thomas as director of the music festival (and later of the city's College of Music) is itself telling. Thomas was well known as a champion of high standards. In matters of repertoire, he drew sharp distinctions between serious and "light" (but still tasteful) classical music, insisting that only the first was suitable for the festival's evening performances.

"Programmes for the evening concerts [should be] pure and clean without being heavy . . . principally made up from standard works of our great masters. Those for the matinees as light as good taste will allow."[4] And to protect both programs from pollution by commercial considerations, Thomas successfully opposed moves to include a prize contest for singing. High standards should also apply to performance practices. The focus should be on the art, not on the performer. Pandering to unrefined audience tastes was no better than using prize money to engage their interest. Preparing for the first festival, Thomas instructed board members to "be sure that a good contralto is engaged . . . one who will not try to cover up her bad singing by shaking her body and smiling at young America."[5] And high standards applied, finally, to the consumption as well as the production of art. As John Kasson documents, Thomas insisted on strict decorum at performances. However some might behave at minstrel shows, those privileged to attend his concerts must concentrate on the music, appreciate it in silence, and eschew demands to repeat popular pieces—demands that were "greedy and in bad taste."[6] Observers agreed that Thomas succeeded in his civilizing mission. "The Musical Festival," Cincinnati's *Commercial Gazette* preened, "has brought to the city those who really love music, those who are educated and refined."[7]

Lest there be any doubt that refined visitors were superior to those who might come for "a jamboree," the *Gazette* added that "the city prefers the musical festival visitors." Artistic and popular music corresponded to different types of people. Some had the sensibility to appreciate orchestral performances of the classical canon, while others took pleasure in lowbrow entertainment. The two should not be mixed. Samuel Covington, vice president of a local insurance company, was appalled to learn that Cincinnati's Park Commission planned to allow a circus to use the Music Hall. Registering his complaint with the Festival Association president, he expressed his "regret to see the buildings so occupied (I had almost written disgraced) as they have been of late, and as it is proposed to occupy them, for the sake of the Musical Festival. . . . At the rate they are moving, respectable people will soon decline to enter them for any purpose. Can't you . . . have this abasement of the buildings stopped?"[8] Given the city's long-standing musical traditions, fencing off classical music as the preserve of high culture was bound to antagonize those who felt excluded. One festival chorus member, having been refused the privilege of escorting his wife to her seat, protested the indignity and went on to question who owned music in Cincinnati. "This feeling is not the usual grumble of singers," he told the festival secretary. "It is the warmth of just indignation at being rated as machines, and not gentlemen and ladies. . . . For twelve years I have been identified with every leading musical event in Cincinnati. . . . The festival is as much mine as yours."[9] New standards could also meet resistance from those who *were* included in the charmed circle of high culture, and yet found the demands of refinement at times unbearable. "Thomas concert at ODeon," a local bookseller and publisher reported in his diary. "A symphony of Beethoven was followed by a concerto by same for orchestra and piano. Was too much for me. I went to sleep."[10] For better or worse, the lines of cultural refinement were becoming clearly drawn, and they largely coincided with class differences. Chamber of Commerce Secretary Sidney Maxwell, in a series of newspaper articles on the city's suburbs, underscored the links among class, residence, and sensibility. Having described in lavish detail the architectural excellence and artistic decoration of houses in Glendale and Avondale—communities "largely of the families of business men"—Maxwell listed the advantages of living in these distant neighborhoods. "It saves the inhabitants from visitors that would otherwise . . . swarm in the streets." In contrast to such riffraff, "the inhabitants are generally intelligent and refined," with "a common cement in similar education and tastes."[11] Theodore Thomas was equally clear on how musical artistry pitted refined classes against the rabble. Referring to the city's Democratic and relatively populist newspaper, Thomas expressed doubt that "the uncompromising programmes for the evening concerts of the Festival" would succeed "in a community when a paper like the *Enquirer* has any influence."[12]

Civic Hierarchy

Another set of invidious distinctions was tied to civic rather than cultural institutions and gauged worthiness in public life rather than in the arts. Here, censure fell not on the unrefined, but on the irrational, the unmanly, and the partisan. More clearly than with cultural distinctions, these contrasts reflected the impact of Cincinnati's perceived economic decline and political disorder.

In major cities across the United States, the 1877 railway strike, the 1886 Haymarket bombing, and the 1894 Pullman boycott greatly amplified the venerable rhetoric that depicted brutish mobs threatening law, order, and decency.[13] These disturbances received ample attention in Cincinnati, but they provided less of a focal point for elite anxieties than the Court House burning, when "the mob [ran] riot, with torch and bloody hand triumphant."[14] As chapter 1 pointed out, commentaries on the riot from both business-oriented and more populist newspapers did not distinguish between respectable, law-abiding workmen who held themselves aloof, and a mob made up of "the idle, giddy, vicious, and criminal."[15] Instead, they found precisely those respectable workmen to have been the largest contingent in the mob. Consistent with popular sociologies of the madding crowd, elites argued that these *normally* decent working men were easily swept away, both by their own inner passions and by the contagious influence of mobs.

Without suitable reforms, the *Commercial Gazette* warned, the judicial system could once more fail and decent men's "impulse may be again unloosed and passions again rage."[16] The loosening reins were both psychological and civil, as passions escaped the control of individual conscience and of public authority.

In contrast, the respectable community leader retained calm judgment and steady nerves. He could, and should, step in during a crisis. In the longer run, he should devise appropriate institutional bulwarks against popular passions. Gas company president (and Civil War hero) General Andrew Hickenlooper cast himself in just this role, advising the mayor on how to deal with disturbances and offering to pay the costs of hiring additional police. And the lessons he drew from the riot were regularly echoed by businessmen in the 1880s and 1890s. "It is dangerous to arouse the passions of the populace, or enlist agencies that cannot be governed and controlled by conservative wisdom and intelligence. The ignorant, vicious and depraved, misinterpreting the purpose, unbridle their passions, the servant becomes the master, and their latent—but always existing—antipathy to the restraints of law and order, finds expression in excesses."[17]

A similar if less alarmist contrast appears in business commentaries on the irrational voter. The same men who could be swept up in a mob could be gulled by political demagogues. The main difference was in the risk of property damage. Local bookstore owner Davis James made the link between gullibility and class in his attack on the 1896 Democratic presidential campaign. "The worst and most unruly element has been arrayed against the law abiding by the [William Jennings] Bryan demagogues. . . . Should Bryan and his anarchistic friends come into power . . . it will be a crushing blow to business." Even in a less partisan mood (criticizing yellow journalist accounts of the sinking of the Maine in 1898), James had the same estimate of popular capacities. The "pernicious influence" of the newspapers has "weight with the unthinking masses. Intelligent people have learned to discount such inflammatory journalism."[18] It followed that those who combined high rank and higher faculties had the highest obligations. Commercial Club members applauded a visiting cleric's dinner speech on "The Responsibility of the Upper Half." After dividing the body politic into reason (located in the head), brave energies (heart and lungs), and those appetites "which by their lower position confess their natural servitude and liability to shame," Bishop Greer urged the head to "govern and control" the rest. "That I take it is the 'upper half' in our American society."[19]

This contrast between the thoughtful and the impulsive members of the body politic overlaps with another boundary in civic life separating men of "character" from the weak and venal. The man of character was outwardly decisive, inwardly disciplined, and utterly trustworthy. His outward decisiveness involved a "manly" bearing and forceful manner, which did not always endear

him to others. One Commercial Club member praised local railroad executive Melville Ingalls as a "born administrative official, and of the school that
believed in . . . commands. Such qualifications are not conducive to enlisting
strong friendships, but they are necessary, in doing great work."[20] Such leading citizens display self-control, steady habits, and serious purpose. Indeed, for
both the businessmen who hired staff at Cincinnati's industrial expositions and
for the businessmen who recommended applicants, "character" in this sense
trumped mere job skills. Reference forms asked a series of questions about candidates' sobriety, work habits, and integrity, but only one about their practical
ability to fill the position.[21] Self-discipline also meant independence, or at least
the fortitude to steer one's own course without undue reliance on, or influence
from, others. One great advantage of the cooperative education program at the
University of Cincinnati, according to the secretary of the city's Metal Trades
Association, was the class of men it attracted to the city. These "sturdy young
gentlemen" were destined for success because, having to work their way through
college, they were "free from mollycoddle and ribbon counter influences."[22] This
combination of direct dealing with others and exacting self-discipline, finally,
made men of character trustworthy. They would neither deceive others nor
allow personal whim or temptations to divert them from honoring their commitments. The highest praise bestowed on the dead by members of Cincinnati's
Chamber of Commerce was that "his word was his bond." With such upstanding
men, legal contracts were mere formalities.

   In this praise of worthy men, reliability, discipline, and strength overlapped
with status distinctions: men of character were gentlemen. In filling industrial
exposition jobs, applicants and recommenders alike linked character to breeding,
offering as an important qualification for a position that the young man came
from "a good family" or belonged to "good society here."[23] Dry goods merchant
Charles Reemelin gave a similar rationale for joining the city's Taxpayers' League
in 1881: he knew the members "to be gentlemen of good character."[24] Character
also distinguished citizens along the lines of gender. The wives and daughters of
local businessmen often played important roles in philanthropy and the arts, but
in definitions of good citizenship they were invisible. Discipline, forcefulness,
and seriousness were manly traits. The close links between character, manliness,
and good citizenship are particularly clear in indictments of Cincinnati city
government under Boss Cox. For local reformer Henry Wright, "the greatest
evil of bossism . . . [is its] depreciation of manliness of the citizens. This country
would never have had the courage to make the fight for independence against
the king of England if our forefathers had been the weaklings the boss system is
developing. . . . If [citizens] will put the premium on manhood rather than on
money, bossism will not long rule our cities and despoil our youth."[25]

A third categorical distinction between the civic elect and the unworthy contrasts those willing to subordinate their own interests to the greater good and those who are selfish and partisan. This was a familiar trope in mugwump politics,[26] and for Cincinnati elites the main focus was once again on municipal misgovernment. City politics, in this view, was corrupt and inefficient because most politicians, many voters, and even some craven businessmen were unable or unwilling to put self-interest aside and pursue the good of Cincinnati. Partisanship might mean thinking only of one's party rather than the commonweal. For Charles Reemelin, speaking at a public meeting of the Committee of 100, "no one has any capacity to judge public questions, who argues them from the party stand-point. He must rise or sink in your estimation just according to the degree to which he rises to the highest ideals of true citizenship, or sinks to the cess-pools of partisanship." Selfishness also had the more familiar meaning of thinking first of one's personal or business interests, as when utility companies in search of favors "corrupt men who are in office."[27] The outcome in either case, according to Commercial Club members, was misgovernment. Public officials came to treat their jobs "as a reward for partisan work" rather than discharging their duty "to do [the] best public service."[28]

In contrast to the scheming Boss Cox, bribe-paying corporations, and toadying political appointees stood disinterested citizens, men who put aside their personal interests for the betterment of the city. Politically, this meant eschewing partisanship. Organizers of the Committee of 100 carefully balanced the number of Democratic and Republican members to demonstrate their commitment to public over party interests, and speakers at the committee's public meetings insisted that nonpartisanship was the cure for what ailed Cincinnati. The city, committee members argued, was like a business. "Are we going to ask when we are electing directors to a bank . . . are you a Democrat or Republican? Not at all. We ask is he honest, is he capable," and, harking back to character, "is he a man of pure life, is he . . . the center of a good family."[29] The Chamber of Commerce applied the same yardstick when backing a nonpartisan police commission in the aftermath of the Court House riot.[30]

The good citizen put his own as well as his party's interests aside in public life. Members of the Commercial Club, according to one of the club's founders, had their eyes set only on the general good. "None . . . have ever been accused or can be accused, justly, of acting for their individual interests. . . . The purpose of the Commercial Club is in accord with the highest form of citizenship."[31] In memorials prepared for deceased members of the Chamber of Commerce and the Commercial Club, this theme is regularly invoked. Julius Dexter's "absolute forgetfulness of self" marks him as an "ideal citizen." Another businessman is commended for "regarding the interests of others no less than his own."[32] It was clearly recognized that success in business required a tight fist and a hard nose. But the good businessman had responsibilities beyond his own firm and his personal wealth. Members of the Commercial Club commemorated William Breed in 1908 because, while "he was born to wealth and to a place in the community," he "shirked none of the responsibilities that were thus put upon him."[33] The same selflessness won praise when displayed in the form of charitable giving. To be "liberal" and "generous" in one's support of orphans and art museums was a virtue; to do so without calling attention to oneself brought a businessman closer still to civic sainthood. Insurance company owner Lewis Glenn earned the admiration of his Chamber of Commerce colleagues because "his charities were numerous and were bestowed without ostentation in that right spirit of not letting the left hand know what the right hand doeth."[34]

As with hierarchies in reason and judgment, so differences in selflessness overlapped with class rank. Studies of Gilded Age reform suggest that the ideal of disinterested citizenship was tied to the "best men" of the community, who by their upbringing and education felt more attuned to public needs and public service.[35] The link between good citizens and good breeding appears in Cincinnati as well. In Sidney Maxwell's contemporary account of the suburbs, the character of "the intelligent and refined" was what ensured that "their influence is expended on such objects as promote the public good," and that explained why the suburbs enjoyed such blessings as "excellent schools" and "wholesome government." Unwholesome government, by contrast, he attributed to the masses: "the increase in the density of population brings with it . . . a growing inability or indisposition to suitably manage public affairs."[36] And woe to the rich political boss who sought to cross status boundaries. George Cox managed to buy a home in elite Clifton, but "of course the Coxes never 'belonged' in Clifton." George had to be tolerated because he was powerful and a Republican, but the ladies shunned his wife.[37] The corrupt officials on the Board of Education, a Committee of 100 speaker argued, were no better. They were "men who it would disgrace their daughters to know; whom no gentle, well-bred woman could speak to without blushing."[38]

BUSINESS IDENTITIES

These distinctions of social worth—in refinement and in civic competence—were elaborated in the context of cultural and civic institutions built by businessmen. Men who belonged to these institutions and who fit the social categories of refined and virtuous citizenship also occupied the upper rungs of Cincinnati's economic hierarchy. But these institutions and categories did more than erect boundaries between businessmen and lower classes. Refinement and civic-mindedness were also important parts of late-nineteenth-century employer identities. Their self-conception as citizen-businessmen distanced employers from mere mechanics. At the same time, this identity helped bring employers together, despite their rivalries, as the responsible civic, cultural, *and* business leaders of Cincinnati.

The importance of this business identity becomes clearer against the backdrop of the 1870s. Chapter 1 showed that a version of the producer ethic lived on in Cincinnati shortly after the Civil War. At least some manufacturers at that time embraced an identity as "mechanics," and it was common to praise them, if less and less for "working side by side" with their employees, then at least for knowing the trade and being "practical men." Many "mechanics and manufacturers" still placed themselves in a separate category from commercial capital and regarded their own interests as being poorly served by mercantile organizations. By the 1890s, manufacturers—well represented in Cincinnati's cultural and civic organizations—rarely identified themselves, and were rarely praised by others, as either mechanics or practical men. Neither label appears in the records of the leading civic associations of businessmen or in the (much more fragmentary) records of the principle organization catering to industrial capital, the Manufacturers' Club. The language of *trade* persists in some settings. Much as civic associations were added to employers' organizational repertoire rather than replacing those based on trade, so manufacturers still referred to themselves by industry. Context matters here. It is in handling strikes or in electing officials to run their employer association, for example, that references to machine tool men or carriage makers are common. But the prevailing *public* rhetoric of the 1890s combines the inclusive "businessman" with the role of "citizen" of Cincinnati.

This shift is bound up with the constituencies and activities of the key civic institutions for individual businessmen—the Commercial Club, the Committee of 100, the Business Men's Club, and a Chamber of Commerce that took up the civic gospel in the 1890s. These organizations brought diverse manufacturers, merchants, managers, and self-employed professionals together as generic businessmen with a putative common interest in boosting Cincinnati. As associations dedicated to improving city governance by putting it on a sound business basis, these clubs also gave businessmen a privileged public role as representatives of the (respectable) community as a whole. The labels used to describe Committee of 100 members are typical. Speaking at one of the committee's public meetings in 1886, H. Wilson Brown (railroad manager and Musical Festival commissioner) presented himself as "a business man" acting in defense of Cincinnati "as a city and as a commonwealth."[39] Looking back ten years later, Thomas McDougall (a founder of the National Association of Manufacturers) made the more general claim that the Committee of 100 was made up of "representative business men," capturing both the cross-section of businesses involved and their self-proclaimed public role.[40] Their economic functions, varied though they may have been, thus gave manufacturers and merchants common civic responsibilities and a shared commitment to the public interest.

Late-nineteenth-century Cincinnati businessmen's emphasis on their common public role rather than their sectional economic interests also drew on older cultural tools from their kit. Business citizenship adapted republican traditions in particular ways as proprietors faced new challenges, and did so in the context of new organizations. Historians have shown how employers gradually abandoned the producer ethic and the participatory ethos of traditional republicanism.[41] Employers rethought republicanism in part because of the challenge of working-class radicalism, a movement whose leaders had adapted these same cultural resources into a critique of wage labor, class inequality, and autocratic management. Employers, in turn, selected and reinterpreted republican ideals to suit *their* interests. What emerged from this retooling looks much like liberalism, with a suspicion of state power, a definition of equality in terms of opportunities for mobility, a sharp separation between politics (where democratic norms apply) and the economy (where they do not), and a wholly individualistic notion of liberty. The timing assigned to this move away from traditional republicanism on the part of employers varies from one scholar and case study to another, but few would date it later than the end of Reconstruction and the labor insurgency of 1877. Ross finds republicanism to have been more persistent in Cincinnati on account of the relatively small scale and proprietary character of capital. By the late 1880s, however, that tradition no longer held. Confronted by industrial and political threats from below, capitalists embraced an ideology of law, order, and liberalism which sharply distinguished the norms appropriate for political as against economic life.[42]

Although this general shift from republicanism to liberalism captures some of Cincinnati employers' emerging "business" identity, there are important departures from the standard story line. Despite the evident decline in a producer ethic and in identification with their trade, a broad sense of calling still runs through proprietors' views of the good businessman. There is also a strong rhetorical emphasis, as in classical republicanism, on the vital need for individuals to subordinate their personal interests to some larger community good. Most importantly, Cincinnati employers in the 1890s retained much of the participatory thrust of republicanism. In each of these areas, moreover, businessmen regularly crossed the liberal boundary between economic and political roles.

In their thinking about what it means to be good businessmen, leading Cincinnati employers of the 1890s voiced a secularized version of Puritan calling, and they did so in ways that bridge rather than separate the economy and the public sphere. This updated sense of calling is most clearly expressed in a characteristic locution used in profiles of local merchants and manufacturers, that they had "an identity with" their business. In the course of his career, says a memorial to John Swasey, he "became thoroughly identified with many interests." "The business career of Mr. Kuerze includes identity with the drug trade," meaning, presumably, pharmaceuticals. Henry Innenhort gained prominence in the coal trade, "with which his identity began in 1872."[43] The phrase conveys both a personal identity and an equivalence of interest—the manufacturer's sense of self was, or should have been, bound up with his business. But employers honoring their colleagues also used the phrase to link business identities and wider civic interests. Thus John Gano, in addition to his success in publishing, achieved a "prominent identity with the Chamber of Commerce," while lumberman John Hartwell "represented in a remarkable degree, in his own personal bearing, the high purposes that prompted [the Chamber of Commerce's] organization."[44] And through this identity with their firms, their trades, and such organizations as the Chamber of Commerce, businessmen became identified with the city as a whole. Theodore Marsh, for example, "was identified not only with [Cincinnati's] prosperity by his [business] interests, but as well with the general welfare of his fellow citizens."[45] For respectable businessmen, these economic and political identities should not conflict. Members of the Commercial Club in 1898 mourned the death of fellow member Julius Dexter, remembering him for his success in business, his generous contributions to cultural institutions, and his leadership on behalf of political reform. Dexter, they wrote, was "first and before all else the Citizen."[46]

As this language of an "identity" with the firm or the city reminds us, the discourse of business citizenship strongly condemns the pursuit of mere self-interest. In *either* economic or political affairs, those who thought first of their personal or partisan interests deserved censure as bad citizens. By contrast, businessmen like the banker Henry Peachey earned praise from the Chamber of Commerce for putting the interests of his company and its clients ahead of his own: "he performed all the duties required of him faithfully and well, never allowing any selfish considerations to [divert] him."[47] The same criterion for approval or reproach applied in civic life. Here too, businessmen warned one another of the corrosive effects of self-interest. "The great danger that threatens us as a people," McDougall told Committee of 100 supporters in 1886, "is the existence of that class among us [whose] meat and drink is corruption in politics."[48] For members of the Business Men's Club, similarly, "interest and zeal in municipal office is not politics." Leadership should instead be in the hands of men like the club's members, "active, patriotic, unselfish business men, of unquestioned social and commercial standing."[49]

These exemplary businessmen, vigilant in keeping their personal interests in check, are surely individualists. In this sense the preferred identity of employers is consistent with the narrative of liberalism displacing republicanism among America's bourgeoisie. Yet Cincinnati proprietors around the turn of the century retained a republican insistence on active participation in civic affairs. Civic action, they still believed, was an essential antidote to corruption and unchecked power in municipal government. And businessmen, by virtue of their prominence, their resources, and their "businesslike" nonpartisanship, had a special obligation to serve the public good in this way. "Every business man in Cincinnati," the Business Men's Club admonished its members, "owes it to himself, his family and to his city to devote a reasonable portion of his time to public affairs. Good citizenship demands this sacrifice on the part of every man. . . . Republics require such service from their citizens in order to exist and our municipalities are but miniature republics made possible by law-abiding and liberty-loving people."[50] It was through his civic, charitable, and political contributions that the businessman, in another favored turn of phrase, lived a "life of usefulness." And here too, far from separating economic from political relations, the employer's usefulness and merit as a good citizen demanded active service to the city as well as to his business.

In arguing that a modified republicanism became an important component of late-nineteenth-century employer identities, I make no claim that these beliefs were new. A sense of identification with one's work and the duty of active citizenship are clearly expressed in Cincinnati documents of the 1830s and 1860s as well. The surprise, rather, is that these themes are still such vital parts of employers' self image. The conventional view of Gilded Age capitalists sees them as staunch liberals of the laissez-faire variety, especially in comparison to their antebellum predecessors.[51] In that laissez-faire vision, economic activity should be neither regulated by the state nor measured by the same standards of legitimacy as apply in democratic politics. Gilded Age liberalism, moreover, celebrated the wider social benefits flowing from the pursuit of narrow individual interests. But this alleged trajectory from republicanism to liberalism clearly does not fit Cincinnati. Further testimony to that city's defiance of historical stereotypes comes from business obituaries. The Chamber of Commerce had a custom of appointing ad hoc committees to prepare memorials for deceased members. These are hardly infallible biographical guides, but they do suggest what businessmen themselves considered praiseworthy in their peers. Comparing all the memorials recorded before the Civil War with a sample of their counterparts in the 1890s shows that civic merits became, if anything, more important components of the worthy life.[52] In both periods, members are most often commended for their business virtues—the efficiency and success of their enterprises, their integrity as businessmen ("his word was as good as his bond"), and their contributions to the Chamber of Commerce or the economic well-being of the city. But there is also a striking increase in references to *both* private and public virtues. Praise for personal character or social charms (a likable man, a loyal friend) appear in 20 percent of the prewar memorials and 70 percent of those in the 1890s. And far from showing a trend toward social Darwinism, the incidence of praise for community virtues (such as political activity and membership in civic organizations) rises from 20 to 30 percent, and the proportion of memorials commending businessmen for their charitable activities grows from 10 to 36 percent. There was also a qualitative change in these notions of calling and civic duty. As late as the 1870s, they are still tied to proprietors' roles as "mechanics and manufacturers," echoing the ideal mechanic of early-nineteenth-century republicanism. In the 1890s and after, calling and citizenship are parts of proprietors' roles as businessmen—a category that excluded even skilled manual labor while encompassing proprietors and managers, employers from different industries, and capitalists from both manufacturing and commerce.

ALIGNING CULTURAL, CIVIC, AND ECONOMIC BOUNDARIES

The distinctions and identities highlighted in business discourse might have varied from one social setting to another. For example, the criteria for distinguishing "us" from "them" used by a machine tool manufacturer talking shop with colleagues in the industry could have little in common with distinctions made by businessmen as they organized the next music festival or plotted the next political assault on Cox's regime. Instead, economic, cultural, and civic boundary work largely coincided. Boundary work in these areas came together through institutions, individuals, and ideas. The Commercial and Business Men's Clubs had multiple agenda. Although comprised overwhelmingly of businessmen, these clubs involved their members in promoting political reform *and* cultural uplift *and* economic growth, all under a single banner of good citizenship. Individual members also commonly belonged to more specialized organizations, active in civic improvement, cultural affairs, or economic boosterism. Some biographical information is available for 137 men who belonged to the Commercial Club between 1880 and 1907. No less than 79 percent of these men also belonged to associations dealing more narrowly with business concerns, and 72 percent belonged to the prestigious Queen City Club. At least 36 percent were involved in more specialized political clubs or service, and 29 percent played leading roles in the city's cultural life.[53]

In ideas as well as in organizational activities and personal involvements, cultural uplift, political reform, and industrial progress went together. Businessmen seem to have applied the same standards for assessing worth—and claiming leadership—in each area. Consider, first, cultural refinement. Paul DiMaggio has argued that in constructing canons of good taste, institutions of music, theater, and dance sharply separated art from commerce and artistic sensibilities from the crass instrumentalism of business.[54] Cincinnati's elite thought differently. They claimed leading roles in each of these spheres, and they moved fluidly among those roles. A newspaper account of an 1894 meeting to discuss municipal art associations captures this intermingling of cultural, economic, and civic hierarchies. Describing the "brilliant gathering of representative Cincinnatians" that took place at the Queen City Club, under the auspices of the Commercial Club, the *Cincinnati Enquirer* reported that "art and literature, as well as the mercantile interests of the Queen City, received homage at the hands of solid citizens. . . . The menu was of the finest and the sociability of the gentlemen present of the closest."[55] Businessmen could simultaneously advance "art and literature" and "mercantile interests" because each goal served the other. A reputation for cultural excellence, many argued, served as a good advertisement for new business. And they seem to have viewed cultural and economic betterment as two sides of the same coin. According to the *Enquirer*, it was the "horny-handed sons of toil," not businessmen, who complained that building a Music Hall elevated the fiddlers above the mechanics.[56] For the wealthy citizens who supported the Music Hall, by contrast, a great virtue of the facility was that it would serve as a home for *both* music festivals and industrial expositions. Both advanced the interests of the city, in part by showcasing the "artistry" of its manufactured products along with it singers and painters. And when Samuel Covington protested the use of the Music Hall by a traveling circus, he explicitly deemed the expositions as well as the festivals defiled by such low-brow entertainment. The Board of Trade concurred.[57]

Civic betterment as well as cultural refinement contributed to business progress. The Court House riot underscored the connection between law and order and economic growth. "If the citizens of Cincinnati do not want to see our trade prostrate at their feet, let them assume control and prevent further scenes of bloodshed."[58] On a more constructive note, business leaders committed to municipal reform stressed its economic payoffs. A local government free from mismanagement, corruption, and inefficiency would help the city compete with its rivals for new investment. It was not just that progress on the civic front benefited the industrial, and vice versa. The categories themselves merged. An insistent theme in meetings of the Committee of 100 likened city government to a business and demanded that the business be run more efficiently. "Cincinnati is a corporation in which we all have a pecuniary interest," Joseph Carbery told one public meeting. "It would amaze you to know," revealed another speaker, "how little business sense is manifested in the running of the corporation known as the city of Cincinnati."[59] Improving municipal government, it followed, required a return to sound business sense. This did not necessarily mean putting business-men in charge. Rather, the very object of political reform merged municipal gov-ernance and sound business, as when the manufacturer and Commercial Club member T. R. Spence called for nonpartisan control of "the business affairs of the community."[60] The Chamber of Commerce affirmed this blending of civic and economic betterment by naming its unit for municipal improvement the "Civic and Industrial Department."

Completing the virtuous circle of high culture, economic progress, and civic reform, leading Cincinnati businessmen shared mugwumps' belief that good gov-ernment required refined character on the part of political leaders. As John Sproat has shown, Protestant elites in many urban centers during this period saw them-selves as the community's "best men," uniquely responsible for protecting govern-ment from venal politicians and disreputable constituents. Many of those living in Cincinnati's affluent "hilltop" neighborhoods agreed that social status not only carried political responsibilities but also served as a warrant for political virtue. Committee of 100 organizers appealed directly to "the best men" of both politi-cal parties as the most promising recruits to a campaign for municipal reform.[61] A standard narrative of Cincinnati's fall from grace under Boss Cox, similarly, attributed it to insufficient civic engagement on the part of the city's "stronger and more respected men."[62] "Until the men of character and of property can be aroused to suitably take care of their own affairs," the Chamber of Commerce's Maxwell warned, "there appears little to be derived from a change in method[s]" of govern-ment. Instead of men who are "brutal in all their ways," offices should be reserved for those qualified by a combination of "character, education, experience, tech-nical capacities [and] previous moral rectitude."[63] The link drawn by men like Maxwell between civic competence, class, and municipal governance was not lost on labor politicians. Where reformers saw civil service rules as protecting office holders from partisanship and corruption, Cincinnati's 1883 labor candidate for mayor saw "the first step towards establishing an aristocracy." Such rules "virtually shut . . . out all laboring men too poor to obtain [anything] better than a common school education from obtaining an office of any consequence."[64]

A strong sense of collective responsibility and local pride helped tie together businessmen's commitments to cultural, political, and economic betterment. In their own view, these men had the calling to play leading roles in each arena. Rail-road president Melville Ingalls's 1885 dinner speech to fellow Commercial Club members reminded them of their multiple obligations. "It used to be thought the duty of a commercial man to attend strictly to his trade, and leave all economic and political questions to the professional man and the idler. Happily, we have outgrown this, and the chief support of our society now are the men who manage our commercial affairs. They have to find time for politics, charities, churches and a countless number of things for which they get no reward or thanks except that of their own conscience and the satisfaction of doing their duty."[65] By merging their responsibilities into a single burden of good citizenship, businessmen like Ingalls also brought into alignment the standards for measuring cultural, political, and economic worth. Local pride, too, unified the goals of reforming politics, enhancing culture, and promoting growth. To a degree echoed only faintly among today's municipal boosters, Cincinnati was the primary anchor for residents' sense of civic identity. Municipal government, not state or federal, is the political community that is featured most often in formal dinner programs and, it seems, during informal discussions at the Commercial Club or Business Men's Club. *Local* festivals stirred hopes that "the Queen City of the West" would become "famous as the great art and musical center of the world."[66] And there was a striking sense of localized economic nationalism in Cincinnati. It is displayed most prominently in the anxious comparisons of the city's manufactures with those of municipal rivals. But it is also suggested by the Chamber of Commerce's organization of economic statistics into "imports and exports"; the Commercial Club's self-proclaimed dedication to the welfare of "our home people"; and commendation of the Commercial Club for its "spirit of local patriotism."[67] With Cincinnati the focus of such "patriotic" feelings, music festivals, charter reform, and booming "exports" all became parts of a common project of civic betterment. And this, in turn, reinforced the ideology of business citizenship that lay at the heart of employers' public identity and associational activities.

BUSINESS CITIZENSHIP AS CLASS CONSCIOUSNESS

Chapter 1 described the ways in which Cincinnati businessmen came to organize and to act together—and apart from their employees. The present chapter has shown how businessmen's boundary work reinforced and gave ideological substance to this class realignment. In their public discourse, capitalists preferred inclusive social categories to identities and interests which set them apart. They identified as businessmen instead of as mechanics or merchants, and they celebrated their common roles as leading citizens. They cultivated these more inclusive business identities, moreover, in part by distancing themselves from lesser men on the basis of cultural refinement and civic competence. As with their organizational affiliations, these cultural maps of the social world broadened horizontal ties and cut vertical ones. In addition, the cultural, civic, and economic boundaries businessmen constructed ran in close parallel. The individuals who displayed good taste and good citizenship also tended to be those exercising economic leadership—the city's respectable merchants, manufacturers, managers, and self-employed professionals.

Class formation is the term that summarizes this increasing alignment between economic position on one side and cultural practices or collective action on the other. The boundary work that contributed to this alignment, in turn, may be labeled the *class consciousness* of Cincinnati businessmen. But where the sociologist or historian may describe how economic positions and cultural practices coincide, "class consciousness" means something more. It refers to similarly placed economic actors' *own* construction of commonalities among themselves and of differences from other social ranks. One distinguishing characteristic of class consciousness in Cincinnati is its vehement repudiation of class. As an economic category for explaining social facts, class had no place. When members of the Committee of 100 or the Business Men's Club sought to explain misgovernment, they emphasized the corrupting influence of self-serving politicians and ignorant voters, not the corrupting influence of wealth or economic power. Gas company president Hickenlooper emphatically rejected the notion that local corporations or rich individual residents were the root cause of trouble; he identified the real problem as ballot stuffing and demagoguery. Social divisions reflected not class inequalities, but differences between respectable, law-abiding citizens and those lacking in one or the other of those two qualifications.[68] As a basis for political action, class had no legitimacy. Understood as the pursuit of sectional advantage at the expense of the larger commonwealth, "class" was held responsible for all manner of urban ills. In this view, class was an artful fiction of demagogues and agitators, one which divided harmonious communities, stirred up conflict, and poisoned politics. Melville Ingalls made the usual contrast when he indicted "the froth of our friend Gompers" and celebrated the victory of Taft in 1908. The election, he crowed, demonstrated "that the attempt to place class issues above the good of the nation is to no avail."[69] As grounds for collective identity, finally, "class" had no relevance. Cincinnati's business leaders defined themselves as representatives of the general community and rejected suggestions that they acted on behalf of any class interest. Members of the Commercial Club or the Business Men's Club were surely aware that they differed in wealth and social standing from manual workers. But they saw themselves as leading *citizens* who stood for the interests of all respectable Cincinnatians. The chief virtue of organizations like the Chamber of Commerce, its secretary claimed, was that it "furnishes a means of giving expression to the average business sentiment of the community"; and "that, in general terms, is the average common sense of the population."[70]

This classless business ideology was nevertheless coupled with social exclusion. In organizing music festivals and attacking municipal corruption, businessmen elaborated distinctions of social worth between high and low culture, selfless citizens and partisans, men of good character and those lacking all scruples. This interweaving of class differences with other criteria for validating privilege and stigmatizing the rabble is a classic example of status closure—a strategy as useful to economic classes as to other social groups. On one side, labor unionists sometimes felt treated like "the scum of society"; on the other, manufacturers like Frederick Geier knew that economic success meant, among other things, that it was time to switch from Zion Evangelical Church to Mt. Auburn Presbyterian.[71] Whereas status closure among workers is apt to divide them along lines of skill and race, here status closure fostered class formation.

PATH-DEPENDENT IDENTITIES

Two final questions are worth raising. First, how sturdy is the claim that business citizenship was the most salient public identity of Cincinnati capitalists? Second, what order can be imposed on the tangled causal roots of that identity?

Business citizenship can be glimpsed largely in the official records of formal organizations and in the words and deeds of the men who were most prominent in Cincinnati's civic, cultural, and business circles. Were these views representative of rank-and-file proprietors? It is impossible to know for sure. But it is possible to listen to those prominent manufacturers and merchants rather than inferring their views from the political economists or the bourgeois editorial writers of the day.[72] It is clear, too, that the basic tenets of business citizenship were shared by some small proprietors like publisher Davis James as well as the large manufacturers who left records of their opinions. And membership in the Business Men's Club suggests that a significant fraction of the city's capitalists either subscribed to or were regularly exposed to the rhetoric of business citizenship.[73]

And why did Cincinnati businessmen define their identities and frame social differences in these particular ways? Purely economic explanations will not do. Nothing in their immediate experiences as dry goods merchants or brewers or bankers fostered business citizenship. A better answer is both more complex and less focused on the economic roles of these men. The selection of identities and frames can be likened to a path-dependent process in which multiple possibilities for drawing boundaries are winnowed down by causes moving in different historical meters. Particularly in the emphasis on the importance of citizenship and the perils of self-interested partisanship, the influence of venerable republican traditions is clear. But as the case of San Francisco will highlight, businessmen can draw on different aspects of republicanism and interpret them in different ways. Historical influences operating on a somewhat shorter time scale further constrained business discourse. Cincinnati's experience of relative economic decline following the Civil War heightened the perceived need for "local patriotism" and collective service to set things right. The slow diversification of investment and separation of ownership and control meant that individual capitalists were less identified with particular firms or trades, which reinforced the shift from a mechanic's identity to the more inclusive "businessman." And the weaker challenge from Cincinnati unions made it more plausible for businessmen to define social problems in terms of good and bad citizenship instead of capital and labor. On a still shorter time scale, the 1884 Court House riot keynoted particular definitions of and remedies for urban unrest. To further complicate this path-dependent account, however, we should remember that elite interpretations of this momentary event did not occur in a vacuum. Particular ways of defining the meaning and lessons of the riot reflected medium-term influences (such as the city's economic decline) and drew on the still older tool kit of republican traditions. Together, these pivotal events and older traditions helped lock in specific frames for employers to define themselves, their roles, and their differences from other groups. So did the utility of these frames. They "worked" to make sense of many of the troubles faced by employers, from riots and delinquency to political corruption. They offered a satisfying replacement for increasingly implausible claims to social worth based on mechanical background and prowess. And as chapter 5 will show, these frames provided businessmen with reassurances that challenges to their authority at work had no legitimacy.

This account has emphasized another medium-term influence on business identities, namely the organizational settings within which employers responded to worker unrest, economic decline, and political corruption. Civic associations enter into the path-dependent selection of identity frames in several ways. We have seen how they steered members toward a more expansive identity as businessmen and endowed that role with the particular status of being a "leading citizen." Cincinnati employers, of course, belonged to a wide array of organizations. Their associational résumés typically included, in addition to civic and cultural associations, a church, one or more fraternal orders, a trade group, and a political party. Civic associations, however, occupied a propitious middle ground for building class solidarity. Trade organizations like the Brewers' Exchange or the Carriage Makers' Club sought to unite competitors in order to regulate their industries. But they also undertook tasks (fixing commodity prices, collecting data from member firms, and setting labor standards, for example) that both highlighted trade identities and made it profitable in the short run for individuals to defect. At the other extreme, fraternal orders brought individuals from different classes together for fellowship and ritual rather than discussion of economic matters. Neither their constituencies nor their agendas highlighted conflicting interests among members. Still, they did not offer fertile soil for *business* identities, either.

The Commercial Club and the Business Men's Club stood in between. They had few members other than businessmen, but that group covered a wide range. And club topics like political reform, public education, transportation facilities, and music festivals were unlikely to spark defection or pit one member's interests directly against another's. The same characteristics of these organizations that favored more encompassing solidarities among businessmen also cut them off from the lower ranks of clerical workers and manual labor. The Committee of 100 in the mid-1880s had as elite a membership as the Commercial Club, but in its efforts to mobilize reform sentiment it still reached out to a wider audience through public meetings. In their lobbying efforts between 1890 and 1910, by contrast, the Chamber of Commerce, the Commercial Club, and (in most cases) the Business Men's Club did not enlist lower-status Cincinnatians as members or as allies.

If studies of comparable contemporary organizations apply as well to an earlier period,[74] the wider network and civic roles of Cincinnati's business organizations would have fostered a broader, more public-spirited vision among members. But there were other ways in which these organizations encouraged a class ideology of business citizenship. One was direct socialization. Some members may have come to club dinners primarily for the food and cigars. But they would still have to listen to speeches highlighting current public issues and emphasizing the clubs' civic responsibilities. It is likely, too, that these clubs operated like other voluntary associations, applying sanctions to get members to do their bit—to serve on working committees, to join delegations to city officials, and to take turns giving dinner talks. The custom of memorializing dead members, too, probably had its effects on the living. Those charged with writing the memorials (a shifting responsibility that, over time, involved many members) were reminded of prescribed standards for appraising the "usefulness" of a life. Perhaps, too, the exercise encouraged them to plan ahead. "Death is constantly reminding us of our frailty, and it behooves us to prepare a good record for ourselves while we live . . . [so] that our departure may be regretted."[75] Civic associations fostered business citizenship, finally, by modeling that ideology. A key feature of this ideal was the blurring of boundaries among cultural, political, and economic worth. The business clubs were organizational counterparts to this cognitive map of the social world. They were active on all three fronts, and bore the characteristics of social club, reform movement, and business association. The generalized quality of these associations—and of the corresponding business identity—carried this influence, as chapter 5 will argue, into the world of work.

4

PRACTICAL CORPORATISM
IN SAN FRANCISCO

Speaking to dinner guests at San Francisco's Commonwealth Club in early 1908, Stanford University president David Starr Jordan lent his authority to a view widely shared among his business audience. "The coolies that come from the class of the homeless laborers of Japan [and] China . . . can not for the most part be made free men and free citizens." Assimilation might eventually occur, but at great cost, because "the final result is to lower the average of the better race."[1] On the subject of *white* labor, by contrast, the Commonwealth Club appears to have been unusually progressive. It accepted the legitimacy of unions, championed arbitration to settle disputes between unions and employers, and organized conferences and publications in which representatives of organized labor and capital presented the public with their views of pressing social issues.

This combination of racist and pro-union rhetoric was common among American workers and is well documented. It is less familiar coming from businessmen. And here San Francisco stands in sharp contrast to Cincinnati. Businessmen in both cities drew clear distinctions between people of greater and lesser civic worth. In Cincinnati, however, the civic elect and damned largely correspond to the class hierarchy. San Francisco businessmen took republican traditions in a different direction, emphasizing the civic threats to good government posed by unfit races and unchecked monopolies. This racialized version of good citizenship reinforced and embellished the cross-class alliance described in chapter 2. It placed white labor and businessmen together in the virtuous middle class, between Asian hordes and rapacious corporations. In business discourse regarding unions, too, we find different criteria than in Cincinnati for inclusion in civic life. With varying degrees of enthusiasm, San Francisco businessmen agreed with the Commonwealth Club that representation of class interests was both legitimate and served the public interest—not, as Cincinnati's business leaders insisted, something fatal to good government. This different sense of labor's and capital's public identities and political entitlements reflects San Francisco businessmen's unusual experience with unions at work: since they could not defeat them, a quasi-corporatist class compromise appeared the next-best thing.

This chapter explores these contrasts to Cincinnati in greater detail. It shows how many San Francisco manufacturers and merchants, drawing from the same republican tool kit as their Cincinnati counterparts, selected different tools with which to construct social hierarchies and civic identities. These selections worked to make sense of highly charged conflicts over racial privilege and monopoly power. They also provided ideological warrant for employers' dealings with unions. However, because San Francisco's businessmen were involved in these conflicts in different ways and sometimes on opposing sides, the ideals of race-based civic rights and class-based representation did not rally them together. There was also a dissenting discourse of business citizenship which periodically challenged employers' pragmatic recognition of labor representation. At the end of chapter 6 we will see how, amid shifts in organizational setting and political opportunities, that minority opinion became the dominant voice of San Francisco business.

RACIAL BOUNDARIES AND CIVIC IDENTITIES

Leading San Francisco manufacturers and merchants, like those in Cincinnati, put republican traditions to use in constructing social hierarchies. As in Cincinnati, moreover, their invidious distinctions of economic worth and political virtue tended to coincide, placing the same sorts of people on the top and bottom of each hierarchy. The specific criteria for praise or stigma in the two cities stand in sharp contrast, however. Accordingly, San Francisco and Cincinnati businessmen drew social maps that grouped people in quite different locations. Most important, race served as the key marker for vice and virtue in both economic and political life in San Francisco.

In the main industrial battlegrounds over Chinese labor in the 1870s and 1880s—the cigar, footwear, and clothing industries—manufacturers were not of one mind on the merits of white as against Chinese employees. We saw in chapter 2 that some willingly hired Chinese laborers, driven by the usual motives: these workers came cheap, did not make "unreasonable demands," and seemed "steady and industrious."[2] Other employers, whether out of high principle or fear of union reprisals, renounced these benefits and employed white labor, sometimes going to considerable trouble to do so. One of the only efforts by manufacturers to establish vocational education for less-skilled labor before the 1890s served the sole purpose of training white cigarmakers to replace those cheap and industrious Chinese.[3] Even outside of these hotly contested trades, many manufacturers and merchants drew clear social boundaries against the Chinese as workers and as citizens.

Historians have documented how American workers of varied national backgrounds "became white" in common opposition to racialized minorities—African Americans above all others, but also Asian immigrants.[4] Prominent San Francisco businessmen constructed boundaries along similar lines. Andrea Sbarboro, president of the Manufacturers' and Producers' Association, extended the city's glad hand to all immigrants, except those from Asia. "We want the Scotchman, who is full of enterprise," he told delegates to the California Chinese Exclusion Convention in 1901. "We want the Englishman, who brings with him capital [and] industry." Sbarboro opened San Francisco's gates to "the industrious and thrifty Italian, who cultivates the fruit, olives, and vines," and even to "the Irish, who build and populate our cities (laughter)." These groups, each in accordance with its national character, all made contributions to San Francisco's economic growth and thus deserved welcome and honor. "Coolies" had no such virtues. Individually, they lacked "thrift and industry" and failed to "improve ... [their] condition." Collectively, they were "a detriment to every country they invade."[5] Cincinnati businessmen also celebrated men of good character, who bettered themselves through skill and self-discipline, as against the shiftless and intemperate. In San Francisco, however, these distinctions lined up more with racial than with class divisions.

The most common charge leveled against the Chinese, by businessmen and union leaders alike, was that they lowered labor standards in the city. "Labor standards" covered a multitude of virtues. Among them were wages and consumption levels. The "Chinaman" placed these in jeopardy because, in the well-worn stereotype, he had no family to feed and his stomach required no more than a little rice to fill. He would work at wages that could not support the basic living standards to which all *real* Americans were entitled, much less allow the accumulation of capital to start a business and move up in the world. Cable manufacturer and perennial president of the Mechanics' Institute Andrew Hallidie condemned this "vast herd of humanity, accustomed to slave in the substratum of life"[6] And opening addresses at the Mechanics' Institute's industrial fairs ritually invoked the same threat. This "constantly increasing foreign horde [is] rapidly monopolizing all departments of labor. Our young and active boys [may] be driven from their employment by a race with whom they cannot compete on any narrow ground in a struggle for existence."[7]

Standards of production as well as consumption were at risk. Manufacturers made invidious comparisons between Chinese and white labor on the grounds that the former undercut workplace dignity and craftsmanship. In this demonology, the Chinese were driving white men from employment not only through low wages but through low moral standards that made factories uninhabitable by respectable men. No less an authority than California's commissioner of labor affirmed that despised races and despicable employees went together. Some owners maintained "model establishments" with "strict rules regarding cleanliness and decorum." Here "well behaved" employees prevailed, and "the hoodlum element is, happily, absent." Less scrupulous employers hired a "mixed, nondescript class, comprising about every nation under the sun," including "Negro" and Chinese workers. "Decent . . . American boys and girls" would not work in such vile places.[8] Other commentators contrasted Chinese laborers with skilled craftsmen. A Union Iron Works partner, for example, claimed that true "artisans" such as himself would refuse to employ the Chinese despite the financial temptations. Hallidie emphasized that the threat was not merely to the income of the "high grade artisan" but to his trade.[9] Because of their "servile" character, Chinese labor even corrupted white *supervisors*. Testifying at U.S. Senate hearings in 1877, cabinetmaker John Condon agreed that white foremen standing "over the Chinese finally acquire such a habit as to prevent them from conducting decently towards white labor. . . . It has the same effect . . . upon the white overseer that slavery had upon the slave-driver."[10]

With this image of Chinese servility and its corrosive effects on authority, economic boundaries begin to shade into political ones. Cincinnati businessmen often contrasted the "best men," who were nonpartisan and civic-minded, with the rabble; in San Francisco, the corresponding boundary between good and bad citizenship divided whites, whether old immigrants or new, from the Chinese. The preoccupation with Chinese men's political as well as economic debilities also helped spread anti-Chinese discourse well beyond the trades in which they found employment. Together with most union officials, many businessmen deemed the Chinese to be threats to good government. According to historian Hubert Bancroft, the leather manufacturer William Merry was committed to "the interests of the city" and believed that "the best man, rather than ardent politicians," should lead. That mugwumpish ideal, however, takes a different turn here. Bancroft approvingly notes Merry's efforts to defend republican government by restricting Chinese immigration.[11] Another Bancroft interviewee, real estate agent Wendell Easton, warned in 1891 against the Chinese "scourge" on the grounds that these foreigners might, through sheer numbers, gain political influence. For Easton, as for David Roediger's white workers, conjuring the common enemy of the Chinese led to an accommodation with some of the less desirable white immigrants. "We have many disagreeable traits to contend with in the Irishman," a real estate agent complained in 1891, "but I would sooner have him with all his bad points than over run this city with Chinese. . . . We have got to look at this from a national and not a selfish point of view."[12] Ten years later, Andrea Sbarboro reaffirmed the link between whiteness and patriotic virtue. The European immigrant, he asserted, not only improves himself economically; he "becomes a worthy citizen. . . . When the country calls, [he is] always ready and willing to defend the flag" or, showing more imperial ambition, "to follow the 'stars and stripes' throughout the world. Can you recall any battle in which the Chinese have raised their hands in defense of 'Old Glory?'"[13]

These racialized boundaries between good and bad citizens put many businessmen and wage earners on the same side. White businessmen, especially small proprietors, participated in the anti-coolie neighborhood associations that proliferated between 1873 and 1876; they lent support to the virulently anti-Chinese Workingman's Party in the late 1870s; and they joined the city's League of Deliverance in the early 1880s.[14] The California Chinese Exclusion Convention held in San Francisco in 1901 gave formal representation to both classes, and this only a few months after some of the city's most bitter industrial disputes. Joining politicians and officials of the city's major unions were delegates from the Merchants' Association, the Board of Trade, the Civic Federation, the Manufacturers' and Producers' Association, and the Municipal Federation of Improvement Clubs. All were organizations dominated by firms with modest assets and local roots.[15]

Political boundary work thus reinforced distinctions of economic worth in allying small employers with, rather than against, white labor. And these divisions between people of greater or lesser civic merit were no mere reflection of economic interests. They extended beyond the industries where white labor faced off against Chinese, they involved businessmen who stood to gain from racial competition in the labor market, and they persisted after Chinese entrepreneurs and wage earners had been marginalized. The independent momentum of attacks on Chinese civic virtue reflects, in part, the push of electoral politics. Alexander Saxton shows how the Democratic Party hoped to win back voters from the Republicans after the Civil War by demonizing the Chinese. Ten years later, Denis Kearney and the Workingman's Party used the same tactic to increase their electoral base beyond the unemployed and less-skilled men most directly affected by Chinese competition.[16] The spread of anti-Chinese rhetoric is no more reducible to political opportunism than to economic interests, however. Political opportunists could also draw on long-standing republican discourse to broaden the appeal of racialized political and economic hierarchies. In putting that discourse to work, they merged these two hierarchies. Mayor James Phelan illustrates this point in assessing the multiple threats posed by the Chinese. Addressing the 1901 Exclusion Convention, the retired banker told delegates that "I regard it as a labor question; I regard it as a race question; I regard it as a national question." Lest anyone still belittle the matter, he deemed it "above and over all, a question involving the preservation of our civilization."[17] Here, Phelan is true to republican understandings of the prerequisites for political virtue. It was in part their putative lack of economic independence and manly skill that incapacitated the Chinese as citizens. Irving Scott, president of the Union Iron Works and, in 1878, of the Mechanics' Institute as well, laid out the basic contrast. He praised skilled, cooperative, and disciplined workers on the grounds that they took those assets "with them into the council chambers and prove[d] that the strength of the republic rests on the producers." The Chinese, in his view, lacked those virtues as producers, and for that reason they could not contribute to good government.[18] In his 1908 address to the Commonwealth Club, David Jordan made the same link between self-reliance and citizenship. "We know that a very large part of the foreign element here is not interested in our form of government, nor interested in the individual taking care of himself."[19] The importance of economic independence for political virtue placed a special obligation on manufacturers. Hallidie reminded Mechanics' Institute members that by employing and improving skilled labor, they would also purify government. "The aim of the patriotic manufacturer, one who has the welfare and elevation of the individual as much at heart as the progress and integrity of the nation . . . is not so much to employ human beings for the sake of the number employed as to employ those who, in their individual capacity, tend to the greater happiness of society."[20] This republican connection between productive skill and good citizenship can also be traced in the other direction. What made the Chinese reprehensible as economic competitors was, in part, their failure to conform to American standards of patriarchy (the men did not support families) and political independence (they were servile and under the "despotic sway" of secretive Chinese fraternal orders).[21] In these varied ways, San Francisco businessmen joined their Cincinnati colleagues in using republican ideals to construct overlapping hierarchies of economic and political worth. Those moral hierarchies divided San Franciscans along racial more than class lines, however.

Republicanism also gave San Francisco businessmen rhetorical ammunition when they turned from the Chinese enemy to another threat to the city's fortunes: "monopoly power." As chapter 2 explained, for those dependent on the railroad to ship goods into the city or to reach national markets, the Southern Pacific's high shipping rates seemed to be strangling the local economy. Because

FIGURE 2. Devilish monopolies and deceitful Chinese combine to cheat White Labor of its cards, each marked by a local trade (cigar making, clothing manufacture, box making, and so on). Virtuous anti-Chinese leagues come to the rescue. *San Francisco Illustrated Wasp* (AP2 N469) May 12, 1882, issue, pp. 296–97. Department of Special Collections, Charles E. Young Research Library, UCLA.

the Southern Pacific made extensive use of Chinese labor, it was also regarded as partly responsible for the city's "coolie hordes." As with the Chinese "problem," antimonopoly discourse spread beyond those directly affected by Southern Pacific rates and employment practices. Most important, the company came to epitomize the corrosive effects of corporate power on good government. The Southern Pacific blocked efforts by business and union leaders to curb immigration and lower shipping rates, and this appeared to be a clear case of an unaccountable monopoly thwarting the democratic voice of the people. The company also earned a reputation for achieving its political ends through backdoor influence and bribery, making it the main exhibit in indictments of government corruption and inefficiency.

These criticisms came together in the long campaign for a new city charter in the late 1890s. Advocates of charter reform sounded much like Cincinnati's "best men." The city's government, according to critics like James Phelan, was one of "extravagance and corruption,"[22] in which officials wasted taxpayers' money and betrayed voters' trust. Most of the proposed solutions, similarly, were standard mugwump fare. Various drafts of a new charter called for civil service rules, at-large elections, a stronger mayor, and curbs on patronage by supervisors. The result, reformers predicted, would be to end graft and put city government on a sound business basis. "A civil service system will be established entitling men to office not for their services to a boss, but for their efficiency."[23] But much more than in Cincinnati, businessmen here frequently used this discourse of civic virtue against some of their own. They attributed San Francisco's ills not only to chaotic government and sinister bosses but to "unjust discrimination in favor of the corporations."[24] The local water company (Spring Valley Water), they claimed, would pay off supervisors to get favorable rates. Monopolists thwarted efforts to rein in corporate power, as when the street railway company "goes to some miserable political boss and he manacles the hands of seven men of [the] board whenever an attempt is made to control the street railroads of this city."[25] And inevitably, the Southern Pacific loomed over them all. "You cannot get into or out of this city unless you pay them tribute. They own all our street railways, except a few, [and] they do not wait until their franchises expire. They go to the Supervisors and have them extended ten years."[26] In the campaign for charter reform, accordingly, advocates held up "corporations" as the main enemies of progress, defying the people's will in order to preserve their economic interests and political clout. These, rather than generic partisanship, were the corrupting forces behind opposition to the charter, and although corrupt politicians came in for plenty of criticism, "the men chosen by the . . . machine will represent the worst of corporate interests."[27] "The people" triumphed in 1898, approving the new charter in November elections, but ongoing conflicts over municipal policy and government corruption kept the rhetoric of honest merchants versus corporate grafters alive. The *San Francisco Examiner* cheered members of the Merchants' Exchange in 1911 for their efforts to lower shipping rates. "The far-sighted business men [realize] that California is in a life and death struggle with the Southern Pacific octopus."[28]

Prominent businessmen like Andrew Hallidie and James Phelan saw the problems of corporate power and Chinese immigration as closely linked. On one side, the Southern Pacific stoutly opposed Chinese exclusion; on the other, the presence of what Phelan called a "bondsman" class, unable to stand up for democratic principles, fueled the growth of unaccountable monopolies.[29] And the dual threats posed by Chinese hordes below and monopoly power above encouraged smaller merchants and manufacturers to think of themselves as part of a virtuous and expansive middle class. Hallidie placed himself in "the great middle," and he identified that broad stratum with the interests of the community as a whole. As against either corporate tyrants or coolie labor, he celebrated skilled white labor and small proprietors as the sources of economic growth, public morality, and good government.[30] Fellow Mechanics' Institute member Frank Pixley agreed. Addressing the opening of the 1884 Industrial Exhibition, Pixley flattered his audience as "you gentlemen of the skilled trades" who "compose the great middle class of society upon whom devolves most of the duties and most of the responsibilities of upholding the Government and maintaining the law. . . . You must shield the community from the crimes and follies of aggressive, insolent wealth, from the actions and greed of corporate power and all the evils necessarily incident to wealth and power. You, too, must guard it from the agitations of the criminal and idle class that rages below."[31] This conception of an exemplary middle class echoes earlier ideals of a producer republic. And this updated republican ideal reinforced the city's distinctive class coalition. By pitting whiteness, civic virtue, and economic worth against the Chinese and the large corporations, the celebration of San Francisco's great middle class conjoined skilled labor and proprietors. Mechanics' Institute president P. B. Cornwall's description of the Institute's membership in 1881 may have been neither accurate nor coherent, but it shows how the category of a virtuous middle lumps the two classes together. Members, he claimed, were "of the scholarly, professional, mercantile, mechanical and laboring classes . . . the great reading, thinking, working middle class."[32]

CLASSES AS CIVIL ACTORS

Even as Cornwall assembled professionals, merchants, manufacturers, and wage earners into a middle class, he continued to use the plural in itemizing the constituents: these were members of different "classes." Businessmen like Cornwall could hardly pretend that San Francisco had no classes. Even had he conveniently forgotten that his middle class included, among others, a distinct laboring class, San Francisco's workers, widely organized into powerful unions, would have regularly refreshed his memory. Professionals, merchants, and manufacturers, similarly, had their own organizations for their own purposes. Still, organization on the basis of common economic positions tells us nothing of how businessmen defined their public identities. Nor does it reveal whether their definitions of legitimate civic actors allowed room for other classes. In Cincinnati, manufacturers and merchants found common ideological ground as business citizens, standing above class and claiming special responsibilities as civic leaders. That identity both muted economic conflicts among capitalists and denied unions any legitimate public role as class representatives.

San Francisco businessmen less often assigned themselves *any* public role, and those that did defined that role in different ways. Certainly, there were business citizens in San Francisco, and their numbers grew after 1911. A quite different civic ideology was more common and more influential, however. As in Cincinnati, it had roots in the local history of business organization; in contrast to Cincinnati, that organization focused more on coping with labor than on reversing industrial decline or reforming municipal government. I summarize this alternative civic ideology as *practical corporatism* because, unlike business citizenship, it legitimized class representation at work and in politics. Practical corporatism, together with anti-Chinese and antimonopoly discourses, also reinforced cross-class ties and divided capital between allies and enemies of organized labor.

One of the implicit principles of practical corporatism is that good citizens include collective actors as well as virtuous individuals. In Cincinnati, of course, public decision making routinely involved organizations like the Business Men's Club along with individual "leading men" whose prominence and probity entitled them to be heard. But these business organizations claimed to speak for the community, not for the collective interests of functional groups. In San Francisco, by contrast, it seems to have been taken for granted in the early twentieth century that individuals in different social categories (finance, shipping, manufacturing; professions; neighborhoods; ethnic groups) had distinct interests and deserved a corporate voice. This characterization of local political culture resembles Philip Ethington's. He finds that by the 1890s, San Francisco had made the transition from "republican liberalism" to "pluralist liberalism." In the latter, public actors are groups and the old republican ideal of a unitary public interest has given way to a frank acknowledgement of group conflict. This shift toward groups as the basic units of liberal politics is also a major theme in the rise of Progressivism.[33] One way in which my account and Ethington's differ is in our explanations for this shift. Ethington interprets the development of group identities based on class, ethnicity, and gender as an outcome of political discourse, as parties struggled to mobilize electoral support. My view is the reverse of this causal sequence. From the 1870s on, the brute facts of class and racial conflict crowded out more individualistic notions of citizenship.

A second assumption of San Francisco's practical corporatism sets it apart from both Ethington's and the standard Progressive version of pluralism: local civic ideology had a clear class-based agenda. Most Progressives (along with Cincinnati's business citizens) expressed strong reservations about class as a basis for public action. In this view, "class feeling" was artificial, conducive to irreconcilable social conflict, and incompatible with the public interest. San Francisco's practical corporatism, by contrast, took classes for granted as legitimate collective citizens and as a natural (if at times disruptive) basis for social conflict. This acknowledgement of class actors and action applied both to work and to politics. At work, employers neither liked unions nor regarded them as having some fundamental right to exist. Nevertheless, most employers viewed them as natural expressions of worker interests and as organizations with whom they had to do business. In politics, similarly, it was taken for granted that working-class interests deserved representation. That might take the form of parties or caucuses in electoral politics, or it might take the form of union representation on public boards and committees.

A third assumption followed: given that unions had to be admitted as public actors, the public interest could not be defined as a classless general interest—much less as the "above-class" interests of the business community. Instead, a typical view was that of members of the Commonwealth Club, that on a range of civic issues there would be "three parties to the problem: The Unions, the Employers, and the Public."[34] What served the public interest, in turn, was *balanced* class organization and *peaceful* negotiation of the class conflicts that would inevitably arise. Both at work and in politics, businessmen often expressed the view that they lagged behind workers in organizing to defend their interests. Rather than catching up and then using their new concerted strength to break labor organizations, businessmen were content to see their own associations as a counterweight to labor's. The greater good, whether in a particular industry or in politics, would be served by this parity in organizational resources. Even the anti-union Employers' Association conceded as much in 1901. "We believe that the organization and the federation of labor should be followed by the organization and federation of employers of labor, to the end that neither party may be tempted to overstep the bounds of right, reason, and justice."[35] The wider industrial or political community would also be well served if both sides settled conflicts through consultation rather than open warfare. Some San Francisco employers certainly took a hard line and engaged in bitter disputes with unions, challenging their very right to exist. But others denounced this fight-to-the-finish mentality on *either* side. Particularly from the late 1890s through 1911, these moderates recognized that capital and labor would inevitably clash. Responsible public action meant working out conflicts peacefully rather than letting them disrupt city life and business. Claiming to represent "a large proportion of the conservative and intelligent business interests of San Francisco," members of the Wholesale and Retail Merchants cheered Mayor Schmitz for his work in mediating disputes between unions and employers. The city's industrial prosperity required that he continue to foster "peaceful and friendly relations . . . between capital and labor."[36]

THE ROOTS OF PRACTICAL CORPORATISM

The assumptions underlying practical corporatism, so unlike those seen in Cincinnati, reflect a different trajectory of class relations and business organization in San Francisco. As chapter 2 made clear, the timing of economic development and labor mobilization in San Francisco led businessmen to focus their attention and associational efforts more on unions than on municipal betterment. Manufacturers, in particular, fell far short of their Cincinnati counterparts in their civic engagement. They formed organizations whose membership and agenda highlighted manufacturers' economic, not civic, roles. Topping that agenda was dealing in more or less "peaceful" ways with well-developed unions. San Francisco merchants had less direct dealings with trade unions, and they dominated organizations (particularly the Merchants' Association) that *did* privilege issues of municipal improvement. But here too, union power taught them that good citizenship and class representation went together. When the Merchants' Association tried to stand "above class," labor used its political clout to pull them back down.

These roots of political corporatism are suggested by its waxing and waning over time. The legitimacy of class representation and the belief that mutual organization and negotiation by class actors serves the public good were most often voiced and most commonly practiced during the period of San Francisco labor's greatest power, from the late 1890s through 1910. As organizational conditions and the political balance of power shifted after 1911, so did business discourse. The roots of practical corporatism are also suggested by more direct evidence of business responses to particular demonstrations of labor power. The most important examples come from industrial relations, where we can see employers coming to embrace practical corporatism. Another example takes us back to the campaign for charter reform. In that political campaign, labor taught merchants that civic improvement could be accomplished only through the efforts of *both* classes' organizational representatives.

Learning Practical Corporatism at Work

San Francisco's reputation as a closed shop city rests on the period from 1901 until World War I, but union power and employer accommodation appeared earlier. Despite temporary reversals, the general trend from the rise of manufacturing in the 1870s was toward union recognition. In a surprisingly large number of industries, employers went beyond this. In construction, brewing, metal working, boots and shoes, and the waterfront trades, they came to accept *industry-wide* collective bargaining as the normal method of managing labor relations. Where employers elsewhere might sign union agreements covering their own workers, it became common practice in San Francisco for organized employers and unions to negotiate terms governing all members of the industry. At a minimum, these terms included wage scales and hours of labor. They often added grievance procedures, so that disputes arising during the life of the contract could be handled without a strike. Typically, the procedures called for unions and employer-association officials to intervene if a disagreement could not be resolved on the spot.

On the employers' side, a pragmatic orientation to industrial relations went along with these practices. Unions, in this view, had their advantages and disadvantages. They could be dictatorial. They could make unreasonable demands, such as calling for wage increases out of line with economic realities or insisting on the closed shop. But they also simplified the task of dealing with labor and could help bring stability to the trade. Members of the Shipowners' Association recommended industry-wide collective bargaining on the grounds that "questions affecting one in his relations with his employees may be settled uniformly," and unions could assist owners in "regulating prices." This pragmatic approach also conceded workers' right to act collectively, but sought balance by having employers do the same. In this, the shipowners noted, "employers have been educated by employees." Finally, most employers with opinions on record considered collective bargaining and grievance procedures sensible means for dealing with the conflicts that inevitably arose at work. At the very least, they were preferable to out-and-out industrial warfare, and gave employers like the shipowners some peace for "a reasonable length of time."[37] The building and the metal trades provide fuller illustrations of these trends and attitudes. The first were well-organized trades in many large cities. The second were among the most belligerent of open shop industries.

Building. San Francisco's construction industry presents in extreme form some essential characteristics of the city's class relations. Employers faced unusually powerful labor organization. Individual building trades unions were generally among the strongest in the late-nineteenth-century United States, thanks to workers' skills, the insulation of construction from national competition, and the acute vulnerability of the industry to work stoppages. Particularly after 1896, San Francisco construction workers took union power several steps further. That was the year in which they organized the Building Trades Council (BTC), a federation of trade unions in the industry. The BTC soon achieved a commanding position vis-à-vis employers and its own constituents. It did so in part through the card system, whereby members could be pulled off a job if business agents discovered anyone at work without a union card. Through persuasive threats to call out other tradesmen in support of any one union, the BTC further increased its leverage with employers. And by judicious pressure on individual contractors to reject "unfair" materials, such as mill work produced in non-union planing mills, the BTC extended the scope of union power and the closed shop throughout the industry.[38]

And what of employers? As in other industries, they were several steps behind labor. Although associations of contractors in specific branches had existed for some time—Master Painters, Bricklayers, Millmen, and the like—only in 1902 did employers organize on an industry-wide basis, in the Affiliated Building Contractors (ABC). Like comparable groups in other industries, the ABC was short lived. The next attempt at joint organization came in 1910 with the Building Trades Employers' Association, a more durable effort. Even within specialized employers' associations, moreover, proprietors often failed to keep a united front. In 1896, for example, demands by painters for a wage increase and recognition of the card system produced mixed reactions among the Master Painters. Some argued for conceding all demands. At the opposite extreme, a few objected to any concessions at all. Charles Bruschke, for example, protested that the union was trying to run his business, and that "they expect me to change the course of my career to satisfy their whims." But the prevailing position within the association was more typical of San Francisco. It called for continuing negotiations with the union, concessions on wages, and a strong stand, later compromised, against the card system.[39]

In justifying this approach to unions, building contractors combined a live-and-let-live attitude with an appreciation of the benefits that came from dealing with the BTC. They had no illusions that strikes could be avoided, and they accepted that in any given strike one side would prevail. In one of the most serious conflicts, a 1900 dispute over the eight-hour day at local planing mills, one mill owner emphasized that "we do not deny them the right to take the stand that they have taken. We also have our rights, and that is why we have taken our stand. If they beat us, then we will have to stand it. If we beat them, then, I suppose, they will have to stand it."[40] This pragmatic recognition of union rights, despite the inconveniences, came more easily because contractors also understood the advantages of a powerful BTC. Owing to its authority over constituent unions and the generally responsible (often dubbed, approvingly, "conservative") leadership of P. H. McCarthy, contractors could count on the BTC to rein in fractious locals. When millmen went out for a wage increase in 1906 without first submitting the demand to arbitration, as required by local procedures, the Affiliated Building Contractors could and did call on the BTC to order them back to work. Contractors also appreciated that the BTC's control gave them fixed wages for known periods of time, and thus the confidence to calculate bids and plan ahead.[41] Moreover, much as it policed its own members, the BTC could help contractors keep one another in line. The fact that contractors viewed this service with favor, rather than merely resigning themselves to it, is indicated by one of the ABC's own initiatives. In order to maintain internal discipline and monopolize business, ABC leaders in 1903 adopted a policy that member contractors should do business only with other members, on penalty of having their building supplies cut off. They approached the BTC with a request that it help the ABC enforce the new policy.[42]

Metal trades. The metal trades offer a tougher test of San Francisco's practical corporatism. Following the breakdown of a short-lived national agreement in 1901, employers across the country organized the National Metal Trades Association and rejected all further dealings with unions. Indeed, the industry became one of the leading centers of the open shop drive that got underway after 1901.[43] The trend in San Francisco, however, was just the opposite.

San Francisco's metal trades typified the city's industrial structure. As of 1900, the 179 firms in the trade averaged only twenty-six employees. Typical, too, was the workforce, skilled men of largely old immigrant stock. Thirty-one percent had Irish backgrounds, 15 percent German, and 13.5 percent English or Welsh.[44] The industry also illustrated patterns of mobilization found elsewhere in San Francisco. Craftsmen not only organized first; they were also precocious in their habits of solidarity, forming a metal trades federation in 1885. The Iron Trades Council (ITC), as it became known, combined union locals of molders, machinists, boilermakers, and other skilled tradesmen, together with less-skilled workers in iron molding.[45] Employers, characteristically, came in second. In response to the ITC, they launched the Engineering and Foundry Association in 1886; it soon foundered. The California Metal Trades Association (CMTA) followed in 1907, and it endured.

It was particularly after 1901 that labor relations in the metal trades diverged from national norms. Most union locals elsewhere went down to defeat in 1901 as employers rallied to the open shop. In San Francisco, by contrast, employers were more divided in 1901. Smaller firms and at least one large one (Fulton Iron Works) conceded union demands for the nine-hour day. Other large enterprises, led by the Union Iron Works, refused to budge.[46] Further concessions came in 1903. Although few firms would sign a formal agreement, most granted union demands for the nine-hour day and a wage hike. The breakthrough came in 1907, when employers formed the CMTA and began to bargain collectively with the ITC. The outcome was a three-year trade agreement covering the entire industry, providing for the eight-hour day and regular grievance procedures. When efforts to renew that agreement threatened to break down in 1910, employers went a step further, agreeing to outside arbitration by a committee of prominent local citizens—a procedure both sides agreed to incorporate into the new contract.[47]

The disputes in 1903, 1907, and 1910 were hard fought, involving work stoppages, lockouts, and ill-feeling. Particularly from 1907 on, however, the CMTA seems to have accepted the ITC as its counterpart ("partner" would be putting it too strongly) for managing industrial affairs. Despite the opportunity offered by the sharp depression of 1907–8, the CMTA made no moves to reverse union gains. It also extended its cooperation with the ITC into new arenas, such as joint lobbying for naval contracts and to promote home industry.[48] This somewhat guarded cooperation reflected the familiar San Francisco view that organization on both sides of industry provided a salutary balance. In President J. M. Robinson's characterization of CMTA goals, "the association is working not to break down the strength of the labor forces, for that is impossible, but to develop within itself a power and influence equally as effective." His successor, Sam Eva, added that this balance of power enabled employers to standardize wages and hours. The agreement with the ITC would also "tend to make the unions more responsible."[49]

These views were anathema to open shoppers in the industry. It is further testimony to San Francisco employers' different approach that even Robinson's and Eva's views struck some CMTA members as too harsh. In 1914, foundrymen split off to form their own association on the grounds that the CMTA was not conciliatory enough.[50] The contrast to Cincinnati is especially striking. That city's Metal Trades Association was a remarkably civic-minded body. Its leaders were active members of the Commercial and Business Men's clubs, and its members showed unusual commitment to the cooperative development of new technology and industrial education programs. They were also adamantly opposed to unions in the industry. Their San Francisco counterparts displayed much less civic virtue, keeping a tight focus on industrial relations to the exclusion of most other issues. Yet out of a pragmatic appreciation of their own interests and of the balance of power locally, they embraced a corporatist approach to the rights and role of labor unions.

There was certainly dissent from these attitudes and practices. Even during unions' peak strength in the city, some employers sought to deny workers the basic right of organized representation. Chapter 2 provided one example, the 1901 campaign of the Employers' Association to strong-arm small employers into repudiating collective bargaining. That campaign failed. Still, it illustrates the division among local businessmen between pragmatists and those who, whether because of national pressures or ideological commitments, opposed unionism. The same division reappeared in 1904 with the formation of San Francisco's Citizens' Alliance. The new organization clearly had national rather than local origins. It was built up by a traveling organizer for the Citizens' Industrial Alliance, and the firms that gave the local body its strongest support, moral and financial, were subdivisions of such national corporations as the American Can Company and the American Steel and Wire Company.[51] And the Citizens' Alliance was anything but pragmatic. Its rhetoric makes Employers' Association members look like level-headed moderates. It made no fine distinction between responsible unionism and union excesses. According to Citizens' Alliance pamphlets, unions were largely responsible for declining investment in San Francisco, and their strikes and boycotts posed a public menace. The Citizens' Alliance would come to the rescue, protecting its members' "inalienable rights to manage their business in such lawful manner as they deem proper, without domination or coercion by any organized movement."[52] But as we saw in chapter 2, the successes of the Citizens' Alliance were few and short-lived.

The inability of the Citizens' Alliance to attract support for its open shop drive is partly a reflection of politics. Key members of the Alliance also played leading roles in the campaign to defeat the Union Labor Party in 1905 by naming a fusion ticket of Democrats and Republicans. Union Labor Party strategists made the most of the connection and won a sweeping electoral victory.[53] Even without the political fallout, however, many business groups simply found the anti-unionism of the Citizens' Alliance to be unreasonable and impractical. After initially lending its support, in 1907 the Chamber of Commerce opted not to be represented on the advisory board of the Alliance. The Merchants' Association took the same position.[54] Individual firms, similarly, preferred to make their peace with unions, and they kept their distance. In 1906, for example, the San Francisco-based Seattle Brewing Co. and the Citizens' Alliance won an injunction against the San Francisco Labor Council and the Brewery Workers for their boycott of the firm's beer. But the company soon reached an agreement with the union, and the Alliance was forced to withdraw its suit.[55]

The center of gravity among San Francisco businessmen was confirmed in 1907, in response to that year's streetcar strike. The dispute was unusual both for its violence, as unionists battled scabs, and for the unyielding refusal to deal with unions on the part of United Railroads president Patrick Calhoun. Calhoun and violent workers alike were criticized as extremists, as unrepresentative of most employers and unions, and as illustrating a pigheaded and counterproductive approach to industrial conflict. Even before the strike broke out, the Real Estate Board pleaded for conciliatory measures and proposed that a committee of citizens hold a peace conference between the two sides. In May, the Labor Council joined two business-dominated civic groups, the Mission Promotion Association and the Civic League, to establish just such a conciliation committee to resolve the strike. Meetings to organize the committee included representatives from the Chamber of Commerce and Merchants' Association as well. In July, finally, civic leaders such as the liberal businessman Harris Weinstock held an "Industrial Peace Conference" to discuss more enlightened methods of handling disputes. The conference included delegates from all the leading business federations (including the Chamber of Commerce, the Merchants' Association, and the

Merchants' Exchange), several employers' associations, and a few unions. Delegates took turns denouncing the "two sets of anarchists" at the top and bottom of the social scale, and praising the "great body of the better element" among capital and labor. For this better element, the proper approach was not Calhoun's. Instead, as the Draymen's George Renner put it, "we should make an honest effort to adjust our differences and this should be done by practical men."[56]

Learning Practical Corporatism in Politics

Most San Francisco employers proved to be practical men. But what of those who had less direct dealings with organized labor, either as employees or direct consumers? For commercial capitalists active in civic affairs, practical corporatism worked for other reasons. These were the men who dominated the city's leading organization of reform-minded businessmen, the Merchants' Association. This body resembled the Commercial and the Business Men's clubs of Cincinnati in its commitment to political reform and civic betterment. In those projects, however, the Merchants' Association had to deal with a labor movement well organized for political as well as industrial self-defense. Union vigilance ensured that the Merchants' Association, in order to advance its agenda, had to abandon the rhetoric of above-class reform and concede regular political representation to unions, as class actors. Charter reform once again provides the best example.[57] It is important for three reasons in addition to its impact on local political institutions. Charter reform was the main focus of reformist businessmen in the 1890s; the campaign for reform unfolded near the beginning of the period in which San Francisco labor exercised its greatest influence; and the reform efforts afford a glimpse of civic leaders abandoning business citizenship for practical corporatism.

By the mid-1890s, reform-minded businessmen like James Phelan and his fellow Merchants' Association members were raising criticisms of municipal government, and these differed little from those voiced in Cincinnati. San Francisco suffered from "boss rule," ballot stuffing, wasteful spending, and lax enforcement of laws against prostitution and gambling. Such misgovernment, they warned, retarded city growth. The solutions they proposed—civil service rules, at-large elections, more powerful "expert" administrators—also resemble those put forward in Cincinnati. A new charter with these provisions went before the voters in 1896. Advocates and critics seem to have divided along class lines. On one side were reformers from the Merchants' Association and Civic Federation, most of whom could also be found in the city's Social Register. On the other side, remnants of the old political machine joined unionists in opposing the charter. They feared that current municipal employees stood to lose their jobs under new civil service rules, and they worried that the shift in administrative power from the Board of Supervisors to a stronger mayor would dilute their influence. Nor did they let reformers' rhetoric of virtuous citizens standing above class partisanship go unchallenged. According to one opponent of Phelan's, "he says that the charter is all right if we elect a good man Mayor—and he is willing to be the Mayor. I have no doubt but Phelan is a good man, but he belongs to the class that by riches seeks to govern and control the masses."[58] Civic Federation president I. J. Truman did little to reassure union critics. Speaking on behalf of civil service measures in the new charter, he emphasized that "the City Hall has many men who would be a success as bricklayers, blacksmiths, farmhands, etc., but . . . are out of place as clerks and accountants."[59]

Thanks to the votes of those bricklayers and blacksmiths, the 1896 charter went down to defeat. Working-class wards came out especially strongly against it. Newly elected Mayor Phelan and the Merchants' Association learned their lesson and set about wooing unions for another try. Phelan's first step was to set up a Committee of 100 to prepare a revised charter, and this time he included BTC president McCarthy and the Seamen's Walter Macarthur. Unions pressed for greater representation, and did so "in language charged with class consciousness."[60] They did not get the full representation they sought, but the issue had become one of how many delegates unions should have, not whether they should be recognized as a needed voice on the committee. In order to win union approval for the new charter, Phelan also asked union leaders to suggest changes in the document. They replied with a variety of amendments to benefit labor: the initiative and referendum, a minimum wage and eight-hour day on municipal work, compulsory education, a free employment bureau, and municipal ownership of public utilities. Here too, unions had to compromise. The new charter, for example, merely permitted public ownership. The key change from 1896, however, was business reformers' acknowledgement that charter provisions had to be negotiated with unions. And in the end, unions got most of what they wanted from charter proponents. In return, they endorsed the charter, which passed with cross-class electoral support in 1898.[61]

In speeches promoting the proper use of the city's new constitution, Phelan affirmed local class alignments and their corresponding standards of civic virtue. The opponents of the charter and of good government, he charged, were "the corporations." As for the improved wages and hours for municipal workers, "whatever encourages labor makes for bettered [*sic*] conditions and permanent growth." His homely example was one dear to the Merchants' Association: higher wages for street sweepers benefited both these wage earners and the community. The association also stuck with this corporatist deal.[62]

Practical corporatism was the dominant script for San Francisco business-men's civic discourse from the late nineteenth century into the second decade of the twentieth. It represented a particular adaptation of republican traditions and a particular way of drawing social boundaries, grouping white labor and small proprietors against the Chinese and monopolies. In the virtuous middle ground between those two evils, a majority of businessmen recognized class representation as inevitable, perhaps legitimate, and in either case conducive to public order. There is a path-dependent logic to this cultural script, with businessmen selecting from a broader discursive repertoire according to pre-vailing social challenges, organizational contexts, and idiosyncrasies of timing and events. Boundary work after the Civil War appropriated some parts of the republican tradition and left others in abeyance. Businessmen highlighted the importance of economic independence and skill as prerequisites for good citi-zenship and good work, and they turned those standards of worth against the Chinese and the large corporations. They had less use for the themes of civic duty or the perils of partisan politics. Their selections proved useful at a time when businessmen confronted particular patterns of racial conflict and formidable pressures from organized labor. And the selections were made in an organiza-tional setting that mobilized businessmen more for dealing with unions than for reversing economic decline, reforming municipal government, or improving cultural amenities. But practical corporatism was never uncontested. Business citizenship, too, was part of the local cultural tool kit, and it was championed by some prominent members of the Merchants' Association. That voice would become the dominant one in San Francisco by mid-1916, in a historical reversal that we will examine at the end of chapter 6.

Part III

TRANSPOSITION

Part 2 focused on businessmen's collective identities and civic ideologies. Part 3 shows how these identities and ideologies crossed institutional borders. For San Francisco, where relations between capital and labor in city politics and the workplace mirrored one another, the empirical question is whether businessmen applied a single model of class representation across a range of industrial and political issues. For Cincinnati, where businessmen nourished their self-image as leading citizens in civic clubs and municipal uplift, far from workaday class relations, the question is more pointed. Did Cincinnati's employers apply their standards for good citizenship to work? For example, did they assess the worthiness of an employee by the same standards used to measure cultural merit or civic competence? Do the criteria for good governance that they applied in attacking Boss Cox reappear in their models of good management?

With some qualifications, the answer for both Cincinnati (chapter 5) and San Francisco (chapter 6) is Yes. The qualifications would be fewer if we had a more complete record of employers' views. Cincinnati employers, alas, resemble their counterparts elsewhere in undergoing a personality change as they moved from civic associations to the workplace. As members of museum boards, charities, and business clubs, they were a voluble lot. They had well-formed opinions about who qualified as a good citizen and what his civic rights and duties were. They expressed those views often and in forms which survive in the archives. They become more reserved on the subject of work. Most of them seem to have given less thought to employee rights and management ideals than to shipping rates. The exceptions involve a few individuals and atypical moments (mainly strikes). San Francisco employers are not much better served by the documentary record. Their formal dealings with labor unions left more of a paper trail, but other records were lost in the 1906 earthquake and fire. In general, historians who have touched on employer conceptions of workplace governance around the turn of the century have relied on the writings of management professionals and the records generated by labor relations bureaucracies—grievance procedures, welfare benefits, hiring and firing guidelines, collective bargaining agreements.[1] Yet these sources miss the smaller, proprietary firms that typified turn-of-the-century Cincinnati and San Francisco.

Making a virtue of necessity, chapters 5 and 6 range beyond the factory gates in search of business ideology regarding work. Chapter 5 begins by exploring public representations of work in Cincinnati's industrial expositions. In showcasing local industry, these expositions suggest what it was about work that manufacturers thought worth celebrating and how they rethought manual workers' contributions to industrial excellence. A second section of chapter 5 examines vocational education. Businessmen's recommendations for training reveal what employee characteristics they deemed worth cultivating, what distinctions they made between more and less "useful" employees, and how these characteristics and distinctions changed over time. The chapter's third section turns to the good employee. I assemble a composite sketch of the kind of worker Cincinnati employers most valued and the benefits they thought they owed that worker (whether or not they actually fulfilled those obligations). A final section considers the negative side of employee rights—the rationale advanced by proprietors for denying their employees the right to union representation and collective bargaining. Chapter 6 uses a parallel strategy for San Francisco. To show the consistency with which businessmen there deployed the model of practical corporatism, I follow them from the "private" to the public sphere where they made use of arbitration to settle industrial disputes, cooperated with unions in the promotion of "home industry," and incorporated class representation into city planning.

The application of businessmen's collective identities and civic ideologies to work illustrates the transposition of cultural scripts, but it also sheds light on comparative and historical treatments of U.S. management. U.S. manufacturers once won wide praise for being innovative and efficient, the human engines of a dynamic and expansive economy. They are rarely described as accommodating or benevolent employers. Comparativists more often note their unusual ruthlessness in labor relations. To a greater degree than their European counterparts, U.S. employers have resisted infringements on their "management prerogatives" by either workers or government. They have also aggressively fought off union efforts to organize employees or win collective bargaining rights, if necessary tolerating or even initiating a high level of violence to get their way.[2] Why? The usual answers put emphasis either on distinctive features of U.S. culture or on generic individual capitalists acting in distinctive economic and political settings. Part 3 shifts attention to variations within the United States, to employers' collective identities, and to the ways in which those identities provided a common script for thinking about work and politics.

Cultural accounts of the "American" approach to management typically begin with what is missing—a feudal past and a hereditary aristocracy. Those absences left U.S. employers with no traditions of noblesse oblige to soften capitalist management. With no counterweight to bourgeois culture, moreover, even those without capital of their own opposed restrictions on the rights of private property. "In contrast to Europe's *haute bourgeoisie,* steeped in aristocratic values that bonded upper and lower ranks in a common social order, America's newly rich seemed all too eager to play Ebenezer Scrooge to working-class Bob Crachits."[3] The other common explanation for employer thinking about management and unions emphasizes the industrial conditions and political opportunities under which these individuals pursued their interests. Given the country's rapid economic growth, Reinhard Bendix argues, U.S. employers were especially disadvantaged by and impatient with any limits on their freedom of action. According to Richard Edwards, because U.S. firms pioneered large-scale corporate organization, they had the resources both to fend off union challenges and to develop alternative, internal mechanisms for labor management. And—to be evenhanded in my selection of targets—I once claimed that the timing of changes in production and management techniques relative to unionization gave employers little incentive to regulate workplace conflicts with the help of unions.[4] As for political opportunities, American employers have been blessed with a highly sympathetic state and relative freedom from working-class electoral threats. Being able to count on government forces as allies against labor organization, and having no need to cultivate moderate unions in order to fend off the Left, they could afford to be uncompromising.[5]

The Cincinnati and San Francisco cases raise some doubts about accounts emphasizing either national culture or the strategic choices of individual capitalists. Attributes of the nation as a whole are poorly placed to explain the differences between these American cities—one in which most employers agreed on the evils and illegitimacy of unions, the other in which a majority of employers saw them as necessary participants in political and industrial governance. Nor is there any reason to think that San Francisco businessmen's views reflected a greater sense of noblesse oblige, or a lesser attachment to property rights, than prevailed in Cincinnati. In principle, variations in the settings for strategic action are more promising causal suspects. The cities had different industrial and political histories that might have steered businessmen in different directions. Some of those differences, however, are the opposite of what scholars would predict. If the pace of industrialization or the presence of larger corporations were decisive, San Francisco's capitalists would have been the ones most defensive of managerial rights and most hostile to unions. The two cities lend more support to the argument that political threats made employers more accommodating at work. Those threats were indeed far greater in San Francisco than in Cincinnati. What mattered in San Francisco, however, was the electoral clout rather than the radicalism of organized labor. Particularly during the reign of the Union Labor Party, municipal government respected union standards and protected workers' right to strike. Without state power at their side, few employers had the gumption to attack trade unionism.

There is a more fundamental reason why cultural traditions and strategic choices are not up to the task of explaining differences between Cincinnati and San Francisco employers. We need to take at least half of the cultural turn and consider how businessmen adapted traditions and defined their interests and opportunities—and did so not just as they pondered their individual economic interests, but as they constructed collective identities. We also need to ask how these collective definitions and identities crossed institutional borders, providing a common framework for evaluating worthy citizens, good employees, and the proper governance of city and workplace. The payoffs from posing and answering these questions can best be seen in two scholarly contexts: debates over the origins of the open shop movement and discussions of historical trajectories in U.S. management ideology.

CIVIC DISCOURSE AND OPEN SHOPS

The beginning of the open shop movement is usually dated to about 1902.[6] Employers had rallied against unions before, but the years between 1900 and World War I featured a more sustained and concerted assault on unions. In this battle, moreover, local capital often received encouragement and support from national organizations, notably the Citizens' Alliance and the National Association of Manufacturers. Local firms also took a harder line. Employers had long fought unions on account of particular demands they made or tactics they used, without ruling out the possibility that *some* demands and tactics might be legitimate. By contrast, the open shop movement rejected any role for unions in workplace governance. It is employers' principled objections to unions, rather than their success in acting on those principles, that I focus on here.

Why did U.S. employers insist on the open shop? The usual answers illustrate an assumption about businessmen that has long since gone out of fashion among historians and sociologists who study labor: that their behavior reflected the rational choices of individuals responding to economic pressures and opportunities. The most common line of argument focuses on the labor process and emphasizes tensions between traditional craft production and employer interests. In order to reap the benefits of new manufacturing techniques—more automatic machinery, reorganized and subdivided work tasks, incentive payment schemes—employers had to break skilled men's customary job controls. Because craftsmen relied on trade unions to defend their workplace powers, breaking craft control meant purging trade unions.[7] Other scholars shift the explanatory focus from workplace to marketplace but retain the same logic of individual calculus. What drove employers to seek maximum control over labor costs, Rowland Berthoff argues, was economic competition and uncertainty. The quest for market control pitted them against unions. In some settings, individual employers might have an incentive to rely on unions to help stabilize output and prices. Thus soft coal producers for a time used trade agreements with the Mine Workers to check ruinous competition. These supportive market conditions, however, were rare and fragile, to the detriment of the American labor movement.[8]

A third perspective on the open shop movement focuses on business organization rather than work or markets. The large corporations that came to dominate the American economy, some argue, had both the resources and the preoccupation with public relations to take a more enlightened approach to labor relations. This might include opening diplomatic relations with "responsible" union leaders, as advocated by the National Civic Federation (NCF). But owing to the adamant opposition of smaller firms, such a class compromise had to wait until the New Deal.[9] Other scholars see the organizational character of capital shaping relations with unions in an entirely different way. They note that the NCF's members rarely practiced in their own firms what they preached in NCF forums. In addition, union shops were more common in trades (such as construction, printing, and garment making) where smaller firms rather than large enterprises prevailed. Corporate organization, in this view, reinforced antiunionism for two reasons. First, the enhanced market power of large firms gave them alternatives to enlisting unions as agents of stability. Second, the increased distance between owner and employees, combined with the greater managerial role of financiers and professionals with no roots in the trade, favored a more cold-blooded calculus in dealings with organized labor.[10] Eventually, corporations in mass production did come to accept unions as partners in stabilization, but this happened under the very different political conditions of the New Deal.

Some of these claims have much to recommend them. Workplace changes, market pressures, and organizational settings surely influenced employer choices. Where these accounts remain incomplete is in treating employers as individual actors and in assuming a straightforward connection between their economic incentives and their perceived interests. In most cases, the pursuit of the open shop was a collective enterprise on the part of middling firms, few of which could stand up to unions by themselves. Without exploring how they developed a common understanding of unions and a common commitment to stick together in fighting them, we cannot fully explain the open shop *movement*. The collective construction of interests by employers is particularly important because the resort to open shop policies reflected experiences with unions over time. For example, a common rationale for rejecting collective bargaining was that unions could not be trusted to honor their side of the agreement. Yet there was no fixed and independent measure of union "responsibility" to which employers could refer. Instead, they had to set that standard—and weigh its importance—for themselves, and they did so not only through individual experiences with unions but through discussions with one another. Studying the settings and substance of that collective discourse thus becomes crucial to understanding the origins of the open shop. One collective setting that has won attention is the trade community. The norms and expectations of trade members, Philip Scranton shows, could powerfully influence how individual employers viewed and responded to unions.[11]

The comparison of Cincinnati and San Francisco demonstrates the comparable importance of employers' common organization and collective identities *outside* their trades, in the civic arena. Part 1 showed how these civic organizations extended ties among Cincinnati businessmen and enhanced their ability to stand together against unions. Part 2 described the corresponding shift away from identification with particular trade communities to a broader discourse of business citizenship. Part 3 explores how that discourse reappears in employers' views of unions, among other workplace issues. In Cincinnati, businessmen applied to employees and unions the same basic categories of good and evil that they embraced in their civic identities. There is a similar continuity in how San Francisco businessmen measured good government in labor relations and in city politics.

Consider, first, the exceptional case of San Francisco. It is an unusual U.S. case in part because most San Francisco employers did not endorse the open shop. It will also surprise those scholars who associate tolerance of trade unions with larger corporations, such as those in the National Civic Federation. According to NCF principles, if labor leaders proved themselves "responsible"—reasonable in their demands, respectful of agreements, willing and able to keep their members in line—they could be partners in a class compromise. In San Francisco, however, it was small proprietors, not big corporations, who embraced collective bargaining and class entente. Unlike NCF members, they also lived up to those principles in their own firms. Both in politics and in labor relations, practical corporatism required—and praised—responsible class organization. This civic ideology depicted the public interest as best served when unions and employer associations corralled individuals on each side and pursued their class interests through orderly negotiation. Reaching and enforcing agreements, whether on working conditions or municipal policy, was the best way to limit threats to economic prosperity and public order.

Cincinnati's business citizenship had no conceptual place for "responsible" unions in labor relations. Like their counterparts in most other industrial centers, Cincinnati manufacturers conceded that unions were legal, with some legitimate functions as mutual aid societies. In workplace governance, however, they stood for class interests, and as in the civic arena, class interests were selfish, partisan, and divisive. As a practical matter, U.S. employers had the luxury of opposing moderate unions because they did not face a more radical threat from the Left. Cincinnati businessmen's civic script provided an additional rationale for lumping together conservative and radical labor activists. They committed the same offense of persuading workers to put class interests ahead of both individual betterment and the public good. Union busting thus became part of a larger project of civic improvement, a righteous common cause for businessmen from different trades and in different competitive positions.

Cincinnati and San Francisco in the early twentieth century thus present two starkly opposed cases. San Francisco after 1911 offers a third case. The concluding section of chapter 6 shows how two key developments in 1911 set the stage for a historical reversal. The merger of major business associations into a new Chamber of Commerce gave San Francisco businessmen the sort of broadly representative, widely engaged collective organization long enjoyed by their Cincinnati counterparts. And local unions' switch from independent labor politics to a Progressive coalition created new opportunities for the business community to popularize the ideal of good government without regard for class. A growing concern over the city's economic competitiveness reinforced these developments. Business leaders' opportunistic responses to critical events in 1916 (the waterfront strike and the Preparedness Day bombing) locked in the new path. At this point we see in San Francisco the same symmetry of political and workplace ideology that we found in Cincinnati, namely classless business citizenship combined with attacks on the legitimacy and rights of unions.

CIVIC DISCOURSE AND MANAGEMENT IDEOLOGY

Examining businessmen's affiliations with class cultures and civic associations has similar benefits for understanding "management ideology." Scholars have asked how employers justify their authority over workers and define the proper ways to govern workplaces. They have also sought to explain the remarkable variation in management ideology across cases and over time. As with the narrower question of the origins of the open shop movement, however, there have been only limited efforts to put this ideological work into the context of employers' class alliances and political identities. For the United States, most of those efforts focus on the early nineteenth century. John Kasson, for example, shows how manufacturers sought to reconcile their republican commitments with the realities of factory production; they did so by assigning themselves responsibility for the moral uplift of employees. Anthony Wallace treats Rockdale manufacturers as members of evangelical political movements as well as profit seekers, and shows how the tensions between those roles fostered paternalism in relations with employees. And both Jonathan Glickstein and Bruce Laurie see the free labor politics of some mid-century manufacturers as shaping their understanding of how to handle workers, including the need to cultivate their moral character and treat them more as colleagues than as subordinates.[12]

It is particularly after the Civil War that the different facets of businessmen's lives—their collective identities and civic roles, on one side, and their views of management on the other—seem to disconnect. This separation between civic identity and management ideology corresponds to the empirical claim examined in part 2, that Gilded Age businessmen coldly detached the treatment of employees from any considerations other than profit and loss. And this disconnection also reflects a theoretical assumption that what drives management ideology are the challenges and opportunities faced by individual employers. In leading surveys of ideological shifts since the late nineteenth century,[13] changes in the social base or collective identities of those who manage play little or no role. According to Stephen Barley and Gideon Kunda, the evolution of management rhetoric reflects the challenges posed by different phases of long economic cycles. During periods of rapid expansion, managers focused on harnessing key innovations in technology and organization. The corresponding rhetorics, such as scientific management after 1900, treated employees as factors of production to be goaded or enticed into working more efficiently. As once-new technologies faced diminishing returns, manufacturers sought to inspire production gains through better treatment of *human* capital—a strategic imperative that gave rise to such management fashions as the "human relations" approach of the 1920s and the enthusiasm for "organizational culture" in the 1980s. Other studies differ in the motives they impute to individual capitalists, but not in their assumption that these motives are the place to look for explaining managerial ideology. Harry Braverman, for example, sees capital as driven to maximize control over the workplace, the better to wring more effort from recalcitrant wage earners. Scientific management served this need by wrenching the mental labor involved in production away from craftsmen and centralizing it in the hands of management.[14] Scholarly interpretations of corporate ideology in the 1920s and 1930s, similarly, emphasize the strategic needs of firms: the rhetoric of employer "stewardship" represented an ideological defense against public criticism of corporate executives as too powerful, arrogant, and unaccountable.[15]

As in all such broad indictments of a literature, there are laudable exceptions. Reinhard Bendix's classic comparative treatment of the development of managerial ideology stresses the importance of the social positions and political needs of industrial elites as a group.[16] The rhetorical defense of employers' authority within the firm in early-nineteenth-century England, for example, was inseparable from the legitimation of an upstart social class of entrepreneurs. As the social composition of those who ruled the workplace changed, so did their collective need to justify their workplace authority and their entitlements in society. Another worthy exception is Yehouda Shenhav's analysis of the early-twentieth-century rise of "rational" management. Here the key movers are mechanical engineers, with their occupational culture celebrating "system" and standardization in the design and use of machinery. By promoting that approach as both applicable to labor relations and a solution for industrial conflict, they reshaped management thinking while elevating their own professional status.[17]

In Cincinnati and San Francisco, the key to "management ideology" before World War I was not a professional community of industrial engineers but a local class of proprietors. And each proprietor's views of work were shaped by more than the challenges and opportunities facing his firm. They also conformed to the conventions of his status group and—what was the same thing for Cincinnati's bourgeoisie—expressed a particular class consciousness.[18] In Cincinnati, moreover, businessmen's class consciousness was constructed in large part through their political roles as good citizens. These links from collective identities to workplace ideologies cannot be taken for granted. Values embraced in politics need not be endorsed (much less actually followed) at work. But the character of business associations and identities in Cincinnati made the boundaries between politics and work unusually porous, so that a single yardstick measured the worth of citizens, clubmen, and employers. Many San Francisco employers followed a different path to the same outcome. The logics governing their political and workplace discourse converged because the same class actors, in the same relations of power, loomed large in both contexts. Practical corporatism offered a single script for legitimating class representation in municipal policy-making and in labor relations.[19] No straight causal line connects political and managerial ideology. The logic of the argument instead emphasizes the alignment of scripts and selection of frames. Whether on the basis of generalized identities or institutional convergence, businessmen had at hand all-purpose recipes for interpreting their problems and rationalizing their actions. From the larger menu of frames for specific tasks, such as stigmatizing unions or evaluating employees, they adopted the ones that conformed to their master recipes.

The pattern is clearest in employer views of unions—unions that, to varying degrees, were potential problems for employers in both cities, and whose virtues and vices could be defined in any number of ways. In San Francisco, the collective organization, responsible leadership, and commitment to peaceful negotiation that marked the good union applied as well to class representation in city planning and civic improvement. In Cincinnati, the hallmarks of the good citizen also defined the terms for denigrating unions. Like political demagogues and mobs, they inflamed partisan spirits rather than demonstrating steady, reasoned judgment; like corrupt political bosses, they pandered to crass self-interest rather than rising above class. And when San Francisco employers made their turn to business citizenship after 1916, they adopted the same language for indicting unions—referring to their victory over the Building Trades Council in 1920, for example, as "more a contribution to civic patriotism than to anything else."[20] The same alignment of scripts across contexts is clear in other aspects of management ideology. Cincinnati employers doubtless found that traditional apprenticeships failed to serve their individual interests. But specific elements of the educational programs that replaced apprenticeship aligned with employers' collective identities as business citizens. They saw the new system as conferring not just technical skills but also the independence and ability to transcend self-interest that marked worthy citizens. Their definition of the good employee, similarly, covered more than just contributions to production. Good employees also displayed the moral character (steady judgment combined with a mixture of personal drive and "identity with" the firm) that businessmen saw in themselves as leading citizens. And offering these employees a "square deal," with clear rules and fair treatment, had little to do with bureaucratic alternatives to the personal touch in governing firms. Instead, these were standards of merit and nonpartisanship owed to good employees even in a small shop—standards which were also familiar from political reform movements.

It may be tempting to dismiss Cincinnati or San Francisco proprietors as representatives of "traditional" management thinking. This would be a mistake. Much as there were continuities between mugwump and Progressive reform politics, so there are between proprietors' workplace ideology and "modern" management. Cincinnati employers like Fred Geier and Lucien Wulsin were neither corporate bureaucrats nor acolytes of Frederick Taylor. But they were very much concerned with "rational" management, including matching employee training to occupational requirements, rewarding workers on the basis of merit, impartially applying fixed rules, and establishing a clear hierarchy of skills and authority. That approach to management directly paralleled their recommendations for good government in the city. And this dual commitment to businesslike efficiency made proprietors like Geier and Wulsin important carriers for the development of "systematic" management thinking. That these carriers have won far less attention than have professional engineers in accounts of management ideology may reflect our tendency to focus on the historical winners rather than the also-rans. Over time, the roots of management ideology in proprietors and their modified republicanism withered. In part, this is the familiar story of management authority moving from owners to professional managers in ever-larger corporations. But here too, we should recall the larger class context. As fewer businessmen combined the roles of local property owner, civic leader, and manager,[21] there were also fewer carriers to move scripts between politics and the workplace. While those carriers thrived, however, they played their roles in the rise of "rational" management.[22] Chapters 5 and 6 take a closer look at the fit between these men's civic roles and managerial ideologies.

5

FROM POLITICS TO WORK

Good Citizens and Model
Employers in Cincinnati

In praising Julius Dexter as an "ideal citizen" of Cincinnati, his fellow Commercial Club members found in his devotion to the public good "the very life of the Republic and the hope of its perpetuity." They added that Dexter was "a man who did not have one conscience for private matters and another for public . . . affairs."[1] Such consistency in the application of moral codes counted as a virtue among Cincinnati's leading citizens. And in their thinking about "private" matters of work, employers applied the same all-purpose cultural script they cultivated in public affairs. I support this claim in three ways in this chapter. First, I identify parallels between business citizenship and employers' workplace ideology—parallels in language, in underlying assumptions, and in categories of analysis. Because this comparative analysis of rhetoric is hardly an exact science, the overall case becomes more persuasive if *multiple* correspondences can be established. The strategy here is to trace parallels between business citizenship and one work arena after another, moving from industrial fairs to employee training, personnel policies, and union representation. Second, I present evidence that employers actually framed and responded to workplace dilemmas in accordance with principles of business citizenship. Such evidence comes closer to revealing transposition in action, as employers interpret problems and choose solutions from a wider menu along lines laid down by their class script. Third, I show that the approach employers took to various workplace matters changed over time in tandem with class formation. They redefined the goals of industrial training and the appropriate solutions for labor unrest, for example, as they shed older identities in favor of business citizenship.

THE PUBLIC FACE OF WORK: CINCINNATI'S INDUSTRIAL EXPOSITIONS

Cincinnati's industrial expositions date back to 1838, when the city's Ohio Mechanics' Institute (OMI) organized a display of local arts, crafts, and manufactures. Held annually until the Civil War, those expositions advertised locally made products, educated "mechanics," and entertained the public. Yearly expositions resumed between 1870 and 1888, with the Board of Trade and the Chamber of Commerce joining the OMI as sponsors.[2] Parades and festivals celebrating local industry continued thereafter, but less frequently and with shifting institutional backing. As the premier effort by local manufacturers to publicize the work they did, these industrial expositions offer clues about how manufacturers constructed their own social identities. They also indicate what it was about manufacturing that proprietors deemed worth celebrating. And shifts in the expos over time show businessmen's civic discourse and their views of work moving in parallel.

Manufacturing Identities

The changing character of manufacturer identities can be seen both in the producers being celebrated at the expositions and in the way their products were presented. The original expositions acted out republican ideals of work. Run solely by the OMI—whose own membership mixed manufacturers and craftsmen— these fairs celebrated the mechanic, the producer-citizen applying art and science to his trade. In anticipation of the 1847 exhibition, the *Daily Times* reminded readers that the people are the "foundation of all honor and power," but to meet this responsibility they must also be "virtuous and intelligent." The OMI and its annual expositions sought to foster those virtues. One way in which they did so was to display the "choicest specimens of the craftsman's skill." Those specimens, exposition organizers hoped, would do more than provide good advertising for local wares. They would also instruct others in craft techniques and, through competition for awards, stimulate mechanics to perfect their arts. Winners received a certificate depicting an artisan in his toga, holding a scroll in one hand and a hammer in the other, with books, scientific instruments, and manufacturing tools arrayed at his feet.[3] In none of these rituals did organizers make clear distinctions between proprietors and skilled labor.

There were still echoes of this republican ideal in the expositions of the early post–Civil War years. But the central actors were increasingly manufacturers, not mechanics, with skilled labor appearing (if at all) only as employees of participating firms.[4] By the 1870s, the OMI itself had come to be run largely by manufacturers, and it now shared sponsorship with the Board of Trade and the Chamber of Commerce. By 1895 and 1900, in discussions about reviving the expositions, the initiative had shifted further, from manufacturers organized in the OMI to the more inclusive Business Men's Club. There are other signs of change in the identity of the expositions' leading actors. Accounts of competitions among exhibitors are more often described as pitting one firm, not one craftsman, against another.[5] The parades that launched each exposition also portray a different set of identities than in the old mechanics' fairs. The typical exposition procession began with city officials and exposition commissioners, followed by floats representing local firms (often led by the proprietor). Then, in place of the independent republican artisan, came the skilled employee, marching with his employer's float or enjoying the exposition as his employer's guest. Consistent with business citizenship, however, this separation of the mechanical arts into businessmen and employees involved no class division. In 1886—not an easy year in which to deny class conflict—the local Knights of Labor assembly asked exposition commissioners to deny space to McCormick Reaper because of an ongoing dispute. The commissioners demurred, taking the high ground that ill-considered demands from *either* labor or capital would be rejected. In the draft of their reply, the commissioners asserted their nonpartisanship by claiming to represent "the interests of both Capital and Labor," but before sending the resolution, they replaced "both capital and labor" with "all citizens."[6]

As the businessman replaced the mechanic as the idol of the exposition and the benefactor of the city, so artisanship ceased to be the object on display. In its place came commodities and, increasingly, entertainments that were more or less detached from productive activities. This shift can be seen in the language used to promote the expos. The main draw in the 1850s—those "choicest specimens of the craftsman's skill"—differed little from "the best specimens of their skill and ingenuity" solicited in 1870, but the latter were described as products of "manufacturers and inventors," not of artisans. By the turn of the century, the commodities on display were the products of "industry," not skilled hands, and their purpose was not to educate but to "spread the fame of the city's manufactures."[7] The competitions for excellence in art and craftsmanship, a centerpiece of expos in the 1850s, were also much diminished by the 1880s. And the character of parade displays followed the same pattern. Floats in the 1870s, while no longer showcasing artisanship, still often included demonstrations of a firm's or industry's manufacturing methods. Mitchell and Rammelsberg Furniture, for example, joined the First Division of 1875's march. In Robert Mitchell's wake came wagons displaying product samples, followed by carriages filled with employees, then a column of "stalwart men" organized into production departments, and finally wagons with craftsmen "practically illustrating their various trades."[8] By the end of the regular expositions in 1888, such displays had all but disappeared. In their place was a franker advertising of Cincinnati products and, increasingly, popular entertainment. In assessing the prospects for a fall festival in 1900, Business Men's Club organizers envisioned something "not on [the] heavy, ponderous lines" of the old expos, but rather a demonstration of local wares combined with "side features" to attract a broader audience.[9] The industrial parade that kicked off the festival fit that bill. Some manufacturers offered amusements unrelated to their trade (such as the jewelers' Egypt display); others advertised their products (such as kegs of Lackman's beer); and some celebrated their contributions to Cincinnati in ways quite abstracted from flesh-and-blood work and workers. Where Mitchell and Rammelsberg in 1875 had paraded their employees by trade and demonstrated manufacturing practices, the lithographers' procession in 1901 included a lavish imitation of a Japanese cherry blossom carnival, with marchers bearing a banner proclaiming the industry's vital statistics: capital invested, wages paid, presses operated, employees on the payroll.[10]

The Civic Worth of Work

In tracing the shift in manufacturer identity from mechanic to businessman, we saw that the public role constructed for businessmen was a broad one, encompassing civic and cultural as well as economic leadership. This same generous view of businessmen's responsibilities was clear in Cincinnati's expositions. Exhibitions of the 1870s and 1880s did not so much abandon as transform the producer republicanism of early industrial fairs. Manufacturers and their wares were celebrated both for their civic worth and their economic value, with those two virtues merged into one.

The fusion of industrial excellence and other public goods was achieved in part through the individuals and associations primarily responsible for Cincinnati's expositions. Key backers of the expositions typically combined this role with civic involvements of different kinds. Sidney Maxwell, a prime mover behind the revival of the expos, also served as secretary of the Chamber of Commerce, participated in Republican Party reform movements, and led efforts to improve local education. Exposition committee member John Goetz joined Maxwell as a member of the Chamber of Commerce and the reform-minded Lincoln Club, in addition to serving as brewer Christian Moerlein's second vice president and son-in-law. And Melville Ingalls added work on behalf of the expos to his busy schedule as railroad president, founder of Cincinnati's Technical School, officer of the Commercial Club, and promoter of the Music Hall.[11] These personal affiliations combined with institutional ones to pull civic and industrial organization closer together. On one side, the expos relied on employers' trade associations and business clubs (such as the Pork Packers' Association, the Board of Trade, and the Commercial Club) to help organize and promote the fairs. On the other side, planning and running the expos gave employers new opportunities for organizing themselves. Preparations in 1875, for example, brought both footwear makers and leather manufacturers together "for the purpose of devising the best means of representing their interests" at the expo.[12] Arrangements in 1888, similarly, helped businessmen extend their networks well beyond the city. Representatives of the main sponsors (OMI, Chamber of Commerce, Board of Trade) created industry-based committees to plan displays, and the heads of these, in turn, tapped others to join the effort. Those same committees also sought to co-opt public officials to serve as "Honorary Commissioners."[13] Thus the business of celebrating work in Cincinnati itself fostered class formation and blurred the boundaries between public and private roles, organizations, and planning. And here again, these effects went hand in hand: dignifying commercial self-interest as public service muted economic frictions among capitalists.

The character of exposition displays further illustrates the merging of civic and industrial worth that characterized business citizenship. Late-nineteenth-century exhibitions joined their predecessors from the 1840s in advertising Cincinnati's industry. By the time of these later exhibitions, however, it is no longer possible to distinguish between promoting local manufactures and advancing the good of the city as a whole. When it proposed to hold an industrial festival in 1900, the Business Men's Club anticipated that the event would "spread the fame of the city's manufactories and widen the market for her wares" while showcasing her as "the most gracious municipal host."[14] What is striking in discussions of the expositions is not just the familiar principle that what benefits business is good for the city. Instead, the very categories used to interpret cultural and political merit fuse in these celebrations of work. The construction of a combined Music Hall and Exposition building had blurred the boundary between high culture and industrial excellence. So did praise of the new building, as when George Nichols called attention to "the scope of its influence, covering, as it does, a wide area, embracing the interests of commerce and civilization as well as those of morals and the art of music."[15] Business leaders like Melville Ingalls also frequently referred to the expositions as examples of the revival of "public spirit" in Cincinnati, sharing this honor with the Committee of 100 and the success of Procter and Gamble.[16] And in some of the exposition parades, successive floats representing stages in the development of Cincinnati made the city's history synonymous with the advance of its commerce and industry (a depiction of public history that survives in the murals which adorn the city's combined Amtrak terminal/museum center complex). This identity of manufacturing with the public sphere extended even to patriotic observances. Following the Spanish-American War, a parade to honor local soldiers gave pride of place to displays of local firms, including the Queen City Coal Company, Fleischmann's Yeast, the Krell Piano Company, and the Foreman Shoe Company. In the *Enquirer*'s headline, not appreciative citizens but "Industry in All Her Splendor Arrays Herself Before the Nation's Heros."[17]

The images of work and manufacturing offered up by Cincinnati employers, then, corresponded to changes in their own identities. The mechanic ceded place to the businessman as Cincinnati's useful citizen; craftsmanship gave way to the products of industry as the objects of public praise; and instructional displays of manufacturing techniques yielded to popular amusements as the chief entertainment. Yet a modified version of the republican link between production and citizenship persisted. In expositions as in business citizenship more broadly, art and industry carried a common measure of civic worth. They did so particularly as manufactures (and manufacturers) came to be redefined in terms of their contributions to general business prosperity, not the processes or products of their craftsmanship.

PRODUCING WORKERS

Cincinnati employers had to deal with some familiar problems of industrial education. How could they ensure that the workers they needed, with suitable skills and attitudes, would be available for hire? What *were* the most appropriate skills and attitudes? As classical republicanism gave way to business citizenship as the dominant idiom of local employers, the answers to those questions changed. Businessmen continued to emphasize the civic content and contributions of vocational training. The character of the well-trained worker, however, increasingly had more to do with loyal and motivated employees than with independent citizens. And by 1900, the civic benefits of training programs lay more in molding a suitable labor force than in building pillars of the republic. Manufacturers' changing approaches to industrial training reveal shifting class identities in another way. As in Cincinnati's expositions, the broadly educated mechanic largely disappears. In his place, separate curricular tracks turn out wage earners and managers specialized in their skills and divided between manual and mental labor.

Changing Approaches to Industrial Education

Formal industrial education in Cincinnati dates back to 1828, when manufacturers and master craftsmen founded the Ohio Mechanics' Institute to advance "the best interests of the mechanics, manufacturers, and artisans, by the more general diffusion of useful knowledge." The OMI offered regular classes, periodic popular lectures, and a library for wholesome reading. These programs aimed to equip young men for self-improvement by combining education in "Mathematical and Physical Sciences" and "Operative Mechanics" with ethical instruction in "History, Metaphysical and Moral Sciences." In this uplifting work, the OMI resembled similar institutes in other industrial cities.[18]

After the Civil War, Cincinnati joined the nation in a gradual movement toward more specialized industrial education. As a first step, Cincinnati public schools introduced manual training in the 1870s.[19] Manual training involved little more than drawing and basic shop work, and educational reformers conceived it as an aid to general education rather than as a way to teach job-specific skills. For that reason, it failed to satisfy growing demands for education geared to the needs of industry. One source of those demands was engineers, architects, and other upwardly mobile professionals seeking a more selective and clearly defined path to acquiring credentials. But manufacturers had other reasons to reform industrial education. They feared that the requirements of factory production— including specialized manual as well as lower-level managerial skills—could not be met through traditional apprenticeship. They also sought training programs that would not expose impressionable youth to union influence, an obvious risk when boys learned the trade from journeymen in the shops.[20]

Cincinnati manufacturers addressed these needs in several ways. One was by organizing new, private schools. The most important was the Technical School, founded, funded, and overseen by members of the Commercial Club. Enrolling its first students in 1882, the Technical School provided a high school education that mixed academics, shop work, and sufficiently advanced courses in mathematics and physical sciences to qualify graduates for admission to engineering colleges. By 1895 the school had 175 students. Another response came from within the OMI. The Institute moved to upgrade the "scientific" content of its educational offerings during the 1880s, organizing a new Department of Science and Arts and adding new courses in chemistry, physics, and engineering. At the same time, OMI directors began discussing a School of Trades to cater specifically to skilled manual workers.[21]

Two other important initiatives came after 1900. The University of Cincinnati launched a cooperative education program in 1906, under which students worked half time in local factories while earning engineering degrees through college classes. Their employers covered the tuition. University of Cincinnati officials and employers in the Business Men's Club and the Metal Trades Association supported the plan in part because it combined academic training with experience in the realities of manufacturing, commerce, and labor relations. That practical training, moreover, would take place in functioning shops which the university could ill afford to duplicate.[22] The second initiative came in 1909, when the public schools began offering vocational training in specific crafts. In this case backing came from a particularly wide range of business organizations, including the Manufacturers' Club, the Chamber of Commerce, the Metal Trades Association, and the Business Men's Club. The problem, they agreed, was a "lack of fundamental training" for boys, which decreased "their efficiency and consequently their earning capacity; it also retards the development of our manufacturing industries."[23] The solution: "continuation schools," for which the city provided buildings, equipment, and instructors. Manufacturers, for their part, sent apprentices who would split their days between school and shop. Participating employers continued to pay their employees' wages while they learned.

Redefining the Goals of Industrial Education

Businessmen deserve most of the credit for these changes. They directed the OMI and the Technical School, and they promoted and helped run the cooperative program and continuation schools. Their agenda for industrial education parallels class discourse in two major ways. First, their educational goals were frankly utilitarian: they wanted not more republican citizens, but workers with more specialized skills. As in other areas, however, businessmen adapted republicanism for new purposes, redefining the character of the individual citizens and the collective goods that education should produce. Second, the egalitarian commitments of republican education yielded to hierarchies of skill and mental capacity, hierarchies that mimic those of civic worth.

The well-trained worker in early OMI programs was a republican producer, a man who combined artisanal skill, economic independence, and equal citizenship. No clear line divided his occupational and his civic virtues, nor his manual labor from either "professional" training or proprietorship. The OMI, its founder promised, would endow "our ingenious artisans and mechanics" with the requisite knowledge "to extend and improve their respective arts beyond any known limits, and raise those who practice them to that rank in society to which their utility entitles them."[24] By enlightening mechanics, moreover, the OMI served the larger civic goods of equality and social order. "God has seen fit," a speaker revealed to OMI members in 1848, "to deposit the best minds where he has placed the richest jewels, under rough coatings and in caverns quite obscure." Such benighted youths "might, by the aid of science and moral truth, be converted . . . into bright ornaments, and instruments of much good, and, instead of distracting our social order, contribute largely to the peace and harmony of society."[25] Echoes of this mechanics' ideal can still be found after the Civil War. A tepid commitment to social leveling reappears in the manual training movement, which criticized the standard curriculum as impractical (who needs Greek?) and elitist, advocating instead a mix of scholastic and practical training for all. And some businessmen at this time still valued industrial education programs for uplifting the character as well as improving the technical skills of pupils. The programs might, for example, civilize "untutored savages, who use their sleeves for spittoons."[26]

Increasingly, however, industrial education was valued more for its narrow utility than its civilizing role. For the individual student, the main goal should be to develop technical skills rather than good character. Employees who had the benefit of "theoretical training" at the OMI, one proprietor opined, "are becoming more and more appreciated by manufacturers." The educated worker gets "greater return for his work," the Metal Trades Association agreed.[27] In this, Cincinnati employers fit the more general pattern found by a U.S. Commissioner of Labor survey in 1902. Most respondents deemed trade and technical school graduates better employees because they were better trained, needed less supervision, and were more productive.[28] This utilitarian turn is clear, too, from business views of the collective benefits of industrial education. Graduates of turn-of-the-century industrial education, like their counterparts in the 1830s, were still considered an important resource for the city, but now in their capacity as a pool of skilled labor rather than as citizens. After J. K. Reynolds, secretary of the manufacturers' Carriage Club, persuaded the OMI to offer classes in carriage drafting in 1892, he framed his thanks in terms of the industry's manpower needs. The program would "supply a felt want in the trades. . . . As an old carriage builder you know our difficulty in finding skilled workers."[29]

Although advocates of industrial education emphasized skill over character and labor force needs over the needs of the republic, they continued to stress the virtues of this education both for the individual employee and for the community. It is here that we can most clearly see the discourse of business citizenship at work. The key changes since the heyday of republicanism involved a narrowing in the virtues associated with the well-educated worker and a redefinition of the civic value of industrial education in terms of business needs. The benefits of vocational training, in this view, accrued both to the individual student and to the community at large. The individual student would acquire the same kinds of virtues that businessmen valued in the good citizen. For example, industrial education helped cultivate the "take charge" workers that employers applauded so enthusiastically. General programs of manual training imprinted habits of self-discipline and hard work; Director Stanwood claimed a similar "habit of industry" for Technical School graduates.[30] Trade-specific vocational training and cooperative education went further. They were geared toward the more ambitious boy, the one who had the potential to take a leading role on the shop floor and perhaps make his way into management. Reynolds commended the Ohio Mechanics' Institute for its course in carriage drafting because it not only met his basic labor needs but also supplied "educated intelligent men [ready] to . . . take charge of our factories."[31] There was more to the well-trained employee than ambition and drive, however. Good workers, like good citizens, had to be willing to make sacrifices for the general good. Herman Schneider, who developed the cooperative program at the University of Cincinnati in consultation with local businessmen, used the example of the locomotive engineer to explicitly link the two ideals. The exemplary engineer displayed "the highest quality of good citizenship; namely, an instant willingness to sacrifice himself for the lives in the train behind him. This makes for the best type of civic responsibility." Schneider and at least some of his business supporters saw cooperative education as fostering that kind of moral character. One way it did so was to weed out the narrowly self-interested student, too snobbish to get his hands dirty. Requiring a summer's hard work in the shop before beginning co-op classes, for example, achieved what the Cincinnati Metal Trade Association's secretary described as "the elimination of the mollycoddle."[32]

These self-reliant co-op students may seem like latter-day republican yeomen. But much as the valued artisan of the early industrial expositions had, by the 1880s, become an employee of the valued firm, so the worth of the well-educated workman lay in his usefulness to the company, not to the wider political community. Businessmen regularly commended trade schools, for example, because they made young men "independent." In part, independence meant having the requisite skills and credentials to earn a living. But perhaps the more important sense of independence involved workplace governance. Industrial education, in substituting for traditional apprenticeships, protected impressionable young men from union influences. With their enhanced human capital, workers would have the ability to "earn a living independent of the support of any trade organization and [would be] mentally indifferent to" those unions.[33] Herman Schneider emphasized another way in which the good character of the well-trained employee contributed to the firm. Within each shop, "the morale of an entire working force is strengthened by the introduction of a few ambitious young employees" like those turned out by the cooperative program.[34]

The wider community also benefited from industrial education, but that community was now redefined. Businessmen particularly stressed the contributions of new educational programs to the local economy—and thus to the greater glory of Cincinnati. "The future development of our industrial interests upon which the growth of our city is so largely dependent will be materially advanced" by vocational training, the Metal Trades Association emphasized in

1909.[35] The well-educated worker would also be a boon to the political community, but mainly by not rocking the boat. One enthusiastic backer of the Commercial Club's Technical School predicted that "the effect of education would be to prevent riots."[36] Metal Trades Association officers praised graduates of continuation schools first and foremost for their "intelligence and skill," but they went on to note that this allowed graduates to "earn enough to be respectable, thus improving the quality of our citizens."[37] In these approaches to industrial education, then, it seems that the OMI's older vision of a public sphere served by educated mechanics had narrowed. But Cincinnati businessmen continued to make this connection. And if the public sphere had narrowed, the private sphere had taken on a wider civic role: businessmen's discussions of education reveal their expansive sense of the public importance of local economic activity and of local economic actors.

Reconstructing Class Boundaries at Work

As Cincinnati employers recast industrial education, they also built into education the business citizen's distinctions of class and social worth. The same categories of status and rationality that ranked Cincinnatians in culture and politics appeared as well in educational reform. In contrast to the ideal of the republican mechanic or even the post–Civil War "practical man," employers frankly acknowledged a fixed division between manual and mental workers, and a need for specialized training appropriate to these stations.

Early OMI leaders' view of education as an egalitarian enterprise dovetailed with their understanding of industrial hierarchy. "Mechanic" was a remarkably capacious category. Laborers performing mere physical labor could not be dignified by the label, nor could passive investors of capital. But in between was a wide range of skill and responsibility, from specialized craftsmen through manufacturers with wide knowledge of a trade and broad responsibility for managing workers. Greater degrees of skill and responsibility justified greater rewards. "A journeyman who can work only under the direction of others, or perform only a simple and not very complicated process, while receiving better pay than a hod carrier or shoveler, gets much less than he who understands all parts of the business, and can direct others."[38] Apart from pay, there is no fundamental difference in kind between these grades of mechanic, and the expectation seems to have been that individuals would progress from lower to higher grade in the course of their careers—with the help of educational institutions like the OMI. Even in this golden age of Cincinnati republicanism, there were pronounced inequalities in the amount and character of education enjoyed by local youth.

The dividing lines were quite different in the 1830s and 1840s than they would be in the 1890s and 1900s, however. Despite some doubts as to the mental content of manual labor,[39] middle-class commentators before the Civil War contrasted "practical" training, which *combined* science, art, and skilled mechanical labor, with the classical education of the leisured gentleman, useful mainly for social display. In Cincinnati this division separated the OMI, catering to "mechanics and manufacturers," from the high school and especially the college classes of the city's gentry. And in Cincinnati, at least, this distinction was still being drawn in the 1870s. It was in the *South,* a contemptuous *Cincinnati Commercial* editorial claimed, that manual labor was stigmatized and that "to be a mechanic was to be degraded . . . filthy, greasy, a mudsill."[40]

The combination of liberal and all-purpose manual training available to most students in the 1870s and 1880s gave way to a sharper split between academic and practical education by the 1890s; these, in turn, further differentiated along specific professional and vocational lines after 1900.[41] With specialization came ranking. In part, this was because the ideal of a cultivated gentleman presumed broad training. Even if prep schools and elite colleges had not become the bastions of liberal education, the split between general and vocational education would have ranked students by their cultural capital. But in Cincinnati, specialization and ranking were more finely calibrated than this by the early twentieth century. At a National Association of Manufacturers' meeting in 1906, Cincinnati machine tool proprietor Ernst DuBrul boasted that his city was well on its way to integrating into a single system the various levels of industrial training. These he identified as all-purpose manual training, trade schools for turning out skilled workers, continuation schools to upgrade some craftsmen into foremen, technical schools to produce superintendents, and university-level technical training.[42]

These multiple tiers corresponded to a full range of occupational trajectories, from the "managers and businessmen" that DuBrul saw graduating from the University of Cincinnati to the "poorer boys" who were adequately served, in Melville Ingalls's view, by manual training programs.[43] The system differed from the republican model in several respects. In place of the earlier commitment to social leveling, industrial education now had a hierarchy of training programs, specialized by economic function and graded by social status. No longer did one pedagogical model, like the manual training programs of the 1870s, fit all students, regardless of background or prospects. Vocational training classes in Cincinnati's public schools after 1900 taught specific occupational skills to future blacksmiths, machinists, and carpenters. They also acquainted pupils with the realities of workplace authority. Staff at the public school's Manual Training Center were designated superintendents, general managers, foremen, and time keepers; practice work earned grades measured in wages; and students could be docked their "wages" for lateness or misbehavior.[44] This type of training, then, differed from the liberal arts track both in curriculum and pedagogy. It was also considered the final stage of education for most of the students enrolled.

Several more tiers, lodged between the graduates of vocational education and the captains of industry, further divided and ranked students. The introduction of continuation schools in 1909 catered to a higher grade of manual worker. Among apprentices, employers identified some as having suitable intelligence and drive to serve as gang bosses or foremen. The continuation schools gave such promising youth additional training suitable for their new responsibilities. For the machinists who accounted for most continuation school pupils, the curriculum included shop arithmetic, geometry, the physics of metalworking ("not the ordinary high-school course in physics dealing with abstract subjects, but physics with reference to the practical problems of the shop"), geography (as illustrated by the sources and shipping routes of shop materials), and instruction in such shop conventions as how to answer questions placed in the foreman's suggestion box.[45]

Others were destined for higher things. The OMI's School of Technology catered to young men with prospects as managers. Its curriculum presented students with more theory and with more instructors who were practicing professionals.[46] In making these and related changes, the OMI recognized that it had to serve two different groups, "the great majority of our young people who are destined for mechanical pursuits, and . . . our young men whose lot it will be to manage manufacturing establishments." The two types would complete different courses of study. The great majority would learn "things in science and mechanics which will be of practical and real value to him in making his living"; those fated to manage would be given the opportunity to "reach for a higher range of scientific education."[47] The University of Cincinnati's cooperative program served future managers of a technically more sophisticated kind. The program offered a full college curriculum and conferred engineering degrees on its graduates. But Schneider and his business allies wanted to guarantee that these future engineers and managers would not be impractical theorists. Having them work in shops half time ensured that they would get plenty of experience with real shops, operating under real commercial pressures. In the end, however, they would join the managerial ranks. Schneider reassured suspicious unionists from local foundries that they had nothing to fear from cooperative education: it had the higher goal of producing engineers, not molders.[48]

Advocates of the hierarchical approach to industrial education praised by DuBrul assumed that industry required very different types of workers, not workers in different stages of their careers. And these different types of workers needed different courses of study, each with a suitable balance between "practical" and "theoretical" training. What we would now call the vocational track emphasized the manual skills and practical knowledge—reading diagrams, taking measurements, judging the behavior of metals when heated, and so on—required by Cincinnati's carriage makers, blacksmiths, and machinists. At the other extreme, the appropriate curriculum for future engineers emphasized classroom over shop work, higher math over practical calculation, and general physics over pragmatic knowledge of how metal cutting tools behaved under stress. While the OMI provided the "primary courses" for beginning craftsmen, it was the University of Cincinnati that offered "the higher course for the making of engineers."[49] In between, there were varying degrees of competence and levels of responsibility, as there had been among "mechanics." But each now represented a distinct grade of worker with distinct educational needs. Perhaps a more striking contrast is that early-twentieth-century businessmen seem to have assumed that these differences were fixed: with some meritorious exceptions, some boys were destined for manual labor, some had the potential to play leading roles on the shop floor, and a few had the aptitude for professional and managerial roles in the enterprise as a whole. Each deserved the best possible education—but an education suited to their likely station. Praising the OMI's vocational training program in 1910, cotton merchant James Hooker noted "the folly of parents giving boys an academic schooling who should be fitting themselves for the practical struggle of life."[50] School superintendent Frank Dyer concurred. Alluding to the increased enrollment in manual training classes in 1911, Dyer explained than an academic education merely "diverted children from work with their hands" at a time when the professions could absorb only small numbers of graduates.[51]

Different ways of thinking about skill went together with different cultural maps of social inequality. OMI founders distinguished between producers and parasites both above and below them—the idle rich and the idle poor. Views had changed by the beginning of the twentieth century. Much as businessmen came to distinguish good citizens from the rabble on the basis of their capacity for reason and steady judgment in politics, so in education for work. Now the crucial boundary divided not the productive citizen from those who did no real work, but manual from mental laborers. Even at the relatively populist OMI, Director John Shearer in 1901 divided students into "scholars and workers."[52] And among mental workers, the invidious republican distinction between productive and unproductive labor was largely gone by the late nineteenth century. Managers and proprietors who were also "practical men," and investors with little background or involvement in the trade, both qualified as respectable businessmen. And they had far more in common with one another and with other mental workers than with craftsmen. As one of the latter complained in 1884, even the poorly paid service worker, doing no manual labor, had higher status than he did. "Socially in this town, a mechanic earning fifteen dollars a week is looked down on by many of what we call society people, while a counter-hopper, earning one half as much, is regarded as a very much better man, not because he knows any more, but because the former is a 'greasy mechanic.'"[53] Central Labor Council officials echoed the complaint in 1901 and connected it explicitly to education. Students at the Technical High School, on the track toward professional engineering or management, "usually . . . become snobs and [are] not willing to cooperate with workmen."[54] For business sponsors of education reform, that social distance could be counted a blessing.

VIRTUOUS EMPLOYEES AND THEIR RIGHTS

As they moved from expos and schools to the workplace, Cincinnati employers did not check business citizenship at the door. Instead, their civic identities are clearly reflected in their definitions of what constitutes a good workplace citizen and what obligations they have to such an employee. The familiar caveat applies with particular force here: my concern is with principles *professed* by employers. Those principles (that valued employees deserve job security, for example) might yield to other considerations (such as cutting costs during depressions), but they appear to have been sincerely held. The best evidence on proprietary employers' beliefs comes from a small but diverse group of owner-managers. Lucien Wulsin (president and part owner of Baldwin Piano), Nelson Strobridge (of Strobridge Lithographing), Frederick A. Geier (chief owner, executive, and patriarch of Cincinnati Milling), Richard LeBlond (LeBlond Machine Tool), and Joseph Hall (Hall Safe and Lock) represented several different industries. What they had in common was their involvement in civic affairs. All belonged to the Commercial Club, Geier and LeBlond were active in municipal reform movements, and Wulsin played a leading role in the city's musical life. Together with scattered information from other sources, these men's opinions suggest how employers assessed the virtues and rights of workers in accord with the master frame of business citizenship.

The Good Employee as Republican Citizen

One of the standard laments of late-nineteenth-century employers was the increasing difficulty of maintaining "the personal touch" with their employees.[55]

Even in Cincinnati, the growing scale of production impeded regular, face-to-face contact between proprietors and workers. Richard LeBlond worked at the bench alongside a handful of employees in the 1890s, and he could no doubt hustle his co-workers along. But this was no longer typical. At the same time, proprietors continued to be closely involved in day-to-day production matters, even when (as with Lucien Wulsin and Frederick A. Geier) they did not start out as crafts-men themselves. They made decisions about product designs, for example, and they helped recruit skilled employees. This combination of direct interest and inability to personally supervise and cajole workers created a real dilemma, one familiar from the management of "high-tech" employees: how can an employer get workers *voluntarily* to devote their efforts and skills to the company? "One man cannot watch it all and that is the reason he has to have the co-operation of the men," a Baldwin Piano vice president argued. His plant manager agreed. "You have to get every man to feel a personal interest in the work."[56]

The available evidence suggests that Cincinnati employers approached this problem much as they did the dilemma of republican virtue. The good employee, first of all, looks very much like the good citizen. On one side, the ideal work-man had—and *ought to* have—strong personal ambitions and drive. The secre-tary of Cincinnati's Metal Trades Association struck a common note in praising employees who needed "no urging to forge ahead."[57] Employment ads, simi-larly, often called for "take charge" individuals, and it was natural that a good mechanic would seek to "improve himself." Thwarting those ambitions would, at best, lead energetic and skillful employees to quit. At worst, it would create openings for union organizers. On the other side, individual abilities and energy had to be put in harness and exercised on behalf of the company. One hallmark of a good workman was his "faithful attention to his daily work . . . and laboring for the interests of the employer."[58] A general goal, accordingly, was the same as in the civic arena. The ideal employee should serve the business as the good citi-zen serves the community. Baldwin's treasurer commended one employee as "a first class man" because "he considers himself as . . . looking after the interests" of the firm. President Wulsin, in recruiting a skilled woodworker, used the same phrase that his fellow Commercial Club members applied to politics. Wulsin expressed his satisfaction that the man was "ready to identify yourself with us," adding that he could be expected to devote his "entire time and best talents" to the firm.[59]

A similar orientation appears in employment contracts. For their skilled craftsmen, some local firms offered individual contracts which spelled out mutual rights and obligations, working conditions, and pay. These agreements demon-strate the close interest taken by proprietors in their leading hands, with Wulsin and Strobridge personally negotiating terms of employment with woodworkers and engravers. The contracts also suggest the value employers attached to workers' "identity" with the firm, emphasizing that employees would do more than simply turn out a piece of work. Each engraver at Strobridge should "promote the interests of [the company] as far as he can," giving them "the best of his talent." Other provisions acknowledged that no *external* supervision could ensure this. Contracts at Strobridge set wages on the assumption that the engraver would have a full week's work. If not, a clause made it the employee's responsibility to tell the bookkeeper so that wages could be adjusted.[60] Proprietors who made arrangements such as these must have assumed that their best craftsmen acted like good citizens, putting self-interest aside for the general benefit of the firm.

This image of the good employee appears, finally, during strikes. Good employees, of course, *do not* strike, so the characteristics of those who stayed and those who quit were measures of a worker's worth. Almost by definition, worthy employees, by remaining on the job, demonstrated their loyalty, and late-nineteenth-century Cincinnati employers were hardly unusual in preferring loyal workers. In the praise of stalwarts and denunciation of renegades, however, two other virtues were closely associated with loyalty, virtues which were also parts of the modified republicanism of business citizens. First, loyalty and skill go hand in hand. In publicizing how little need they had to settle with strikers, Cincinnati brewers emphasized that most of the work could be done with the few "good men" still employed, directing the work of green hands. One garment trade proprietor made the point explicit during an 1896 strike by cutters. It is "not the best artisans [who] are in this agitation, but only men of mediocre ability."[61] Second, loyalty reflects the calm and reasoned judgment of the good citizen. Cincinnati stove manufacturers, hoping to lure strikers back to work during an 1884 dispute, sent a letter to every molder in the city, making an invidious comparison which paralleled the distinction between responsible citizen and partisan mob. The employers claimed to have spoken "with our most intelligent and thoughtful workers," who were willing to deal with the companies in a "just and business-like manner." Many of these good men, alas, were "compelled to lose a great portion of [their] valuable working time" on account of strikers "who are blinded by prejudice, controlled by impulse."[62] Proprietors acknowledged that employees, like ordinary voters, could be swept up in the emotions of a strike. A return to work was a return to reason. According to another clothing manufacturer during the 1896 dispute, "our men are not Anarchists, but mainly German, frugal, high principled and industrious, who will come to their senses soon enough."[63]

In some ways this framework for understanding labor relations resembles the reassuring employer doctrine of a harmony of interests between labor and capital. But as in the civic arena, the kingdom of virtue was an exclusive one. It was mainly skilled workers, and only those with the proper character, who qualified as good employees. Those who lacked enterprise, self-discipline, and reason were no more welcome workplace participants than their counterparts among the urban rabble. During the World War I boom years, LeBlond Machine Tool supervisors, in consultation with Richard LeBlond, kept records tracking employee departures. All former employees were not equal. One category included "undesirables" who engaged in strikes or were incompetent. A separate category identified the more virtuous individuals, who left in hopes of "bettering" themselves. Even the blacklist maintained by the Cincinnati Metal Trades Association implies a view of employer loyalty as a matter of personal commitment and character rather than natural harmony between labor and capital. The list included the usual "dangerous agitators or disturbers," but it also included men who had "broken faith" with their employer, some of whom were allowed to work again after making the proper apologies. Others would remain shut out "until they remove[d] the stain from their character."[64]

Cincinnati manufacturers surely gauged good employees by productivity as well as character. This is consistent with the general trend toward utilitarian criteria in evaluating an employee's worth.[65] Yet character often seems to crowd out more "modern" standards for evaluating employees in Cincinnati, even into the early twentieth century. Certainly "character" does not yet refer to a bundle of *characteristics* that can be tested for suitability, enhanced by training, and matched to appropriate tasks. Nor has the good employee yet been whittled down to the efficient task worker of scientific management, his worth measured by output and his character irrelevant (so long as he is responsive to wage incentives). Cincinnati proprietors of the 1890s and early 1900s instead seem to have thought of the good employee much as they liked to think of themselves.[66] Both were part of an elite of high character, sober judgment, and selfless devotion to the business. Certainly, in recommending candidates for employment in the industrial expositions, employers gave rather short shrift to the applicants' credentials or expertise, merely noting in some cases than they "knew their business" and were "industrious." They gave at least as much attention to their character. The priorities are suggested by one merchant's reference for a woman, declaring her to be honest and trustworthy. Added to the letter, in fine print squeezed above the signature, is the additional information that she might be suitable for a position in the Ladies Toilet Room.[67] Nor did these recommendations merely reflect busy employers with nothing more to say. Some used printed forms, prepared by exposition officials, with specific questions about job candidates. Out of ten questions, one asks if the applicant has sufficient education and ability for the position. Most assess character. Is the individual industrious? Any bad habits?

Addicted to liquor? Do they have "integrity"? Is there any reason not to employ the individual in a position of trust?

Employee Rights

What rights did these worthy citizens of industry enjoy? How did employers think they *should* encourage and reward an "identity" with the firm? Their most important obligations were to give valued employees job security, promotion opportunities, and a "square deal." Although these promises fell short of binding commitments, they illustrate assumptions about workplace citizenship that businessmen carried over from their civic endeavors.

A worthy employee, identified with the firm, seems to have been thought entitled to regular employment.[68] One clue comes from want ads. A wide variety of companies advertised openings in the local newspapers. They rarely attempted to lure potential applicants with anything beyond good pay, but when they did, the enticement was almost always job security (for example, "a permanent position" or "steady work for a good man"). Similarly, trying to interest elementary school students in apprenticeships as machinists, the Metal Trades Association promised "steady employment all seasons of the year."[69] There are other indications that these appeals reflected a widely endorsed principle. Chamber of Commerce memorials, for example, seldom mention the deceased's virtues *as an employer*. When they do, however, the commendation is for providing regular employment. On his death in 1899, Frederick Burckhardt won praise for his policy "that satisfactory service rendered, assured an employee a life position."[70] Leading firms might go to considerable lengths to retain their best men. Colleagues eulogized Joseph Hall for procuring orders for different products in order to keep his skilled locksmiths employed during hard times. Joseph Nurre, seeking the moral high ground during a strike at his picture frame factory, insisted that "he had tried to keep his men steadily employed even when times were dull and when other factories had dispensed with the services of their workers."[71] Cincinnati Milling Machine's Frederick A. Geier, similarly, honored the principle that "every employer has a responsibility to try to keep men uniformly employed."[72]

There is an obvious ulterior motive for keeping the best men on when business drops off: they might otherwise be lost to rival firms or unavailable when conditions improve. There are also echoes of an older republican ideal linking employment, steady work, and economic independence. But it is important to look more closely at what entitled these "best men" to regular employment, and here we find the republican ideal altered in the direction of business citizenship. Much as the citizen mechanic celebrated in early industrial expositions evolved into the skilled employee, so the turn-of-the-century worker's "self-sufficiency" was at best a matter of job security within a firm. And in the quid pro quo of "steady work for a good man," it was character as much as technical competence that counted. A skilled woodworker, negotiating his pay with Wulsin, both deferred to the company president and invoked a common understanding that job security was part of the package. "I leave it to your own judgment what [a fine craftsman] is worth, where steady work is given" and where the employee, in turn, displays "regularity in business."[73] Steady work went to steady *workers.* And just as the good employee was an exclusive category, so only a select few earned its rewards.

If the worthy employee resembled the employer's self-image as one invested in the firm, uncommonly competent, and steady in character, surely he should have been entitled to more than a secure job. He should also have been able to improve himself, to demonstrate his worth and ambition and be given greater responsibility (and pay) over time. Cincinnati proprietors seem to have agreed. In no known case before 1900 did they systematize job ladders and procedures for promoting from within. Such internal labor markets are the creations of more bureaucratized management in larger firms,[74] and they ran against the spirit and beyond the means of the city's proprietors. Cincinnati Milling's employee handbook took a less formal approach, offering to "point out the path" which "will help you make good."[75] Wulsin steered his employees along that path with a slightly heavier hand. In his response to one employee who had protested his demotion from finish work to staining, he insisted that for a young man still learning, five dollars an hour was fair. "Naturally, as you progress, you will be advanced in proportion as you become valuable to the factory. Continue to make yourself useful and to take an interest in your work and be assured you will be treated with proper consideration." The focus here is still more on character and "identity with the firm"—as divined by the proprietor—than on the mastery of any specific skills. The president of a local message company in 1899 struck a similar balance: "the messengers who are bright and active are promoted."[76]

The invocation of both usefulness and improvement recalls a basic dilemma of business citizenship. In work as in politics, how could the virtues of individual drive and ambition be combined with an identification with the city or firm? One answer was through education, and some firms supplemented public offerings with in-house programs. Consistent with the principle that the good employee was committed to both *self*-improvement and to the interests of the company, Baldwin Piano and Strobridge Lithographing gave selected employees paid leave to tour other factories and learn the best manufacturing practices.[77] That knowledge would be useful to employer and worker alike. Employers' efforts to combine self-improvement with service to the company also appear in debates among Baldwin managers over the introduction of piecework. Vice President J. W. Macy, who had himself come up from the ranks of skilled Baldwin piano makers, argued that payment by results could indeed stimulate output, but that it was better to stick with day wages. The latter, he emphasized, presupposed honesty and loyalty to the firm, but could also create resentment among the most skillful workers if all employees received the same compensation. Piecework, by contrast, rewarded industry, but it also appealed to a narrower self-interest and undercut cooperation among workers of differing ability and initiative. Macy's solution was to establish a hierarchy of day rates to reward skill and "habits of industry" without stimulating self-interest and competition among the men.[78]

Did Cincinnati employers concede to worthy employees, even in principle, rights of participation, along with security and self-improvement at work? They did, and here too, the standards of business citizenship reappear in the work setting. Cincinnati's business leaders, after all, had a rather circumscribed model of participation even in the political realm. Responsible citizens certainly had an obligation to involve themselves in civic and political uplift. But these citizens were to act as disinterested individuals, not as members of partisan groups or classes. Among individuals, moreover, only those of good character were to be called to politics, and civil service or charter reform curbed the influence of political parties. This ideal, in short, championed responsible citizenship, not popular democracy.

A similar model of governance appears in the workplace. The qualifying citizens are few, their participation is better characterized as engagement with the firm than promotion of their own interests, and *collective* or partisan representation is out of the question. Baldwin Piano executives in 1912 straddled the line between participation and "identity with the firm" when they acknowledged the need to "arouse the old Hamilton enthusiasm" at one of their plants, for which purpose managers should "go around the factory and talk about business with our men."[79] Cincinnati Milling wanted more than talk, offering annual prizes for employee suggestions that yielded improvements or savings.[80] But even in these large firms, where "the personal touch" was beyond reach, company officials insisted that discussions about the business must occur on an individual basis, "man to man." One Baldwin vice president rejected a proposal to hold regular lunch or dinner meetings to hear employee suggestions. "I do not agree with this Utopian scheme of getting people down and feeding them and having a good time. I can find out what I want to know a great deal better by going around and talking to a man individually."[81] The corollary in labor relations, as we will see, was "individual dealing" rather than collective bargaining.

This model of participation certainly did not tie Cincinnati employers' hands. But they did concede, in principle, *some* limits on their right to do as they pleased with their employees. Here, as in mugwump politics, fairness and non-partisanship rather than democratic participation checked managerial authority. Employers summarized the principle as "the square deal."[82] Treat employees with decency, treat them the same, and keep personal feelings out of it. Perhaps disturbed as much by the inconvenience as by the underlying cause of a messenger strike, local businessmen criticized the company's president because he "won't treat the boys fairly. . . . I believe in living and letting others live, and I think if anybody is acting arbitrarily it is Mr. Page."[83] Wulsin insisted on the same principle, even if it meant refusing to allow an employee paid leave for national guard service. "Having nearly 500 employees in our factories, it is absolutely necessary that every one of them be treated on the same basis."[84]

The square deal provided a measure of fair play and predictability to workplace authority. In trade journals, this predictability was sometimes linked to highly rule-bound management, as in praise for Frederick Taylor's piece-rate system on the grounds that its "moral effect" was to encourage "the feeling that substantial justice is being done them."[85] Cincinnati proprietors had a different view. As with other employee rights, the square deal was not yet a matter of formal procedure or fixed rule, much less union contract. It remained instead a rule of thumb, with roots more in general principles of good citizenship than in company bureaucracy or professionalized management. And as the principles of good citizenship had changed since the Civil War, so had the character of the worthy employee's rights. The virtues of the artisan celebrated in Cincinnati's early expositions and at its Mechanics' Institute had much to do with his larger role in the community and the trade. He was, after all, both a pillar of the republic and a representative of progress in the manufacturing arts. The merits of the good employee at the end of the century have little to do with either his civic role or his relationship to a larger craft community. By 1900 he is instead a good citizen of the workplace—a steady employee, invested in the firm, ambitious to move up. Thus, as Cincinnati employers extended their own identities across industries and emphasized more strongly the wider civic contributions of business, they regarded workers as having *fewer* legitimate ties beyond the firm. Among those broader ties, connections to labor unions had the least legitimacy.

UNION WRONGS AND RIGHTS

Late-nineteenth-century Cincinnati employers frequently and forcefully expressed their preference for the open shop. In doing so, they did not introduce a whole new language of anti-unionism. But they did draw *selectively* from a long-standing repertoire, and the themes they emphasized most strongly corresponded to the civic ideals which were at the heart of their class identity. It is these themes, and not the causes or the success of employer anti-unionism, that concern me here.

Employers were no more consistent in practicing what they preached about unions than they were about job security or promotion opportunities. In a few industries, notably the construction trades and printing, employers regularly negotiated wages and working conditions with unions. By contrast, proprietors in the machine tool industry—as a group, perhaps the strongest devotees of business citizenship—ran open shops from the early days of the industry. Elsewhere, collective bargaining waxed and waned with changes in industrial conditions and the balance of power, although by the early 1900s, it was more the exception than the rule. Such variations in practices, however, belie a narrower range of views about workers' right to union representation. On one side, those who refused to deal with unions often accepted employees' right to join them—so long as they did so for the purposes of mutual insurance and fraternity rather than collective bargaining or striking. On the other side, those who did sign agreements with unions not only did so grudgingly (as their periodic efforts to win open shops indicate). They also showed the greatest resistance when demands moved from higher wages to union work rules and the closed shop—the very issues emphasized by uncompromising anti-unionists in their calls for the open shop. Clothing manufacturers made the distinction explicit in 1896 when, in response to demands for the closed shop at one establishment, they locked out cutters in all member firms. Because the dispute "did not affect either wages or hours of labor . . . [we] will not do anything until the cutters return to their positions again as individuals, and not as an allied body of men."[86]

Consistent open shoppers and reluctant collective bargainers alike also advanced the same basic arguments about the evils of unions. These arguments represent choices from an extensive rhetorical menu for demonizing unions. Some rhetorical options, regularly invoked before the Civil War, were rarely voiced by late-nineteenth-century employers. During the religious revival of the late 1830s and 1840s, for example, evangelical proprietors deemed unions to be atheistic influences with which no pious owner would (and no pious employee should) deal.[87] But I have found no case of local manufacturers expressing the same view after 1880. The widespread derision which greeted George Baer's 1902 claim to divine right against coal mining unions suggests that Cincinnati employers were probably typical in repudiating unions on secular grounds. Also missing from local employer discourse during this period were attacks on unions as secret and conspiratorial societies, a common view among their predecessors during the hue and cry over the Molly Maguires in the mid-1870s. Perhaps more surprising, Cincinnati employers did not make much use of a more modern argument: that unions hamper efficient production. As we saw, employers associated union agitators and strikes with workers of lesser skill and lower intelligence. In that sense, a victory for unions would have been bad for business. The claims popularized by scientific management in the early 1900s, however—that unions condoned deliberate restriction of output and that union work rules undermined efficiency in the division of labor and the use of new technology—were rare among late-nineteenth-century Cincinnati employers.

The themes that Cincinnati manufacturers did emphasize are much more consonant with business citizenship than with either divine right or managerial efficiency. Their main criticisms depicted unions as mobs, as tyrants, as outsiders, and as purveyors of class feeling. In each of these overlapping indictments, the core virtues of business citizenship, embodied by the good employee as well as the virtuous employer, were seen to be jeopardized.

Unions as Mobs

The pairing of unions and mobs is a regular feature of employer commentary. Not surprisingly, the association was strongest during labor disputes. Diary entries by local publisher Davis James are typical. James dismissed Cincinnati railroad strikers in 1877 as groups of "rioters . . . thieves and tramps." Their Chicago counterparts, Davis added, were nothing but a "mob . . . made up of the worst characters of society, the very sewer of the human family." That imagery mirrors a wider hysteria over the 1877 uprising, but James does not change his views over the next twenty years. Participants in the 1894 Pullman strike are still "rioters," not legitimate strikers.[88]

Stigmatizing unions as marauding mobs follows a venerable tradition. Elites of all sorts prefer to think of rebellions against their authority as the work of deranged individuals and rabid crowds.[89] Cincinnati businessmen had additional reasons to capitalize on (or exaggerate) reports of violence during strikes. Doing so could win public sympathy and provide the legal grounds for an injunction.[90] But this interpretation of strikes also resonated with Cincinnati employers' sense of themselves as good business citizens. For one thing, it engaged their commitment to "law and order." Business leaders saw themselves as defenders of public authority and the rule of law. And the same rhetoric, used by the Committee of 100 to lambaste rioters (and corrupt politicians), was turned against strikers (and labor leaders) as well. For the Brewers' Association, for example, it was a fine line between political upheaval and mob violence during a strike. When the Knights of Labor Trades Assembly backed a brewers' strike in 1881, the owners felt obliged "to call the attention of every citizen of this community to this institution, in order to fight it with all possible means before it has assumed such terroristic features as the 'National Convention' of the French Revolution." Over twenty years later, the city's Employers' Association sounded the same warning in arguing against a proposed anti-injunction bill. "It means to legalize all the unlawful measures of organized labor engaged in strikes. It means the legalization of the picket, of the boycott and of mob rule with all its terrors."[91] Two local circumstances reinforced this view of strikes. The Court House riot heightened fears of the mob, and an acute sense of the city's economic decline meant that even peaceful strikes were easily construed as threats to the public good.

The identification of strikes with mob terror corresponded to another principle of business citizenship: its celebration of the rational man, sound in character and steady in judgment. Employers sharply distinguished such good citizens from strikers, with their lesser skill, intelligence, and character—"the poorer element among workmen," in Wulsin's 1902 summation.[92] The poorer element, regrettably, could infect the better. Strikers had the character of a mob because they overwhelmed the sober judgment of good employees who would otherwise remain on the job. Most construction workers, as members of the Builders' Exchange charged during an 1882 dispute, "do not want to strike, but have been overridden by a party of men who do not deserve the name of mechanics."[93] Nor was it only during strikes that unions empowered "the poorer element" over workers of good judgment. The Committee of 100, the Commercial Club, and the Business Men's Club, as chapter 3 showed, regularly criticized political corruption and machine politics in the city. As "the best men" suited for civic leadership, they also viewed Boss Cox and his political henchmen as men of low character. The cordial relationship between Cox's regime and powerful local unions in the building trades (and, to add insult to injury, these were *Irish*-dominated unions) reinforced business citizens' dim view of labor organizations. So did the fact that the Central Labor Council opposed the civil service rules that figured prominently in businessmen's reform agenda.[94] Clearly, unions were not just bad for business. They were incompatible with public order and good citizenship, corrupting politics and workers alike.

Unions as Tyrants

Unions most clearly embodied the spirit of the mob during strikes. Whether in industrial peace or war, Cincinnati businessmen also associated unions with tyranny. The preferred term was union *dictation,* victimizing both employers and employees. In the case of employers, union interference with management prompted the greatest outrage.[95] Proprietors generally did not charge that union recognition and work rules jeopardized efficiency. Their complaints instead involved a testy insistence on running their own businesses. These were enterprises they often claimed to have built from scratch and with which they personally identified. To this strong sense of ownership they added the business citizen's concern for proper governance. A rolling-mill owner, speaking in 1882 after a meeting of employers, issued a characteristic declaration of independence from unions. We "will not be hampered and oppressed by the [union's] tyrannical usurpation and flagrant inroads upon natural rights of self-control of property."[96] Cincinnati employers summoned up similar indignation at union tyranny over their employees. The good employee resembled the business citizen in his independence. He had the ability and character to exercise his own judgment at work. By virtue of his skillful and loyal service, moreover, he had regular employment and thus a measure of economic independence. Unions tyrannized employees in both respects. They forced workers to strike against their own will and good sense, and in so doing they undermined their self-reliance. In fighting unions, businessmen thus claimed to be defending their employees' manhood and economic independence. The stakes were high. According to the secretary of Cincinnati's Employers' Association, union control of the city's typographers led them to forsake even their family responsibilities. "God knows how many thousand wives within the past four years," on account of typographers' strikes, have "stood over steaming washtubs, have scrubbed the dirty floors of public buildings, have worked at anything they could get to do, in order to support, not only themselves and their families, but in order to feed their husbands, whose loyalty to the union forced them upon a strike and forbade them from pursuing their calling and earning an honest livelihood."[97]

Whether dictating to employers or to workers, unions thus took on the characteristics of "bossism" that business citizenship decried in municipal government. Political and union bosses alike trampled on individual rights in their corrupt pursuit of self-interest. And this indictment of both unions and city bosses tightly linked their political and economic offenses. It was the employee's right as a *citizen* to earn a livelihood. That link between a "right to work" and economic independence, on one side, and good citizenship, on the other, helps account for some of the more inflammatory attacks on unions as threats to the nation. Successive presidents of the National Association of Manufacturers, for example, denounced unions generally as "lawless organizations" (President Pope) and as "treason, pure and simple" (President Kirby). Cincinnati employers avoided these rhetorical excesses, but still proclaimed it their civic duty to "protect their employees in their right to be free and independent as American citizens."[98]

Unions as Outside Agitators

Cincinnati employers occasionally leveled accusations of dictation at their own employees, but they usually reserved the term for "outsiders." The 1882 building trades dispute, employers charged, was "not a strike of the carpenters. It was a strike of a one-man power for the control both of the carpenters and their employers. . . . [We do] not propose to accept any terms dictated by outside parties." Disruptive industrial action at Baldwin Piano, Wulsin insisted, was usually the work of "the restless, anarchistic walking and talking delegate, whose business it is to create trouble."[99] Outside agitators, of course, are the usual suspects when conflict erupts despite the natural harmony of interest between labor and capital. But where, in addition, good employees are thought to identify with and subordinate their self-interest to the firm, unions become a reprehensible obstacle to direct dealing between employer and employee.

Historians have noted cases where the late-nineteenth-century employer's hostility was directed not at unions per se, but at union procedures and representatives that appeared to be imposed from outside the local community.[100] Cincinnati employers from the 1880s on drew the lines differently. Those who did accept collective bargaining sometimes welcomed the involvement of national union officials in settling disputes fomented by local hotheads, as shoe manufacturers did in their short-lived arbitration agreement. Those who broke off collective bargaining did not do so because of meddling by extralocal union officials. The more common dividing line anticipated the standard open shop formula. Employers claimed not to object to hiring unionists. But they insisted that they would "deal with the members as individuals and not as a union" and would meet only with their own employees.[101] Adhering to this policy could involve some make-believe. When harness makers demanded union recognition and a wage increase in 1892, employers refused the former and announced that they would consider the wage request as coming from individual employees.[102] The principle itself, however, remained clear: unions must remain outside the workplace and excluded from its governance.

Cincinnati employers' critique of outside interference shows a greater preoccupation with control than with efficiency. We rarely hear the voice of the professional manager complaining that unions resisted cost-effective manufacturing methods such as piecework schemes or new machinery. Instead, we hear the proprietor, heavily invested in his firm, becoming bitterly resentful of challenges to his freedom to do as he pleased with "his own." Rather than focusing on production techniques, the usual warning was that unions threatened to "take the entire management of our business from us."[103] What made outside control all the more galling was proprietors' strong conviction that they, and not union officials, had the competence and character to run their firms. Machine tool manufacturer J. C. Hobart made the contrast clear. Unions put power in the hands of "men who by natural endowment or education are totally unfit to properly wield it. The result has been the abuse of this power, threatening the continued prosperity of the country and even the permanence of its free institutions."[104] This sharp distinction between the suitability of proprietors and union officials to exercise industrial authority should sound familiar. It replicates the boundaries constructed by business citizens between "the best men" of the community, properly called to public service, and those unworthy of political authority.

Unions as the Source of Class Conflict

Portrayals of unions as mobs, as tyrants, and as outside agitators reflected the importance for business citizens of the rational individual, constitutional government, and identification with the larger civic or workplace community. The last major charge against unions was that they stirred up "class feeling." This indictment can be seen as part of a widely shared and recurrent American denial that European class divisions are to be found in the New World. Cincinnati businessmen would have agreed with Tocqueville—and with most contemporary politicians—that, although the United States certainly has economic inequalities, it has neither cohesive nor permanent classes. Rich and poor do not, and should not, form groups with shared cultures and political interests, in part because individuals achieve wealth or fall into poverty on the basis of their singular talents and industry.[105] The charge that unions promote class division involves two specific arguments, however. One is that they limit individual self-improvement. The second is that they encourage individuals to think in terms of selfish class interests rather than the greater good.

Many San Francisco employers regarded unions (and employers' associations) as natural expressions of class interests. Their Cincinnati counterparts adopted a more constructionist perspective, well before it was fashionable to do so: unions themselves *created* class differences. In this view, individual workers, both by right and in fact, could "better themselves" by improving their skills and redoubling their efforts. The good employee, as we saw, would certainly strive to do so, and his employer was to reward him accordingly. Unions, however, sought to impose a uniform rate of wages and output. If they succeeded, the brighter and more ambitious workman would be denied the opportunity to demonstrate his superiority and move ahead. Thus employers' frequent insistence that they would pay their men "what they were worth." Rejecting union wage demands in 1882, employers in the building trades claimed that they advanced wages voluntarily, increasing pay "in proportion as [employees] earned money for them."[106] A leading carriage maker gave the same argument an entrepreneurial twist. "The men that are now going into business for themselves are the ones who are not tied to labor organization leaders, but the ones who work for their families."[107] Here again, framing unions as enemies of individual merit highlighted not problems of efficiency, but the fundamental American right to self-improvement.

The claim that unions aroused class hostilities also mirrored the business citizen's contempt for "partisanship," itself a legacy of republican abhorrence for putting class ahead of the commonweal. The Metal Trades Association secretary embellished this basic charge with other rhetorical flourishes, framing unions, in addition, as outsiders and leeches on productive citizens. Surveying a year's worth of strikes, he blamed "the activities of thirty-five well paid non-residents of Cincinnati who were sent here to preach the doctrine of class hatred and to promote every known species of discontent in the hope that a steady stream from the pockets of the great army of workers in this city might be diverted to channels which are controlled by them." His report goes on to make the link to unworthy politicians, who similarly promoted "class legislation" and played up class jealousies for partisan gain.[108] Whether in politics or industrial relations, such appeals to sectional and selfish interests were entirely illegitimate. In 1878, organizers of the Builders' Exchange were careful to distinguish their nonpartisan employers' association from less reputable bodies. It is not a "trade union," one member stressed, "formed to enact arbitrary rules and regulations; it is not a combination having one-sided aims." Nor is it a clique formed in the "improper interest of any particular . . . part of the community," or an organization to promote "the interest of particular classes to the prejudice of others."[109] The message of the Chamber of Commerce in the 1890s is the same, except that now the classless interests of the country *are* those of business. Calling on all members to help end strikes in sympathy with Pullman employees, officials added that "the Cincinnati Chamber of Commerce, politically considered, is strictly non-partisan. It is an organization for the promotion of business interests irrespective of classes or sections."[110]

With unions judged incompatible with both individual self-improvement and good government, it is easy to see how employers could take the next rhetorical step, framing unions as incompatible with U.S. citizenship. In this, Cincinnati employers had much in common with later business attacks on unionism, from the "American plan" of the 1920s to the anticommunist crusades of the 1950s. There is, however, a more historically specific character to anti-union rhetoric in late-nineteenth-century Cincinnati. Their alleged partisanship, moblike disposition, and disrespect for constitutional authority gave unions all the characteristics of political "bossism" abhorred by business citizens. The salutary difference was that employers, mostly unsuccessful in defeating Boss Cox, were generally able to purge union bossism from industrial relations.

From Class Arbitration to Classless Civic Uplift

These selections from America's extensive repertoire of anti-union discourse correspond closely to Cincinnati employers' class identity as business citizens. In tandem with class formation, there were also two shifts in their understanding of how unions related to the larger civic community. First, modest disagreements among economic elites over the virtues of arbitration vanished. In relations between employer and employee, business citizens increasingly deferred to the individual proprietor. Unions thus lost allies in support of collective bargaining. Particularly after 1900, however, there was a second shift. In the wider political community, unions *gained* legitimacy as civic actors, *if* they demonstrated that they, too, could be good business citizens.

Scholars have argued that as economic changes rendered free labor republicanism obsolete, liberals of the 1880s and 1890s came to accept the reality of industrial conflict and endorsed arbitration as a way to settle the inevitable disputes.[111] At first glance, Cincinnati seems to fit this picture. In the mid-1880s, members of the Board of Trade made several efforts to arbitrate disputes, particularly in cases likely to have a serious impact on the local economy. Arbitration also received considerable attention during the United Labor Party's 1886 electoral campaign. The 1880s were a time of growing labor unrest, and arbitration seemed a sensible solution. Businessmen were familiar with the practice. Since 1839, the Chamber of Commerce had relied on its Arbitration Committee to resolve disputes among members. Arbitration by responsible third parties fit some tenets of good citizenship as well. The arbitrators represented the larger interests of the community over and against shortsighted and selfish disputants. They also fit the role of worthy citizens—"gentlemen of recognized standing in the community, cool-headed, dispassionate men," as the Ohio Bureau of Labor Statistics described mediators from the Board of Trade.[112]

From the 1880s, however, the trend in Cincinnati was in the opposite direction. Builders refused arbitration in 1882; the most developed local arbitration system, in the boot and shoe industry, suffered setbacks in 1884 and collapsed in 1885. By 1893, Commercial Club members were a skeptical audience for a guest speaker praising Canada's system for arbitrating industrial disputes. Fred Geier declared it imprudent to submit private industry to public authority, particularly when, as in the United States, labor unions had no legal obligation to act responsibly.[113] In industries where employers did, at least occasionally, deal with organized labor, grievance procedures involving employer and union representatives continued to occur, and these were sometimes labeled "arbitration." After the 1880s, however, arbitration by neutral third parties won some business support only in rare disputes that severely disrupted the local economy, namely, the Western Union strike in 1899 and the streetcar strike in 1913.[114]

This change in practices and attitudes reflects, in part, proprietors' fractious insistence on managing their own affairs without interference from outsiders. But it also corresponds to the rise of business citizenship. Arbitration takes for granted the legitimacy of unions as well as capital. It also presumes the right of public figures or authorities to stand apart from (and above) both of them. In its effort to mediate a dispute between stove molders and their employers in 1884, a Board of Trade spokesman claimed to represent the view of "the citizen" that "the Union workers and the manufacturers" should resolve their differences.[115] Business discourse, however, rejected any such separation between the interests of citizens and the interests of employers. And against that general community interest stood unions, representing partisanship and outside "dictation." It made no sense to concede power to unions through arbitration schemes, much less concede them legitimacy as equal partners in industrial governance.

In matters of public policy, by contrast, some Cincinnati employers showed increasing willingness to cooperate with labor leaders if, like good business citizens, unions could rise above class and separate their contributions as civic boosters from any role at work. Although business leaders identified themselves with the public interest, no such assumptions applied to their union counterparts. This asymmetry—and the contrast with San Francisco—is suggested by the organization of city directories. San Francisco's 1890 directory groups labor unions and employers' associations together under the common heading of "Protective Associations." Cincinnati's directory subdivides "Societies and Associations" into three sections, one for fraternal orders, one for trade unions, and one for "public bodies," including employers' associations, benevolent societies, and social clubs. Still, business leaders would admit unions as legitimate public, not industrial, actors to the extent that they embraced the language of civic betterment. That acknowledgement signaled a transition in Cincinnati from mugwump liberalism to Progressivism.

The Central Labor Council made its first move toward business citizenship in 1893. Adopting and publicizing a new "Declaration of Independence," the council abandoned the language of class struggle and declared its commitment to the "education and social advancement" of all the "working classes." The next year, Central Labor Council leaders recommended electoral cooperation on behalf of candidates nominated by a reformist citizens' committee "in order that the gang of boodlers which now infest the city may be ousted by an overwhelming majority and honesty in municipal government take the place of corruption."[116] The Chamber of Commerce returned the favor while also pointing out the prerequisites for cooperation. The chamber's Board of Directors agreed to let union leaders address them on the proper observance of Labor Day in 1895. It went on to say that the chamber "heartily greets and welcomes the representatives of labor, and stands ready at all times to cooperate with the working classes of our city in their efforts for maintaining their rights and privileges as free American workmen and in all demands that are consistent with fair, honorable and just methods."[117]

The American rights and just demands of business citizens ruled out contentious issues of class. Common civic enterprises could be launched in other areas, however. As the youngest and most liberal of the city's business clubs, the Business Men's Club proved most cooperative and won the Central Labor Council's praise as a progressive organization. In the view of Business Men's Club leaders, Cincinnati's sluggish economic growth and the era's "indiscriminate attacks" on business required both sides to bury the hatchet. "Capital and labor constitute essential parts of industry and . . . without their friendly cooperation, neither can progress." The club did not go so far as to recommend collective bargaining, however—pointedly encouraging cooperation on behalf of economic growth between "industry" and "the rank and file of all labor." And one month later, it came out in opposition to an eight-hour-day legislative bill for federal employees. But in matters of civic betterment rather than industrial relations, the Business Men's Club frequently invited and accepted the cooperation of the council, as in efforts to revise the municipal code and to plan redevelopment of the city's canal.[118]

One area for cooperation is especially instructive. Early efforts to provide vocational training through Cincinnati's private Technical School and through public schools faced opposition from unions. They feared that programs turning out journeymen in larger numbers and without union supervision would undermine labor standards. The National Association of Manufacturers did little to allay these fears, declaring its support for "trade schools properly protected from the domination and withering blight of organized labor." But unionists and businessmen reached common ground in Cincinnati, as they did nationally. On one side, unions stopped pressing the issue of labor standards raised by industrial education. On the other, having training programs run by elected school boards rather than by the Technical School provided some reassurance to unions. So did the OMI's policy of not permitting its pupils to be recruited as strike breakers. The Central Labor Council formally endorsed the city's continuation schools in 1910.[119] By treating industrial education as an issue of civic betterment rather than workplace control, then, unions won acceptance from "progressive" businessmen as legitimate members of the community, entitled to a voice when local leaders discussed the issue.

Employers' commentary on unions offers a final example of the correspondence between generalized class identities cultivated in the civic arena and ideological perspectives on work. The core tenets of business citizenship paralleled employers' choice of anti-union rhetorics, just as they had paralleled employers' celebration of manufacturing, their designs for industrial education, and their models of the good employee. And as in those other case studies, the patterns of change over time confirm the argument for class formation as a key to cultural transposition. The emergence of a common, "classless" business identity among employers, together with the sharpening of status distinctions between classes, undermined the premises of arbitration. Within this framework, it made no sense to treat class conflicts as inevitable, to assign both sides legitimacy, or to elevate some community interests and leaders above business, with at least moral authority to mediate disputes. These principles were, by contrast, the conventional wisdom under San Francisco's practical corporatism.

6

FROM WORK TO POLITICS

Representing Class in San Francisco

San Francisco's civic leaders launched yet another charter reform campaign in 1910. The agenda of the Charter Reform Convention included familiar Progressive proposals, such as improved procedures for initiatives, referenda, and recalls; nonpartisan elections; and greater government control over city franchises. A Committee of Nine took charge, composed mainly of prominent business figures like Harris Weinstock of the Commonwealth Club and C. H. Bentley from the Chamber of Commerce. Two committee members, however, Andrew Gallagher and Walter Macarthur, represented labor. Their inclusion signaled the need to win union support in the upcoming election. That tactical consideration, in turn, supported a broader assumption that economic associations deserved recognition as legitimate political actors. Reporting on the committee's plan to convene a meeting of such associations, the *San Francisco Examiner* referred to the "quasi public organizations, such as the Merchants' Exchange, Bar Association, the Building Trades and Labor Councils . . . and various improvement clubs" that had been invited. These would be among the "representatives of sixty public bodies" that helped design the new charter.[1]

This matter-of-fact acceptance of class organizations as serving representative functions in politics *and* industry would have struck Cincinnati businessmen as a pernicious mingling of public and class interests, one that would be corrosive of the civic good. Yet it made sense to many San Francisco businessmen. They had ample experience with organized labor's power on the job and in the voting booth. And they had learned that recognizing unions through collective bargaining in the workplace and regular consultation in municipal politics had

advantages. Earlier chapters explored these two faces of labor power and business accommodation. This chapter shows that these parallel experiences blurred
the boundaries between workplace and political class representation. Practical
corporatism, I argue, resembled Cincinnati's business citizenship in its transposable character—but for reasons that had more to do with institutional symmetry
than generalized identities. Accordingly, the burden of the chapter is to illustrate
the broad applicability of businessmen's implicit notions of good citizenship and
of the proper relationship between class and the public interest. The illustrations
include employers' use and views of arbitration; their efforts to "sell" San Francisco
through expositions and the promotion of home industry; and their approaches
to city governance, particularly their responses to municipal corruption. These
are fields which range from "private" industrial relations to highly public political reform. In each case, however, we see the distinction between industrial and
political organization blurred, and class representation treated as conducive to
the public good. The emphasis in this chapter shifts slightly from that of the
previous chapter. In Cincinnati, the empirical surprise lay less in the content of
business citizenship than in its application to work issues. In San Francisco, the
surprise is that a group of U.S. proprietors endorsed practical corporatism at
all—this was far from the American norm—rather than the fact that this script
crossed boundaries between work and politics. The corresponding scholarly goal
is to document this surprising pattern, marshaling diverse examples where San
Francisco businessmen acknowledged class representation and its contributions
to community welfare.

Support for class representation was not unanimous. Chapter 4 showed that
businessmen had less ideological and organizational common ground in San
Francisco than in Cincinnati, and one point of sharp disagreement concerned
the representative rights of organized labor. Much as in Cincinnati, where traces
of class formation appear in discourse about expos or industrial education, so
echoes of San Francisco's peculiar class alignments can be heard in business
discussions of arbitration and municipal corruption.[2] Businessmen's practical
corporatism in these areas also conforms to the timing of class formation.
Arbitration, city promotion, and governance practices are most clearly organized around class representation from the late 1890s through 1910, when
labor's dual power peaked. The years after 1911 form a contrasting period.
From this point, manufacturers and merchants begin to unify through new,
or newly invigorated, civic institutions, and discourse shifts in the direction of
business citizenship. By the end of 1916, business citizenship is being applied
to industrial relations, with the repudiation of arbitration, and to politics, with
the curtailment of union rights. This historical reversal is examined in the final
section of this chapter.

ARBITRATING CLASS CONFLICT

The use of arbitration in labor relations is a good place to begin testing the applicability of San Francisco's practical corporatism. Employers, after all, might deal with unions grudgingly, but do so through direct collective bargaining with union representatives. Arbitration goes further, having third parties help resolve disputes and set new employment conditions. In some variants, it assigns this role to quasi-public authorities, with civic groups or trusted government officials mediating between labor and capital. Both in relinquishing direct control and in accepting public intervention, San Francisco proprietors took an unusual approach to industrial relations between the early 1900s and World War I. The distinctive character of their approach, and its conformity to underlying principles of practical corporatism, can be seen in contrast to the fate of arbitration in Cincinnati.

Arbitration was discussed and occasionally practiced in late-nineteenth-century America.[3] Particularly during the tumultuous 1880s, it appeared to be a sensible method for dealing with industrial conflict. Employers and unions alike, some businessmen argued, could be selfish and hotheaded. A constructive role, accordingly, could be played by neutral arbiters, men who stood coolly above the fray and helped warring factions reach reasonable compromises. Such worthy citizens made a sincere effort to play this role in several disputes during the mid-1880s, particularly in cases thought likely to have a serious impact on the local economy. In Cincinnati, however, arbitration had all but disappeared from employers' repertoire by 1900. That change, I have argued, corresponds to changing assumptions about class relations. Most forms of arbitration make unions the legitimate voice of employees and give them formally equal status to capital: the arbitrator's task is to mediate between representatives of both sides. In this way, arbitration also draws a clear line between the partisan interests of labor *and* capital, each of which may be shortsighted and unreasonable, and the neutral public. By the 1890s, however, most Cincinnati employers repudiated any such representative role for unions, and they did not distinguish public from business interests.

Far from disappearing, arbitration in San Francisco became commonplace after 1900. Arbitration took different forms, and businessmen used the term loosely, but it always added further steps to regular collective bargaining. If those directly involved could not resolve a dispute, it would be referred for "arbitration." Consistent with practical corporatism's model of negotiation between balanced powers in industry, the arbitration might be conducted by officials of the relevant employers' association and union. While these representatives took control of the controversy, the disputants would be expected to maintain the status quo rather than engage in disruptive strikes or lockouts. This much is little different from industry-wide collective bargaining—rare enough in the United States, but relying little on genuine third parties. In some local variants of industry-wide bargaining, however, the two sides could call in an outside arbitrator to break deadlocks. During a 1903 streetcar strike, the United Railroads and the Carmen's Union agreed to set up a "board of arbitration" composed of one representative of the company, one from the union, and a third to be chosen by these two. The Building Trades Employers' Association and the Building Trades Council adopted a similar scheme in 1914.[4]

Other local arbitration schemes took this reliance on third parties still further. Sometimes the "third party" was a labor federation. As early as 1890, Andrew Hallidie commended the new Federated Trades (soon to become the Labor Council) because "it promises to have a conservative and restraining influence on impatient members, and to conciliate differences between the employer and the employed."[5] Others put this theory into practice. In 1902, the owners of a hat-making factory called on the Labor Council to mediate a strike; the gas company had the council intervene in a dispute with the Gas Workers' Union; and the California Tanners' Association worked with the Labor Council to settle a strike at one of its firms.[6] In recognition of this new responsibility, the Labor Council changed its rules in 1904 to require that all members submit demands to the council for approval before directing them at employers. Building contractors relied on the BTC for this kind of arbitration. To a lesser degree, waterfront employers did the same with the City Front Federation.[7]

San Francisco industrial relations featured yet another type of arbitration, where the third party was a civic association. During one 1900 strike, for example, the Builders' Association proposed arbitration by the Merchants' Association—a proposal accepted, with caveats, by the BTC's McCarthy on the grounds that "these men are business men and have the city's welfare at heart."[8] A year later, the Merchants' Association itself backed the Municipal League (made up of representatives from the city's improvement clubs) as a mediator between the Employers' Association and striking unions.[9] During the strike-filled summer of 1907, leading labor and business organizations formed a "joint conciliation committee" to provide this sort of neutral arbitration on a wider scale. The committee brought together representatives from the Chamber of Commerce, the Merchants' Association, the Manufacturers' and Producers' Association, and the Civic League, on one side, and the Labor Council on the other. They devised a plan to deputize subcommittees, each with a labor and a business figure, to meet with the warring parties in several ongoing disputes. Their charge in each case—ironworks, street railroads, laundries, telephones—was to elicit each side's proposals for a settlement and to attempt mediation.[10] These examples of arbitration had an ad hoc character, with business and labor leaders trying to douse fires as they broke out. The practice was more institutionalized in the metal trades. In 1910, the inability of the California Metal Trades Association and the Iron Trades Council to agree on a new contract threatened an industry-wide strike. In response, Harris Weinstock of the Commonwealth Club proposed an arbitration board composed of twelve employer representatives nominated by the Chamber of Commerce and twelve put forward by the Labor Council. This Industrial Conciliation Board helped forestall a strike in 1911 and made recommendations (not always followed) in several subsequent disputes.[11]

These arrangements—even when they failed to avert strikes—showcase San Francisco businessmen's distinctive assumptions about class and citizenship. Where Cincinnati employers treated unions as illegitimate outsiders, arbitration constructed labor relations around the principle of mutual organization and representation. The goal was not to purge one party from industrial relations but to balance one against the other. Each stage of arbitration, whether it involved meetings between officials of unions and employers' associations outside the firm or third-party mediation between the two, enacted this model of balanced representation. The standard formula in arbitration plans acknowledged both classes, encouraged their formal organization, and assigned those organizations equal weight in deliberations. Thus a proposal made at a Merchants' Association dinner would have convened meetings of officials from the association and the Chamber of Commerce with presidents of the Building Trades and Labor Councils, "representing the business interests on one hand and the labor interests on the other." These would work out the details for a court of arbitration, with four delegates from each side and one additional, neutral member.[12] Two by two, four by four, the representatives of capital and labor would be given responsibility for resolving their conflicts.

Arbitration also applied different assumptions about the contributions of organized labor to industrial peace. According to Cincinnati businessmen, unions promoted partisan interests, and partisanship had no place in political or industrial governance. Supporters of arbitration believed that unions could act "responsibly." Employers' willingness to have higher-level union officials or labor federations serve as arbitrators presumed (or hoped) that they could act as checks on impetuous employees or militant local lodges. "Responsible" action might mean siding with employers against unruly unionists, as when leaders of the Labor Council and the local Glass Blowers' Union demanded that striking boys honor the existing contract. Pending arbitration, officials insisted, work must continue; in the meantime, they tried to mediate between employers and the boys.[13] Such cooperative behavior, however, neither signaled weakness nor called into question the union's rightful role as representative of labor's class interests. This use of unions also implies what Hallidie made explicit: an appreciation for their role in enforcing the rule of law in industry. The rules themselves might be irritating, but at least they were fixed and imposed on all competitors, thus allowing for planning.

Particularly when arbitration involves ostensibly neutral third parties, whether civic associations or government officials, it also takes a different view of the relationship between class and the public interest. In contrast to Cincinnati, here the public good was neither monopolized by business nor subverted by unions. Both parties to arbitration put their more or less self-interested claims on the table for steadier hands to sort out. Neither side's uncontested sway was deemed beneficial to the community. "Industrial peace in itself does not always mean true welfare for the community," according to a joint statement from labor and business leaders at the 1907 Industrial Peace Conference. Mere peace "may go hand in hand with an abject status of labor, or with economic conditions prohibitive to capital. This committee seeks an industrial peace founded upon just and stable relations between capital and labor. To labor[,] a fair wage commensurate with our high degree of civilization . . . proper protection and true economic and social opportunity; to capital, stability of conditions affecting it [and] . . . reasonable interest on investment."[14]

Arbitration, finally, offered hope that the ideal of good citizenship embraced by practical corporatism could be achieved. Labor and capital could best serve the public good, not by renouncing self-interest, but by settling their conflicts peacefully. Advocates saw the "public interest" as jeopardized by uncompromising industrial warfare waged by either side. In 1907, the Civic League and labor leaders alike denounced "the sentiment of 'fight to a finish' . . . shared equally by the agitators in the ranks of labor and capital."[15] Responsible leaders of labor and capital were supposed to condemn these agitators, and they did. "There [are] two elements in this city that wanted to fight," according to one business speaker at the Industrial Peace Conference, "one element at the top of the social column, the other at the bottom of the social column. . . . Between the anarchist at the top . . . and the anarchist at the bottom . . . [stands] the great body of the better element." A colleague from the Draymen's Association agreed. "Everything should not be charged to unionism. Capital in many instances is just as much to blame."[16] On this point the premises of arbitration come together. The public interest is distinct from any one class, and it is best served when both sides are well organized, hold their less responsible members in check, and use mechanisms for resolving disputes without disrupting the city's affairs. To the extent that labor federations or business clubs could provide these mechanisms, they were dignified as "public bodies," representing a community interest above the play of balanced class forces. San Francisco's 1905 "Citizens' Law and Order League" captures the divergence from the assumptions of business citizenship. The name alone may lead students of Cincinnati to expect a business-led vigilance committee rallying classless citizens against labor unions. Part of this hypothesis is correct. The league was rooted in the city's improvement clubs, which were made up largely of small businessmen in particular neighborhoods. But the league did not claim to defend a classless public order against labor agitators and radicals. Instead, it defined itself as "an organization of the disinterested general public as a buffer between organized capital and organized labor."[17]

In recommending arbitration, the Industrial Peace Conference's praise of "the great body of the better element" standing between high- and low-class anarchists echoes businessmen's celebration of a virtuous middle hemmed in by the immoral corporations and uncivilized Chinese. As with racist and antimonopoly politics, arbitration affirmed a common ground for responsible unionists and proprietors. In arbitrating disputes, both showed their good citizenship in its practical corporatist guise, not denying their class roots but representing class interests in a spirit of compromise and with a willingness to discipline the anarchists in their ranks.

Calls for arbitration embodied San Francisco's class alignments in another way: they divided businessmen among themselves. Arbitration was a key point on which the conflicts of 1901 turned. Even as Mayor Phelan gave employers the support of city police, he pushed them to accept arbitration to resolve disputes. The Employers' Association refused, and it pressured trade-based organizations to do the same. That repudiation of arbitration, in turn, cost the Employers' Association support among smaller employers and "civic minded" businessmen in the city's improvement clubs and Merchants' Association.[18] The split here divided a minority of larger firms from proprietary capital on the issue of collective bargaining. Arbitration could also divide the latter groups over their "right to manage." Consider the 1900 planing mill strike. The Building Trades Council prompted this dispute by trying to extend the eight-hour day and union shop from construction sites to the local mills which supplied lumber. Owners refused, and the resulting strike threatened to starve construction work of material. Organized building contractors, by now accustomed to dealing with the BTC, urged mill owners to allow the Merchants' Association to arbitrate between them and the BTC. The millmen replied that outside arbitrators had neither the right nor the competence to become involved in their business decisions. "The Merchants' Association is incapable of judging the merits of the strike," one owner complained to the Examiner. "Its members are not familiar with the situation and cannot appreciate the position the mill owners are in." And regardless of how knowledgeable an arbitrator might be, some things were none of their business. When it came to whom they would hire and how long they would work, "the mill owners haven't anything to arbitrate."[19] This claim to an inviolable right to manage, free from outside interference, is a staple of U.S. employer rhetoric. The National Association of Manufacturers' journal *American Industries* regularly dismissed arbitration because it gave authority to ignorant outsiders, because matters of right and wrong should not be negotiated, and because an arbitration decision could not be enforced on irresponsible unions anyway.[20] In San Francisco, however, only a minority acted on this view between 1901 and 1916. Whether or not they came to accept arbitration in principle, the mill owners eventually joined the majority and accepted it in practice.

There is a further lesson in the fact that mill owners, among many others, finally came around. One of the things that most powerfully recommended arbitration to members of the Merchants' Association or the Municipal League was precisely its promise as a check on those employers with a "fight to a finish" mentality. It offered recalcitrants a face-saving alternative to direct dealing with unions, both by giving groups like the Merchants' Association a mediating role and by wrapping arbitration in the flag of civic patriotism. By the time of the highly disruptive and sometimes violent 1907 streetcar strike, these virtues of arbitration seem to have become widely accepted among San Francisco businessmen. Most of the leading business associations strongly condemned street railroad czar Patrick Calhoun for his refusal to accept arbitration, and the Industrial Peace Conference was launched in part to lobby for this alternative. Reminding conference attendees that "all industrial peace is based on good citizenship," commerce secretary Oscar Strauss particularly condemned those, like Calhoun, who "take the position, when a conflict is imminent, [that] there is nothing to arbitrate." Calhoun did not back down. But in Strauss's recommendation of arbitration we see a conception of good citizenship that includes organized labor and capital. And in endorsing that recommendation, Conference members ruefully acknowledged that an irresponsible minority—men who were *not* "good patriotic citizens"—existed on *both* sides of industry.[21]

SELLING SAN FRANCISCO

San Francisco businessmen had ample reason to promote their city, and they were not shy about doing so. In the 1850s and 1860s, the major goals were to attract population and investment from back east; in the late nineteenth century, there was a major push to reinvigorate the city's manufacturing; and in the early twentieth century, key concerns included fending off West Coast rivals and celebrating the city's rebirth from the 1906 earthquake. Commercial exhibitions and a home industry movement helped meet these goals. Both were largely the work of businessmen, and their approach to selling San Francisco provides another illustration of the uses of practical corporatism.

Annual industrial fairs began in 1865 under the auspices of the Mechanics' Institute. They had much in common with Cincinnati's expositions. Organizers saw them as advertisements for the city. They also hoped the exhibitions would educate skilled workers and trumpet mechanics' contributions to the city's economic growth and republican virtue. The fairs were "the people's colleges, where farmers and mechanics improve their education" and thereby enhance their social position. "Let it not be forgotten that our greatest statesmen, discoverers, inventors, scholars, and artists, have sprung from the ranks of Labor, and not from the Silk Stocking classes." And as in Cincinnati, these fine republican sentiments faded. Showcasing the techniques, products, and moral worth of mechanics gave way to boosterism and popular entertainment. "The people of this city should have learned to appreciate the true educational value of these Industrial Fairs," the Mechanics' Institute president lamented in 1899. Alas, what they wanted were "amusements similar in nature to those found in the dime museum or vaudeville entertainments."[22] Increasingly, the people got what they wanted.

In other respects, however, San Francisco businessmen took a different approach to promoting their city. Particularly from the mid-1890s, they solicited the participation of unions in their efforts. Cincinnati's Business Men's Club welcomed the support of the city's Central Labor Council in municipal improvement, but they did not treat the council as speaking for a different class; organized labor earned admission to civic planning only by checking at the door its role in representing members at work. For the businessmen organizing the 1915 Panama Pacific International Exposition, by contrast, unions' representative functions at work and in politics were explicit and went hand in hand. Directors of the exposition may not have signed a contract with the Building Trades and Labor Councils, but they did negotiate employment conditions on exposition work. The directors also recognized that business could not have it both ways, winning union cooperation in civic affairs while insisting on the open shop. The exposition board, accordingly, squelched calls from the Merchants' and Manufacturers' Association (organized in 1914 by veterans of earlier open shop drives) to use non-union labor on city construction projects.[23] A public contretemps at the 1909 Portola Festival may have reminded them of this link. In most respects, preparations for the festival followed local customs. A coalition of business and labor groups planned the event, including the Merchants' Association and Chamber of Commerce for business, and the BTC, printers' union, and Teamsters for labor. But when it came to the opening parade, unions declined the invitation to march, protesting the festival's displays of Asian art and culture.[24]

The promotion of home industry was a theme in the earliest Mechanics' Institute fairs. By showcasing locally manufactured goods, fair organizers hoped to make city residents aware that they had alternatives to imports from back east.

More self-standing and urgent campaigns for home industry developed in the mid-1890s, prompted by widely publicized statistics showing that the city had grown in population but declined slightly in manufacturing activity. Led by prominent local industrialists, including Henry Scott of the Union Iron Works and the ubiquitous Andrew Hallidie, business responded by organizing the Manufacturers' and Producers' Association in 1895. Over the next several years, the association arranged exhibitions of local products and advertised the virtues of buying them in preference to East Coast goods. Similar efforts under other auspices continued until World War I.[25] For participants in these campaigns, patronage of local commodities was a civic duty, a way to promote the good of San Francisco as a whole. This rhetoric was, of course, common enough in Cincinnati as well. Where San Francisco's campaigns differed was in the way they defined the beneficent results of buying local products and in the social base of the campaigners themselves.

The standard pitch for buying local gave particular prominence to those benefits that would accrue to labor. A full-page ad in 1910 reminded "Native Sons and Daughters" that they should show their "love for and loyalty to [their] State" by patronizing home industries. By listing local firms that made common products—from baby carriages and overalls to faucets and furniture—it helped these patriotic consumers do their duty. The ad also highlighted the merits of this patriotic consumption. Half of the advantages listed in the ad emphasized improvements in the local economy generally—increased population, business revenues, property values, and so on. The other half emphasized how local consumption benefited wage earners, offering up projections of the average number of new hands that could be hired and the corresponding increase in wages paid.[26]

These campaigns differed from those in Cincinnati in another way, involving the cooperation of business groups and labor organizations. As would be expected in San Francisco, businessmen squabbled over the inclusion of unions. At the 1895 convention which gave birth to the Manufacturers' and Producers' Association, several sessions featured debates over labor participation. A former city supervisor began the debate, arguing that it was of "the greatest importance that labor should be represented in a convention like this. . . . It would be wise for the Committee on Credentials . . . to see that there are enrolled in the list of delegates at least one actual employee from every trade and occupation here represented. . . . If these delegates cannot be appointed by the Trades Councils, it would be well for us to call upon employers to choose one of their employees." A resolution then carried "that the various trades workmen may select a representative for each line of industry, [who will] meet with the Executive Committee at stated times for the purpose of consultation." The next day, delegates went on to waive the membership assessment of $5 for workingmen. The convention stalemated, however, on the further step proposed by Andrew Furseth of the Sailors' Union. Furseth urged delegates to formally endorse labor unions as making an important contribution to local prosperity. At least one delegate insisted that unions were, instead, impediments to growth. A compromise resolution evenhandedly indicted abuses by both unions and monopolies and took the unexceptionable view that *if* unions benefited the local economy, they were good things. Ultimately that compromise ended up tabled by general consent, but delegates from the Labor Council continued to speak for "the workingmen."[27] The association also affirmed that in promoting San Francisco manufacturing, proprietors and skilled men were natural allies. The initial call for new members by the association's business leaders invited manufacturers and "producers" to rally around, and it emphasized that the latter term was "meant to include the workingman as well as the employer." Convention speakers added that both sorts of producers deserved the favor of San Francisco consumers and protection from unfair competition—including both East Coast corporations and convict labor. And to fight such a "degradation of free and honest labor," the Manufacturers' and Producers' Association at times called on the Labor Council to boycott local firms selling convict-made goods.[28]

This class collaboration would continue in later movements for home industry. When the Mission Promotion Association took up the cause in 1910, it invited the Labor Council to participate. The same practice appears within individual industries. The Metal Trades Association joined forces with the Iron Trades Council in 1908 to persuade city officials to buy local products for the water system, making common cause against such East Coast corporations as General Electric. The two sides continued their collaboration in bids for Navy orders, with the Iron Trades Council compromising on wage scales in order to win shipbuilding contracts. Out of these ad hoc efforts grew a more permanent "promotion committee." Similar arrangements appear in printing, shoe manufacturing, and clothing.[29] The 1910 Home Industry League, finally, helped centralize many of these cross-class initiatives. Through the league, businessmen worked with Labor Council representatives to win the purchase of local manufactures for such municipal projects as the civic center and city hall. They also recognized that organized labor brought more than self-interest to the partnership: its political clout made it a valuable ally in lobbying city officials.[30] The practical corporatism that worked for running San Francisco industry worked as well to sell it.

Expositions and campaigns for home industry provided forums for proprietors to squabble with one another as well as to ally with unions. We saw that by the 1880s, Cincinnati fairs subsumed "mechanics" and merchants within a general identity as business boosters. In San Francisco's expositions, manufacturers occupied a separate and lesser place. Even in many of the Mechanics' Institute's own fairs, the mechanical arts had less prominence than agricultural displays, artwork, and entertainment. At the 1881 fair, local newspapers noted that "the mechanical exhibit is . . . especially lacking, nor is the manufacturing interest well represented. Each year this portion of the Fair, undoubtedly the most important, has decreased in interest and effect. On the other hand the Art Gallery and exhibit of curious and interesting specialties and candy-making has grown with the years."[31] The *Examiner*'s gushing account of the 1887 fair, similarly, described first the musical offerings, then the art gallery, and then the products of rural California. The machinery exhibit came dead last, with attention focused on its "wagons, threshing machines, and agricultural implements." Small wonder that in the fair's traditional welcoming speech, successive Mechanics' Institute presidents urged listeners to pay mechanics more respect, if only to promote local manufacturing.[32] The institute's fairs, in turn, were separate from and considerably less lavish than the city's commercial expositions—the 1894 Midwinter Festival, the 1909 Portola Festival, and the 1915 Panama Pacific Exposition. These celebrated San Francisco's role as commercial hub and gateway to foreign lands, not a center of manufacturing excellence. The 1894 fair, originally named "The Commercial World's Fair," featured representations of everyday life in such exotic colonial outposts as Egypt, Africa, and Hawaii. The theme of the 1909 festival was the rebirth of San Francisco after the 1906 earthquake, symbolized by a reenactment of Gaspar de Portola's discovery of the Bay Area.[33] And not coincidentally, the planning as well as the exhibits of these fairs gave little space to manufacturers. As the Mechanics' Institute emphasized in a somewhat huffy public statement, it played no role in the planning of the 1915 exposition.[34]

The campaign for home industry offered still more opportunities for mutual recrimination among businessmen. The same 1895 convention of manufacturers at which a majority voted to include representatives of labor also featured harsh words for local merchants. "The wholesale and retail dealers have an antique and apparently hereditary prejudice against articles of home make," the convention secretary charged, further suggesting that it would take pressure from working-men to cure dealers of their prejudices.[35] In 1911, similarly, the Home Industry League aligned itself with local workers and against the false economies preached by advocates of government efficiency. The league had been pushing the Board of Public Works to award a streetcar contract to a local firm. The Downtown Association protested that this went too far: city officials should choose the low-est bidder. In their rejoinder, league speakers particularly emphasized that one of the low bidders from the East Coast had withdrawn its proposal on learning that contractors would have to honor the eight-hour day and a minimum wage of three dollars a day. Low bids, they implied, were not necessarily the best for all the city's classes. The league expressed similar frustration with Mayor James Rolph's choice of an out-of-town bid on civic center work.[36] In Cincinnati, more efficient city administration was part of a general project of civic betterment backed by broadly representative business associations. In efforts on behalf of home industry in San Francisco, manufacturers and workers lined up against business advocates of good government and suggested a different way of measuring the community good.

GOVERNING SAN FRANCISCO

The assumptions of practical corporatism can be seen, finally, in two arenas for the practice of good citizenship: civic improvement associations and responses to political corruption during the Union Labor Party administration. In Cincinnati, campaigns for community betterment and clean government acted out the ideal of municipal administration by individuals of good character, free from class partisanship. Leading San Francisco businessmen saw matters differently. Civic associations could best advance their goals if they worked with rather than stood above class interests; political corruption *and* the uncompromising fight against it were symptomatic of one-sided class rule, to be cured by more balanced and responsible collective representation for all classes. And rather than bringing businessmen together, this model of good citizenship aligned some of the city's economic elite with unions and against rival businessmen.

Where business reformers pursued plans for municipal improvement through electoral politics, it obviously paid to involve unions. Bond issues or charter reforms had to be put to vote, and unions swung working-class voters. We saw in chapter 4 that the 1898 charter reform succeeded where prior efforts had failed because Merchants' Association leaders negotiated its provisions with unions and thereby won their support. A drive for improvement bonds followed the next year, with business clubs and delegates from labor's trade councils—"associations interested in the progress of the city"—meeting together to organize a campaign committee. Civic Federation meetings to promote bond issues in the early 1900s, similarly, tended to include representatives from neighborhood clubs, the Merchants' Association, and the Building and Labor Councils,[37] Among business reformers, James Phelan took the lead in his solicitude for organized labor, marching in their parades, contributing to their funds for striking miners, and endorsing their rallies for labor rights.[38] Courting labor made sense not only because unions delivered votes, but also because the industrial and political strengths of the unions were well integrated. As mayor, Phelan learned this lesson the hard way. His use of police against strikers in 1901 helped the Union Labor Party win a solid majority on the city council in 1903.

Even outside of electoral politics, business leaders treated union federations as entitled to a voice in civic betterment. In their role as representatives of city workers they were no different from organizations acting on behalf of other social interests, including neighborhoods, professions, and merchants. Consider, for example, the 1889 Commercial Convention. The event brought together business leaders from along the Pacific Coast as well as San Francisco's own Manufacturers' Association, Produce Exchange, and Board of Trade. Delegates discussed trade-related issues, including government subsidies for ocean mail service, plans for the proposed Nicaraguan Canal, and policies of the Interstate Commerce Commission. A Cincinnati reader of this account would find nothing out of place—until seeing that the Federated Trades had applied for the admission of five representatives to the convention and that the application was likely to be approved without dissent.[39] The lack of dissent was unusual for San Francisco, but the final outcome was not. Civic organizations and public meetings run by local businessmen often invited prominent union officials to serve as delegates, or they at least consulted with them. Why? Although it is impossible to say whether most businessmen believed that workers *deserved* a corporate voice in civic improvement efforts, the basic model of class representation was certainly familiar from work and electoral politics. And whatever the inner thoughts of participants in the matter, this was the model generally followed in practice, with unions taking their place alongside business organizations as civic actors, charged with articulating and negotiating the interests of their constituents. They did so in relatively small matters, as when the Chamber of Commerce in 1908 urged the Labor Council to send a representative to a conference on harbor improvements. They did so in matters of greater import, as when the post-earthquake Committee of Reconstruction combined business associations with presidents of the Labor Council, the BTC, and the Carpenters' Union.[40] And there was no conflict here, as there was in Cincinnati, between responsibly representing class interests and contributing to the community good. As Phelan put it in welcoming delegates to the 1901 Chinese Exclusion Convention—Chinese exclusion being very much a community good in the minds of most whites—"we have men here representing commerce and labor; we have them representing the field, the mine, and the orchard; we have them representing skilled and unskilled industry; but, above all, we have them here as American citizens, representing our American institutions."[41]

Episodes of government corruption give political actors opportunities to fine-tune their standards of good citizenship. They can judiciously weigh what counts as outrageous, who belongs on either side of the moral divide, and what countermeasures are justified. In Cincinnati, the contrast drawn by businessmen between political virtue and corruption coincided with class divisions, and the preferred cure was leadership by virtuous and nonpartisan men. Their San Francisco counterparts allocated praise and blame along different lines and offered different solutions. We have seen that they put far more emphasis on "monopolies" or "wealthy corporations" as corrupting influences, with the usual suspects—the Southern Pacific, the street railways, Spring Valley Water—denounced for using bribes and political muscle to get preferential treatment. In their efforts to clean up the mess, moreover, business reformers allied with union leaders against the bosses. Reform Democrats like Phelan did so in order to purge "Blind Boss" Buckley in the early 1890s, and the Merchants' Association did so to win voter approval for structural reforms in 1898.

The graft scandal that emerged in early 1906 provided a tougher test of this alliance. Unionists had been the junior partners in Phelan's reform coalition; now the Union Labor Party ran city hall. In the 1890s, union officials had not been taking bribes; in 1906 it was the party's chief figures who were the initial targets of prosecution. The scandal, then, would appear to have offered businessmen an excellent opportunity. The rallying cry of clean, nonpartisan government could have been used to pull factions of capital together, end "class rule" by labor, and restore to businessmen the upper hand in city politics. Instead, a majority of business leaders continued to endorse balanced and responsible class representation, condemning the excesses and fanaticism of *both* corrupt unionists and zealous prosecutors.

The Union Labor Party's Eugene Schmitz had won the mayor's office in 1901 and 1903, but his party controlled few other positions. That changed dramatically in 1905. Using the recent open shop campaign by the Citizens' Alliance to motivate working-class voters and some skeptical union leaders, the party swept the election. With solid control of the city's Board of Supervisors, party leader Abe Ruef orchestrated a system of bribes for political favors. Under Ruef's scheme, a "French restaurant" (offering a mixed menu of fine food and prostitution) needing to renew a license, or a street railway company seeking a new route, would hire him as its attorney. Ruef then distributed a portion of his substantial attorney's fee among supervisors and the mayor to ensure approval of the request. Exposure of the scheme can be credited to sugar magnate Rudolph Spreckels and publisher Fremont Older. Spreckels's wealth financed the private detectives who entrapped supervisors, while Older's *San Francisco Bulletin* gave the scandal wide publicity. And together with district attorney William Langdon, they turned the corrupt board to their own purposes. By threatening individual supervisors with indictment, they procured the testimony needed to convict Schmitz and Ruef. By leaving the captive supervisors in office, they secured appointments of their own choosing, including Schmitz's interim replacement.[42]

Much as business organizations in 1901 first rallied behind the Employers' Association in its battle with unions, so in 1906 did they initially applaud the investigation and prosecution of graft. The investigative trail, however, soon led from bribe-takers like Schmitz and Ruef to bribe-givers like the United Railroad's Calhoun and the telephone company's Louis Glass. As businessmen got caught in the district attorney's net, what had been praised as conscientious law enforcement began to look like fanaticism. Part of the problem, as hesitant businessmen portrayed it, was the district attorney's tactics: leaving grafters in public office to "cooperate" with prosecutors hardly seemed the best route to clean government. More important, the scandal disrupted commerce and impaired the ability of the city government to resolve the 1907 streetcar strike. The resulting backlash reached "the city's most exclusive clubs," where members rallied to the defense of the prosecution's business victims and snubbed prosecutors and their allies, including James Phelan and Rudolph Spreckels. Critics of the prosecution also began to withdraw their accounts from Spreckels's First National Bank and their advertisements from Older's *Bulletin*. The Merchants' Association was more direct, denouncing as overly zealous the legal attacks on "remote figures" in the scandal.[43] H. E. Huntington joined the fray as well, making a straightforward case for the business advantages that came with political stability. He claimed in an interview that, given the choice, he would prefer Schmitz to the reformer Phelan as mayor. "Schmitz in his weakness can at times be controlled by some people," Huntington calculated, "while Phelan, with his anarchistic views, has too much misapplied brains to be influenced."[44]

These reminders that prosecutors could be as dangerous to orderly government as grafters echoed reactions by moderate businessmen to the streetcar strike. Their evenhanded opposition to fanaticism, in turn, established common ground with responsible labor unions. The two sides certainly had some different motives. Building Trades Council officials hoped to salvage their political leverage, while business moderates sought to defend their own colleagues. They agreed, however, on the evils of extremism in fighting corruption, much as in regulating industrial relations. And both sides "felt more comfortable with the old order in which politics was acknowledged to be a matter of power bloc against power bloc."[45] That old order, although shaken, continued to shape efforts to replace Schmitz. Looking ahead to the fall 1907 election, district attorney Langdon appealed to the major business associations and labor federations to choose a common candidate to run. The Merchants' Association issued a similar appeal, calling on Republican, Democratic, and labor union "parties" to set aside "all personal and partisan consideration" and agree on a single candidate. In the short run, no such collaboration was possible. Both sides spurned Langdon in protest against his continued manipulation of the Board of Supervisors.[46] Like the business community, moreover, the labor movement had its pro-prosecution faction. The Labor Council, and particularly Teamsters' leader Michael Casey and the Sailors' Walter Macarthur, were delighted to see old enemies like Calhoun come under the gun. These splits on both sides made it impossible for business organizations and labor unions to cooperate in the 1907 election. P. H. McCarthy ran on the Union Labor Party ticket, but without united labor backing, and finished a weak second to acting mayor Edward Taylor, who ran as the candidate of the Democratic Party and the "Good Government League." In the election two years later, however, McCarthy showed that he had learned his lesson, cultivating support from the Labor Council along with his own BTC.[47] By this time, moreover, several business groups were willing to rejoin the coalition. Fearing that the city's reputation and trade suffered from the prosecution and political instability, business gave considerable support to the Union Labor Party ticket. Retailers formed a "McCarthy Businessmen's Association," while McCarthy eased the concerns of manufacturers by emphasizing his impeccable credentials as a "business unionist." Even in 1911, with the Union Labor Party in decline and nonpartisan elections required under the new charter, assembling the Good Government League ticket was the work of class representatives acting in concert. The municipal conference preparing the ticket solicited delegates from "all classes and political factions" and specifically set aside three seats for union leaders.[48]

Much as with the campaign against the Chinese and the call for arbitration, then, the response to municipal graft ended up allying "the great middle" against the "anarchists"—whether these were impractically upright businessmen like Phelan or left-leaning unionists like Casey and Macarthur. And here too, it was this middle, rather than the business community, that was identified with civic virtue. Early in the graft scandal, Harris Weinstock made the case for fighting corruption to an appreciative Merchants' Association audience. "With the big businessman a briber and a dealer in corruption; with the typical business man neglectful of his civic duties; with the mass of wage-earners led away by social demagogues and political pirates, wherein . . . lies the hope of our cities?"[49] His answer—more civic spirit!—could have come from the mouth of any Cincinnati businessman. But Weinstock's indictment was careful to make labor agitators *and* big business the culprits. And his appeal for civic unity, like his plan for industrial arbitration, called for the collaboration of "typical" businessmen with responsible union leaders like McCarthy. The 1909 election appeared to put that coalition back in power. It would be defeated for the final time two years later, during a realignment in political and class relations that put an end to San Francisco's practical corporatism.

A THIRD CASE: SAN FRANCISCO'S HISTORICAL REVERSAL, 1911–16

In June 1916, four thousand San Francisco dockworkers joined a Pacific Coast waterfront strike for higher wages and overtime pay. The Waterfront Employers'

Union, in an effort to unload cargo, recruited non-union labor, housing them in floating barracks to keep them away from unionists. But strikebreakers could not be fully quarantined, and their confrontations with strikers sometimes turned violent. San Francisco's revitalized Chamber of Commerce soon weighed in, denouncing unionists for violating existing contracts and for disrupting the city's commerce. The solution, according to the chamber, was the open shop. Employers required the right to hire union or non-union men, as they pleased.[50] Nor would the chamber any longer accept arbitration as a solution for the disputes of that summer. Concerned that labor and capital appeared to be squaring off for a destructive fight, Mayor Rolph proposed a familiar San Francisco expedient. The labor federations and the Chamber of Commerce would each choose five members to speak for labor and capital, and Archbishop Edward Hanna would select a neutral bloc of five clergymen to "act as a balance." This arrangement, Rolph predicted, would avert industrial warfare. The Labor Council, the Waterfront Federation, and the Building Trades Council all endorsed Rolph's proposal. Organized businessmen refused. The Restaurant Owners' Association's spokesman declared that they had reached "the conclusion that they [could] operate only as open shops." The Chamber of Commerce's Board of Directors unanimously endorsed the same principled objections to arbitration. Unions, President Frederick Koster allowed, had every right to exist. Unionism as practiced in San Francisco, however, no longer served the public interest. In these disputes, Koster continued, "the issues are the open shop against the closed shop; the maintenance of law and order . . . against violence, coercion, [and] intimidation. . . . These issues are not arbitrable."[51]

Koster and his colleagues did their best to put these new principles into practice. In response to the waterfront strike, they organized a "Law and Order Committee" within the Chamber of Commerce, echoing business vigilance committees from San Francisco's early years. The committee sought an injunction against the strikers and hired private guards to protect scabs. It also pressured employer associations on the front line of the waterfront battle to insist on the right to hire non-union labor as a condition for taking strikers back. That position prevailed, and strikers returned to work in late July. The committee also contributed funds to support employers in battles over the open shop among culinary workers and structural iron workers.[52] And it waged a campaign to curb union power by force of law, putting an antipicketing ordinance on the November 1916 ballot. The campaign wove together calls for local patriotism, law and order, and an end to union coercion. A full-page newspaper ad appearing shortly before the election illustrates the committee's approach. According to the ad, "picketing invariably leads to violence. . . . There is no such thing as PEACEFUL picketing any more than there can be LAWFUL lynching."

Then followed an itemization of beatings and verbal abuse by picketers in the culinary workers' and longshoremen's strikes. The ad neatly juxtaposed the community's welfare against class conflict ("the public streets must not be used for private strife") and urged all "patriotic citizens" to protect themselves and serve the city by voting for the ordinance.[53] By a sound margin, the measure passed.

The year 1916 marks a break with San Francisco's practical corporatism. In matters of industrial relations, a broadly based organization of businessmen now declared the open shop, rather than unionism, to be necessary for advancing the city's interests. Advocates of the open shop also prevailed politically, by framing unions as a threat to law and order. The only familiar feature of the 1916 offensive was that, like its predecessors in 1901 and 1904, it failed to drive unions from strongholds. Unfortunately for San Francisco labor, this time failure reflected little more than bad timing. The tremendous wartime expansion in local manufacturing once more gave labor unions the upper hand. But it also shifted the center of labor power from construction to metalworkers in shipbuilding and munitions, workers who were newer to "responsible" unionism. By the time the boom ended in 1919, employers had had ample opportunity to confirm that powerful unions, even under conservative leadership, could not be relied on to impose discipline on the labor force. Businessmen took up where they had left off in 1916, defeating longshoremen in 1919, imposing the open shop in the metal trades in 1920, and breaking unionism in the building trades a year later. They did so through some new organizations, notably the Industrial Association. Many of the key actors, however, had familiar faces. Chamber of Commerce activists figured prominently in the postwar offensive; large firms with national ties also played leading roles, as they had in 1901.[54]

Did San Francisco thus follow along the same path as Cincinnati, but twenty years behind? Certainly not. The city's business community pursued a course all its own between the 1880s and the early 1910s, one never covered by Cincinnati. That alternative path, as I argued in chapters 2 and 4, was rooted in features of local race relations, labor power, and employer organization that had no counterparts in Cincinnati. The business community's reorientation in the years before World War I should not be viewed as delayed development, but as historical reversal. Treating this reversal as a distinct case reveals that the causal factors at work in the city's new trajectory are consistent with my account of the earlier one. In the period after 1911, changes in race relations, labor power, and civic organization are crucial influences on business class alignments; salient problems, organizational settings, and critical events lock in businessmen's civic identities; and business citizenship supports a righteous anti-unionism.

Toward Unity

The Chinese, joined by the Japanese in the early 1900s, continued to be the victims of scapegoating and segregation in early-twentieth-century San Francisco. Organized labor took the lead, working to deny both groups employment and lobbying to extend to other Asians the laws that barred Chinese immigration. White San Franciscans, including many businessmen, also continued to confine Asians to specific residential areas and schools. What had changed was that racial antagonisms no longer redirected industrial conflict as they had in the 1870s and 1880s. The industries which relied most heavily on Chinese labor—especially those making shoes and cigars—went into sharp decline, and trade union opposition largely succeeded in keeping Asian workers out of industrial jobs. As a result, frictions over de-skilling or increasing concentration of capital came less and less frequently to throw small proprietors and skilled workers together in "white" opposition to large firms. This particular obstacle to business unity had been lowered.[55]

The character of San Francisco labor's power also changed after 1911. Unions retained their full strength in the workplace through World War I, and this unavoidable fact still divided conciliatory employers from aspiring open shoppers. Politically, however, labor disarmed, abandoning the Union Labor Party and entering a Progressive coalition behind Mayor Rolph. To some extent, they were pushed. By 1911, the Union Labor Party had been discredited by corruption and by the listless mayoral administration of the Building Trade Council's P. H. McCarthy. Faced with a choice between McCarthy and the charismatic Rolph, a sizable minority of San Francisco workers bolted and contributed to Rolph's overwhelming victory in 1911. Other considerations pulled labor into Progressive politics. Rolph, despite being a wealthy shipper, had a record of cooperating with unions and criticizing partisans of the open shop. In office, too, he scrupulously avoided giving city support to belligerent employers. And statewide, the policy of supporting Progressives paid off. Under Governor Hiram Johnson, labor won laws that they had long and unsuccessfully sought, including the eight-hour day for women and workmen's compensation.[56] These gains came at a high price, however. For San Francisco labor—and the labor movement nationwide under Woodrow Wilson—hitching their fortunes to Progressives also meant sharing their defeats, most dramatically after World War I. The 1911 electoral realignment under Rolph also created new opportunities for San Francisco capital. He promised changes long sought by business reformers, which included adopting the principle that technical expertise, not partisan affiliation, would be the basis for government appointments and policy making. And even businessmen indifferent to Rolph's reform platform welcomed an end to the Union Labor Party's "class rule."[57]

Beyond electoral politics, new challenges gave local businessmen other reasons to rally together. In the short term, the 1906 earthquake and fire was the occasion for many solemn declarations that businessmen should put selfish interests aside for the sake of rebuilding. Businessmen were also spurred to unite by the realization that San Francisco faced increasing competition for new investment from rival West Coast cities, and San Francisco appeared to be losing that competition to upstarts like Los Angeles. Nothing about these challenges ensured that merchants and manufacturers would agree on new standards of good citizenship. But increasingly, new organizations institutionalized those standards and brought diverse businessmen together on their behalf.

Signs of change appear as early as 1904, when the committee to plan for the Panama Pacific International Exposition was first organized. Although small in membership, the committee built a broader base through mass meetings to raise funds and generate enthusiasm for its projects. First among them was preparing for the 1915 exposition, but the committee also played a leading role in cultural improvement (notably, construction of the opera house), creation of a new civic center, and promotion of the gospel of government efficiency. By focusing attention on these issues, the exposition committee provided a rallying point and helped redefine businessmen's responsibilities as quasi-public leaders of the community. Like Cincinnati's Commercial Club and Business Men's Club, moreover, the committee popularized a vision of civic improvement as a classless, nonpartisan enterprise.[58]

A clearer shift in patterns of business organization came in 1911, with the reconstruction of San Francisco's Chamber of Commerce. The new body merged the city's four leading business organizations, the old Chamber of Commerce, the Merchants' Association, the Downtown Association, and the Merchants' Exchange, and it claimed an initial membership of two thousand. By mid-1916, following an energetic recruitment campaign and the stimulus provided by the waterfront strike, the chamber boasted a roster of six thousand. It also merged the functions, previously divided among specialized organizations, of commercial development, political reform, and civic improvement. With its broad business constituency and expansive agenda, the new chamber put members to work on many of the same kinds of activities long pursued in Cincinnati. These included efforts to systematize philanthropy, foster cultural institutions like the symphony, improve municipal efficiency, and extend vocational education programs. In one striking symbol of reunification under the mantle of civic patriotism, the chamber even gave a warm welcome to William Sproule, president of the much-loathed Southern Pacific, as he recited the company's many and valuable contributions to San Francisco's progress.[59]

From Practical Corporatism to Business Citizenship

By 1916, then, the conditions that supported practical corporatism had come undone. Organized labor had demobilized as an independent political force after 1911, opting instead to join a cross-class Progressive coalition. Around the same time, businessmen had begun organizing more broadly under the banner of class-less civic betterment. And the city's relative economic fortunes were of growing concern. In these altered circumstances, manufacturers and merchants were born again as business citizens, with a corresponding reframing of unions as threats to the public good. As in Cincinnati, business citizenship was hardly new. The reframing of identities and enemies is better thought of as a selective appropria-tion of existing cultural scripts. As businessmen organized in new ways amid new threats and opportunities, what had been a minority discourse in San Francisco came to be more widely adopted.

Reframing the public interest involved not changes in specific policies so much as a shift in the reigning model for the proper relationship between class and governance. The once-dominant view of organized class representation as essential to the public interest—or at least to public peace—retreated. The major business organizations instead came to depict government as a neutral agency standing above class conflict and partisanship. This shift can be seen in preparations for the 1915 Panama Pacific International Exposition. Exposition committee members took care not to directly antagonize labor, even quashing calls for the open shop on exposition construction sites. But they also made an important distinction. On the one hand, the committee informally conceded union conditions on construction work. On the other, committee leaders refused to put those concessions into a signed contract. As a *public* body, President Moore insisted, the committee could not give organized labor any official recognition or preference over non-union labor.[60] By denying formal recognition to organized labor, Moore detached the public interest from class representation—even while identifying the exposition committee, composed almost exclusively of business leaders, with the higher public good.

That reinterpretation of class and citizenship became more explicit in com-mentary on industrial relations. Here businessmen forthrightly yoked community needs to their own goals. And here they reframed union rights as not merely dif-ferent from but opposed to the public interest. The Merchants' and Manufacturers' Association was one voice linking San Francisco's faltering economic position to self-serving unions. There was a "small percentage of our total population who are inclined to obstruct" new industry, the association charged, and that small percent-age consisted of union leaders. The path to renewed growth seemed clear, and the association proposed to lead the way. It would "oppose restriction of output, sympathetic strikes, lockouts and boycotts" and "secure for employers and employees the freedom of individual contract." Frederick Koster, speaking on behalf of the far more influential Chamber of Commerce, endorsed the same view. Businessmen had to free the city from the "industrial and political disease" of union control, control which had "throttle[d] the commercial freedom of San Francisco."[61]

Amid the 1916 waterfront strike, the Chamber of Commerce portrayed unions as threatening the public interest in a second way, by endangering "law and order." This is a venerable charge in American business rhetoric, dating back at least to the citizens' committees and the law and order leagues that proliferated in response to the strikes of 1877 and 1886.[62] San Francisco, in this respect as in so many others, had defied U.S. norms in the 1890s and early 1900s. The city's own "Law and Order League" in 1905 dedicated itself to mediating between unions and employers in order to resolve disputes. In the years leading up to World War I, however, businessmen increasingly voiced doubts about union leaders' reliability. And during both the waterfront strike and the campaign to limit picketing, they branded unions as the source of damage to persons and property.

Unions, then, endangered both commercial development and law and order. These public goods, moreover, stood above class. Putting an end to picketing, for example, was "not a class question, but one of civic decency."[63] And who better to defend classless civic decency but organized capital? No group could be more "safely trusted with public responsibilities," the chamber's executive officer assured diners at the inaugural banquet, and "none is more respected." The aim, according to Koster, was "to establish by the influence and work of a united citizenship the power necessary for San Francisco's advancement commensurate with her greatness. It requires only sufficient local patriotism to substitute order for disorder, and reason, common sense, and action for negligence, indifference, and inertia."[64] Applying this script specifically to industrial relations, Koster neatly equated business associations, the public interest, and freedom from unions. "The position of the Chamber of Commerce could hardly be misunderstood. It resolves itself down to one thing—the maintenance of Law and Order. That is all . . . the maintenance of the principle of the Open Shop amounts to."[65]

The Chamber of Commerce played a key role in this reorientation of business discourse. It had a broad membership of local merchants and manufacturers; it had an organizational commitment to civic uplift; and it provided a platform for ideological entrepreneurs like Koster to define civic uplift in particular ways. His success in doing so also owed a great deal to two serendipitous events. The immediate spur to a renewed open shop drive came from the waterfront strike. That strike combined several challenges to San Francisco employers' customary tolerance. First, waterfront employees refused to handle materials made by non-union labor. That insistence on closed shop conditions, backed by the threat of a boycott, went beyond what local employers considered legitimate union behavior. Second, the strike took place in violation of an existing contract. In the past, pragmatic businessmen had accepted union power in part because unions generally had conservative leadership and acted as a stabilizing force. This strike may have persuaded many moderate employers that they could no longer count on responsible unionism. Third, by tying up San Francisco's waterfront, the strike appeared to confirm what veterans of unsuccessful open shop drives in the past had argued, namely that unions put the city's commercial development at risk. More important was the bombing at San Francisco's July 22 Preparedness Day parade. The bombing outraged San Franciscans of all classes. But it was used with great skill by Koster's Law and Order Committee to rally opinion against unions as threats to public peace. Launching a "Committee of 100" local notables on behalf of "decent citizenship," Koster and his colleagues presented the bombing as just the latest example of union violence. "Recent disturbances upon the water front were accompanied by violence. Intimidation was practiced on merchants and their employees and an intolerable situation resulted. . . . This spirit of lawlessness in the community logically terminated in the damnable bomb outrage on Saturday." The Law and Order Committee did its best to keep that logic in the public view—even by suppressing evidence exonerating Tom Mooney for the bombing.[66]

San Francisco between 1911 and 1916 thus confirms arguments made in earlier chapters. The cumulative historical sequence that inhibited business unity before 1911 (described in chapter 2) was itself reversed. Race relations no longer put the interests of capitalists at loggerheads. Labor's switch from independent party to Progressive coalition opened the door to a political rhetoric of classless municipal improvement. Having to deal with relative economic decline made that rhetoric particularly useful. And through the 1915 exposition committee's mass meetings and the reconstructed Chamber of Commerce, businessmen came together in organizational settings where the gospel of civic uplift was constantly preached and often practiced. Those settings, in turn, were a key factor in the reconfiguration of businessmen's public personae. Much as we saw in chapter 4, the character of challenges, the organizational means to meet them, and the opportunistic use of fortuitous events locked in new identities. After 1911, however, that path-dependent selection favored business citizenship. Businessmen increasingly had to confront economic slowdown; they did so under the leadership of the new Chamber of Commerce; and that leadership successfully keynoted the 1916 waterfront strike and parade bombing to rally local capital against "class rule." With business citizenship triumphant, finally, local capital turned against unions at work, decisively marking an end to San Francisco exceptionalism.

CONCLUSIONS

This book identified sharp contrasts between two cities in businessmen's solidarity, civic discourse, and views of labor. Each part of the book took up the corresponding puzzle. How did businessmen with varied interests achieve substantial unity in Cincinnati while their San Francisco counterparts remained divided? Why did these two business communities take republican tradition in such different directions, especially in the ways they distinguished good government, and good citizens, from bad ones? How did public ideologies show up at work, favoring a virulent anti-unionism in Cincinnati (as in most of the United States) and a seemingly un-American accommodation with unions in San Francisco? Although bourgeois solidarity, civic discourse, and views of labor were all aspects of class formation in these cases, it was useful to analytically distinguish the three and treat them in separate chapters. The introductions to each part of the book connected these questions to wider comparative and historical debates about U.S. bourgeois solidarity (were American capitalists unusually fragmented?), class discourse (did Gilded Age businessmen set themselves apart in championing the virtues of individual self-interest and laissez-faire policy?), and management ideology (why have U.S. employers been so insistent on unilateral control and so hostile to unions?).

My conclusion translates the three puzzles back into the theoretical framework developed in the introduction. The development of common organization and ideology among capitalists illustrates generic problems in the study of social movements and social inequality. Why do individuals come to organize and act together on the basis of particular shared attributes—work situation, nationality, residence, religion, sexual preference—rather than in other alignments, on other common grounds? How do some identities and frames—cultural scripts for identifying who we are and what distinguishes us from others—prevail over other ways of drawing boundaries and endowing those boundaries with meaning? The application of bourgeois ideology to work, in turn, illustrates the broader question of transposition. Under what conditions does a set of identities and frames cultivated in one institutional context get applied in others? Although there are no all-purpose answers to these questions, here I advocated two starting points for analysis. One is to think in terms of a path-dependent process in which wider menus are winnowed down and particular social alignments and identities locked in over time. The second is to pay particular attention to organizational contexts. Here neoinstitutionalism joins the literature on social movements and class formation. Institutions selectively group individuals and construct common interests among them; they foster particular identities and frames and embed them in organizational routines; and the identities they favor *may* make social actors particularly effective carriers of cultural scripts across institutional settings. Applying each of these guidelines to Cincinnati and San Francisco illuminated social mechanisms that might appear in a wider range of cases.[1]

Consider, first, bourgeois class formation. I argued that we can recognize class formation when collective action or cultural practices line up with economic positions. That alignment involves a twofold movement. On one side, concerted action or similarities in lifestyle *across* class lines diminish; on the other, they extend among individuals of similar economic rank. Applying this standard to particular cases will not produce an unequivocal conclusion that class formation either did or did not happen. Businessmen may have little in common with manual workers in the character and location of their homes, but still watch the same TV programs; they may come together through service organizations, but continue to vote or pray in different ways. Here comparison simplifies matters. By juxtaposing two or more cases and focusing attention on particular collective actions and cultural practices, we can at least identify clear differences in patterns of class formation and attempt to explain them. The comparison of Cincinnati and San Francisco highlighted particularly stark differences in the character of joint organization and relations with labor. Cincinnati merchants and manufacturers moved from organization on the basis of sector and trade to more inclusive, citywide association. They also acted together to enforce open shops in most industries. Their San Francisco counterparts showed far less unity. The city's manufacturers more often stood apart from merchant-led civic groups, at times favoring instead cross-class organizations to fight the Chinese or boost the local economy. And far from rallying together against labor, industrial relations divided an accommodating majority of smaller firms from a handful of aggressively open shop corporations. Voluntary associations and labor rela-tions do not, of course, exhaust the categories of "collective action and cultural practices." There are indications, however, that the comparative picture in these areas extends to others. In Cincinnati, late-nineteenth-century cultural boundar-ies, institutionalized in musical societies and embedded in canons of taste, also brought varied economic elites together and distinguished them from wage earn-ers. Cultural markers of class difference are less evident in San Francisco, with arbiters of good taste frequently decrying the poor manners and indifference to high culture displayed by wealthy city residents.

The differences between these cases are clear. The puzzle is to explain them, and here orthodox accounts of class formation offer little help. We certainly find many of the economic transformations commonly thought to divide classes. Firms grew larger and production saw advances in technology and the division of labor. And however slowly and unevenly, these changes weakened personal ties between employers and employees, increased friction over work practices, and widened the gap in wealth and authority between the few and the many. Class differences in economic resources, in turn, supported polarization in other areas: businessmen moved to affluent hilltop communities, for example, while most workers stayed behind in the city basin. The obvious objection to this narrative is that similar trends can be found in San Francisco, from changes in manufac-turing methods to shifts in residence. The conclusion comes as no surprise: as is often remarked of workers, changes in economic circumstances are not sufficient conditions for class formation.

Differences in class formation between Cincinnati and San Francisco, I ar-gued, are better explained using tools from the literature on social movements. One such tool has been developed in studies of recruitment, which examine how the relative salience of competing affiliations encourages or blocks mobilization. For example, an individual's changing social networks may detach her from the restraints of some ties (such as to parents or to a conservative church) and con-nect her to activist communities. Over time, such shifts in social ties can lead to closer identification with and reliance on fellow activists, together with an escalating willingness to take risks for the cause.[2] The social movement literature also emphasizes the importance of interaction over time between challengers and elites, as initial responses by authorities—repressive or co-opting, resolute or vacillating, united or divided—alter the course of mobilization, such as by nar-rowing or expanding the breadth of opposition.[3] The same point can be turned around to focus on elites, whose organizational efforts, coalitions, and strategic choices will be shaped by the perceived character of threats from below. What is perhaps clearer in class formation than in most studies of social movements is the long-term, path-dependent quality of this interaction, as social ties and strategic responses called forth at one time become reinforced by and embedded in formal organizations and procedures.

This checklist of influences on social movement mobilization guided my comparison of class formation in Cincinnati and San Francisco. A short version of that account starts with the relative salience of competing group ties (class versus race), continues with the interaction of elites and challengers (weaker or stronger labor movements), and concludes with the feedback effects of business organization (general civic associations versus trade-based organizations to deal with labor). It turned out that the economic transformations which appeared to offer little explanatory leverage did matter, but as mediated by race. De-skilling, the division of labor, and the increasing scale of production fueled conflicts in both cases. In San Francisco, however, the interaction of demographic and industrial change redirected those conflicts. Instead of workers generally and employers collectively squaring off over the powers and privileges of skill, the position of the Chinese in key industries created common ground for white craftsmen and smaller proprietors in opposition to large factories and degraded Chinese labor. This racial dynamic was one key factor favoring the persistence of cross-class ties in San Francisco, as compared with the cleaner class divisions of Cincinnati labor relations. It also fostered particularly strong unions in San Francisco, as white workers of varied skills and ethnic backgrounds joined forces against the Chinese. Conflict between a powerful labor movement and business elites might be expected to polarize social relations along class lines. Instead, strong and aggressive unions further divided San Francisco employers. They did so directly, as businesses insulated from competitive pressures and vulnerable to union reprisals made their peace, while larger firms in national markets chafed under union standards and their inability to rally fellow businessmen behind the open shop. They did so indirectly, as manufacturers formed trade associations to deal with their better-organized workers. The importance of this institutional path becomes clear in comparative perspective. The challenges faced by Cincinnati employers in the 1880s and 1890s appeared to come more from economic decline and urban disorder—exemplified by the Court House riot and political corruption—than from unions, and their most important organizational efforts focused on these concerns.

The final piece in my account of class formation stressed the implications of these divergent organizational moves. They mattered, in part, because they grouped businessmen differently. Cincinnati's business clubs enlisted a broad cross-section of the city's proprietors, while San Francisco's manufacturers, underrepresented in reform associations, organized in separate trades to cope with labor. Organizational settings mattered, too, because of their different agenda. Cincinnati's civic clubs directed members' attention away from divisive short-term interests and toward such putative common goals as cultural uplift and administrative reform. San Francisco's businessmen, by contrast, were more actively involved in organizations that highlighted their labor market interests vis-à-vis unions—interests which divided them from other groups of businessmen.

Contrasts in the ways that businessmen organized among themselves and related to labor tell only part of the story of bourgeois class formation. Part 2 turned to bourgeois discourse, examining differences in businessmen's construction of boundaries and definition of civic identities. One goal was to show how this boundary work complemented the class alignments described in part 1. We saw Cincinnati businessmen drawing invidious distinctions on the basis of cultural worth and civic merit, distinctions that coincided with class divisions. In this cultural work, they adapted republican traditions in particular ways. They lionized the engaged individual citizen who stood above class and demonstrated independent character and reasoned judgment, in contrast to the selfish, the gullible, and the irrational. The latter traits they associated with manual workers and immigrants, men who lined up for the political machine or got swept up in mobs. San Francisco proprietors took republicanism in a different direction. Emphasizing the importance of independent citizenship, they drew boundaries against the Chinese for their economic debasement and political servility—but also against the monopolies that corrupted government and overrode the voice of the people. This discourse celebrated not a cultural elite of leading citizens but a virtuous middle class encompassing white labor and small business.

Part 2 also contrasted the very different civic ideologies to which Cincinnati's businessmen and a majority of San Francisco's proprietors subscribed. Mirroring elite boundary work against the rabble, Cincinnati's businessmen constructed a class identity around standards of good citizenship. They claimed for themselves the virtues of nonpartisanship, professed their responsibility for civic leadership, and identified their own interests with those of the city as a whole. This ideology, I argued, was both widely shared and institutionalized in local business clubs. And even while it forcefully rejected the relevance or legitimacy of class in social life, this collective identity deserves the label "class consciousness." No such consensual civic ideology, embodied in broadly representative civic associations, is to be found among San Francisco businessmen. Particularly from the late 1890s into the early 1910s, however, a majority of them subscribed to a practical corporatism. They recognized class as the most important axis for conflict at work and in politics. They allowed for a civic good independent of either labor or capital, one best served when each side was compactly organized, responsibly led, and firmly committed to resolving differences through peaceful negotiations. That matter-of-fact acceptance of class representation smoothed the way for collective bargaining in labor relations and corporatist consultation in municipal politics.

But it also divided conciliatory employers from those whose market position or ideological commitments pitted them against unions.

In accounting for these differences, my general sociological approach began by noting that a broad but not inexhaustible repertoire of ideological tools is available to make sense of challenges, draw social boundaries, and construct public identities. Ann Swidler's "tool kit" analogy is appropriate, with two caveats. First, it may underestimate the range of options. Even single "tools" like republicanism can be honed and deployed in quite different ways. Second, the analogy may overestimate the freedom with which actors choose their tools.[4] The alternative is not to impute internalized cultural directives, but rather to identify external constraints on the selection of tools. And in assessing those constraints, a different metaphor—that of path dependency—also proves useful, directing attention to historical influences, moving in different temporal rhythms, that winnow out some tools and lock in others, tracing a path from wide repertoire to specific performance.

The particular forces selecting identities and frames will vary from one case to another. For the Cincinnati and San Francisco bourgeoisies, I emphasized the role of salient problems, keynoting events, and organizational contexts for action. The relative prominence of economic decline and "boss rule" as compared with powerful unions and despotic monopolies meant that Cincinnati and San Francisco businessmen had quite different problems on their plates. These were not the inventions of cultural discourse. Instead, they both shaped understandings of what needed to be done and steered businessmen into civic or industrial organization. Early moves in each direction were reinforced by critical events. The Court House riot of 1884 traumatized Cincinnati elites, underscoring their sense that political corruption and mob violence were the dangers to be confronted. The riot provided a persistent frame through which they later interpreted new events (for example, was this or that disturbance a Court House riot-in-the-making?). The failure of San Francisco's 1896 Charter Reform campaign and the 1901 Employers' Association lockout—each defeated by organized labor—similarly locked in an understanding that working-class power was the key challenge for business leaders, and one not to be solved by either ignoring or trying to defeat unions. Institutional settings reinforced these divergent paths. The most important sites for collective organization among Cincinnati businessmen were associations that privileged general civic issues and actively engaged members in those matters, even if they had initially come for the wine, cigars, and good company. San Francisco businessmen, and especially the city's manufacturers, were of necessity more involved in trade-based organizations dedicated to labor relations. With the key problems defined in these ways, underscored by critical events, and dealt with through these organizations, business citizenship and practical corporatism "worked" as public identities and interpretive frames. And much as it may become increasingly costly to reverse earlier economic choices, "investments" in these civic identities and frames discouraged backsliding. The status that came to active members of Cincinnati's business clubs, for example, stigmatized overt displays of narrow self-interest. Industry-wide agreements with unions, similarly, would reinforce a commitment to effective organization on both sides in order to enforce its terms.

The factors narrowing the choices from wider discursive menus do not necessarily fall into neat temporal sequences—salient problems coming before keynoting events, events before organization, and so forth. Nor is it possible to measure the relative causal weights of what is present (or lacking) in the cultural tool kit, of events that keynote particular problems, and of the organizational settings in which actors tackle those problems. What I have tried to do instead is construct an analytical narrative of cumulative causation which is consistent *both* with differences between cases and the sequence of business mobilization over time within each case. And here too, the explanatory approach bridges studies of social movements and theories of class formation. In its more flexible form, class analysis also begins with multiple possibilities. The question is not just whether class formation will "happen" or not, but in what social contexts, involving which specific class fractions, and along what ideological lines. Social movement scholars, similarly, are agnostic as to whether or not aggrieved individuals will mobilize collectively, in what particular alliances, and on the basis of what animating identities and diagnostic frames. Some of the influences on mobilization, moreover, mirror those at work in bourgeois class formation. Movement organizers, like business leaders, pitch particular interpretations of and remedies for social problems.[5] Some of these interpretations may be powerfully boosted by events (the use of troops against peaceful demonstrators, for example) which seem to confirm some diagnoses of the situation and discredit others. Whether potential participants actually join in protest, in turn, depends in part on their formal and informal social ties. If those ties bring them into contact with activists, in the company of friends, and distance them from competing obligations and inhibitions, they will be moved toward participation in two ways. First, they will get regular exposure to the movement's interpretive framework. Second, they will have the social support needed to take on the risks of protest. And in good path-dependent fashion, initial forays into movement activities and organizations can lock in early choices by forging bonds and constructing identities that participants become reluctant to give up. Institutionalized networks can play a similar role in class formation. Civic organizations and industrial associations connected businessmen in particular ways (across sectors or to fellow brewers or shoe manufacturers); defined particular agendas (cultural uplift or collective bargaining); and supported particular definitions of a worthy member (the engaged citizen or the responsible employer). In these ways, they helped lock in different public identities.

These mechanisms for the path-dependent selection of cultural scripts help explain why social actors adopted certain identities and frames, and not others. They are less relevant to the puzzle addressed in part 3: Why do scripts sometimes transpose across institutions? Sociologists remind us that collective identities and interpretive frames deployed in one context (such as politics) need not have any relevance in another (such as industrial relations). Historians make Gilded Age businessmen a case in point. They allegedly erected a high wall between political and economic relations: what might be appropriate in government, such as democratic participation, played no legitimate role in the exercise of property rights. Yet we found that some scripts did cross the boundary between politics and work. In Cincinnati, the standards businessmen used to define their civic identities and measure the corresponding worth of others reappeared in the ways they celebrated local industry, trained and evaluated employees, and stigmatized unions. For San Francisco employers, similarly, the formula used to justify class representation at work applied as well to municipal politics.

How to explain these transpositions? For San Francisco, neoinstitutionalists have a ready answer. They emphasize the "logics of appropriateness"[6] that govern the applicability of cultural scripts across institutions. If the logics are not *too* different, actors may make use of "foreign" scripts as they pursue their interests in new settings. In San Francisco, logics of appropriateness converged because of similar alignments of class actors, in similar relations of power, in both industrial relations and politics. A common script of practical corporatism readily applied in each sphere. This neoinstitutionalist argument can be seen as encompassing a familiar claim about working-class formation. Where wage earners find themselves subordinated both in the state (denied the vote) and at work (denied the right to join unions or contest management authority), they are more likely to develop class consciousness, or what in institutionalist terms might be described as a single interpretive frame for diagnosing exploitation throughout society. For San Francisco businessmen, confronting powerful unions both at work and in electoral politics fostered a similarly pervasive script for defining who were legitimate social actors and how best to manage their relations. A quite different mechanism accounts for transposition in Cincinnati. There, the key was not similarly aligned institutions but generalized identities. Through their participation in the city's civic clubs, businessmen acted out the same code of good citizenship, in company with many of the same fellow actors, as they boosted the economy, reformed city government, sponsored high culture, and claimed social status. The dense and multivalent social networks built into Cincinnati's business associations, then, not only bridged differences among capitalists (part 1) and locked in a particular civic ideology (part 2). They also made businessmen effective carriers of cultural scripts, with an all-purpose identity exercised in a wide range of social tasks. A hat that fit so well as they moved from promoting investment to fighting Boss Cox and subscribing to art museums was not cast off as they turned their attention to labor.

This interpretation of transposition in Cincinnati might appear to confirm the virtues of social capital. Local businessmen transcended parochial interests and narrowly bounded solidarities through participation in citywide civic associations. And although Putnam does not explain why social capital generated in one association or another should spread its beneficent influences elsewhere,[7] I have offered one reason: that the character of businessmen's collective identities made them especially capable carriers of the civic gospel from one institution to another. As applied to labor relations, however, the portable script of good citizenship loses its charm, having fueled a virulent anti-unionism. If cooperation and at least a wary trust in labor relations are measures of civic virtue, we find it not in Cincinnati but among San Francisco's relatively disengaged businessmen. Practical corporatism was neither a high-minded nor an enthusiastically embraced creed. And if business citizenship had a dark underside of anti-unionism, practical corporatism grew out of a long causal sequence that included racist mobilization against the Chinese. Yet San Francisco businessmen could be surprisingly reasonable, by U.S. standards, in their relations with labor. As long as unions remained vigilant in politics as well as the workplace, most employers conceded the value of a rough equity in class power, whether in setting wages or deciding matters of public policy. Had the status quo held in the labor movement, this practical corporatism might have become more firmly locked in place by the accretion of organizations and procedures for joint consultation. And to stretch out this counterfactual still further, San Francisco's recipe for class relations might have proved more resilient than the New Deal alternative. The latter system lodged collective bargaining in firms rather than industries and based representation rights on voting individuals rather than the constituents of an organized class.[8] These characteristics made the New Deal system particularly fragile. It was especially vulnerable to global competition, because plant-based bargaining pitted each employer's need for flexibility against unionism itself. And it made it more difficult to retain collective bargaining rights as employers began to actively contest NLRB elections. Practical corporatism promises an alternative. By conceding class representation, it gives unions more security, yet also allows individual employers some managerial discretion so long as they adhere to the general terms of industry-wide agreements.[9]

That rosy scenario, of course, was never put to the test. Developments in San Francisco after 1911 offer, instead, a test of my comparative arguments. As the final section of chapter 6 showed, the city moved in the direction of Cincinnati—and the rest of the country—between 1911 and 1916. This was not a matter of San Francisco, having gotten a late start, finally catching up. The city's businessmen had followed a different trajectory altogether before 1911, organizing and interpreting class relations in ways never seen in Cincinnati. The period after 1911 is better viewed as a historical reversal, but the reasons for that reversal are consistent with the account of Cincinnati. They also affirm the usefulness of social movement and neoinstitutionalist insights when assessing class formation, class identities, and cultural transposition. Consider, first, bourgeois unity. San Francisco's "exceptional" class alignments, I argued, emerged from the intertwining of racial cleavages and industrial change, the political and economic clout of labor, and the detachment of many businessmen from civic organizations. In the sociological language of this chapter, the key differences from Cincinnati involved the relative weight of competing social cleavages, the character of challenges faced by businessmen, and the organizational settings in which they addressed those challenges. It is useful to have a well-matched case to further assess the argument, and San Francisco between 1911 and 1916 offers such a case. By 1911, racial divisions were more marginal to relations *among employers.* Although unions remained formidable adversaries in the workplace, labor's independent political influence suffered with the demise of the ULP and unions' entrance into a Progressive alliance with Mayor Rolph. Particularly in the aftermath of the 1906 earthquake, moreover, businessmen were increasingly preoccupied with the challenge of maintaining San Francisco's economic supremacy on the West Coast as rival cities like Los Angeles, Portland, and Seattle gained ground, and as many manufacturers opted to rebuild across the bay in Oakland. The launching of a broadly representative business organization in 1911, the revamped Chamber of Commerce, was in part a response to these new challenges. The chamber, in turn, helped unify the city's bourgeoisie both through its expanded agenda and its aggressive membership drives over the next five years.

The new Chamber of Commerce also selectively favored a different public identity for its members. The image of San Francisco businessmen as leading citizens, tirelessly working for the city's good without regard for class interests, had long been part of the local repertoire, associated particularly with the Merchants' Association. So long as proprietors had to regularly deal with unions at work and labor representatives in government, however, that image could not crowd out practical corporatism. Business citizenship was boosted by organized efforts to rebuild from the earthquake and prepare for the 1915 exposition. The reborn Chamber of Commerce, both in its practical activities and its official discourse, further promoted and popularized this civic identity. And in that way it also played a role, comparable to Cincinnati's Commercial Club and Business Men's Club, in transposing business citizenship to work. Merging the specialized activities of prior business organizations, it brought under one roof the tasks of economic improvement, political lobbying, and cultural uplift. And the multipurpose language of above-class civic betterment soon turned on unions, increasingly stigmatized as selfish class actors strangling the city's growth and condoning mob violence. These changes in the definition of problems to be solved and in the organization to solve them came together in (and received a final push from) two critical events which "confirmed" the new diagnosis of unions: the June waterfront strike and the July Preparedness Day bombing.

Breaking out these post-1911 developments as a separate case does more than offer a comparative test of the larger argument. It also prompts us to rethink the metaphor of "switch points" in path-dependent historical explanations. The year 1916 appears to be the point at which employers turn, with greater unity, against organized labor. That characterization is misleading, however. It attributes special causal weight to momentary, if also momentous, events, the disruptive June strike and the July 22 parade bombing. This illustrates a more general problem with the metaphor of switch points. The metaphor is typically paired with that of "paths" in path-dependent historical explanations. This style of interpretation has much to recommend it. It helps sociologists think more historically, in terms of causes whose effects turn on their sequence and their combination over time. As I have applied it to collective identities and frames, it also alerts us to the ways in which particular outcomes are selected from broader possibilities and congealed in social organization. And it directs our attention to the interplay of long- and short-term causal forces. But on this last point, the metaphor of path dependency can be misleading, contrasting the short-term serendipitous happenings which set history on a new path, and the long haul, in which various mechanisms lock in a particular historical trajectory.[10] San Francisco reminds us of how old new paths can be. Long-running historical developments, predating any "switches" to a new path, may bequeath viable alternatives which are then spotlighted by events and promoted by opportunistic actors.[11]

In San Francisco, this alternative path in effect reversed the sequence which divided businessmen. The key elements of this reversal were the extrusion of racial cleavages from competitive relations among San Francisco capitalists, labor's retreat from independent politics, and a shift in the constituency and agenda of businessmen's collective organization. These cumulative developments made available certain organizational and discursive resources—a revamped Chamber of Commerce and a widely broadcast language of business citizenship. There remained historical tasks for actors like chamber president Frederick Koster. Along with other chamber leaders, he seized on the waterfront strike in June to drive home San Francisco unions' threat to the city's economy, and through his Law and Order Committee within the Chamber of Commerce, put the organization's resources to work in fighting strikes. The parade bombing and alleged threat from "anarchists" like Mooney provided a further opportunity, eagerly grasped, to discredit militant unions and rally business and middle-class support for the chamber's new path. The reward for businessmen in the short run was passage of an antipicketing ordinance in the November 1916 elections. World War I temporarily stalled this business offensive, but the postwar Industrial Association would finish what the Law and Order Committee began, helping impose the open shop in key industries such as metal working, construction, and shipping in 1919–21. It is impossible to say if this vigorous employer counteroffensive would have happened in the absence of the 1916 strikes and bombing. But it would be a mistake to focus on these critical events to the exclusion of preparatory work done by prior developments in race relations, labor power, and civic organization.[12] Instead of juxtaposing momentary happenings with long-term trajectories, it is important to recognize that such prior historical shifts give the passing event its significance, both to the actors that interpret it and for subsequent change.

To what extent do the conclusions in these three areas—businessmen's unity, civic discourse, and views of labor—apply in our own time? The details, not surprisingly, are quite different, but some of the underlying social mechanisms and cultural themes reappear. Questions of bourgeois unity are now far more important to answer at the national than the local level. Businessmen still organize and act together in cities as well as nationally, but for both the firms and the outcomes that matter most, the local stage does not have the importance it had a century ago. At the national level, however, we can still find comparable mechanisms for transcending parochial viewpoints and conflicting interests—particularly in policy institutions which bring business leaders together, direct their attention to issues affecting more than one industry, and confer honor on those able to take the long, "statesmanlike" view.[13] In part through such institutions, and in part because of perceived challenges from global competition and protracted economic slowdown (a transnational version of Cincinnati's economic decline), there also appears to have been some reconciliation in the 1970s and 1980s between large corporations and smaller employers, factions of capital that had been divided by their different approaches to government regulation and New Deal labor relations.[14]

Under what banner has that reconciliation occurred? Economic and political leaders still draw on the themes of business citizenship. Celebrations of business as conducive to the public good, for example, remain with us, often backed by large tax subsidies from local and state governments eager to attract investments. Charges of "class warfare," similarly, are quick to follow the occasional reminder that government policies often benefit the rich or harm the poor. But Cincinnati proprietors, adapting older republican norms, tightly linked the public contributions of capital to the civic responsibilities of individual entrepreneurs. That link is largely broken in today's neoliberalism. Business still serves the greater good, but through resolute attention to shareholder value[15] rather than through public responsibilities personally shouldered by top executives. And although this ideology is certainly hawked in think tanks and business school curricula, it is not clear that the substance of the ideology can be traced to organizational characteristics of those think tanks or business schools.

Contemporary views of work and unions, too, reflect a mix of legacies from business citizenship and entirely different selections from the cultural repertoire. The late-nineteenth-century Cincinnati employer applied his standards of citizenship in evaluating workers and constructing "the square deal." His late-twentieth-century counterpart also applied to the workplace neoliberalism's celebration of markets untrammeled by the state. Innovative and flexible employers, business magazines preached, slashed bureaucracy, empowered rather than regulated valued workers, and encouraged employees to exercise the freedom—and assume the risks—of entrepreneurship within the context of a large company.[16] As for views of organized labor, current "union avoidance" campaigns draw from an extensive repertoire. They denounce unions, in good neoliberal fashion, as impediments to flexibility and enterprise. But defenders of the "right to work," like earlier business citizens, also shun unions as selfish organizations, concerned more with collecting dues than fostering individual opportunity. And as in a still-older paternalism, unions are depicted as outsiders to the company family.[17] In accounting for these themes in contemporary anti-unionism, however, the primary mechanisms of transposition highlighted in this study are conspicuously absent. Businessmen do not confront a powerful labor movement either in politics or the workplace, much less in both—the institutional convergence seen in San Francisco. Nor is workplace ideology much shaped by businessmen who, like those in Cincinnati, *combine* the roles of civic leader, local property owner, and managing authority within their own firm. Instead, management rhetoric more strongly reflects the training and fashions of professionals and consultants. For these men and women, the influence of civic identity in the workplace is much more remote. Business citizenship thus shapes current thinking about labor not through its transposition to work but through its contributions to our inherited ideological repertoire.

What is missing from that repertoire is San Francisco's practical corporatism. And therein lies one source of pessimism for those who value workers' right to representation. However much readers and authors might prefer to end books on an upbeat note, my account offers a somber reminder that historical reversals do not come easily. We have ample evidence that U.S. employers usually have the upper hand over unions in the absence of strong political counterweights. We know, too, that since the 1960s they have more frequently used that advantage to keep unions out of the workplace. Both their choices and their ability to impose them, in turn, reflect a confluence of global challenges, political opportunities, organizational resources, and inherited frames for making sense of things—each with formidable historical roots and together operating to lock in particular approaches to labor. These are obstacles that cannot be overcome simply by more effective recruitment on the part of a revitalized labor movement, even if more effective recruitment were to become the norm. Nor is it enough to counteract employers' workplace advantages with political power, a strategy that has fostered labor resurgences in the past. What would be necessary is for these things to happen together, and over a sufficiently long time, so that employers could come to accept a different civic ideology—at first grudgingly, and then eventually out of habit and long investment in ancillary organizations and procedures. In the more institutionalist language I have used in this book, there would need to be an alignment of political clout and workplace militancy for long enough to push business thinking onto a new path, granting legitimacy to class representation and class accommodation—something like practical corporatism, without the racist underpinnings. San Francisco suggests it could happen in America. It also reminds us that the odds are long.

Notes

INTRODUCTION

1. *New York Times,* March 16, 2003; PR Newswire Service, September 18, 2006; *New York Times,* March 10, 1996.

2. *New York Times,* November 29, 2000, November 28, 2005; unionfacts.com/ads.cfm, accessed December 16, 2006.

3. Hochschild 1995; Newman 1999; Young 2004; Sandage 2005.

4. Gerteis and Savage 1998; Lamont 2000.

5. Dubofsky 1975; Gutman 1977; Schneirov, Stromquist, and Salvatore 1999.

6. Jacoby 1991; Gerber 1997; Friedman, forthcoming.

7. I regularly refer to these proprietary employers as "businessmen" rather than using gender-neutral terms (such as "business owners"). This is appropriate for two reasons. First, in my archival work, women never appeared as either owners of firms or members of the business organizations that figure prominently in my account. Second, masculinity ("manhood") was itself a prized attribute of the successful entrepreneur and leading citizen. The gendered label is thus consistent with both the facts and the ethos of the period.

8. United States. Census Office, Eleventh Census (1890), Manufactures, xxxv. For more detailed comparative data on the cities' industrial profiles, see the introduction to chapter 2 below.

9. Burawoy 1985, 5.

10. For example, qualitative research continues to find cultural differences—in life style, in cultural capital, in cognitive maps of social inequality—between individuals from working-class and middle-class backgrounds (Kefalas 2003; Holt 2000; Lareau 2003; Ortner 2003). Studies of elites show that class background or class networks still can be the basis for social solidarities (Schwartz 1987; Domhoff 2002). And there is ample evidence that class still shapes government policy, and vice versa, as in the funding and effects of public education (Weir 2002; Aronowitz 2003).

11. These hierarchies may be based on market assets (property, skill), as Weber emphasized, or on organizational position, as Wright (1989) and others have added.

12. Treating class formation as an alignment between cultural practices and economic position echoes Bourdieu's (1993) notion of homologies across fields. One important difference is that I consider these homologies mere possibilities. Cf. Katznelson 1986; Hall 1992.

13. Sklar 1988; Adams 1995; Lipset and Marks 2000.

14. Offe and Wiesenthal 1980. See also Lembcke 1995.

15. Harris 2000; Pearson 2004; Millikan 2001.

16. Hoffecker 1974; Horowitz 1976; Ingham 1978; Couvares 1984; Beckert 2001.

17. Historical studies that answer this description include Jaher (1982); Livingston (1986); Roy (1991); and critics of "corporate liberalism" such as Weinstein (1968); Kolko (1967). Sociologists of the contemporary capitalist class share the same preference: Mintz and Schwartz (1981); Useem (1984); Domhoff (2002).

18. Beckert (2001a) draws the line between the nineteenth-century lower middle class and the "bourgeoisie," with the latter enjoying greater security and freedom from manual

work, as well as larger incomes. The smallest businesses would likely fall below this line, and that social distinction is appropriate for cities like New York, where the firms were bigger and the fortunes larger. My rudimentary distinction between professionals and businessmen on one side and wage earners on the other makes sense for Cincinnati and San Francisco, both characterized by small-to-middling-sized capital. It is also a reasonable starting point because it corresponds to distinctions made by actors at the time. Some taxonomic problems in class analysis (best described by Wright [1989]) are thus of less concern for this study.

19. Surveys include Berlanstein (1993); Joyce (1995); Hall (1997); Lembcke (1995); Portes (2000); Eley and Nield (2000).

20. Katznelson 1981. Keeping an open mind about the content of class discourses means allowing for situations in which workers or businessmen are culturally distinct but do not identify themselves as members of a distinct class—or even, as in Cincinnati, emphatically repudiate such an identity. See Bottero 2004; Savage, Bagnall, and Longhurst 2001.

21. Examples include Sewell (1980); Jones (1982); Rosenzweig (1983); Wilentz (1984); Steinberg (1999).

22. Somers 1997, 88; Steinmetz 1992, 501.

23. Somers 1997; Rose 1997; Steinberg 1996.

24. Recent compilations surveying the state of the art include Aminzade (2001); Meyer, Whittier, and Robnett (2002); Diani and McAdam (2003); Snow, Soule, and Kriesi (2004); Davis et al. (2005).

25. Bettie 2003; Ortner 2003.

26. Melucci 1989; Gamson 1992; Taylor and Whittier 1992; Polletta and Jasper 2001.

27. Snow 1986; Williams and Kubal 1999; Benford and Snow 2000; Snow 2004.

28. The relationship between collective identity and social ranking is addressed less by social movement scholars than by students of inequality, such as Parkin (1979); Bourdieu (1984); Lamont (1992).

29. Theoretical discussions of boundary work include Bourdieu (1984) and Lamont (2000) on class, and Cornell and Hartman (1998) on race. On boundary work and identity more generally, see Lamont and Fournier (1992); Brubaker and Cooper (2000); Lamont and Molnár (2002).

30. Hanagan 1994; Tilly 2005; Sen 2006.

31. Douglas 1986; Friedland and Alford 1991; Lamont and Fournier 1992; Lamont and Molnár 2002.

32. Friedland and Alford 1991, 249.

33. Arthur 1994; Haydu 1998; Mahoney 2000. Empirical examples from the study of ethnic identities include Brubaker (2005) and Ruane and Todd (2004).

34. Traugott 1985, 15.

35. Events that serve as touchstones for identity construction are likely to be "recognized as notable by contemporaries" and may "impart . . . an unforeseen direction to social development." They may also be effective in part because they activate themes already existing in the cultural repertoire or provide interpretive anchors in unsettled times. There is no reason to assume, however, that they result in "a durable transformation of structures"—one hallmark of that narrower class of historical events explored by Sewell (1996, 843).

36. Skocpol 1992; Clemens 1997; Armstrong 2002.

37. Schwartz 1987. Useem (1987) adds that such individuals not only gain a wider view but also face sanctions against appearing provincial and narrowly self-interested.

38. Friedland and Alford 1991; DiMaggio 1992; Lamont 1992.

39. Halle 1984. Clemens (1996) makes the related point that organizational forms may convey frames for understanding the social world and may embody identities.

40. And as in path dependency, initial moves can become self-reinforcing. For example, embracing a particular ethnic identity may lead an individual to make choices—of where to shop and whom to associate with—which draw boundaries even more sharply along ethnic lines.

41. Benford 1997; Ferree et al. 2002. My own cases lead me to emphasize particular mechanisms that lock in identities. There are other mechanisms, such as the commemorative rituals highlighted by students of "collective memory" (Olick and Robbins 1998; Spillman 1998).

42. On republicanism, see Trachtenberg (1982); Livingston (1994); Foner (1996); Friedman (1998). For corporate liberalism and Progressive reform, see Thimm (1976); Sklar (1988); Zunz (1990); Watts (1991); Ernst (1995).

43. Ingham 1991; Hoffecker 1974; Eggert 1993; Gilkeson 1986; Licht 1995; Isaac 2002.

44. Sewell 1992.

45. Friedland and Alford 1991; Clemens and Cook 1999.

46. Unlike Sewell's schemas, these transposable frameworks are not theoretical solutions to the structure-agency problem. Nor are they peculiarly responsible for social change, which is their role in institutional theory: transposition can as easily reinforce existing relations of power.} But as in both Sewell and institutionalism, they do vary from one social context to another, and they are transposable by social actors.

47. Wallace 1972.

48. Spencer 1984.

49. Wiley and Alexander 1987; Goffman 1959.

50. Putnam 2000.

51. Engelbourg 1980; Portes and Sensenbrenner 1998.

52. Scott (2001) provides an overview and sorts out the different flavors of institutionalism.

53. Lamont and Thévenot 2000.

54. Friedland and Alford 1991; Clemens and Cook 1999.

55. Hochschild 1997. Another rich case study of how institutional scripts can both blur and clash is Heimer and Staffen (1998).

56. Koditschek 1990.

57. Classic comparative studies that illustrate this argument include Lipset 1983; Dahrendorf 1959.

58. Jacoby 1991; Kirk 1994; Adams 1995; Gerber 1997.

59. Berthoff 1964; Bendix 1974; Haydu 1988; Sisson 1991.

60. Lipset 1986; Jacoby 1991.

61. Adams 1995; Haydu 1997; Robertson 2000.

62. There was a national class of business leaders emerging in the 1890s and early 1900s, but their social ties, formal organizations, and worldviews were distinct from local bourgeoisies'. Livingston 1986, chap. 4; Roy 1991; Licht 1995, 108.

63. Burawoy 1989; Goldstone 1997; Mahoney and Rueschemeyer 2003.

64. Haydu 1998.

PART I. SOLIDARITIES

1. Wiebe 1967; Roy 1997; Stern 1994; Thimm 1976.

2. *American Industries,* March 2, 1903; Bowman 1989; Streeck 1991.

3. Jaher 1982; Folsom 1981; Beckert 2001; Dawson 2004.

4. The higher the rung of the social ladder, the more WASP its occupants, but less elite business circles also were disproportionately WASP. See Cohen (1990) and Rosenzweig (1983) on Worcester; Bruchey (1976) on Baltimore; Zunz (1982) on Detroit; Folsom (1981) on Scranton; and, more generally, Miller (1952b).

5. Tocqueville 1969, 557.

6. Livingston 1986, 243.

7. Sklar 1988, 164.

8. On this point, Putnam and Skocpol agree. Gamm and Putnam 1999; Skocpol 1999.

9. On various class coalitions rooted in "whiteness," see Saxton (1990); Jacobson (1998).

10. The best example is Beckert (2001). See also Harris 2000; Dawson 2004; Millikan 2001; Couvares 1984; Ingham 1978; Hoffecker 1974; Bruchey 1976; Rammelkamp 1978; Frisch 1972; Folsom 1981; Eggert 1993; Horowitz 1976; Hirsch 1980.

11. These trade identities are best chronicled in the work of Philip Scranton (1989, 1997). On free labor republicanism, see Gutman 1977; Faler 1981; Dubofsky 1999; Glickman 1997.

12. This is a key theme in Ross's account of class formation in Cincinnati. I would add that countermobilization against labor in particular was weaker in Cincinnati than elsewhere, mainly because labor's own challenge paled in comparison to that in other industrial cities.

13. Wiebe 1967; Gamm and Putnam 1999; Skocpol 1999.

14. Charles (1993, 16) considers the Masons an exception to the cross-class character of fraternal orders. Case studies concur: Dumenil 1984, 12–13; Orr and McNall 1991; Zunz 1990, 204–6.

15. Ingham (1978, 213) suggests that fraternal orders played a more important role in the lives and civic endeavors of elites in smaller cities than in industrial centers like Pittsburgh, with its array of social clubs and civic associations catering exclusively to the bourgeoisie.

16. Stromquist 1987.

17. Ross 1985, 83, 131.

18. Blumin 1989; Archer and Blau 1993; Gilkeson 1986.

19. Beckert 2001. Similar themes appear in Jaher's (1982) account of the re-formation of urban elites. For Jaher, however, the crucial movement is from elite economic power (or economic divisions) to coherent (or divided) political organization and cultural leadership. In Beckert's account, solidarity among economic actors is the problem, and political and cultural institution-building is the solution. Livingston (1986) sides more with Beckert in emphasizing the unifying role of political ideology.

20. McCarthy 1982; Couvares 1984; Jaher 1982; DiMaggio 1992.

21. Beckert 2001; Rammelkamp 1978; Schneirov 1984, 194–95; Horowitz 1976; Ratcliff, Gallagher and Ratcliff 1979. For an earlier era, see Hall (1982); Siskind (2002).

22. Mann 1993, 220–21.

23. Trade associations could support cooperative relations *within* an industry, as Scranton (1989; 1997) emphasizes. But as theorists of social capital remind us, the close ties that build trust within a community also erect barriers to wider collective action (Woolcock 1998).

24. In particular cases, businessmen *do* often put their differences aside in the face of labor mobilization, but there are likely to be other contingencies that account for this response. Studies invoking labor challenges as keys to business unity include Beckert (2001); Millikan (2001); Bonnett (1956).

1. BUSINESS UNITY IN CINCINNATI

1. Cincinnati Chamber of Commerce, Forty-sixth Annual Report (1895), 56.

2. Cincinnati Chamber of Commerce, Forty-sixth Annual Report, 112. Comparisons with Cleveland and Pittsburgh are calculated from the U.S. Census, Manufactures, 1900.

3. Ross 1985, 221.

4. The persistence of proprietary management and local control helps qualify Ross's picture of a historical march toward corporate organization in the nineteenth century.

The sheer size of firms grew, and they were less commonly owned by a single founder. The unevenness of this trend, moreover, certainly contributed to the fragmentation of worker experience and mobilization which concerns Ross. For understanding business culture, however, the close links between ownership, management, and residence are more important than the sheer numbers of employees or partners.

5. I am describing the late-nineteenth-century assimilation of Germans and the Irish in relative terms. The very top of the class hierarchy remained disproportionately WASP, and both German and Irish Americans had some niches where they congregated, including brewing (German) and construction (Irish). Compared to the position of eastern or southern European immigrants at this time, however, no sharp status division barred Cincinnati's German and Irish descendants from business ownership, political office, or cultural life. See Shapiro and Sarna 1992; Dannenbaum 1984; Miller 1968.

6. Most worked instead in domestic and personal service (3,316) or trade and transportation (1,152). United States Bureau of the Census 1904, Table 43.

7. Miller 1968; Anderson 1979.

8. For similar patterns in other cities, see Couvares (1984); Gilkeson (1986); Ingham (1991); Licht (1995); Stern (1994).

9. Ohio Mechanics' Institute, Memorabilia, Box 72, Folder 1, "Sketch of the History of the Ohio Mechanics' Institute" by George Kendall, Cincinnati, 1853, 6.

10. *Cincinnati Enquirer,* October 22, 23, 1870.

11. Address by Sidney Maxwell to the Women's Art Museum Association, "The Manufactures of Cincinnati," March 11, 1878. Reprinted in Cincinnati Chamber of Commerce, Annual Report for 1878.

12. Report of the Third Cincinnati Industrial Exposition, 1872, 7.

13. Morrison 1886, 193; Wright 1993.

14. Montgomery 1981; Trachtenberg 1982; Glickman 1997.

15. Ross 1985, 221, 224.

16. Ohio Bureau of Labor Statistics Annual Report, 1877, 216, 226; hereafter cited as BLS.

17. Ohio BLS, 1877, 228; Downard 1973; Wing 1964.

18. The character and business membership of Cincinnati's fraternal orders can be gleaned from Ford and Ford (1881, 214–15); Wittke et al. (1941, 282); and the rosters in By-Laws of Kilwinning Lodge, No. 356, Free and Accepted Masons, 1870 (Cincinnati Historical Society); By-Laws of McMillan Lodge, No. 141, Free and Accepted Masons, 1872 (Cincinnati Historical Society); *Masonic Review* February 1871, 58, March 1872, 374, December 1884, 312.

19. Greve 1904, 2:193.

20. *Cincinnati Enquirer,* April 11, 1869.

21. Miles Greenwood, quoted in *Cincinnati Enquirer,* April 1, 1869. By only a narrow vote, organizers opted not to underscore the point by naming their new institution the "Manufacturers' Board of Trade." *Cincinnati Enquirer,* February 26, April 11, 1869.

22. *Cincinnati Daily Gazette,* May 22, 1875.

23. *Cincinnati Enquirer,* December 11, 1884.

24. *Cincinnati Commercial,* November 10, 1873.

25. Morrison 1886; Ohio BLS, 1877, 228, 1884, 285; Strobridge Lithographing Company; *Cincinnati Daily Gazette,* August 25, 1876; Duggan 1977; Wing 1964; Ross 1985.

26. *Cincinnati Commercial,* December 17, 1874; *Cincinnati Enquirer,* June 28, September 4, 1877, December 30, 1882, October 15, 1899.

27. Cincinnati Chamber of Commerce, 1874 Report, 39.

28. Ohio BLS, 1885, 235.

29. *Cincinnati Enquirer,* January 1, 1884, June 24, 1885.

30. In the twenty-two years before the economic slump of 1873, Cincinnati manufacturing output shot up 211 percent. Over the twenty years between 1873 and the onset of

the next major depression, local output increased only 66 percent. Calculated from Ohio BLS, 1894, 112.

31. In 1850, the value of manufactured goods produced in Hamilton County totaled over $20 million, compared to 16.7 in Allegheny County (Pittsburgh), 2.6 in Cook County (Chicago), and 0.9 in Cuyahoga (Cleveland). Cook and Allegheny pulled ahead of Cincinnati by the 1870 census and Cuyahoga neared parity in 1900. Data is from U.S. Census, Manufactures. Because city data is unavailable in the earlier census reports, I use county data throughout the time period for consistency.

32. *Cincinnati Enquirer*, March 14, 1890. The Chamber of Commerce Annual Reports are a good place to follow the fortunes of Cincinnati business and the anxieties of Cincinnati businessmen. See also Miller 1968, 69.

33. Ross 1985, 252–53; United States Bureau of Labor, *Third and Tenth Annual Reports.*

34. *Cincinnati Enquirer*, July 27, 1877. Local observers made the same claim about the relative moderation of Cincinnati labor in the 1886 strikes: Greve 1904, 1:1005; Morris 1969, 155, 167, 280.

35. Cincinnati Chamber of Commerce, May 6, 1886.

36. Cincinnati Chamber of Commerce and Merchants' Exchange 1889, 39 For a general survey of elite concerns, see Miller 1968.

37. Lakes 1988, 41–44, 48–49; Anderson 1979.

38. Accounts of the riot include Stern (1984); Schweniger (1999); Rodabaugh and Ohio Valley Folk Research Project (1962).

39. *Commercial Gazette,* March 30, 1884. My interpretation of the riot differs from Ross's. Ross makes the riot part of Cincinnati labor's larger rebellion; I emphasize that contemporary observers did not view the upheaval in terms of class or labor (whether union or non-union).

40. *Commercial Gazette,* March 29, 1884.

41. March 31, 1884.

42. *Cincinnati Enquirer,* April 1, 1869, April 1, 1882; *Cincinnati Commercial,* December 13, 1867, November 24, 1868.

43. Morris 1969, 217; Ross 1985, 274–79.

44. Ross 1985, chap. 12; Miller 1968, 62–63; Ansell and Burris 1997, 19–21.

45. Ross 1985, 312.

46. Goss 1912, 254–55; Wright 1905; Foraker 1932, 82–83.

47. The best source is Miller (1968).

48. Wright 1905, 76, 107; Miller 1968.

49. Musselman 1975, 39, 129; Central Labor Council (Cincinnati), March 1, 1892.

50. Warner 1964, 160–63, 188.

51. Ross 1985.

52. *Cincinnati Daily Gazette,* August 25, 1876.

53. Morrison 1886, 191.

54. Ohio BLS, 1884, 222.

55. *Cincinnati Enquirer,* October 18, 1881, May 4, 1901; Commercial Club of Cincinnati, Minutes, October 13, 1882; Lakes 1988, 55.

56. Ross 1985, 221.

57. *Cincinnati Enquirer,* April 7, 1901; Downard 1973, 99–102; Brody 1980; Cochran 1972, 163–64.

58. These categorizations are based mainly on the Ohio Bureau of Labor Statistics Annual Reports.

59. Morris 1969, 135–38; *Cincinnati Commercial,* March 12, September 9, 1868; December 17, 1874; *Cincinnati Enquirer,* June 28, 1877, December 16, 1879; Downard 1973, 89.

60. *Cincinnati Enquirer,* October 2, 5, 7, 1869, March 8, 11, 1884; Ohio BLS, 1880, 105–7, 1884, 283; Morris 1969, 143, 188–90.

61. Ohio BLS, 1882, 255–61; *Cincinnati Enquirer,* January 1, May 6, June 5, 24, 1884, November 24, December 1, 1885, January 5, 9, 1886, August 23, 26–27, October 9, 10, 1889.

62. Downard 1973, 49, 80; *Cincinnati Commercial,* November 10, 1873.

63. Cincinnati Metal Trades Association, Minutes, March 7, April 26, 1900, March 1, 1906.

64. *Cincinnati Enquirer,* April 9, 1887.

65. Zimmerman 1981; United States Commissioner of Labor 1893, 110; Bennett 1937, 396–97; *Cincinnati Enquirer,* April 22, 1894; Ford and Ford 1881, 253–56; Wittke et al. 1941, 460–63; Greve 1904, 1, 923–26; Spraul 1976.

66. Couvares 1984; Levine 1988; Kasson 1990; Archer and Blau 1993.

67. Ford and Ford 1881, 253, 254; Boyer 1978; Beisel 1997; McCarthy 1982.

68. *The Courier,* May 1892, Cincinnati Musical Festival Association Records (Cincinnati Historical Society), Box 1, Folder 4.

69. *Cincinnati Daily Gazette,* January 10, 1874.

70. Ohio Mechanics' Institute, 1876 Annual Report of the Board of Directors, 13; Spraul 1976; Howe 1978.

71. Zimmerman 1981, 33.

72. Ford and Ford 1881, 253–56; Howe 1978.

73. Commercial Club Minutes, July 27, 1880, October 15, 1904; *Cincinnati Enquirer,* September 28, 1880; Miller 1968, 51.

74. Commercial Club Minutes, December 24, 1994; January 23, 1892; *Cincinnati Enquirer,* February 13, 1891; Cincinnati Chamber of Commerce, March 21, 1891.

75. *Cincinnati Enquirer,* March 27, 28, 1884; McDougall 1896; Wright 1905, 28–30; Julius Dexter Papers (Cincinnati Historical Society), Box 2, Folder 14, Material Pertaining to the Committee of 100.

76. Hickenlooper, Personal Reminiscences, 2:522, 599; McDougall 1896; Anderson 1979, 302, 316–21; Committee of One Hundred 1886a; Committee of One Hundred 1886d.

77. Anderson 1979, 455–58.

78. Committee of One Hundred 1886a, 5.

79. Business Men's Club [Cincinnati Club] Records (Cincinnati Historical Society), Organizational Papers, "Inaugurated. The Young Men's Business Club."

80. Goss 1912, 280–82; Leonard 1927, 1:156–57; *Cincinnati Enquirer,* April 26, 1900, January 21, December 31, 1904; Business Men's Club Records, Annual Report, 1907–8.

81. Cincinnati Chamber of Commerce, December 1, 15, 1908; Business Men's Club, Annual Report for the Year Ending October 31, 1909, 40; Miller 1968, 157–58.

82. *Cincinnati Enquirer,* December 11, 1892; Business Men's Club Records, Annual Report, 1904–5; Roster and Classified Business Directory, November 1, 1911, 159; Committee Minutes, February 10, 1912, Address by William Redfield.

83. Miller 1968; Wiebe 1962; Thelen 1972.

84. Chamber of Commerce Records, March 17, 1894; Chamber of Commerce Minutes, January 2, February 6, 1900; Commercial Club Minutes, December 29, 1908; Business Men's Club, 1909 Annual Report, 40.

85. *Cincinnati Enquirer,* April 19, 1905.

86. Commercial Club Collection, "List of Members," and Business Men's Club Annual Reports. Information on business activities comes from city directories, supplemented with biographical information from Goss (1912); Greve (1904); Leonard (1927). Business Men's Club officers may not have been typical, but there are no complete rosters of club members from which to sample the rank and file.

87. Scholars like Bonnett, Watts, and Voss emphasize just these associations when they treat late-nineteenth-century employer mobilization as a response to working-class protest. Bonnett 1922; Watts 1991; Voss 1993.

88. *Cincinnati Enquirer,* February 2, 1904.

89. Bonnett (1922); Smith (1983); and Fine (1995) offer overviews. Case studies of open shop organization include Yarmie (1991); Klug (1993); Harris (2000); Millikan (2001); and Pearson (2004).

90. *Cincinnati Enquirer,* January 16, 1904; Business Men's Club, Code of Regulations, By-Laws, and House Rules, undated, 53; Records, Minutes, December 20, 1912.

91. *Cincinnati Enquirer,* September 19, 22, 1905, January 30, August 15, 1907; Central Labor Council, Minutes, September 11, 1906, March 12, 1907; American Industries, August 15, 1904.

2. RACE AND CLASS ALIGNMENTS IN SAN FRANCISCO

1. Barth 1975.

2. Ethington 1994, 425.

3. Decker 1978, 63–66, 186; McWilliams 1949; Roberts 2000; Walker 2000; Tygiel 1977.

4. In 1852, over 50 percent of the city's residents were foreign born; in 1870, 62 percent of skilled and 81.4 percent of unskilled workers were foreign born, with the largest contingent—the Irish—accounting for only 20.9 percent and 25.7 percent of these strata. Decker 1978, 171–75; Ethington 1994, 49; Erie 1975, 141; Burchell 1979.

5. Chen 2000; Decker 1978, 159–60; United States Census, 1870, Population, Table 8.

6. United States Census, 1860, 1870, 1880, 1890, Manufacturing; United States Census, 1870, Population, Table 32; Shumsky 1972, 24–25.

7. Ryan 1936; Chatom 1915; Franks 1985.

8. Issel and Cherny 1986, 111; *The Argonaut,* July 12, 1884; Ethington 1994, 63–64.

9. Hittell 1878, 459.

10. Shumsky 1972; Barth 1975; Decker 1978.

11. Mechanics' Institute of San Francisco, September 26, 1864.

12. *San Francisco Examiner,* November 11, 1884.

13. Ibid., February 3, 1903; Ryder 1954; Decker 1978.

14. "Commercial Decline of San Francisco," *The Wave,* February 9, 1895.

15. Hallidie, Addresses and Reports, 1875 Annual Report to the Mechanics' Institute, p. 4.

16. San Francisco Commercial Club n.d., p. 23.

17. Hennings 1961, 8; Issel 1988.

18. San Francisco Examiner, June 4, 8, 1892.

19. Decker 1978, 311n44; Shumsky 1972, 54.

20. Gordon, Edwards, and Reich 1982; Mink 1986; Gerstle 2001; Reed 2002.

21. Montgomery 1979; Robertson 2000.

22. U.S. Census, 1870, Population, Table 8, and Manufactures, Table 32; Bristol-Kagan 1982, chap. 5, 22–24.

23. Hittell 1882, 442, 509; Bristol-Kagan 1982; Chiu 1960.

24. *San Francisco Chronicle,* May 13, 1870, July 16, 1870.

25. California State Senate, Special Committee on Chinese Immigration 1878, 116; Chiu 1960; Saxton 1971.

26. *San Francisco Examiner,* July 24, 1878, February 22, 1879, May 4, 1882, March 9, 15, 16, July 9, August 6, 1884, December 1, 1885, January 3, 1886, January 27, 1887, April 4, 1906; California Bureau of Labor Statistics, 1891–92, 55.

27. *San Francisco Examiner,* February 22, 1879.

28. United States Senate 1877, 489–93.

29. Hallidie Papers, Folder 10, "Commercial Decline of San Francisco," from *The Wave,* February 9, 1895.

30. *San Francisco Examiner,* May 15, July 8, 1882, December 31, 1890; *San Francisco Chronicle,* May 13, 1870; Chen 2000, 67, 182–83.

31. United States Senate 1877; Saxton 1971; Chen 2000; Gyory 1998.

32. Bristol-Kagan 1982, chap. 4, 3, and chap. 5, 26–28; Chiu 1960, 181.

33. Choy, Dong, and Hom 1995; Lee 1999.

34. Saxton 1971, 259–65; Issel and Cherny 1986, 127; Cross 1935, 125; United States Senate 1877, 323.

35. San Francisco Chamber of Commerce Records, Frederick Koster, "Law and Order and the San Francisco Chamber of Commerce: An Address," February 1918, Mss 870, Box 3, Folder 33.

36. For general sources of craft union strength, see Jackson (1984). For their application to San Francisco, Knight (1960); Cross (1935).

37. Among skilled manual occupations, the Irish accounted for 20.9% in 1870 and 9.1 percent in 1890. Germans filled another 15.4 percent of these jobs in 1870 and 12.6 percent in 1890. The English and Welsh came in third, at 6.0 percent and 7.4 percent. Erie 1975, 141, 195; Tygiel 1977, 29.

38. California BLS, 1887–88, 128–31.

39. Miller 1968, 123; Giannini 1975, 1.

40. Schwartz 1995, 46.

41. *San Francisco Examiner,* June 20, 1886, September 3, 1904, November 30, 1910; Cross 1935, 182.

42. International Brotherhood of Boiler Makers and Iron Ship Builders of America, November 1, 1907, April 1, 1908; *Labor Clarion,* October 23, 1908; *San Francisco Examiner,* June 5, July 8, 1907.

43. Knight 1960, 8; Cross 1935, 167, 229; Varcados 1968, 67–68; Eaves 1910.

44. Saxton 1965, 422.

45. Erie 1975, 164; Saxton 1971.

46. Bean 1952; Giannini 1975; Kazin 1987.

47. *Labor Clarion,* November 29, 1912.

48. Lipset and Marks 2000.

49. *San Francisco Examiner,* November 5, 1900, October 29, 1902, February 27, 1910; Knight 1960.

50. California BLS, 1893, 52.

51. San Francisco Examiner, March 3, 1892.

52. Citizens' Alliance of San Francisco n.d., 4; Kazin 1987, 115–16; Knight 1960, 131–33.

53. *San Francisco Examiner,* April 20, May 28, 1904; Knight 1960, 143–45, 152–54; Kazin 1987, 117.

54. The best overview is Knight (1960, 49–90).

55. *San Francisco Examiner,* August 7, 1901, May 24, 1903, June 2, 1906; Giannini 1975, 54.

56. *San Francisco Examiner,* May 8, July 4, 1901.

57. Ibid., July 10, 17, 29, 30, August 6, 1901.

58. Ibid., August 13, 17, 30, September 9, 11, October 3, 1901.

59. Ibid., April 11, 1902.

60. Bean 1952; Kazin 1987.

61. Scott 1985, 97.

62. San Francisco Examiner, April 18, 1872.

63. Cincinnati Chamber of Commerce 1969, 9; Fletcher 2003.

64. Bean 1952, 126–27; Issel and Cherny 1986, 120–22; Blackford 1993, 49–55.

65. Senkewicz 1985; Decker 1978.

66. The Commercial Club's "List of Members from Organization" (Commercial Club Papers, Box 42) included 140 men; the economic affiliation of 3 could not be identified. I applied the same procedure to San Francisco (Merchants' Association, Official List of

Members, 1896; San Francisco Chamber of Commerce Records, Box 6, Folder 69), using city directories to track down club members. The labels used in these directories can be ambiguous (e.g., "cabinet maker"). When in doubt, I classified an individual as a manufacturer.

67. Information about the organizational activities of Commercial Club and Merchants' Association members is assembled from scattered biographical sources, such as local histories, newspaper obituaries, and Historical Society biography files. This information is undoubtedly incomplete. There is no reason to think, however, that San Francisco local newspapers, obituaries, and biography files have significantly greater omissions and thus make Merchants' Association members appear less engaged than they really were.

68. Johnson 1886; Decker 1978, 125–27; Issel and Cherny 1986, 137.

69. *The Argonaut,* June 27, 1885; Harris Weinstock in the *Merchants' Association Review,* June 1905, 5; Decker 1978, 125–27.

70. Hittell 1878, 458–59; Decker 1978, 241–42.

71. Commercial Club of Cincinnati, March 21, 1899 letter from Secretary Harry Laws to William Cooper Procter, Box 20, Secretary's and Treasurer's Correspondence, Folder 4; *San Francisco Examiner,* October 13, 1898.

72. Merchants' Association of San Francisco 1910, 4; Decker 1978, 241.

PART II. IDENTITIES

1. Arnesen 1996, 49. For an older example of the classic view, see Hofstadter (1948) on "captains of industry."

2. These comparative generalizations appear, at different resolutions, in Sawyer (1952); Sutton et al. (1956); Shafer (1991); Dobbin (1994); Dawley (2005).

3. Trachtenberg 1982; Wilentz 1984; Furner 1993; Montgomery 1993; Friedman 1998; Foner 1998.

4. Fraser and Gerstle 2005, 21.

5. Thimm 1976; Watts 1991; Nasaw 2005.

6. Case studies connecting business communities with urban reform include Blackford (1993); Hoffecker (1974); Sawislak (1995); Schneirov (1999); Ingham (1991); Beckert (2001); Quigley (2002); Isaac (2002). On continuities and differences between Gilded Age and Progressive reform, see Hofstadter (1955); Hays (1964); Warner (1964); Sproat (1968); Thelen (1972); Buenker (1973); McFarland (1975); Schiesl (1977); Boyer (1978); Schneirov (1998).

7. Blumin (1989, 9–10) notes the paradox of individualism as the defining characteristic of mid-nineteenth-century middle-class consciousness. Because I see late-nineteenth-century businessmen's claims to stand above class as boundary work and identity construction, they do not appear as much at odds with class consciousness.

8. Weinstein 1968; Lustig 1982; Sklar 1988; Ernst 1995.

9. The specific alternatives to republicanism also differ from one account to another. Gutman 1977; Livingston 1986; Stromquist 1987; Furner 1993; Friedman 1998.

10. Business Men's Club, Annual Report, 1904–5, p. 13.

11. Smith (1997) argues that America's civic ideals include "ascriptive inequalitarianism" as well as democratic republicanism and liberalism, and he sees this third tradition as a lamentably rich resource for racial discrimination. In San Francisco, one can see how republicanism, with its high standards for worthy citizens and producers, can itself be mobilized for racist practices. Another good illustration is Gerteis's (2002) study of racial boundaries in the Knights of Labor.

12. Weinstein 1968; Sklar 1988; Ernst 1995.

13. On the NCF, see Weinstein (1968) and Cyphers (2002).

14. *Practical corporatism* in this sense is what Kimeldorf (1999, 181n53), describing American workers' "business syndicalism," calls an "organizational logic of mobilization" rather than a clearly articulated theory of industrial action.

3. BUSINESS CITIZENSHIP IN CINCINNATI

1. *Cincinnati Enquirer,* September 6, 1882.

2. Gutman 1977; Griffen and Griffen 1980; Hirsch 1980; Blumin 1989; Stromquist 1987.

3. On "cultural capital" and social inequality, see Bourdieu (1984); Lamont (1992); DiMaggio (1992). Historians have made the same point. See Levine 1988; Kasson 1990; Bushman 1992.

4. February 7, 1873 letter from Thomas to George Ward Nichols, president of the Musical Festival Association. Cincinnati Musical Festival Association Records, Box 1, Folder 14.

5. Thomas to Nichols, January 20, 1873.

6. Kasson 1990, 237.

7. Quoted in Spraul 1976, 199.

8. Covington to Nichols, February 22, 1873, Musical Festival Association Records, Box 1, Folder 16.

9. William Avery to W. W. Taylor, May 14, 1878, Musical Festival Association Records, Box 4, Folder 1.

10. James Diaries, May 23, 1891.

11. Maxwell 1974 [1870], 26, 96, 99.

12. Thomas to Lawrence Maxwell, February 6, 1881, Musical Festival Association Records, Box 5, Folder 6.

13. Slotkin 1985; Leach 1994.

14. Committee of One Hundred 1886d, 19.

15. *Commercial Gazette,* March 30, 1884.

16. April 1, 1884. McPhail (1991) surveys views of the rampaging lower orders.

17. Hickenlooper Papers, Personal Reminiscences, II, 519.

18. James Diaries, November 2, 1896, February 25, 1898.

19. Commercial Club Collection, Box 3, Minutes, October 15, 1910.

20. Commercial Club of Cincinnati, Box 59, Schmidlapp memorial for Ingalls, 1914.

21. Centennial Exposition of the Ohio Valley and Central States, 1888, Box 4, Folders 6–9.

22. Cincinnati Milacron, Part 2, Series "Misc. Folders," Box M–N, Cincinnati Metal Trades Association.

23. March 19, 1888 application from James Bradford, Jr.

24. Reemelin 1892, 249.

25. Wright 1905, 175. On masculinity and character, see Hilkey (1997).

26. Hofstadter 1955; Sproat 1968; Thelen 1972; McFarland 1975. "Mugwump" was the name given to Republicans who bolted their party in 1884, believing the Democratic candidate Grover Cleveland to be more committed to clean government than was James Blaine. Historians apply the term more broadly to cover elite reformers in the 1870s and 1880s who advocated government by the "best men."

27. Committee of One Hundred 1886b, 4, 16.

28. Commercial Club Minutes, June 25, 1887.

29. Committee of One Hundred 1886a, 3, 24.

30. Cincinnati Chamber of Commerce, March 15, 1886; Anderson 1979.

31. Commercial Club of Cincinnati, Albert Voorheis, quoted in undated newspaper clipping, Box 64, Scrapbooks, Folder 5.

32. Commercial Club Minutes, November 10, 1898; Chamber of Commerce Records, March 2, 1877.

33. Commercial Club Records, Scrapbooks, Box 64, Folder 51.

34. Cincinnati Chamber of Commerce, March 26, 1888.

35. Sproat 1968; Thelen 1972.

36. Maxwell 1974 [1870], 99; letter to the Columbus Board of Trade, printed in *Cincinnati Enquirer,* November 22, 1890.

37. Harlow 1950, 281–82.

38. Committee of One Hundred 1886c, 27.

39. Committee of One Hundred 1886b, 14–15.

40. McDougall 1896.

41. Rodgers 1974; Montgomery 1981; Wilentz 1984; Glickstein 1991; Watts 1991; Rodgers 1992; Foner 1996; Friedman 1998.

42. Ross 1986; Ross 1985, 271–72.

43. Chamber of Commerce Records, March 27, 1888, July 7, 1903, December 15, 1904.

44. Chamber of Commerce Records, February 27, 1898, July 22, 1890.

45. Ibid., October 16, 1889.

46. Commercial Club Minutes, November 10, 1898.

47. Cincinnati Chamber of Commerce, October 2, 1891.

48. Committee of One Hundred 1886c, 16–17.

49. Business Men's Club, 1904–5 Annual Report, 13; 1907–8, 19.

50. Business Men's Club, 1904–5 Annual Report, 13.

51. Benedict (1996) and Cohen (2002), among others, discuss ways in which this stereotype is overdrawn.

52. I examined all 11 pre–Civil War memorials and a random sample of 33 from the 132 printed during the 1890s.

53. I emphasize "no less than" and "at least" because there are so many gaps in the biographical data. More complete information would doubtless raise these figures substantially. Examples of business associations to which Commercial Club members belonged are the city's Chamber of Commerce, Manufacturers' Association, and a variety of industry-specific trade groups. Political involvements include serving on the city's school board; joining the Blaine or Lincoln Clubs; or contributing time or money to the Associated Charities. Cultural service, finally, might take the form of membership in the Literary Club or helping organize the yearly music festival. Sources on memberships include city directories, biographical profiles in local histories, newspaper indexes, organization rosters, and obituaries. I would have examined the multiple affiliations of Business Men's Club members, but club records list only its officers.

54. DiMaggio 1992.

55. *Cincinnati Enquirer,* April 22, 1894.

56. December 11, 1884.

57. Cincinnati Musical Festival Association Records, Box 1, Folder 16, letter from Covington to Nichols; Box 2, Folder 21, Board of Trade resolution; Spraul 1976; Howe 1978.

58. *Cincinnati Enquirer,* March 30, 1884.

59. Committee of One Hundred 1886a, 24, 19.

60. Commercial Club of Cincinnati, Minutes, February 27, 1887.

61. Committee of One Hundred 1886c, 10.

62. Wright 1905, 8; Miller 1968.

63. *Cincinnati Enquirer,* November 22, 1890, quoting letter to the Columbus Board of Trade; Committee of One Hundred 1886b, 6–7.

64. *Cincinnati Enquirer,* March 26, 1883.

65. Ibid., November 13, 1885.

66. Ibid., February 23, 1881.

67. Commercial Club Collection, Box 64, Scrapbooks, Folder 5, undated clipping from the early 1900s quoting Commercial Club president Albert Voorheis; Box 15, Speakers' Presentations 1893–1918, November 7, 1908 speech by William Howard Taft.

68. Hickenlooper, Personal Reminiscences, II, 554. This indictment of class shows again Cincinnati businessmen's rhetorical debts to the republican tradition. See also Thimm 1976; Watts 1991; Burke 1995; Gilkeson 1986.

69. Commercial Club Collection, Box 3, Minutes, November 5, 1908.

70. Maxwell Papers, Box 1, Folder 4, April 6, 1891 letter from Maxwell to J. H. Fisher.

71. *Cincinnati Enquirer,* June 15, 1880; Schwartz 1995, 20–21.

72. Examples of this historiographical strategy include Thimm (1976); Livingston (1986); Sklar (1988).

73. In 1900 the U.S. Census found 5,582 manufacturing establishments in Cincinnati. At that time the Business Men's Club claimed one thousand members (Goss 1912, 280). Many of these were not manufacturers, but the ratio suggests that a significantly higher proportion of businessmen belonged to civic associations than manual workers did to labor unions (around 10 percent at this time).

74. Useem 1982.

75. Cincinnati Chamber of Commerce Records, December 18, 1875.

4. PRACTICAL CORPORATISM IN SAN FRANCISCO

1. Commonwealth Club of California, vol. 3, no. 1 (January 1908), 84–85.

2. Hittell 1882, 442.

3. California Bureau of Labor Statistics (BLS), 1887–88, 257.

4. Roediger 1991; Jacobson 1998.

5. California Chinese Exclusion Convention 1901, 37–38.

6. Hallidie, Addresses and Reports, 1877, 5.

7. Mechanics' Institute of San Francisco, 16th Report, 1881, 36.

8. California BLS, 1889–90, 93.

9. Dillon 1984, 3–4; Hallidie, 1877 Annual Report to the Mechanics' Institute, 5.

10. United States Senate 1877, 347.

11. Merry n.d., 6.

12. Bancroft 1891–92, Wendell Easton file, 109.

13. California Chinese Exclusion Convention 1901, 38.

14. Bristol-Kagan 1982, 32–34; Chiu 1960, 92; Saxton 1971, 118.

15. California Chinese Exclusion Convention 1901; Ethington 1994, 371.

16. Saxton 1971, 259–65; Saxton 1990, 294–95; Issel and Cherny 1986, 125–27.

17. California Chinese Exclusion Convention 1901, 27.

18. Mechanics' Institute of San Francisco, 13th Report, 1878, 6.

19. Commonwealth Club of California, vol. 3, no. 1 (January 1908), 85.

20. Mechanics' Institute of San Francisco, 1877, 6.

21. United States Senate 1877, 47, 9–10.

22. *San Francisco Examiner,* August 13, 1896.

23. Ibid., November 1, 1896, quoting the retired merchant Horace Davis.

24. Ibid., October 22, 1896, quoting James Phelan.

25. Ibid., October 23, 1896, quoting attorney H. P. Van Duzer.

26. Ibid., September 16, 1896, quoting Van Duzer.

27. Ibid., October 20, 1897. For other points of friction between local businessmen and the Southern Pacific, see Issel and Cherny (1986), 121–22.

28. *San Francisco Examiner,* February 18, 1911.

29. Hennings 1961, 8–9.

30. Hallidie papers, Folder 6, address to the Manufacturers' Association, c. 1895, and Folder 7, "A Study of Skilled Occupations."

31. Mechanics' Institute of San Francisco, 19th Report, 1884, 20.

32. Mechanics' Institute of San Francisco, 16th Report, 1881, 22. On the producer republic, see Faler (1981); Glickman (1997); Johnston (2003).

33. Ethington 1994; Hofstadter 1955; Wiebe 1967; Furner 1993; Clemens 1997. I differ from Ethington in emphasizing that politicians put republican traditions to work in their construction of social boundaries. For that reason, one need not choose between "the republican synthesis" and Ethington's argument that political parties ratified group identities.

34. Commonwealth Club of California, vol. 5, no. 2 (April 1910), 16. This tripartite formula was a common one among the progressive (or "corporate liberal") minority of pre–World War I businessmen in the United States. Its leading advocate was the National Civic Federation. Green 1973 [1956]; Weinstein 1968; Cyphers 2002.

35. Statement by Employers' Association spokesman M. F. Michael, *San Francisco Examiner,* May 9, 1901.

36. *San Francisco Examiner,* September 28, 1905.

37. Commonwealth Club of California, vol. 5, no. 2 (April 1910), 19.

38. Cross 1918, 337–38; Ryan 1936; Knight 1960, 286–90; Kazin 1987.

39. *San Francisco Examiner,* March 10–April 9, 1896. Quotation from Bruschke, April 5.

40. Ibid., August 6, 1900.

41. Ibid., October 5, 12, 1906; Tygiel 1977, 123.

42. *San Francisco Examiner,* February 8, 1903.

43. Montgomery 1987; Haydu 1988; Harris 2000.

44. Issel and Cherny 1986, 55–57.

45. Cross 1935, 167.

46. *San Francisco Examiner,* September 25–25, November 12, 19, 20, 1901.

47. Cross 1918, 283–84.

48. *San Francisco Examiner,* October 28, 1908; Knight 1960, 214–16.

49. *San Francisco Examiner,* January 26, 1911, February 12, 1911.

50. Cross 1918, 280–81.

51. Kazin 1987, 115–16; Knight 1960, 131–33.

52. Citizens' Alliance of San Francisco n.d., 4; Citizens' Alliance of San Francisco n.d; Citizens' Alliance of San Francisco n.d.

53. Bean 1952, 58–59.

54. San Francisco Chamber of Commerce Records, Minutes, August 27, 1907; Merchants' Association Records, Reports and Minutes, September 27, 1907.

55. *San Francisco Examiner,* December 30, 1906.

56. Ibid., July 25, April 25, May 10, 1907.

57. Kazin 1987, 40–43; Issel and Cherny 1986, 141–52; Ethington 1994, 387–98.

58. *San Francisco Examiner,* October 16, 1896, quoting Patrick Reddy. On labor opposition to the 1896 charter, see also Kazin (1987, 41).

59. Quoted in Issel and Cherny 1986, 142.

60. Issel and Cherny 1986, 151; Issel 1977; *San Francisco Examiner,* August 3, 1897; McDonald 1986, 211.

61. *San Francisco Examiner,* February 7, 1898; Erie 1975, 307–8, 310–13.

62. *San Francisco Examiner,* November 4, 6, 1899.

PART III. TRANSPOSITION

1. Milton 1970; Bendix 1974; Jacoby 1985; McQuaid 1986; Wren 1994; Guillén 1994; Shenhav 1999.

2. Lipset 1986; Jacoby 1991; Kirk 1994; Adams 1995; Fagge 1996; Gerber 1997. The apparent exception is the New Deal industrial relations system, in which large corporations in the mass production sector seem to have accepted collective bargaining for a time. The extent to which they did so in voluntary pursuit of stability (Gordon 1994) or in grudging deference to militant unionism and a relatively pro-labor federal government (Dubofsky 1994) remains in dispute.

3. Dawley 2005, 164.

4. Bendix 1974; Edwards 1979; Haydu 1988.

5. Adams 1995; Haydu 1997.

6. Bonnett 1922; Smith 1983; Klug 1993; Fine 1995; Harris 2000; Millikan 2001.

7. This basic narrative can be found in the classic work of David Montgomery (1979) and David Brody (1960). Howell Harris (2000) questions this link between attacking craft control and repudiating unions. Philadelphia metal trades manufacturers preserved craft-based production but still sought to rid themselves of union interference.

8. Berthoff 1964; Johnson 1979; Bowman 1989. Robertson (2000) adds a political dimension to this same market logic: it was federal restrictions on the ability of firms to regulate competition that forced employers to opt for unilateral rather than joint control.

9. Wiebe 1962; Weinstein 1968; Ramirez 1978; Sklar 1988; Furness 1990; Gordon 1994; Cyphers 2002; Dawley 2005.

10. Ozanne 1967; Thimm 1976; Loveday 1983; Blackford 1991. Where corporate managers more often differed from smaller proprietors was in their alternatives to unions, including employee welfare programs and representation plans (Jacoby 1985; Nestor 1986; Tone 1997).

11. Scranton 1983, 1989; Calvert 1967; Bensman 1980; Stern 1994.

12. Kasson 1976; Wallace 1972; Glickstein 1991; Laurie 1998.

13. Milton 1970; Barley and Kunda 1992; Guillén 1994; Abrahamson 1997.

14. Braverman 1974.

15. Brady 1972 [1943]; Milton 1970; Marchand 1998.

16. Bendix 1974.

17. Shenhav 1999. See also Guillén 1994; Gantman 2005.

18. Ingham (1991, 98) makes a similar point regarding status conventions: "the labor/management ideas of these independent iron and steel owners were the product of both the market position of their mills and the values and culture of their class."

19. Mandell (2002) points to a comparable transposition of scripts from family life to early-twentieth-century welfare capitalism, without discussing the underlying mechanisms that made this possible.

20. Issel and Cherny (1986, 96), quoting the newsletter of the Industrial Association.

21. Appropriately, this shift is the starting point for Zunz's account of the impact of middle management on work culture (Zunz 1990).

22. On similarities and differences between models of "rational" management in the late nineteenth and late twentieth centuries, see Haydu and Lee (2004).

5. FROM POLITICS TO WORK: CINCINNATI

1. Commercial Club of Cincinnati, Minutes, November 10, 1898.

2. Spiess 1970; Chamberlin 1888.

3. Ohio Mechanics' Institute, Annual Reports of the Board of Directors, 1858 Report, 12; Exhibition Records, Box 82, Folder 5.

4. Compare Ross (1985, 233–35), who argues that the shift is not from mechanic to businessman but from mechanic to impersonal technology. Given the continuing

prominence of leading firms and proprietors in exposition displays and parades, it seems more accurate to say that the shift is to businessmen and business generally rather than to technology itself.

5. *Cincinnati Enquirer,* September 6, 1882; Ross 1985, 235.

6. Centennial Exposition Records, Box 12, Folder 6, Assorted Material from 1878–86 Expositions, "Resolution Relative to Trades Unions."

7. *Cincinnati Enquirer,* April 26, 1900; Chamber of Commerce Annual Reports, 1870, 8.

8. *Cincinnati Daily Gazette,* September 8, 1875.

9. *Cincinnati Enquirer,* April 26, 1900. See also Spiess 1970, 186.

10. *Cincinnati Enquirer,* September 21, 1901.

11. Commercial Club Collection, Box 59, Member Memorials; Greve 1904, 2:44–48, 231; Cincinnati Chamber of Commerce, February 4, 1899.

12. *Cincinnati Daily Gazette,* October 25, November 2, 11, 1875.

13. Centennial Exposition Records, Box 1, Folders 1, 2, 5 and 6.

14. *Cincinnati Enquirer,* April 26, 1900.

15. Quoted in Miller 1968, 31.

16. *Cincinnati Enquirer,* October 7, 1886. Glassberg (2000) and Rammelkamp (1978) find similar patterns in other late-nineteenth-century cities.

17. *Cincinnati Enquirer,* September 9, 1898.

18. Cohen, B. 1990; Hamel 1962; Gilkeson 1986; Hogan 1985; Fisher 1967; Kornblith 1983.

19. Nichols 1877; *Cincinnati Daily Gazette,* May 22, 1875; Lakes 1988.

20. Calvert 1967; United States Commissioner of Labor 1893; United States Commissioner of Labor 1902; Barlow 1967; Fisher 1967; Cremin 1964.

21. Commercial Club Collection, Minutes, June 13, October 13, 1882, October 16, 1886, October 17, 1887; Secretary's Files and Treasurer's Correspondence, Folder 41, Report of Committee on Technical School, December 21, 1895; *Cincinnati Enquirer,* June 25, 1901; Lakes 1988, 72–82; Ohio Mechanics' Institute, Annual Reports of Directors, 1882, 17–18, 1883, 15, 1887, 6.

22. Gingrich 1907; Schneider 1907; Manley 1907; Park 1943; Wing 1964, 188–89.

23. May 21, 1909 letter from the Metal Trades Association to the superintendent of public schools, reprinted in United States Commissioner of Labor 1911, 200.

24. Ohio Mechanics' Institute, Memorabilia, Box 72, Folder 1, "Sketch of the History of the Ohio Mechanics Institute" by George Kendall, 1853, 6.

25. Ohio Mechanics' Institute, Annual Reports, vol. 120, 1839 Report, 17, 29.

26. Barlow 1967, 32–33; *Cincinnati Daily Gazette,* November 11, 1876.

27. Ohio Mechanics' Institute, Biography Records, Professor Shearer materials, Box 20, Folder 21, April 1910 letter from James Hooker; Cincinnati Metal Trades Association, July 29, 1908.

28. United States Commissioner of Labor 1902, 369–95.

29. Ohio Mechanics' Institute, Board of Directors Minutes, vol. 6, July 5, 1892 letter from Reynolds to Miller.

30. United States Commissioner of Labor 1893, 613.

31. Ohio Mechanics' Institute, Board of Director Minutes, vol. 6, July 5, 1892.

32. Schneider 1915, 13; Manley 1907, 840.

33. Cincinnati Metal Trades Association, July 29, 1908 letter to Robert Wuest.

34. Park 1943, 96.

35. United States Commissioner of Labor 1911, 200.

36. Commercial Club of Cincinnati, Box 1, Minutes, April 19, 1884.

37. Cincinnati Milacron, Papers, Part 2, "Misc. Folders," Box M–N, Cincinnati Metal Trades Association Folder, letter to Wuest summarized at July 29, 1902 meeting.

38. *Cincinnati Daily Gazette,* December 26, 1873.

39. Glickstein 1991, 71–81; Rice 2004.

40. *Cincinnati Commercial,* December 29, 1865; Aaron 1992; Lakes 1988, 17.

41. Barlow 1967, 42–60; Calvert 1967; Fisher 1967, chap. 4.

42. National Association of Manufacturers 1906, 61; DuBrul 1910. On shifting educational hierarchies, see Cremin (1964), 42–60; Fisher (1967), 108. For developments in Philadelphia similar to those in Cincinnati, see Scranton (1986); Dawson (1999).

43. *Cincinnati Enquirer,* November 13, 1885.

44. Lakes 1988, 104.

45. United States Commissioner of Labor 1911, 202, 204.

46. Ohio Mechanics' Institute, 1882 Annual Report, Commencement Address by L. M. Hosea; Lakes 1988, 59–61.

47. Ohio Mechanics' Institute, 1883 Annual Report, 14, 15.

48. Schneider 1907, 409; Manley 1907, 840–41; Park 1943.

49. Cincinnati Metal Trades Association, December 20, 1905, presentation by University of Cincinnati president Dabney.

50. Ohio Mechanics' Institute, Biography Records, Professor Shearer materials, letter from James Hooker.

51. Lakes 1988, 133. On the relationship between class hierarchy and the ratio of theory to practice in contemporary education, see Bourdieu (1996).

52. *Cincinnati Commercial,* May 12, 1901; Hamel 1962, 56.

53. Ohio BLS, 1884, 293.

54. Central Labor Council, Minutes, March 25, 1901.

55. Brody 1980; Nelson 1975.

56. Wulsin Family Papers, Box 242, Executive Manufacturing Committee Reports, 1913, 11 and Box 179, Folders 1, 16, Employment Contracts, and Box 167, Folder 5, undated "History of the Baldwin Piano Co"; Ohio Mechanics' Institute, Memorial Files, Box 19, Folder 24.

57. Manley 1907, 840.

58. *American Industries,* May 1, 1907: 6; Wulsin Family Papers, Box 241, EMC Reports, Dec. 12, 1910 memo from Macy.

59. Wulsin Family Papers, Box 241, Executive Manufacturing Committee Minutes, May 7, 1913; Box 241, EMC Minutes, Box 182, Folder 5, August 4, 1892 letter to Bullard; Box 184, Folder 7, November 12, 1902 letter to Decker. Harris (2000, 59–61) finds that Philadelphia metal trades employers took a different approach, one emphasizing "tough love" more than fostering an "identity" with the firm.

60. Strobridge Lithographing Company, Box 9, Folder 1, Employment Contracts.

61. *Cincinnati Enquirer,* December 16, 1879, March 13, 1896.

62. Ibid., May 4, 1884.

63. Ibid., March 13, 1896. Statements by employers to newspaper reporters are influenced by public relations considerations, but in comments such as those about "old hands" who "have thrown a good thing away" (April 24, 1883), there is an unmistakable note of surprise and regret.

64. LeBlond Machine Tool Company, Box 25, Entrance/Exit Journal, 1916; Cincinnati Metal Trades Association Minutes, March 18, 1903.

65. Jenks 1957; Jacoby 1985; Watts 1991.

66. There is not enough evidence from Cincinnati to identify employer views of the good female employee, but she would probably have looked rather different from the worthy male employee—one of whose virtues, after all, was "manliness."

67. Centennial Exposition Records, Box 4, Folder 6–7, April 4, 1888 letter from H. J. Vinton.

68. On this point, the scraps of evidence from Cincinnati are consistent with discussions in contemporary trade magazines. "Between the workman and the factory there is always an unwritten, but fully acknowledged, contract of good and faithful service on the part of the artizan [sic], and of continued employment on the part of the factory" (Roland 1898, 220). They also fit Philadelphia metal trades employers (Harris 2000, 68–70).

69. Quoted in Wing 1964, 186. No date given, but c. 1905.

70. Chamber of Commerce Annual Report 1899, 317.

71. *Cincinnati Enquirer,* April 24, 1883; Cincinnati Chamber of Commerce, March 15, 1899.

72. Quoted in Schwartz 1995, 50.

73. Wulsin Family Papers, Box 179, Folder 1, April 4, 1893 letter from Robert Pfeifer to Wulsin.

74. Jacoby 1985.

75. Undated employee handbook, probably from the early 1920s, with penciled revisions suggesting that it was a legacy from some time earlier. Cincinnati Milacron, Part 1, "Old Timers," Box 1, Folder 1.

76. Wulsin Family Papers, Box 184, Folder 10, October 1, 1903 letter from Wulsin to Will Kilgour; *Cincinnati Enquirer,* July 27, 1899.

77. Wulsin Family Papers, Box 192, Folder 14, letter re: Employees' Scholarship Traveling Fund, and Box 241, EMC Minutes, Report for Period Ending June 30, 1909; Strobridge Lithographing Company Records, Box 9, Folder 4, employment contracts.

78. Wulsin Family Papers, Box 242, EMC Reports, May 30, 1906 report attached to May 7, 1913 Minutes; Box 241, Dec. 12, 1910 Minutes.

79. Ibid., Box 242, EMC Reports, June 3, 1912 meeting.

80. Nestor 1986, 127.

81. Wulsin Family Papers, Box 242, EMC Reports, June 3, 1912 meeting.

82. United States Senate Committee on Education and Labor 1885, II, 122, III, 8; Houser 1927; Hicks 1941, 112–15.

83. *Cincinnati Enquirer,* July 27, 1899.

84. Wulsin Family Papers, Box 182, Folder 7, June 17, 1902 letter to Captain Harry Bryan.

85. "The Taylor Differential Piece-Rate System," *Engineering Magazine* January 1901: 629.

86. *Cincinnati Enquirer,* March 13, 1896.

87. Wallace 1972.

88. James 1852–1933, July 24, 26, 1877, July 7, 1894 entries; Luskey 2003.

89. McPhail 1991; Leach 1994.

90. There was also ample legal precedent for treating unions as threats to public safety. See Forbath 1991; Dubofsky 1999.

91. *Cincinnati Enquirer,* July 25, 1881, January 25, 1904.

92. Wulsin Family Papers, Box 184, Folder 8, March 25, 1902 letter to Congressman J. H. Bromwell.

93. Ohio BLS, 1882, 36.

94. Musselman 1975, 39, 129, 141, 144.

95. This was the most common objection to trade unions in an 1889 survey of Ohio manufacturers (Ohio BLS, 1889, 75).

96. *Cincinnati Enquirer,* April 10, 1882.

97. *American Industries,* September 15, 1909, 29.

98. *Cincinnati Enquirer,* December 4, 1901, quoting local shoe manufacturers. Pope and Kirby are quoted by Wiebe (1962, 169).

99. Ohio BLS, 1882, 36; Wulsin Family Papers, Box 184, Folder 8, March 25, 1902 letter to J. H. Bromwell.

100. Scranton 1989, 23, 207; Ingham 1991, 130–37.

101. Central Labor Council Minutes, April 30, 1892, reporting on brewery owners.

102. *Cincinnati Enquirer,* March 13, 1892.

103. Ibid., March 13, 1880, quoting a cigar manufacturer.

104. Hobart 1903.

105. Burke 1995.

106. *Cincinnati Enquirer,* May 7, 1882.

107. Ibid., December 11, 1886.

108. Cincinnati Metal Trades Association Minutes, March 5, 1914.

109. *Cincinnati Enquirer,* January 23, 1878.

110. Cincinnati Chamber of Commerce, June 29, July 13, 1894.

111. Furness 1990; Schneirov, Stromquist, and Salvatore 1999.

112. Ohio BLS, 1882, 31.

113. Ohio BLS, 1882, 36, 1885, 235; *Cincinnati Enquirer,* January 1, 1884; Commercial Club Collection, Box 15, Speakers' Presentations, 1893–1918, Adam Shortt, Civil Service Commissioner, Ottawa, Canada, "Canadian Method of Settling Industrial Disputes," November 15, 1893.

114. *Cincinnati Enquirer,* July 27, 1899; Park 1943, 109–11; Miller 1968, 223–24.

115. *Cincinnati Enquirer,* August 23, 1884.

116. Miller 1968, 123–124; Central Labor Council Minutes, March 20, 1894.

117. Chamber of Commerce Records, August 30, 1895.

118. Business Men's Club Records, Committee Minutes, February 13, 29, March 13, 1912; Central Labor Council Minutes, January 9, 1900, June 20, 1911.

119. *Cincinnati Enquirer,* May 4, 1901; Schneider 1907, 409; the National Association of Manufacturers is quoted by Cremin 1964, 38; United States Commissioner of Labor, Twenty-fifth Annual Report, 204, 218; Central Labor Council Minutes, March 31, 1914.

6. FROM WORK TO POLITICS: SAN FRANCISCO

1. *San Francisco Examiner,* March 27, 1910.

2. San Francisco manufacturers paid relatively little attention to industrial education, leaving the initiative more to professional educators. Industrial education also lagged behind commercial training, especially in the public schools. See Peterson 1985, 20, 67–68; Kantor 1988; Katznelson and Weir 1985, 153–62. Although these points illustrate San Francisco manufacturers' lack of civic engagement and difficulties overcoming free-rider problems, they also rule out a substantive comparison of Cincinnati and San Francisco businessmen's recipes for industrial education.

3. Akin 1967; Furness 1990; Friedman 1998; Schneirov, Stromquist, and Salvatore 1999.

4. *San Francisco Examiner,* March 31, April 7, 23, 1903; May 13, 1914.

5. Hallidie Papers, Folder 7, "A Study of Skilled Labor Organizations," 6.

6. *San Francisco Examiner,* October 19, November 14, 1902; January 5, 1903.

7. Ibid., September 3, 1902; San Francisco Riggers and Stevedores Union, Minutes, April 22, 1912.

8. *San Francisco Examiner,* August 19, 1900.

9. Ibid., July 6, September 9, 11, 1901.

10. Ibid., May 10, 1907.

11. Ibid., November 11, 1910; San Francisco Industrial Conciliation Board 1910; United States Senate, Commission on Industrial Relations 1916, vol. 6, 5235–37; Cross 1918, 283–84.

12. Merchants' Association, vol. 10, no. 120 (August, 1906), 9.

13. *San Francisco Examiner,* September 21, 1909.

14. Ibid., June 26, 1907.

15. Quoted by Knight 1960, 188.

16. *San Francisco Examiner,* July 25, 1907.

17. Ibid., June 4, 1905.

18. Ibid., May 7, July 2, 29, 30, August 6, September 9, 11, 1901.

19. Ibid., August 21, 1900.

20. *American Industries,* September 15, 1902, 10; December 1, 1902, 9; August 15, 1903, 5–7.

21. *San Francisco Examiner,* July 25, 1907.

22. Mechanics' Institute of San Francisco, *Mechanics' Fair Daily Press,* August 18, 1871, August 14, 1865; Mechanics' Institute of San Francisco, 1899, 14; Leishman 1999.

23. Todd 1921, 325; Issel and Cherny 1986, 168; Bolton 1997, 190–92. The Merchants' and Manufacturers' Association concerned itself primarily with economic development. The Merchants' Association was a different organization—larger, more influential, and more preoccupied with general civic improvement.

24. *San Francisco Examiner,* April 29, 1909; Glassberg 2000, 162.

25. *San Francisco Examiner,* March 20, 21, June 19, July 13, August 11, 1895.

26. Ibid., September 28, 1910.

27. Ibid., March 20, 21, 22, 23, 1895.

28. Ibid., April 27, March 20, August 11, 1895; June 16, 1900.

29. Knight 1960, 214–16; *San Francisco Examiner,* October 28, November 1, 3, 1908, and April 27, 1909.

30. *San Francisco Examiner,* February 27, June 12, 1910; March 14, 1912.

31. Ibid., August 5, 1881.

32. Ibid., September 1, 1887; September 12, 1883.

33. Chandler and Nathan 1993, 4, 19, 26; Merrill 1970; Brechin 1999, 245–48.

34. *San Francisco Examiner,* August 21, 1913; Glassberg 2000.

35. *San Francisco Examiner,* March 8, 1895.

36. Ibid., December 15, 1911; March 14, 1912; June 19, 1913.

37. Ibid., December 2, 1899; September 13, 22, 1903.

38. Tygiel 1977, 359.

39. *San Francisco Examiner,* August 30, 1889.

40. Ibid., May 9, 1908; Blackford 1993, 48.

41. California Chinese Exclusion Convention 1901, 27.

42. Bean 1952; Kazin 1987, chap. 5.

43. Bean 1952, 261–63; Kazin 1987, 132–33.

44. *San Francisco Chronicle,* December 11, 1906.

45. Kazin 1987, 132.

46. *San Francisco Examiner,* July 11, 12, 1907; Merchants' Association Records, Reports and Minutes, September 12, 1907.

47. Kazin 1987, 137–39, 181–83.

48. Issel and Cherny 1986, 157–58; Kazin 1987, 182; *San Francisco Examiner,* June 11, 1911.

49. Merchants' Association, vol. 9, no. 106 (June 1905), 5.

50. *San Francisco Examiner,* June–August, 1916; Levi 1973.

51. *San Francisco Examiner,* August 11, 12, 18, 20, 1916; San Francisco Chamber of Commerce Minutes, August 15, 1916.

52. San Francisco Chamber of Commerce Records, Box 3, Folder 34, July 10, 1916 speech by Koster; *San Francisco Examiner,* July 12–18, 22, 23, August 2, 1916.

53. *San Francisco Examiner,* November 1 (original emphasis), 6, 1916.

54. Issel and Cherny 1986, 96; Kazin 1987, chap. 9; Kimeldorf 1988; Haydu 1997, chap. 4.

55. Giannini 1975; Cherny 1994; Chen 2000; Bristol-Kagan 1982. There are exceptions outside of manufacturing, notably white owners and employees of laundries (*San Francisco Examiner,* April 4, 1906).

56. Kazin 1987; Saxton 1965; Issel and Cherny 1986, 166–76.

57. *San Francisco Examiner,* September 15, 22, 1911, February 6, 1912; Saxton 1965, 430–35; Levi 1973, 55–56, 129–30; Issel and Cherny 1986, 159–62; Kazin, 1987.

58. Issel and Cherny 1986, 167–77; Bolton 1997.

59. On membership, see *San Francisco Examiner,* May 1, 1913, and Chamber of Commerce Records, Box 3, Folder 34, undated typescript on the open shop, 61-A. On the varied activities of the chamber, see San Francisco Chamber of Commerce Records, Minutes, October 27, November 24, 1911, May 22, June 26, September 15, 1915, September 19, 1916; *San Francisco Examiner,* April 9, May 9, December 12, 1912; Ryan 1936, 129–30; Issel 1988.

60. Todd 1921, 329.

61. The Merchants' and Manufacturers' Association is quoted in Cross (1918), 243–44; Knight (1960, 305) quotes Koster.

62. Bonnett 1956.

63. *San Francisco Examiner,* November 6, 1916, quoting Koster.

64. Ibid., December 7, 1911.

65. San Francisco Chamber of Commerce Records, Koster, "Law and Order and the San Francisco Chamber of Commerce: An Address," February 1918, Ms 870, Box 3, Folder 33, pp. 8, 12.

66. *San Francisco Examiner,* July 25, 1916; Levi 1983.

CONCLUSIONS

1. Finding similar social mechanisms in a variety of cases is quite different from concocting generalizable explanations, because those mechanisms are set in motion and combine in distinctive ways from one case to another. See Steinmetz 2004; Stinchcombe 2005.

2. McAdam 1988; Futrell and Simi 2004.

3. Tarrow 1998; McAdam, Tarrow, and Tilly 2001.

4. Swidler 1986. Swidler rightly urges us to investigate how "cultural resources are reappropriated in new contexts," and she goes on to argue that "publicly available meanings facilitate certain patterns of action" (283). I reverse that emphasis, arguing that certain organized patterns of action select publicly available meanings.

5. Snow et al. 1986; McAdam, McCarthy, and Zald 1996; Snow 2004.

6. Clemens 1997.

7. Putnam 2000.

8. On these characteristics of the New Deal system, see Fraser and Gerstle (1989); Brody (1993). O'Brien's (1993) discussion of "responsible unionism" in the New Deal argues that unions gained recognition as semipublic agents deserving some state protection. This differs from the explicit link between workplace and political representation found in practical corporatism. And although unions certainly functioned as collective agents in New Deal industrial relations, representative rights are based on individual voting preferences rather than organizational (or class) membership.

9. Sisson 1991; Haydu 1998.

10. David 1986; Mahoney 2000.

11. Haydu 1998; Orren and Skowronek 2004.

12. In Pierson's typology of "long-term processes," this account most closely resembles "threshold effects" where the causes have long been at work but the effects occur in short order (2004, 83–86). My narrative offers two caveats. One is to pay more attention to the interaction of long-term causes and short-term triggers. The other is to include the role of strategic actors in bringing those causes and triggers together. Sewell (1996), looking forward from "events," shows how they may be thought of as transforming structures. My argument looks backward, at how *past* structures shape the meaning and effects of an event.

13. Useem 1987; Schwartz 1987. Some claim to have found comparable trends at the level of transnational capitalism: Sklair 2001; Carroll and Fennema 2002.

14. Fraser and Gerstle 1989; Akard 1992; Prasad 2000, 19.

15. Fligstein and Shin 2005.

16. Haydu and Lee 2004.

17. These are just some of the themes in anti-union campaigns. Another one is a simple appeal to self-interest: you will be worse off if you elect the union. Mehta and Theodore 2005.

Works Cited

Aaron, D. 1992. *Cincinnati, Queen City of the West, 1819–38.* Columbus: Ohio State University Press.

Abrahamson, E. 1997. The Emergence and Prevalence of Employee Management Rhetorics: The Effects of Long Waves, Labor Unions, and Turnover, 1875–1992. *Academy of Management Journal* 40, no. 3 (June): 491–533.

Adams, R. 1995. *Industrial Relations under Liberal Democracy.* Columbia: University of South Carolina Press.

Akard, P. J. 1992. Corporate Mobilization and Political Power: The Transformation of U.S. Economic Policy in the 1970s. *American Sociological Review* 57, no. 5 (October): 597–615.

Akin, William E. 1967. Arbitration and Labor Conflict: The Middle Class Panacea. *Historian* 29, no. 4 (August): 565–83.

American Industries: Journal of the National Association of Manufacturers.

Aminzade, R. R., et al., eds. 2001. *Silence and Voice in the Study of Contentious Politics.* New York: Cambridge University Press.

Anderson, C. E. 1979. The Invention of the "Professional" Municipal Police: The Case of Cincinnati, 1788 to 1900. Ph.D. diss., University of Cincinnati.

Ansell, C. K., and A. L. Burris. 1997. Bosses of the City Unite! Labor Politics and Political Machine Consolidation, 1870–1910. *Studies in American Political Development* 11, no. 1 (Spring): 1–43.

Archer, M., and J. R. Blau. 1993. Class Formation in Nineteenth-Century America: The Case of the Middle Class. *Annual Review of Sociology* 19: 17–41.

Armstrong, E. A. 2002. *Forging Gay Identities: Organizing Sexuality in San Francisco, 1950–1994.* Chicago: University of Chicago Press.

Arnesen, E. 1996. American Workers and the Labor Movement in the Late Nineteenth Century. In *The Gilded Age: Essays on the Origins of Modern America,* ed. C. W. Calhoun, 39–61. Wilmington, Del.: Scholarly Resources Books.

Aronowitz, S. 2003. *How Class Works: Power and Social Movement.* New Haven, Conn.: Yale University Press.

Arthur, W. B. 1994. *Increasing Returns and Path Dependence in the Economy.* Ann Arbor: University of Michigan Press.

Bancroft, H. H. 1891–92. Chronicles of the Builders. C-D 457. Bancroft Library, University of California, Berkeley.

Barley, S. R., and G. Kunda. 1992. Design and Devotion: Surges of Rational and Normative Ideologies of Control in Managerial Discourse. *Administrative Science Quarterly* 37, no. 3 (September): 363–99.

Barlow, M. L. 1967. *History of Industrial Education in the United States.* Peoria, Ill.: C. A. Bennett.

Barth, G. 1968. Metropolitanism and Urban Elites in the Far West. In *The Age of Industrialism in America: Essays in Social Structure and Cultural Values,* ed. F. C. Jaher, 158–87. New York: Free Press.

———. 1975. *Instant Cities: Urbanization and the Rise of San Francisco and Denver.* New York: Oxford University Press.

Bean, W. 1952. *Boss Ruef's San Francisco.* Berkeley: University of California Press.

Beckert, S. 2001. *The Monied Metropolis: New York City and the Consolidation of the American Bourgeoisie, 1850–1896.* Cambridge: Cambridge University Press.

——. 2001a. Propertied of a Different Kind: Bourgeoisie and Lower Middle Class in the Nineteenth-Century United States. In *The Middling Sorts: Explorations in the History of the American Middle Class,* ed. B. J. Bledstein and R. D. Johnston, 285–95. New York: Routledge.

Beisel, N. 1997. *Imperiled Innocents: Anthony Comstock and Family Reproduction in Victorian America.* Princeton, N.J.: Princeton University Press.

Bendix, R. 1974. *Work and Authority in Industry: Ideologies of Management in the Course of Industrialization.* Berkeley: University of California Press.

Benedict, M. L. 1996. Law and the Constitution in the Gilded Age. In *The Gilded Age: Essays on the Origins of Modern America,* ed. C. W. Calhoun, 289–308. Wilmington, Delaware: Scholarly Resources Books.

Benford, R. D. 1997. An Insider's Critique of the Social Movement Framing Perspective. *Sociological Inquiry* 67, no. 4 (November): 409–30.

Benford, R., and D. A. Snow. 2000. Framing Processes and Social Movements: An Overview and Assessment. *Annual Review of Sociology* 26: 311–39.

Bennett, C. A. 1937. *History of Manual and Industrial Education, 1870–1917.* Peoria, Ill.: Manual Arts Press.

Bensman, D. 1980. Economics and Culture in the Gilded Age Hatting Industry. In *Small Business in American Life,* ed. S. W. Bruchey, 352–65. New York: Columbia University Press.

Berlanstein, L. R., ed. 1993. *Rethinking Labor History.* Urbana: University of Illinois Press.

Berthoff, R. 1964. The "Freedom to Control" in American Business History. In *A Festschrift for Frederick B. Artz,* ed. D. Pinkney and T. Ropp, 158–80. Durham, N.C.: Duke University Press.

Bettie, J. 2003. *Women without Class: Girls, Race, and Identity.* Berkeley: University of California Press.

Blackford, M. G. 1991. *A History of Small Business in America.* New York: Twayne.

——. 1993. *The Lost Dream: Businessmen and City Planning on the Pacific Coast, 1890–1920.* Columbus: Ohio State University Press.

Blumin, S. M. 1989. *The Emergence of the Middle Class: Social Experience in the American City, 1760–1900.* Cambridge: Cambridge University Press.

Bolton, M. 1997. Recovery for Whom? Social Conflict after the San Francisco Earthquake and Fire, 1906–1915. Ph.D. diss., University of California, Davis.

Bonnett, C. E. 1922. *Employers' Associations in the United States: A Study of Typical Associations.* New York: Macmillan.

——. 1956. *History of Employers' Associations in the United States.* New York: Vantage Press.

Bottero, W. 2004. Class Identities and the Identity of Class. *Sociology* 38, no. 5 (December): 985–1003.

Bourdieu, P. 1984. *Distinction: A Social Critique of the Judgement of Taste.* Cambridge, Mass.: Harvard University Press.

——. 1993. *The Field of Cultural Production.* New York: Columbia University Press.

——. 1996. *The State Nobility: Elite Schools in the Field of Power.* Stanford, Calif.: Stanford University Press.

Bowman, J. R. 1989. *Capitalist Collective Action: Competition, Cooperation, and Conflict in the Coal Industry.* Cambridge: Cambridge University Press.

Boyer, P. 1978. *Urban Masses and Moral Order in America, 1820–1920.* Cambridge, Mass.: Harvard University Press.

Brady, R. A. 1972 [1943]. *Business as a System of Power.* Freeport, N.Y.: Books for Libraries Press.

Braverman, H. 1974. *Labor and Monopoly Capital: The Degradation of Work in the Twentieth Century.* New York: Monthly Review Press.

Brechin, G. 1999. *Imperial San Francisco: Urban Power, Earthly Ruin.* Berkeley: University of California Press.

Bristol-Kagan, L. 1982. Chinese Migration to California, 1851–1882: Selected Industries of Work, the Chinese Institutions, and the Legislative Exclusion of a Temporary Labor Force. Ph.D. diss., Harvard University.

Brody, D. 1980. Labor and Small-Scale Enterprise during Industrialization. In *Small Business in American Life,* ed. S. W. Bruchey, 263–79. New York: Columbia University Press.

——. 1993. Workplace Contractualism in Comparative Perspective. In *Industrial Democracy in America: The Ambiguous Promise,* ed. N. Lichtenstein and H. J. Harris, 176–205. Washington, D.C. and New York: Woodrow Wilson Center Press and Cambridge University Press.

Brubaker, R. 2005. Ethnicity without Groups. In *Remaking Modernity: Politics, History, and Sociology,* ed. J. Adams, E. S. Clemens, and A. S. Orloff, 470–92. Durham, N.C.: Duke University Press.

Brubaker, R., and F. Cooper. 2000. Beyond Identity. *Theory and Society* 29, no. 1 (February): 1–47.

Bruchey, E. S. 1976. *The Business Elite in Baltimore, 1880–1914.* New York: Arno Press.

Buenker, J. 1973. *Urban Liberalism and Progressive Reform.* New York: Charles Scribner's Sons.

Burawoy, M. 1985. *The Politics of Production: Factory Regimes under Capitalism and Socialism.* London: Verso.

——. 1989. Two Methods in Search of Science: Skocpol versus Trotsky. *Theory and Society* 18, no. 6 (November): 759–805.

Burchell, R. A. 1979. *The San Francisco Irish, 1848–1880.* Manchester: Manchester University Press.

Burke, M. J. 1995. *The Conundrum of Class: Public Discourse on the Social Order in America.* Chicago: University of Chicago Press.

Bushman, R. L. 1992. *The Refinement of America: Persons, Houses, Cities.* New York: Vintage Books.

Business Men's Club (Cincinnati Club). Records. Cincinnati Historical Society.

California. Bureau of Labor Statistics. *Biennial Reports.* Sacramento.

California Chinese Exclusion Convention. 1901. *Proceedings and List of Delegates.* San Francisco: Star Press.

California State Senate. Special Committee on Chinese Immigration. 1878. *Chinese Immigration: Its Social, Moral, and Political Effect.* Sacramento: State Office.

Calvert, M. A. 1967. *The Mechanical Engineer in America, 1830–1910: Professional Cultures in Conflict.* Baltimore: Johns Hopkins University Press.

Carroll, W. K., and M. Fennema. 2002. Is There a Transnational Business Community? *International Sociology* 17, no. 3 (September): 393–419.

Centennial Exposition of the Ohio Valley and Central States, 1888. Centennial Exposition Records. Mss 654. Cincinnati Historical Society.

Central Labor Council (Cincinnati). Records. University of Cincinnati Library.

Chamberlin, M. W. H. 1888. History of Cincinnati Expositions. *New England Magazine* 6, no. 35 (September): 474–79.

Chandler, A., and M. Nathan. 1993. *The Fantastic Fair: The Story of the California Midwinter International Exposition, Golden Gate Park, San Francisco, 1894.* San Francisco: Pogo Press.

Charles, J. 1993. *Service Clubs in American Society: Rotary, Kiwanis, and Lions.* Urbana: University of Illinois Press.

Chatom, P. 1915. Industrial Relations in the Brewery, Metal, and Teaming Trades of San Francisco. Ph.D. diss., University of California, Berkeley.

Chen, Y. 2000. *Chinese San Francisco, 1850–1943: A Trans-Pacific Community.* Stanford: Stanford University Press.

Cherny, R. W. 1994. Patterns of Toleration and Discrimination in San Francisco: The Civil War to World War I. *California History* 73, no. 2 (Summer): 131–41.

Chiu, P. 1960. Chinese Labor in California, 1850–1880: An Economic Study. Ph.D. diss., University of Wisconsin.

Choy, P. P., L. Dong, and M. K. Hom, eds. 1995. *Coming Man: Nineteenth-Century American Perceptions of the Chinese.* Seattle: University of Washington Press.

Cincinnati Chamber of Commerce and Merchants' Exchange. 1889. *Dedicatory Exercises at the Opening of the New Building of the Cincinnati Chamber of Commerce.* Cincinnati: Cincinnati Chamber of Commerce.

Cincinnati Chamber of Commerce. Minutes of the Board of Directors 1848–1925, Mss fC 443m. Cincinnati Historical Society.

——. Records of Meetings of the Cincinnati Chamber of Commerce 1839–1917, Mss fC 443g. Cincinnati Historical Society.

——. *Annual Report.* Cincinnati: Cincinnati Chamber of Commerce.

Cincinnati Commercial.

Cincinnati Daily Gazette.

Cincinnati Enquirer.

Cincinnati Metal Trades Association. Minute Books, 1900–1915. Cincinnati: In possession of Robert Manley.

Cincinnati Milacron. Papers. Cincinnati Historical Society.

Cincinnati Musical Festival Association. Records. Mss 529, 566. Cincinnati Historical Society.

Citizens' Alliance of San Francisco. N.d. *Constitution and By-Laws.* San Francisco: Citizens' Alliance of San Francisco.

——. N.d. *A Few of the Things Done by the Citizens' Alliance of San Francisco.* San Francisco: Bureau of Publicity, Citizens' Alliance of San Francisco.

——. N.d. *The Open Shop.* San Francisco: Bureau of Publicity, Citizens' Alliance of San Francisco.

Clemens, E. S. 1996. Organizational Form as Frame: Collective Identity and Political Strategy in the American Labor Movement, 1880–1920. In *Comparative Perspectives on Social Movements: Political Opportunities, Mobilizing Structures, and Cultural Framings,* ed. D. McAdam, J. D. McCarthy, and M. N. Zald, 205–26. New York: Cambridge University Press.

——. 1997. *The People's Lobby: Organizational Innovation and the Rise of Interest Group Politics in the United States, 1890–1925.* Chicago: University of Chicago Press.

Clemens, E. S., and J. M. Cook. 1999. Politics and Institutionalism: Explaining Durability and Change. *Annual Review of Sociology* 25: 441–66.

Cochran, T. 1972. *Business in American Life: A History.* New York: McGraw-Hill.

Cohen, B. 1990. Worcester, Open Shop City: The National Metal Trades Association and the Molders' Strike of 1919–1920. In *Labor in Massachusetts: Selected Essays,* ed. K. Fones-Wolf and M. Kaufman, 168–98. Westfield, Mass.: Institute for Massachusetts Studies.

Cohen, N. 2002. *The Reconstruction of American Liberalism, 1865–1914.* Chapel Hill: University of North Carolina Press.

Commercial Club of Cincinnati. Papers, 1880–1973. Cincinnati Historical Society.

Committee of One Hundred. 1886a. *Public Meeting of Committee of One Hundred of Cincinnati in the Odeon, February 11, 1886.* Cincinnati: Robert Clarke and Co.

———. 1886b. *Second Public Meeting of Committee of One Hundred of Cincinnati in the Odeon, February 25, 1886.* Cincinnati: Robert Clarke and Co.

———. 1886c. *Proceedings of the Association of the Committee of One Hundred Held in the Odeon March 26, 1886.* Cincinnati: Robert Clarke and Co.

———. 1886d. *Proceedings of the Association of the Committee of One Hundred of Cincinnati at the First Annual Meeting, Held in the Odeon October 5th, 1886.* Cincinnati: Robert Clarke and Co.

Commonwealth Club of California. *Transactions.* San Francisco.

Cornell, S. E., and D. Hartman. 1998. *Ethnicity and Race: Making Identities in a Changing World.* Thousand Oaks, Calif.: Pine Forge Press.

Couvares, F. G. 1984. *The Remaking of Pittsburgh: Class and Culture in an Industrializing City, 1877–1919.* Albany: State University of New York Press.

Cremin, L. A. 1964. *The Transformation of the School: Progressivism in American Education, 1876–1957.* New York: Vintage Books.

Cross, I. B. 1918. Collective Bargaining and Trade Agreements in the Brewery, Metal, Teaming, and Building Trades of San Francisco, California. *University of California Publications in Economics* 4, no. 4 (May): 233–364.

———. 1935. *History of the Labor Movement in California.* Berkeley: University of California Press.

Cyphers, C. J. 2002. *The National Civic Federation and the Making of a New Liberalism, 1900–1915.* Westport, Conn.: Praeger.

Dahrendorf, R. 1959. *Class and Class Conflict in Industrial Society.* Palo Alto, Calif.: Stanford University Press.

Dannenbaum, J. 1984. *Drink and Disorder: Temperance Reform in Cincinnati from the Washingtonian Revival to the WCTU.* Urbana: University of Illinois Press.

David, P. A. 1986. Understanding the Economics of QWERTY: The Necessity of History. In *Economic History and the Modern Economist,* ed. W. N. Parker, 30–49. Oxford: Basil Blackwell.

Davis, G., D. McAdam, R. Scott, and M. Zald, eds. 2005. *Social Movements and Organization Theory.* New York: Cambridge University Press.

Dawley, A. 2005. The Abortive Rule of Big Money. In *Ruling America: A History of Wealth and Power in a Democracy,* ed. S. Fraser and G. Gerstle, 149–80. Cambridge, Mass.: Harvard University Press.

Dawson, A. 1999. The Workshop and the Classroom: Philadelphia Engineering, the Decline of Apprenticeship, and the Rise of Industrial Training, 1878–1900. *History of Education Quarterly* 39, no. 2 (Summer): 143–60.

———. 2004. *Lives of the Philadelphia Engineers: Capital, Class, and Revolution, 1830–1890.* Burlington, Vt.: Ashgate.

Decker, P. R. 1978. *Fortunes and Failures: White Collar Mobility in Nineteenth-Century San Francisco.* Cambridge, Mass.: Harvard University Press.

Dexter, J. Papers, Mss qD526. Cincinnati Historical Society.

Diani, M., and D. McAdam. 2003. *Social Movements and Networks: Relational Approaches to Collective Action.* New York: Oxford University Press.

Dillon, R. H. 1984. *Iron Men: Peter, James, and Michael Donahue.* Point Richmond, Calif.: Candela Press.

DiMaggio, P. 1992. Cultural Boundaries and Structural Change: The Extension of the High Culture Model to Theater, Opera, and the Dance, 1900–1940. In *Cultivated Differences: Symbolic Boundaries and the Making of Inequality,* ed. M. Lamont and M. Fournier, 21–57. Chicago: University of Chicago Press.

Dobbin, F. 1994. *Forging Industrial Policy: The United States, Britain, and France in the Railway Age.* Cambridge: Cambridge University Press.

Domhoff, G. W. 2002. *Who Rules America? Power and Politics.* Boston: McGraw Hill.

Douglas, M. 1986. *How Institutions Think.* Syracuse, N.Y.: Syracuse University Press.

Downard, W. L. 1973. *The Cincinnati Brewing Industry: A Social and Economic History.* Columbus: Ohio University Press.

Dubofsky, M. 1975. *Industrialism and the American Worker, 1865–1920.* Arlington Heights, Ill.: AHM Publishing.

——. 1994. *The State and Labor in Modern America.* Chapel Hill: University of North Carolina Press.

——. 1999. The Federal Judiciary, Free Labor, and Equal Rights. In *The Pullman Strike and the Crisis of the 1890s: Essays on Labor and Politics,* ed. R. Schneirov, S. Stromquist, and N. Salvatore, 159–78. Urbana: University of Illinois Press.

DuBrul, E. F. 1910. Supplemental Report on the Co-operative System of Industrial Education. *American Industries* 11, no. 1 (August): 26–28.

Duggan, E. P. 1977. Machines, Markets, and Labor: The Carriage and Wagon Industry in Late Nineteenth Century Cincinnati. *Business History Review* 51, no. 3 (Autumn): 308–25.

Dumenil, L. 1984. *Freemasonry and American Culture.* Princeton, N.J.: Princeton University Press.

Eaves, L. 1910. *A History of California Labor Legislation with an Introductory Sketch of the San Francisco Labor Movement.* Berkeley: University Press.

Edwards, R. 1979. *Contested Terrain: The Transformation of the Workplace in the Twentieth Century.* New York: Basic Books.

Eggert, G. G. 1993. *Harrisburg Industrializes: The Coming of Factories to an American Community.* University Park: Pennsylvania University Press.

Eley, G., and K. Nield. 2000. Farewell to the Working Class? *International Labor and Working Class History* 57 (Spring): 1–30.

Engelbourg, S. 1980. *Power and Morality: American Business Ethics 1840–1914.* Westport, Conn.: Greenwood Press.

Erie, S. P. 1975. The Development of Class and Ethnic Politics in San Francisco, 1870–1910: A Critique of the Pluralist Interpretation. Ph.D. diss., University of California, Los Angeles.

Ernst, D. R. 1995. *Lawyers against Labor: From Individual Rights to Corporate Liberalism.* Urbana: University of Illinois Press.

Ethington, P. J. 1994. *The Public City: The Political Construction of Urban Life in San Francisco, 1850–1900.* Cambridge: Cambridge University Press.

Fagge, R. 1996. *Power, Culture, and Conflict in the Coalfields: West Virginia and South Wales, 1900–1922.* Manchester: Manchester University Press.

Faler, P. G. 1981. *Mechanics and Manufacturers in the Early Industrial Revolution: Lynn, Massachusetts, 1780–1860.* Albany: State University of New York Press.

Ferree, M. M., W. A. Gamson, J. Gerhards, and D. Rucht. 2002. *Shaping Abortion Discourse: Democracy and the Public Sphere in Germany and the United States.* Cambridge: Cambridge University Press.

Fine, S. 1995. *"Without Blare of Trumpets": Walter Drew, the National Erectors' Association, and the Open Shop Movement, 1903–1957.* Ann Arbor: University of Michigan Press.

Fisher, B. M. 1967. *Industrial Education: American Ideals and Institutions.* Madison: University of Wisconsin Press.

Fletcher, S. 2003. Public Dreams, Private Means: Cincinnati and Its Southern Railway, 1869–1901. *Journal of Transportation History* 24, no. 1 (March): 38–58.

Fligstein, N., and T.-J. Shin. 2005. Shareholder Value and Changes in American Industries, 1984–2000. Unpublished paper, http://sociology.berkeley.edu/faculty/FLIGSTEIN/fligstein_pdf/Transformation6_edit_tshin.pdf.

Folsom, B. W., Jr. 1981. *Urban Capitalists: Entrepreneurs and City Growth in Pennsylvania's Lackawanna and Lehigh Regions, 1800–1920.* Baltimore: Johns Hopkins University Press.

Foner, E. 1996. Free Labor and Nineteenth-Century Political Ideology. In *The Market Revolution in America: Social, Political, and Religious Expressions, 1800–1880,* ed. M. Stokes and S. Conway, 99–127. Charlottesville: University Press of Virginia.

———. 1998. *The Story of American Freedom.* New York: W. W. Norton.

Foraker, Julia B. 1932. *I Would Live It Again: Memories of a Vivid Life.* New York: Harper and Brothers.

Forbath, W. E. 1991. *Law and the Shaping of the American Labor Movement.* Cambridge, Mass.: Harvard University Press.

Ford, H. A., and K. B. Ford. 1881. *History of Cincinnati, Ohio, with Illustrations and Biographical Sketches.* Cleveland: L. A. Williams.

Franks, J. S. 1985. Boot and Shoemakers in Nineteenth-Century San Francisco, 1860–1892: A Study in Class, Culture, Ethnicity, and Popular Protest in an Industrializing Community. Ph.D. diss., University of California, Irvine.

Fraser, S., and G. Gerstle, eds. 1989. *The Rise and Fall of the New Deal Order, 1930–1980.* Princeton, N.J.: Princeton University Press.

———, eds. 2005. *Ruling America: A History of Wealth and Power in a Democracy.* Cambridge, Mass.: Harvard University Press.

Friedland, R., and R. R. Alford. 1991. Bringing Society Back In: Symbols, Practices, and Institutional Contradictions. In *The New Institutionalism in Organizational Analysis,* ed. W. Powell and P. DiMaggio, 232–63. Chicago: University of Chicago Press.

Friedman, G. 1998. *State-Making and Labor Movements: France and the United States, 1876–1914.* Ithaca, N.Y.: Cornell University Press.

———. Forthcoming. The Decline of the American Labor Movement: Explanations and Implications for United States Industrial Relations. In *New Directions in Industrial Relations,* ed. M. Borrel. Berkeley: University of California Press.

Frisch, M. H. 1972. *Town into City: Springfield, Massachusetts, and the Meaning of Community, 1840–1880.* Cambridge, Mass.: Harvard University Press.

Furner, M. O. 1993. The Republican Tradition and the New Liberalism: Social Investigation, State Building, and Social Learning in the Gilded Age. In *The State and Social Investigation in Britain and the United States,* ed. M. J. Lacey and M. O. Furner, 171–241. Cambridge: Woodrow Wilson Center Press and Cambridge University Press.

Furness, M. O. 1990. Knowing Capitalism: Public Investigation and the Labor Question in the Long Progressive Era. In *The State and Economic Knowledge: The American and British Experiences,* ed. M. O. Furner and B. Supple, 241–86. Cambridge: Cambridge University Press.

Futrell, R., and P. Simi. 2004. Free Spaces, Collective Identity, and the Persistence of U.S. White Power Activism. *Social Problems* 51, no. 1 (February): 16–42.

Gamm, G., and R. D. Putnam. 1999. The Growth of Voluntary Associations in America, 1840–1940. *Journal of Interdisciplinary History* 29, no. 4 (Spring): 511–57.

Gamson, W. A. 1992. The Social Psychology of Collective Action. In *Frontiers in Social Movement Theory,* ed. A. D. Morris and C. M. Mueller. New Haven, Conn.: Yale University Press.

Gantman, E. R. 2005. *Capitalism, Social Privilege, and Managerial Ideologies.* Aldershot, Eng.: Ashgate.

Gerber, L. G. 1997. Shifting Perspectives on American Exceptionalism: Recent Literature on American Labor Relations. *Journal of American Studies* 31, no. 2 (August): 253–74.

Gerstle, G. 2001. *American Crucible: Race and Nation in the Twentieth Century.* Princeton, N.J.: Princeton University Press.

Gerteis, J. 2002. The Possession of Civic Virtue: Movement Narratives of Race and Class in the Knights of Labor. *American Journal of Sociology* 108, no. 3 (November): 580–615.

Gerteis, J., and M. Savage. 1998. The Salience of Class in Britain and America: A Comparative Analysis. *British Journal of Sociology* 49, no. 2 (June): 252–74.

Giannini, R. V. 1975. San Francisco, Labor's City: 1900–1911. Ph. D. diss., University of Florida.

Gilkeson, J. S., Jr. 1986. *Middle-Class Providence, 1820–1940.* Princeton, N.J.: Princeton University Press.

Gingrich, C. S. 1907. The Cooperative Engineering Course at the University of Cincinnati from the Manufacturers' Standpoint. Proceedings of the Fifteenth Annual Meeting of the Society for the Promotion of Engineering Education. New York.

Glassberg, D. 2000. Civic Celebration and the Invention of the Urban Public. *Mid-America* 82 (1–2): 147–72.

Glickman, L. B. 1997. *A Living Wage: American Workers and the Making of Consumer Society.* Ithaca, N.Y.: Cornell University Press.

Glickstein, J. A. 1991. *Concepts of Free Labor in Antebellum America.* New Haven, Conn.: Yale University Press.

Goffman, E. 1959. *The Presentation of Self in Everyday Life.* Garden City, N.Y.: Doubleday Anchor.

Goldstone, J. 1997. Methodological Issues in Comparative Macrosociology. *Comparative Social Research* 16: 107–20.

Gordon, C. 1994. *New Deals: Business, Labor, and Politics in America, 1920–1935.* Cambridge: Cambridge University Press.

Gordon, D. M., R. Edwards, and M. Reich. 1982. *Segmented Work, Divided Workers: The Historical Transformation of Labor in the United States.* Cambridge: Cambridge University Press.

Goss, C. F. 1912. *Cincinnati: The Queen City, 1788–1912.* Chicago: S. J. Clarke.

Green, M. 1973 [1956]. *The National Civic Federation and the American Labor Movement, 1900–1925.* Westport, Conn.: Greenwood Press.

Greve, C. T. 1904. *Centennial History of Cincinnati and Representative Citizens.* Chicago: Biographical Publishing.

Griffen, C., and S. Griffen. 1980. Small Business and Occupational Mobility in Mid-Nineteenth-Century Poughkeepsie. In *Small Business in American Life,* ed. S. W. Bruchey, 122–41. New York: Columbia University Press.

Guillén, M. F. 1994. *Models of Management: Work, Authority, and Organization in a Comparative Perspective.* Chicago: University of Chicago Press.

Gutman, H. 1977. *Work, Culture, and Society in Industrializing America.* New York: Vintage Books.

Gyory, A. 1998. *Closing the Gate: Race, Politics, and the Chinese Exclusion Act.* Chapel Hill: University of North Carolina Press.

Hall, J. R., ed. 1997. *Reworking Class.* Ithaca, N.Y.: Cornell University Press.

——. 1992. The Capital(s) of Cultures: A Nonholistic Approach to Status Situations, Class, Gender, and Ethnicity. In *Cultivated Differences: Symbolic Boundaries and the Making of Inequality,* ed. M. Lamont and M. Fournier, 257–85. Chicago: University of Chicago Press.

Hall, P. D. 1982. *The Organization of American Culture, 1700–1900: Private Institutions, Elites, and the Origins of American Nationality.* New York: New York University Press.

Halle, D. 1984. *America's Working Man: Work, Home, and Politics among Blue-collar Property Owners.* Chicago: University of Chicago Press.

Hallidie, A. S. Papers. Ms 916. California Historical Society.

Hallidie, A. Addresses and Reports. Bancroft Library. University of California, Berkeley.

Hamel, D. B. 1962. A History of the Ohio Mechanics' Institute, Cincinnati, Ohio. D.Ed. diss., Ohio State University.

Hanagan, M. P. 1994. New Perspectives on Class Formation: Culture, Reproduction, and Agency. *Social Science History* 18, no. 1 (Spring): 77–94.

Harlow, A. F. 1950. *The Serene Cincinnatians.* New York: Dutton.

Harris, H. J. 2000. *Bloodless Victories: The Rise and Fall of the Open Shop in the Philadelphia Metal Trades, 1890–1940.* Cambridge: Cambridge University Press.

Haydu, J. 1988. Employers, Unions, and American Exceptionalism: A Comparative View. *International Review of Social History* 33 (1): 25–41.

——. 1988. Trade Agreement vs. Open Shop: Employers' Choices Before WWI. *Industrial Relations* 28, no. 2 (Spring): 159–73.

——. 1997. *Making American Industry Safe for Democracy: Comparative Perspectives on the State and Employee Representation in the Era of World War I.* Urbana: University of Illinois Press.

——. 1998. Making Use of the Past: Time Periods as Cases to Compare and as Sequences of Problem Solving. *American Journal of Sociology* 104, no. 2 (September): 339–71.

Haydu, J., and C. Lee. 2004. Model Employers and Good Government in the Late Nineteenth and Late Twentieth Centuries. *Sociological Forum* 19, no. 2 (June): 177–202.

Hays, S. P. 1964. The Politics of Reform in Municipal Government in the Progressive Era. *Pacific Northwest Quarterly* 55, no. 4 (October): 157–69.

Heimer, C. A., and L. R. Staffen. 1998. *For the Sake of the Children: The Social Organization of Responsibility in the Hospital and the Home.* Chicago: University of Chicago Press.

Hennings, R. E. 1961. James D. Phelan and the Wilson Progressives of California. Ph.D. diss., University of California, Berkeley.

Hickenlooper, A. Papers, Mss H628. Cincinnati Historical Society.

Hicks, C. J. 1941. *My Life in Industrial Relations: Fifty Years in the Growth of a Profession.* New York: Harper and Brothers.

Hilkey, J. 1997. *Character Is Capital: Success Manuals and Manhood in Gilded Age America.* Chapel Hill: University of North Carolina Press.

Hirsch, S. E. 1980. From Artisan to Manufacturer: Industrialization and the Small Producer in Newark. In *Small Business in American Life,* ed. S. W. Bruchey, 80–99. New York: Columbia University Press.

Hittell, J. S. 1878. *A History of the City of San Francisco and Incidentally of the State of California.* San Francisco: A. L. Bancroft.

——. 1882. *The Commerce and Industries of the Pacific Coast of North America.* 2nd ed. San Francisco: A. L. Bancroft.

Hobart, J. C. 1903. The Employment Department of Employers' Association Work. *American Industries,* 1 July, 1–2.

Hochschild, A. R. 1997. *The Time Bind: When Work Becomes Home and Home Becomes Work.* New York: Metropolitan Books.

Hochschild, J. 1995. *Facing Up to the American Dream: Race, Class, and the Soul of the Nation.* Princeton, N.J.: Princeton University Press.

Hoffecker, C. E. 1974. *Wilmington, Delaware: Portrait of an Industrial City, 1830–1910.* [Charlottesville]: University Press of Virginia.

Hofstadter, R. 1948. *The American Political Tradition and the Men Who Made It.* New York: Vintage Books.

——. 1955. *The Age of Reform.* New York: Vintage Books.

Hogan, D. J. 1985. *Class and Reform: School and Society in Chicago, 1880–1930.* Philadelphia: University of Pennsylvania Press.

Holt, D. B. 2000. Does Cultural Capital Structure American Consumption? In *The Consumer Society Reader,* ed. J. B. Schor and D. B. Holt, 212–52. New York: New Press.

Horowitz, H. L. 1976. *Culture and the City: Cultural Philanthropy in Chicago from the 1880s to 1917.* Lexington: University Press of Kentucky.

Houser, J. D. 1927. *What the Employer Thinks: Executives' Attitudes toward Their Employees.* Cambridge, Mass.: Harvard University Press.

Howe, B. J. 1978. Uniting the Useful and Beautiful: The Arts in Cincinnati. *The Old Northwest* 4, no. 4 (December): 319–36.

Ingham, J. N. 1978. *The Iron Barons: A Social Analysis of an American Urban Elite, 1874–1965.* Westport, Conn.: Greenwood Press.

——. 1991. *Making Iron and Steel: Independent Mills in Pittsburgh, 1820–1920.* Columbus: Ohio State University Press.

International Brotherhood of Boiler Makers and Iron Ship Builders of America. Boiler Makers' *Journal.*

Isaac, L. 2002. To Counter "The Very Devil" and More: The Making of Independent Capitalist Militia in the Gilded Age. *American Journal of Sociology* 108, no. 2 (September): 353–405.

Issel, W. 1977. Class and Ethnic Conflict in San Francisco Political History: The Reform Charter of 1898. *Labor History* 18 (Summer): 341–59.

——. 1988. "Citizens Outside of Government": Business and Public Policy in San Francisco and Los Angeles, 1890–1930. *Pacific Historical Review* 58 (May): 117–46.

Issel, W., and R. Cherny. 1986. *San Francisco, 1865–1932: Politics, Power, and Urban Development.* Berkeley: University of California Press.

Jackson, R. M. 1984. *The Formation of Craft Labor Markets.* Orlando, Fla.: Academic Press.

Jacobson, M. F. 1998. *Whiteness of a Different Color: European Immigrants and the Alchemy of Race.* Cambridge, Mass.: Harvard University Press.

Jacoby, S. M., ed. 1991. *Masters to Managers: Historical and Comparative Perspectives on American Employers.* New York: Columbia University Press.

——. 1985. *Employing Bureaucracy: Managers, Unions, and the Transformation of Work in American Industry, 1900–1945.* New York: Columbia University Press.

——. 1991. American Exceptionalism Revisited: The Importance of Management. In *Masters to Managers: Historical and Comparative Perspectives on American Employers,* ed. S. M. Jacoby, 172–200. New York: Columbia University Press.

Jaher, F. C. 1982. *The Urban Establishment: Upper Strata in Boston, New York, Charleston, Chicago, and Los Angeles.* Urbana: University of Illinois.

James, D. L. Diaries, 1852–1933. Mss 858. Cincinnati Historical Society.

Jenks, L. H. 1957. Business Ideology. *Explorations in Entrepreneurial History* 10, no. 1 (October): 1–7.

Johnson, J. C. 1886. Statement. Banc Mss C-D 331. Bancroft Library. University of California, Berkeley.

Johnson, J. P. 1979. *The Politics of Soft Coal: The Bituminous Industry from World War I through the New Deal.* Urbana: University of Illinois Press.

Johnston, R. D. 2003. *The Radical Middle Class: Populist Democracy and the Question of Capitalism in Progressive Era Portland, Oregon.* Princeton, N.J.: Princeton University Press.

Jones, G. S. 1982. The Language of Chartism. In *The Chartist Experience: Studies in Working-Class Radicalism and Culture, 1830–60*, ed. J. Epstein and D. Thompson, 3–58. London: Macmillan.

Joyce, P., ed. 1995. *Class*. Oxford: Oxford University Press.

Kantor, H. A. 1988. *Learning to Earn: School, Work, and Vocational Reform in California, 1880–1930*. Madison: University of Wisconsin Press.

Kasson, J. F. 1976. *Civilizing the Machine: Technology and Republican Values in America, 1776–1900*. New York: Grossman Publishers.

——. 1990. *Rudeness and Civility: Manners in Nineteenth-century Urban America*. New York: Hill and Wang.

Katznelson, I. 1981. *City Trenches: Urban Politics and the Patterning of Class in the United States*. New York: Pantheon.

——. 1986. Working-class Formation: Constructing Cases and Comparisons. In *Working-class Formation: Nineteenth-century Patterns in Western Europe and the United States*, ed. I. Katznelson and A. R. Zolberg, 3–41. Princeton, N.J.: Princeton University Press.

Katznelson, I., and M. Weir. 1985. *Schooling for All: Class, Race, and the Decline of the Democratic Ideal*. Berkeley: University of California Press.

Kazin, M. 1987. *Barons of Labor: The San Francisco Building Trades and Union Power in the Progressive Era*. Urbana: University of Illinois Press.

Kefalas, M. 2003. *Working-Class Heroes: Protecting Home, Community, and Nation in a Chicago Neighborhood*. Berkeley: University of California Press.

Kimeldorf, H. 1988. *Reds or Rackets? The Making of Radical and Conservative Unions on the Waterfront*. Berkeley: University of California Press.

——. 1999. *Battling for American Labor: Wobblies, Craft Workers, and the Making of the Union Movement*. Berkeley: University of California Press.

Kirk, N. 1994. *Labour and Society in Britain and the USA: Challenge and Accommodation, 1850–1939*. Aldershot, Eng.: Scolar Press.

Klug, T. A. 1993. *The Roots of the Open Shop: Employers, Trade Unions, and Craft Labor Markets in Detroit, 1859–1907*. Ph.D. diss., Wayne State University.

Knight, R. E. L. 1960. *Industrial Relations in the San Francisco Bay Area, 1900–1918*. Berkeley: University of California Press.

Koditschek, T. 1990. *Class Formation and Urban-Industrial Society: Bradford, 1750–1850*. Cambridge: Cambridge University Press.

Kolko, G. 1967. *The Triumph of Conservatism: A Reinterpretation of American History, 1900–1916*. Chicago: Quadrangle Books.

Kornblith, G. J. 1983. *From Artisans to Businessmen: Master Mechanics in New England, 1789–1850*. Ph.D. diss., Princeton University.

Labor Clarion. San Francisco Labor Council and the California State Federation of Labor.

Lakes, R. D. 1988. From Manual Training to Trade Instruction: The Evolution of Industrial Education in Cincinnati, 1886–1920. Ph.D. diss., Ohio State University.

Lamont, M. 1992. *Money, Morals, and Manners: The Culture of the French and the American Upper-Middle Class*. Chicago: University of Chicago Press.

——. 2000. *The Dignity of Working Men: Morality and the Boundaries of Race, Class, and Immigration*. New York and Cambridge, Mass.: Russell Sage Foundation and Harvard University Press.

Lamont, M., and M. Fournier, eds. 1992. *Cultivating Differences: Symbolic Boundaries and the Making of Inequality*. Chicago: University of Chicago Press.

Lamont, M., and L. Thévenot, eds. 2000. *Rethinking Comparative Cultural Sociology: Repertoires of Evaluation in France and the United States*. Cambridge: Cambridge University Press.

Lamont, M., and V. Molnár. 2002. The Study of Boundaries in the Social Sciences. *Annual Review of Sociology* 28: 167–95.

Lareau, A. 2003. *Unequal Childhoods: Class, Race, and Family Life.* Berkeley: University of California Press.

Laurie, B. 1998. The "Fair Field" of the "Middle Ground": Abolitionism, Labor Reform, and the Making of an Antislavery Bloc in Antebellum Massachusetts. In *Labor Histories: Class, Politics, and the Working-Class Experience,* ed. E. Arnesen, J. Greene, and B. Laurie, 45–70. Urbana: University of Illinois Press.

Leach, E. E. 1994. Chaining the Tiger: The Mob Stigma and the Working Class, 1863–1894. *Labor History* 35, no. 2 (Spring): 187–215.

LeBlond Machine Tool Company. Records, Mss 982. Cincinnati Historical Society.

Lee, R. G. 1999. *Orientals: Asian Americans in Popular Culture.* Philadelphia: Temple University Press.

Leishman, N. 1999. The Mechanics' Institute Fairs, 1857 to 1899. *The Argonaut* 10, no. 2 (Fall): 40–57.

Lembcke, J. L. 1995. Labor History's "Synthesis Debate." *Science and Society* 59, no. 2 (Summer): 137–73.

Leonard, L. A. 1927. *Greater Cincinnati and Its People: A History.* New York: Lewis Historical Publishing.

Levi, S. C. 1973. San Francisco's Law and Order Committee, 1916. *Journal of the West* 12, no. 1 (January): 53–70.

———. 1983. *Committee of Vigilance, the San Francisco Chamber of Commerce Law and Order Committee, 1916–1919: A Case Study in Official Hysteria.* Jefferson, N.C.: McFarland.

Levine, L. W. 1988. *Highbrow/Lowbrow: The Emergence of Cultural Hierachy in America.* Cambridge, Mass.: Harvard University Press.

Licht, W. 1995. *Industrializing America: The Nineteenth Century.* Baltimore: Johns Hopkins University Press.

Lipset, S. M. 1983. Radicalism or Reformism: The Sources of Working-class Politics. *American Political Science Review* 77, no. 1 (March): 1–18.

———. 1986. North American Labor Movements: A Comparative Perspective. In *Unions in Transition: Entering the Second Century,* ed. S. M. Lipset, 421–52. San Francisco: Institute for Contemporary Studies.

Lipset, S. M., and G. Marks. 2000. *It Didn't Happen Here: Why Socialism Failed in the United States.* New York: W. W. Norton.

Livingston, J. 1986. *Origins of the Federal Reserve System: Money, Class, and Corporate Capitalism, 1890–1913.* Ithaca, N.Y.: Cornell University Press.

———. 1994. *Pragmatism and the Political Economy of Cultural Revolution, 1850–1940.* Chapel Hill: University of North Carolina Press.

Loveday, A. J., Jr. 1983. *The Rise and Decline of the American Cut Nail Industry: A Study of the Interrelationships of Technology, Business Organization, and Management Techniques.* Westport, Conn.: Greenwood Press.

Luskey, B. 2003. Riot and Respectability: The Shifting Terrain of Class Language and Status in Baltimore during the Great Strike of 1877. *American Nineteenth Century History* 4, no. 3 (Fall): 61–96.

Lustig, R. J. 1982. *Corporate Liberalism: The Origins of Modern Political Theory, 1890–1920.* Berkeley: University of California Press.

Mahoney, J. 2000. Path Dependence in Historical Sociology. *Theory and Society* 29, no. 4 (August): 507–48.

Mahoney, J., and D. Rueschemeyer, eds. 2003. *Comparative Historical Analysis in the Social Sciences.* New York: Cambridge University Press.

Mandell, N. 2002. *The Corporation as Family: The Gendering of Corporate Welfare, 1890–1930*. Chapel Hill: University of North Carolina Press.

Manley, J. M. 1907. Shop Practice in the Engineering Course of the University of Cincinnati. *American Machinist* 30, no. 1 (13 June): 840–41.

Mann, M. 1993. *The Sources of Social Power*. Vol. 2: of *The Rise of Classes and Nation-States, 1760–1914*. Cambridge: Cambridge University Press.

Marchand, R. 1998. *Creating the Corporate Soul: The Rise of Public Relations and Corporate Imagery in American Big Business*. Berkeley: University of California Press.

Maxwell, S. D. 1974. *The Suburbs of Cincinnati*. New York: Arno Press.

McAdam, D. 1988. *Freedom Summer*. New York: Oxford University Press.

McAdam, D., J. D. McCarthy, and M. N. Zald, eds. 1996. *Comparative Perspectives on Social Movements: Political Opportunities, Mobilizing Structures, and Cultural Framings*. Cambridge: Cambridge University Press.

McAdam, D., S. Tarrow, and C. Tilly. 2001. *Dynamics of Contention*. New York: Cambridge University Press.

McCarthy, K. D. 1982. *Noblesse Oblige: Charity and Cultural Philanthropy in Chicago, 1848–1929*. Chicago: University of Chicago Press.

McDonald, T. J. 1986. The Parameters of Urban Fiscal Policy: Socioeconomic Change and Political Culture in San Francisco, 1860–1906. Berkeley: University of California Press.

McDougall, T. 1896. *Address of Hon. Thomas McDougall of Cincinnati—November 18th, 1896*. Cincinnati Historical Society.

McFarland, G. W. 1975. *Mugwumps, Morals, and Politics, 1884–1920*. Amherst: University of Massachusetts Press.

McPhail, C. 1991. *The Myth of the Madding Crowd*. New York: A. de Gruyter.

McQuaid, K. 1986. *A Response to Industrialism: Liberal Businessmen and the Evolving Spectrum of Capitalist Reform, 1886–1960*. New York: Garland.

McWilliams, C. 1949. *California: The Great Exception*. New York: A. A. Wyn.

Mechanics' Institute of San Francisco. Annual Reports. Mechanics' Institute Library.

———. Mechanics' Fair Daily Press. Mechanics' Institute Library.

———. Reports of the Industrial Exhibition. Mechanics' Institute Library.

Mehta, C., and N. Theodore. 2005. *Undermining the Right to Organize: Employer Behavior during Union Representation Campaigns*. Washington, D.C.: American Rights at Work.

Melucci, A. 1989. *Nomads of the Present: Social Movements and Individual Needs in Contemporary Society*. Philadelphia: Temple University Press.

Merchants' Association of San Francisco. 1910. *A Year of Civic Work*. San Francisco: Merchants' Association of San Francisco.

Merchants' Association Records. Ms 871. California Historical Society.

Merchants' Association. Review. Bancroft Library. University of California, Berkeley.

Merrill, L. O. 1970. The Portola Celebration. In *West Coast Expositions and Galas*. No. 5 in the Series of Keepsakes. San Francisco: Book Club of San Francisco.

Merry, W. L. N.d. Statement. Banc Mss C–D 328. Bancroft Library. University of California, Berkeley.

Meyer, D., N. Whittier, and B. Robnett, eds. 2002. *Social Movements: Identity, Culture, and the State*. New York: Oxford University Press.

Miller, W. 1952b. The Recruitment of the American Business Elite. In *Men in Business: Essays on the Historical Role of the Entrepreneur*, ed. W. Miller, 328–37. New York: Harper Torchbooks.

Miller, Z. L. 1968. *Boss Cox's Cincinnati: Urban Politics in the Progressive Era*. New York: Oxford University Press.

Millikan, W. 2001. *A Union against Unions: The Minneapolis Citizens' Alliance and the Fight Against Organized Labor, 1903–1947*. Minneapolis: Minnesota Historical Society Press.

Milton, C. R. 1970. *Ethics and Expediency in Personnel Management: A Critical History of Personnel Philosophy*. Columbia: University of South Carolina Press.

Mink, G. 1986. *Old Labor and New Immigrants in American Political Development: Union, Party, and State, 1875–1920*. Ithaca, N.Y.: Cornell University Press.

Mintz, B., and M. Schwartz. 1981. Interlocking Directorates and Interest Group Formation. *American Sociological Review* 46, no. 6 (December): 851–69.

Montgomery, D. 1979. *Workers' Control in America: Studies in the History of Work, Technology, and Labor Struggles*. Cambridge: Cambridge University Press.

——. 1981. *Beyond Equality: Labor and the Radical Republicans, 1862–1872*. Urbana: University of Illinois Press.

——. 1987. *The Fall of the House of Labor: The Workplace, the State, and American Labor Activism, 1865–1925*. Cambridge: Cambridge University Press.

——. 1993. *Citizen Worker: The Experience of Workers in the United States with Democracy and the Free Market during the Nineteenth Century*. New York: Cambridge University Press.

Morris, J. M. 1969. The Road to Trade Unionism: Organized Labor in Cincinnati to 1893. Ph.D. diss., University of Cincinnati.

Morrison, A. 1886. *The Industries of Cincinnati*. Cincinnati: Metropolitan Publishing.

Musselman, B. L. 1975. The Quest for Collective Improvement: Cincinnati Workers, 1893 to 1920. Ph.D. diss., University of Cincinnati.

Nasaw, D. 2005. Gilded Age Gospels. In *Ruling America: A History of Wealth and Power in a Democracy*, ed. S. Fraser and G. Gerstle, 123–48. Cambridge, Mass.: Harvard University Press.

National Association of Manufacturers. 1906. *Proceedings of the Eleventh Annual Convention*. New York: National Association of Manufacturers.

Nelson, D. 1975. *Managers and Workers: Origins of the New Factory System in the United States, 1880–1920*. Madison: University of Wisconsin Press.

Nestor, O. W. 1986. *A History of Personnel Administration, 1890 to 1910*. New York: Garland.

Newman, K. S. 1999. *No Shame in My Game: The Working Poor in the Inner City*. New York: Knopf and the Russell Sage Foundation.

Nichols, G. W. 1877. *Art Education Applied to Industry*. New York: Harper.

O'Brien, R. 1993. "Business Unionism" versus "Responsible Unionism": Common Law Confusion, the American State, and the Formation of Pre–New Deal Labor Policy. *Law and Social Inquiry* 18, no. 2 (Spring): 255–96.

Offe, C., and H. Wiesenthal. 1980. Two Logics of Collective Action: Theoretical Notes on Social Class and Organizational Form. *Political Power and Social Theory: A Research Annual* 1: 67–115.

Ohio Mechanics' Institute. Records. Cincinnati: University of Cincinnati.

Ohio State Bureau of Labor Statistics. *Annual Reports*. Columbus, Ohio.

Olick, J. K., and J. Robbins. 1998. Social Memory Studies: From "Collective Memory" to the Historical Sociology of Mnemonic Practices. *Annual Review of Sociology* 24: 105–40.

Orr, J. R., and S. G. McNall. 1991. Fraternal Orders and Working-Class Formation in Nineteenth-Century Kansas. In *Bringing Class Back In: Contemporary and Historical Perspectives*, ed. S. G. McNall, R. F. Levine, and R. Fantasia, 101–17. Boulder: Westview Press.

Orren, K., and S. Skowronek. 2004. *The Search for American Political Development*. New York: Cambridge University Press.

Ortner, S. B. 2003. *New Jersey Dreaming: Capital, Culture, and the Class of '58.* Durham, N.C.: Duke University Press.

Ozanne, R. 1967. *A Century of Labor-Management Relations at McCormick and International Harvester.* Madison: University of Wisconsin Press.

Park, C. W. 1943. *Ambassador to Industry: The Idea and Life of Herman Schneider.* Indianapolis: Bobbs-Merrill.

Parkin, F. 1979. *Marxism and Class Theory: A Bourgeois Critique.* New York: Columbia University Press.

Pearson, C. 2004. Making the "City of Prosperity": Engineers, Open-Shoppers, Americanizers, and Propagandists in Worcester, Massachusetts, 1900–1925. *Labor History* 45, no. 1 (February): 9–36.

Peterson, P. E. 1985. *The Politics of School Reform, 1870–1940.* Chicago: University of Chicago Press.

Pierson, P. 2004. *Politics in Time: History, Institutions, and Social Analysis.* Princeton, N.J.: Princeton University Press.

Polletta, F., and J. M. Jasper. 2001. Collective Identity and Social Movements. *Annual Review of Sociology* 27: 283–305.

Portes, A. 2000. The Resilient Importance of Class: A Nominalist Interpretation. *Political Power and Social Theory* 14: 249–84.

Portes, A., and J. Sensenbrenner. 1998. Embeddedness and Immigration: Notes on the Social Determinants of Economic Action. In *The New Institutionalism in Sociology,* ed. M. C. Brinton and V. Nee, 127–49. New York: Russell Sage Foundation.

Prasad, M. 2000. The Politics of Free Markets: The Rise of Neoliberal Economic Policy in Britain, France, and the United States. Ph.D. thesis, University of Chicago.

Putnam, R. 2000. *Bowling Alone: The Collapse and Revival of American Community.* New York: Simon and Schuster.

Quigley, D. 2002. "The proud name of 'Citizen' has sunk": Suffrage Restriction, Class Formation, and the Tilden Commission of 1877. *American Nineteenth Century History* 3, no. 2 (Summer): 69–92.

Ramirez, B. 1978. *When Workers Fight: The Politics of Industrial Relations in the Progressive Era, 1898–1916.* Westport, Conn.: Greenwood Press.

Rammelkamp, J. S. 1978. St. Louis: Boosters and Boodlers. *Missouri Historical Society Bulletin* 34 (4): 200–210.

Ratcliff, R. E., M. E. Gallagher, and K. S. Ratcliff. 1979. The Civic Involvement of Bankers: An Analysis of the Influence of Economic Power and Social Prominence in the Command of Civic Policy Positions. *Social Problems* 26, no. 3 (February): 298–313.

Reed, A., Jr. 2002. Unraveling the Relation of Race and Class in American Politics. *Political Power and Social Theory* 15: 265–74.

Reemelin, C. 1892. *Life of Charles Reemelin.* Cincinnati: Weier & Daiker.

Rice, S. P. 2004. *Minding the Machine: Languages of Class in Early Industrial America.* Berkeley: University of California Press.

Roberts, B. 2000. *American Alchemy: The California Gold Rush and Middle-Class Culture.* Chapel Hill: University of North Carolina Press.

Robertson, D. B. 2000. *Capital, Labor, and State: The Battle for American Labor Markets from the Civil War.* Lanham, Md.: Rowman and Littlefield.

Rodabaugh, J. H., and Ohio Valley Folk Research Project. 1962. *The Cincinnati Riot of 1884.* Ohio Valley Folk publications, New Series no. 91. Chillicothe, Ohio: Ohio Valley Folk Research Project, the Ross County Historical Society.

Rodgers, D. T. 1974. *The Work Ethic in Industrial America, 1850–1920.* Chicago: University of Chicago Press.

———. 1992. Republicanism: The Career of a Concept. *Journal of American History* 79, no. 1 (June): 11–38.

Roediger, D. 1991. *The Wages of Whiteness: Race and the Making of the American Working Class.* London: Verso.

Roland, H. 1898. Effective Systems of Finding and Keeping Shop Costs. *Engineering Magazine* 16, no. 2 (November): 207–14.

Rose, S. O. 1997. Class Formation and the Quintessential Worker. In *Reworking Class,* ed. J. R. Hall, 133–66. Ithaca, N.Y.: Cornell University Press.

Rosenzweig, R. 1983. *Eight Hours for What We Will: Workers and Leisure in an Industrial City, 1870–1920.* Cambridge: Cambridge University Press.

Ross, S. J. 1985. *Workers on the Edge: Work, Leisure, and Politics in Industrializing Cincinnati, 1788–1890.* New York: Columbia University Press.

———. 1986. The Politicization of the Working Class: Production, Ideology, Culture and Politics in Late Nineteenth-Century Cincinnati. *Social History* 11, no. 2 (May): 171–95.

Roy, W. G. 1991. The Organization of the Corporate Class Segment of the U.S. Capitalist Class at the Turn of This Century. In *Bringing Class Back In: Contemporary and Historical Perspectives,* ed. S. G. McNall, R. F. Levine, and R. Fantasia, 139–63. Boulder, Colo.: Westview Press.

———. 1997. *Socializing Capital: The Rise of the Large Industrial Corporation in America.* Princeton, N.J.: Princeton University Press.

Ruane, J., and J. Todd. 2004. The Roots of Intense Ethnic Conflict May Not in Fact Be Ethnic: Categories, Communities, and Path Dependence. *Archives Européens de Sociologie* 45 (2): 209–32.

Ryan, F. L. 1936. *Industrial Relations in the San Francisco Building Trades.* Norman: University of Oklahoma Press.

Ryder, D. W. 1954. *Men of Rope: Being the History of the Tubbs Cordage Company.* San Francisco: Historical Publications.

San Francisco Chamber of Commerce Records. Mss 870 and 871. California Historical Society. San Francisco.

San Francisco Chamber of Commerce. 1916. *Law and Order in San Francisco: A Beginning.* San Francisco: San Francisco Chamber of Commerce.

San Francisco Chronicle.

San Francisco Commercial Club. N.d. *History, By-Laws, Roster.* San Francisco: San Francisco Commercial Club.

San Francisco Examiner.

San Francisco Industrial Conciliation Board. 1910. *Rules and By-Laws.*

San Francisco Riggers and Stevedores Union. Records. Labor Archives and Research Center, San Francisco State University.

Sandage, S. A. 2005. *Born Losers: A History of Failure in America.* Cambridge, Mass.: Harvard University Press.

Savage, M., G. Bagnall, and B. Longhurst. 2001. Ordinary, Ambivalent, and Defensive: Class Identities in the Northwest of England. *Sociology* 35 (4): 875–92.

Sawislak, K. 1995. *Smoldering City: Chicagoans and the Great Fire, 1871–1874.* Chicago: University of Chicago Press.

Sawyer, J. E. 1952. The Entrepreneur and the Social Order: France and the United States. In *Men in Business: Essays on the Historical Role of the Entrepreneur,* ed. W. Miller, 1–22. New York: Harper Torchbooks.

Saxton, A. 1965. San Francisco Labor and the Populist and Progressive Insurgencies. *Pacific Historical Review* 34, no. 4 (November): 421–38.

———. 1971. *The Indispensable Enemy: Labor and the Anti-Chinese Movement in California.* Berkeley: University of California Press.

——. 1990. *The Rise and Fall of the White Republic: Class Politics and Mass Culture in Nineteenth-Century America.* London: Verso.

Schiesl, M. J. 1977. *The Politics of Efficiency: Municipal Administration and Reform in America, 1800–1920.* Berkeley: University of California Press.

Schneider, H. 1907. The Cooperative Course in Engineering at the University of Cincinnati. Proceedings of the Fifteenth Annual Meeting of the Society for the Promotion of Engineering Education. New York.

——. 1915. *Education for Industrial Workers: A Constructive Study Applied to New York City.* New York: World Book Company.

Schneirov, R. 1984. Class Conflict and Municipal Reform in Chicago. In *German Workers in Industrial Chicago,* ed. J. Jentz, 183–205. DeKalb: Northern Illinois University Press.

——. 1998. *Labor and Urban Politics: Class, Conflict, and the Origins of Modern Liberalism in Chicago, 1864–1897.* Urbana: University of Illinois Press.

——. 1999. Labor and the New Liberalism in the Wake of the Pullman Strike. In *The Pullman Strike and the Crisis of the 1890s: Essays on Labor and Politics,* ed. R. Schneirov, S. Stromquist, and N. Salvatore, 204–32. Urbana: University of Illinois Press.

Schneirov, R., S. Stromquist, and N. Salvatore, eds. 1999. *The Pullman Strike and the Crisis of the 1890s: Essays on Labor and Politics.* Urbana: University of Illinois Press.

Schwartz, J. E. 1995. *Fred A. Geier, 1866–1934.* Cincinnati: James A. D. Geier.

Schwartz, M., ed. 1987. *The Structure of Power in America: The Corporate Elite as a Ruling Class.* New York: Holmes and Meier.

Schweniger, J. M. 1999. "Sustaining the Civil Authorities": The Ohio National Guard and the Cincinnati Riot of 1884. *Queen City Heritage* 57, no. 1 (Spring): 3–20.

Scott, M. 1985. *The San Francisco Bay Area: A Metropolis in Perspective.* 2nd ed. Berkeley: University of California Press.

Scott, W. R. 2001. *Institutions and Organization.* Thousand Oaks, Calif.: Sage Publications.

Scranton, P. 1983. *Proprietary Capitalism: The Textile Manufacture at Philadelphia, 1800–1885.* Cambridge: Cambridge University Press.

——. 1986. Learning Manufacture: Education and Shop-Floor Schooling in the Family Firm. *Technology and Culture* 27, no. 1 (January): 40–62.

——. 1989. *Figured Tapestry: Production, Markets, and Power in Philadelphia Textiles, 1885–1941.* Cambridge: Cambridge University Press.

——. 1997. *Endless Novelty: Specialty Production and American Industrialization, 1865–1925.* Princeton, N.J.: Princeton University Press.

Sen, A. 2006. *Identity and Violence: The Illusion of Destiny.* New York: W. W. Norton.

Senkewicz, R. M. 1985. *Vigilantes in Gold Rush San Francisco.* Stanford, Calif.: Stanford University Press.

Sewell, W. H., Jr. 1980. *Work and Revolution in France: The Language of Labor from the Old Regime to 1848.* Cambridge: Cambridge University Press.

——. 1992. A Theory of Structure: Duality, Agency, and Transformation. *American Journal of Sociology* 98, no. 1 (July): 1–29.

——. 1996. Historical Events as Transformations of Structures: Inventing Revolution at the Bastille. *Theory and Society* 25, no. 6 (December): 841–81.

Shafer, B. E., ed. 1991. *Is America Different? A New Look at American Exceptionalism.* Oxford: Clarendon Press.

Shapiro, H. D., and J. D. Sarna, eds. 1992. *Ethnic Diversity and Civic Identity: Patterns of Conflict and Cohesion in Cincinnati since 1820.* Urbana: University of Illinois Press.

Shenhav, Y. 1999. *Manufacturing Rationality: The Engineering Foundations of the Managerial Revolution.* New York: Oxford University Press.

Shumsky, N. L. 1972. Tar Flat and Nob Hill: A Social History of Industrial San Francisco during the 1870s. Ph.D. diss., University of California, Berkeley.

Sidney Maxwell. Papers, Mss qM465, 668, 763. Cincinnati Historical Society.

Siskind, J. 2002. *Rum and Axes: The Rise of a Connecticut Merchant Family, 1795–1850.* Ithaca, N.Y.: Cornell University Press.

Sisson, K. 1991. Employers and the Structure of Collective Bargaining: Distinguishing Cause and Effect. In *The Power to Manage? Employers and Industrial Relations in Comparative-Historical Perspective,* ed. S. Tolliday and J. Zeitlin, 256–71. London: Routledge.

Sklair, L. 2001. *The Transnational Capitalist Class.* Oxford: Blackwell.

Sklar, M. J. 1988. *The Corporate Reconstruction of American Capitalism, 1890–1916: The Market, the Law, and Politics.* Cambridge: Cambridge University Press.

Skocpol, T. 1992. *Protecting Soldiers and Mothers: The Political Origins of Social Policy in the United States.* Cambridge, Mass.: Harvard University Press.

———. 1999. How Americans Became Civic. In *Civic Engagement in American Democracy,* ed. T. Skocpol and M. P. Fiorina, 27–80. Washington, D.C. and New York: Brookings Institution Press and Russell Sage Foundation.

Slotkin, R. 1985. *The Fatal Environment: The Myth of the Frontier in the Age of Industrialization, 1800–1890.* New York: Atheneum.

Smith, F. W. 1986. *The Amazing Storm: Business Answers to the Labor Question, 1900–1920.* New York: Garland.

Smith, R. M. 1997. *Civic Ideals: Conflicting Visions of Citizenship in U.S. History.* New Haven, Conn.: Yale University Press.

Snow, D. A. 2004. Framing Processes, Ideology, and Discursive Fields. In *The Blackwell Companion to Social Movements,* ed. D. Snow, S. A. Soule, and H. Kriesi, 380–412. Malden, Mass.: Blackwell.

Snow, D. A., S. A. Soule, and H. Kriesi. 2004. *The Blackwell Companion to Social Movements.* Malden, Mass.: Blackwell.

Snow, D., E. B. Rochford Jr., S. K. Worden, and R. D. Benford. 1986. Frame Alignment Processes, Micromobilization, and Movement Participation. *American Sociological Review* 51, no. 4 (August): 464–81.

Somers, M. R. 1997. Deconstructing and Reconstructing Class Formation Theory: Narrativity, Relational Analysis, and Social Theory. In *Reworking Class,* ed. J. R. Hall, 73–105. Ithaca, N.Y.: Cornell University Press.

Spencer, E. G. 1984. *Management and Labor in Imperial Germany: Ruhr Industrialists as Employers, 1896–1914.* New Brunswick, N.J.: Rutgers University Press.

Spiess, P. D., II. 1970. Exhibitions and Expositions in Nineteenth-Century Cincinnati. *Cincinnati Historical Society Bulletin* 28, no. 3 (Fall): 170–92.

Spillman, L. 1998. When Do Collective Memories Last? *Social Science History* 22, no. 4 (Winter): 445–77.

Spraul, J. 1976. Cultural Boosterism: The Construction of Music Hall. *Cincinnati Historical Society Bulletin* 34, no. 3 (Fall): 189–203.

Sproat, J. G. 1968. *"The Best Men": Liberal Reformers in the Gilded Age.* New York: Oxford University Press.

Steinberg, M. W. 1996. "The Labour of the Country Is the Wealth of the Country": Class Identity, Consciousness, and the Role of Discourse in the Making of the English Working Class. *International Labor and Working-Class History* 49 (Spring): 1–25.

———. 1999. *Fighting Words: Working-Class Formation, Collective Action, and Discourse in Early Nineteenth-Century England.* Ithaca, N.Y.: Cornell University Press.

Steinmetz, G. 1992. Reflections on the Role of Social Narratives in Working-class Formation: Narrative Theory in the Social Sciences. *Social Science History* 16, no. 3 (Fall): 489–516.

———. 2004. Odious Comparisons: Incommensurability, the Case Study, and "Small N 's" in Sociology. *Sociological Theory* 22, no. 3 (September): 371–400.

Stern, J. S., Jr. 1984. It Was the Best of Times; It Was the Worst of Times. *Queen City Heritage* 42, no. 1 (Spring): 3–12.

Stern, M. J. 1994. *The Pottery Industry of Trenton: A Skilled Trade in Transition, 1850–1929.* New Brunswick, N.J.: Rutgers University Press.

Stinchcombe, A. L. 2005. *The Logic of Social Research.* Chicago: University of Chicago Press.

Streeck, W. 1991. Interest Heterogeneity and Organizing Capacity: Two Logics of Collective Action? In *Political Choice: Institutions, Rules, and the Limits of Rationality,* ed. R. M. Czada and A. Windhoff-Héritier, 161–98. Boulder: Westview Press.

Strobridge Lithographing Company. Records, Mss 518. Cincinnati Historical Society.

Stromquist, S. 1987. *A Generation of Boomers: The Pattern of Railroad Labor Conflict in Nineteenth-century America.* Urbana: University of Illinois Press.

Sutton, F., et al. 1956. *The American Business Creed.* Cambridge, Mass.: Harvard University Press.

Swidler, A. 1986. Culture in Action: Symbols and Strategies. *American Sociological Review* 51, no. 2 (April): 273–86.

Tarrow, S. 1998. *Power in Movement: Social Movements and Contentious Politics.* Cambridge: Cambridge University Press.

Taylor, V., and N. E. Whittier. 1992. Collective Identity in Social Movement Communities: Lesbian Feminist Mobilization. In *Frontiers in Social Movement Theory,* ed. A. D. Morris and C. M. Mueller. New Haven, Conn.: Yale University Press.

Thelen, D. P. 1972. *The New Citizenship: Origins of Progressivism in Wisconsin, 1885–1900.* Columbia: University of Missouri Press.

Thimm, A. L. 1976. *Business Ideologies in the Reform-Progressive Era, 1880–1914.* [No city given], Alabama: University of Alabama Press.

Tilly, C. 2005. *Identities, Boundaries, and Social Ties.* Boulder, Colo.: Paradigm.

Tocqueville, A. d. 1969. *Democracy in America.* Garden City, N.Y.: Doubleday Anchor.

Todd, F. M. 1921. *The Story of the Exposition; Being the Official History of the International Celebration Held at San Francisco in 1915 to Commemorate the Discovery of the Pacific Ocean and the Construction of the Panama Canal.* New York: G. P. Putnam.

Tone, A. 1997. *The Business of Benevolence: Industrial Paternalism in Progressive America.* Ithaca, N.Y.: Cornell University Press.

Trachtenberg, A. 1982. *The Incorporation of America: Culture and Society in the Gilded Age.* New York: Hill and Wang.

Traugott, M. 1985. *Armies of the Poor: Determinants of Working-Class Participation in the Parisian Insurrection of June 1848.* Princeton, N.J.: Princeton University Press.

Tygiel, J. 1977. Workingmen in San Francisco, 1870–1901. Ph.D. diss., University of California, Los Angeles.

United States. Census Office. *Census.* Washington, D.C.: U.S. Government Printing Office.

United States Bureau of the Census. 1904. *Special Report: Occupations.* Washington, D.C.: U.S. Government Printing Office.

United States Commissioner of Labor. 1893. *Industrial Education.* Eighth Annual Report of the Commissioner of Labor, 1892. Washington, D.C.: U.S. Government Printing Office.

————1902. *Trade and Technical Education.* Seventeenth Annual Report, 1902. Washington, D.C.: U.S. Government Printing Office.

————. 1911. *Industrial Education.* Twenty-Fifth Annual Report, 1910. Washington, D.C.: U.S. Government Printing Office.

United States Senate. Commission on Industrial Relations. 1916. *Final Report and Testimony.* Washington, D.C.: U.S. Government Printing Office.

United States Senate Committee on Education and Labor. 1885. *Report of the Committee of the Senate upon the Relations between Capital and Labor.* Washington, D.C.: U.S. Government Printing Office.

United States Senate. 1877. *Senate Report no 689, Joint Special Committee on Chinese.* 44th Congress, 2nd session. Washington, D.C.: U.S. Government Printing Office.

Useem, M. 1982. Classwide Rationality in the Politics of Managers and Directors of Large Corporations in the United States and Great Britain. *Administrative Science Quarterly* 27: 199–226.

————. 1984. *The Inner Circle: Large Corporations and the Rise of Business Political Activity in the U.S. and U.K.* New York: Oxford University Press.

————. 1987. The Inner Circle and the Political Voice of Business. In *The Structure of Power in America: The Corporate Elite as a Ruling Class,* ed. M. Schwartz, 143–53. New York: Holmes and Meier.

Varcados, P. 1968. Labor and Politics in San Francisco, 1880–1892. Ph.D. diss., University of California, Berkeley.

Voss, K. 1993. *The Making of American Exceptionalism: The Knights of Labor and Class Formation in the Nineteenth Century.* Ithaca, N.Y.: Cornell University Press.

Walker, T. R. 2000. Economic Opportunity on the Urban Frontier: Wealth and Nativity in Early San Francisco. *Explorations in Economic History* 37: 258–77.

Wallace, A. F. C. 1972. *Rockdale: The Growth of an American Village in the Early Industrial Revolution.* New York: W. W. Norton.

Warner, H. L. 1964. *Progressivism in Ohio, 1897–1917.* Columbus: Ohio State University Press.

Watts, S. L. 1991. *Order against Chaos: Business Culture and Labor Ideology in America, 1880–1915.* New York: Greenwood Press.

Weinstein, J. 1968. *The Corporate Ideal in the Liberal State: 1900–1918.* Boston: Beacon Press.

Weir, M. 2002. The American Middle Class and The Politics of Education. In *Postwar Social Contracts under Stress: The Middle Classes of America, Europe, and Japan at the Turn of the Century,* ed. O. Zunz, L. Schoppa, and N. Hiwatari, 178–203. New York: Russell Sage.

Wiebe, R. H. 1962. *Businessmen and Reform: A Study of the Progressive Movement.* Cambridge, Mass.: Harvard University Press.

————. 1967. *The Search for Order, 1877–1920.* New York: Hill and Wang.

Wilentz, S. 1984. *Chants Democratic: New York City and the Rise of the American Working Class, 1788–1850.* New York: Oxford University Press.

Wiley, M. G., and C. N. Alexander, Jr. 1987. From Situated Activity to Self-Attribution: The Impact of Social Structural Schemata. In *Self and Identity: Psychosocial Perspectives,* ed. K. Yardley and T. Honess, 105–18. Chichester: John Wiley & Sons.

Williams, R. H., and T. J. Kubal. 1999. Movement Frames and the Cultural Environment: Resonance, Failure, and the Boundaries of the Legitimate. *Research in Social Movements, Conflicts and Change* 21: 225–48.

Wing, G. 1964. *The History of the Cincinnati Machine Tool Industry.* D.B.A. diss., Indiana University.

Wittke, C. F., ed. 1941. *The History of the State of Ohio.* Columbus: Ohio State Archaeological and Historical Society.

Woolcock, M. 1998. Social Capital and Economic Development: Toward a Theoretical Synthesis and Policy Framework. *Theory and Society* 27, no. 2 (April): 151–208.

Wren, D. A. 1994. *The Evolution of Management Thought.* 4th ed. New York: John Wiley and Sons.

Wright, E. O. 1989. *The Debate on Classes.* London: Verso.

Wright, H. C. 1905. *Bossism in Cincinnati.* Cincinnati: Henry Wright.

Wright, S. 1993. Procter Heir Responsible for Benefits, Dedication. *Business Record,* October 18–24.

Wulsin Family Papers. Mss 844. Cincinnati Historical Society.

Yarmie, A. 1991. The Right to Manage: Vancouver Employers' Associations, 1900–1923. *BC Studies* 90 (Summer): 40–74.

Young, A. A., Jr. 2004. *The Minds of Marginalized Black Men: Making Sense of Mobility, Opportunity, and Future Life Chances.* Princeton, N.J.: Princeton University Press.

Zimmerman, B. 1981. "To Add to the Enjoyment of its Citizens." *Cincinnati Historical Society Bulletin* 39, no. 1 (Spring): 33–45.

Zunz, O. 1982. *The Changing Face of Inequality: Urbanization, Industrial Development, and Immigrants in Detroit, 1880–1920.* Chicago: University of Chicago Press.

———. 1990. *Making America Corporate, 1870–1920.* Chicago: University of Chicago Press.

Index